This item is to be returned or renewed on or before the latest date above. It may be borrowed for a further period if not in demand. To renew items call in or phone any Warwickshire library, or renew on line at www.warwickshire.gov.uk/wild

Discover • Imagine • Learn • *with libraries*

www.warwickshire.gov.uk/libraries

Warwickshire
County Council

Mokona Apapa

D1464639

Translator - Anita Sengupta
English Adaption - Carol Fox
Copy Editor - Amy Kaemon
Retouch & Lettering - Fawn Lau
Cover Artist - Raymond Swanland
Cover Layout - Gary Shum

Editor - Jake Forbes
Managing Editor - Jill Freshney
Production Coordinator - Antonio DePietro
Production Manager - Jennifer Miller
Art Director - Matt Alford
Editorial Director - Jeremy Ross
VP of Production & Manufacturing - Ron Klamert
President & C.O.O. - John Parker
Publisher & C.E.O. - Stuart Levy

Email: editor@TOKYOPOP.com
Come visit us online at www.TOKYOPOP.com

A  Manga

TOKYOPOP® is an imprint of Mixx Entertainment, Inc.
5900 Wilshire Blvd. Suite 2000, Los Angeles, CA 90036

ISBN: 1-892213-79-6

First TOKYOPOP® printing:June 2003

10 9 8 7 6 5 4 3 2 1
Printed in the USA

I FEAR I MIGHT MAKE THINGS DIFFICULT
FOR YOU, YOUNG SAKURA...

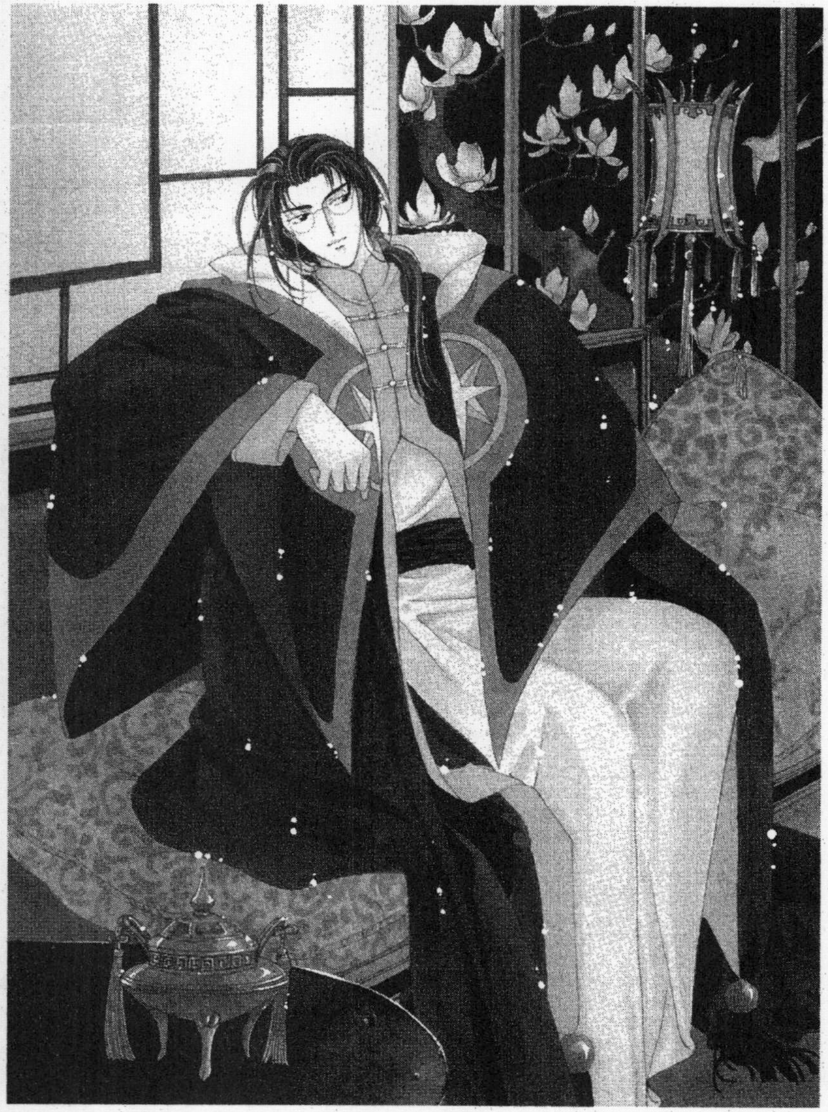

BUT I'M SURE YOU'LL BE ALL RIGHT.

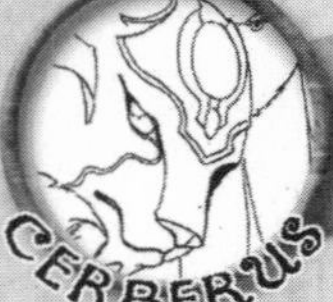

CERBERUS

Kero's true form is a lot bigger. Unlike Yukito, Kero knows about his true form. His symbol of power is the sun.

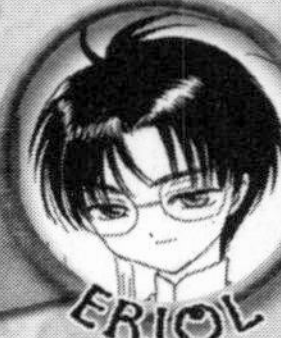

ERIOL

He just transferred into my class from England. Eriol is very polite and mature for his age. He seems to be very interested in me and my friends.

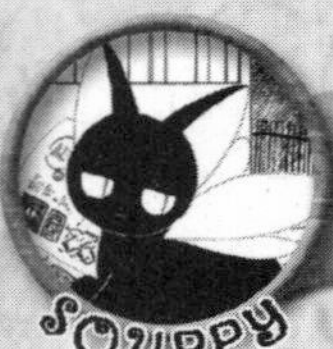

SOUPPY

He's a talking cat-like creature that lives with Eriol. He's very wise and likes his peace and quiet. I've never met him.

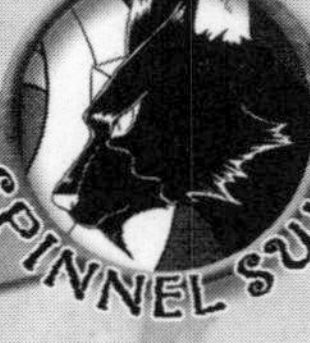

SPINNEL SUN

This fearsome winged panther appears in my dreams. [Sakura doesn't know this, but Spinnel Sun is Souppy's true form!]

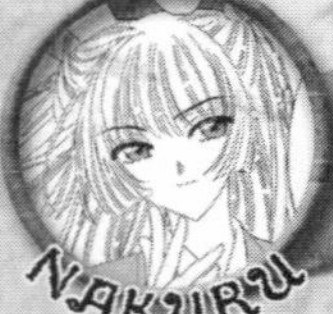

NAKURU

This obnoxious girl just transferred into Toya's class. I think she has a crush on him. She doesn't like Yukito at all. Talk about bad taste!

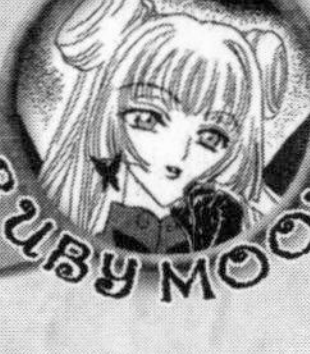

RUBY MOON

This beautiful woman with butterfly wings also keeps appearing in my dreams. [Actually, she's not male or female but is Nakuru's true form.]

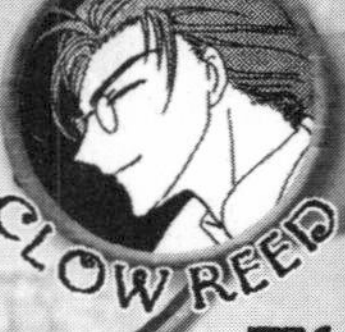

CLOW REED

He made the Clow Cards and created Kero and Yue. Even though he's been dead for many years, his presence is still hovering over Tomoeda.

THE STORY SO FAR...

I finally did it! I confessed my feelings to Yukito at the school festival. And you know what? He helped me realize that while I do love him, it's more of a family love than a romantic love. But if Yukito isn't the one for me, who is? At least Yukito has a special friend in my brother, Toya. Toya gave him his magical power to keep Yukito's true form, Yue, alive. Oh yeah! Toya's awake now, but he's...different. Even though he's still the same loving brother he always was, he's always sleepy and is a little slow on the uptake. But I must admit—now that he doesn't pick on me as much, I kinda miss Toya the bully! The presence of Clow is still testing me with magical challenges, too. No one knows why. The only clues I have are in my dreams. Whatever's going on, it has to stop. Now.

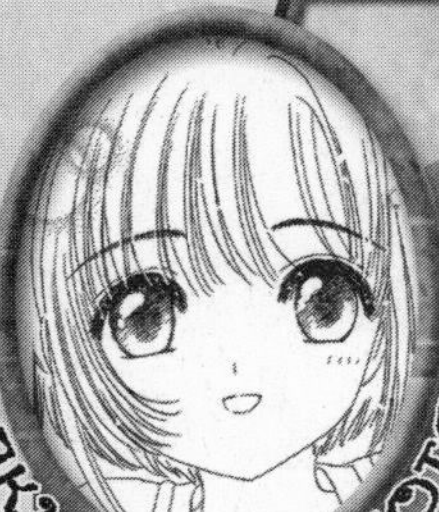

SAKURA KINOMOTO

I'm just your average fifth grader. I love P.E., I'm not too crazy about math (but I'm starting to get it), and . . . oh, yeah! I spent the last year collecting these magic Clow Cards. Now that I've found them all and passed the test, I'm Master of the Clow!

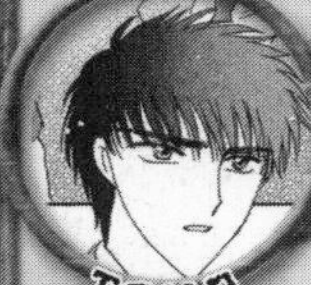

TOYA

He's my stupid brother. Even though he picks on me, I know he really cares. Magic must run in my family 'cuz people say Toya has a sixth sense.

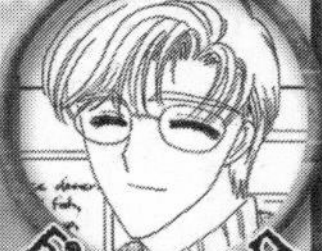

FUJITAKA

That's my dad. He teaches archaeology at the university, which means he's really smart. He's a good cook, too. I love him a lot.

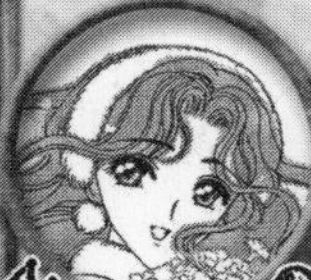

NADESHIKO

She's my mom. Isn't she pretty? She passed away when I was little, but it feels like she's still watching over us.

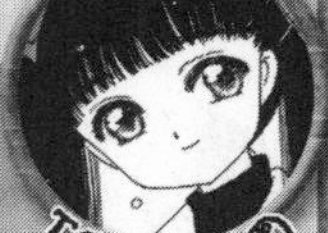

TOMOYO

She's my best friend. I don't know why, but she's always videotaping my battles. She also makes all of my costumes. Her mom and my mom were cousins.

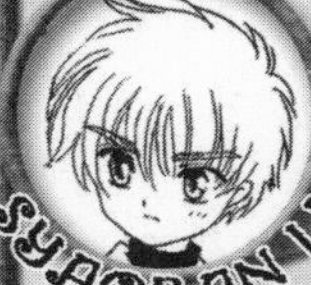

SYAORAN LI

Syaoran used to be my rival, but now we're good friends. He was going to go back to Hong Kong, but he ended up staying in Tomoeda for a while longer. He's been acting funny around me lately. I wonder why...

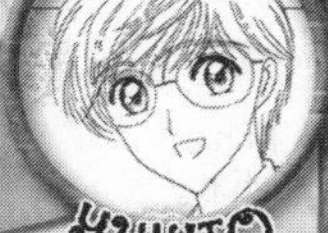

YUKITO

Isn't he just to die for! I don't know why he likes my brother so much, but I don't mind, 'cuz that means he comes over a lot. He's smart, kind, handsome, and he has a healthy appetite!

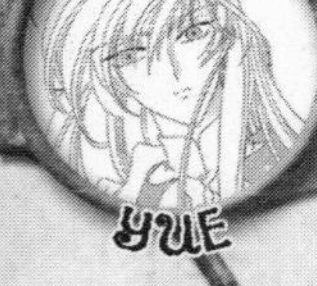

YUE

This is Yukito's true form. He's known as the Judge and his symbol of power is the moon. I'm a little scared of him, even though I'm kinda his boss.

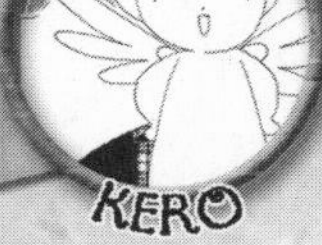

KERO

He may look like a plushie toy, but he's really the ancient, magical Guardian Beast. He gives me advice on all my adventures 'cuz he's really smart. Actually, he's more of a smart-aleck!

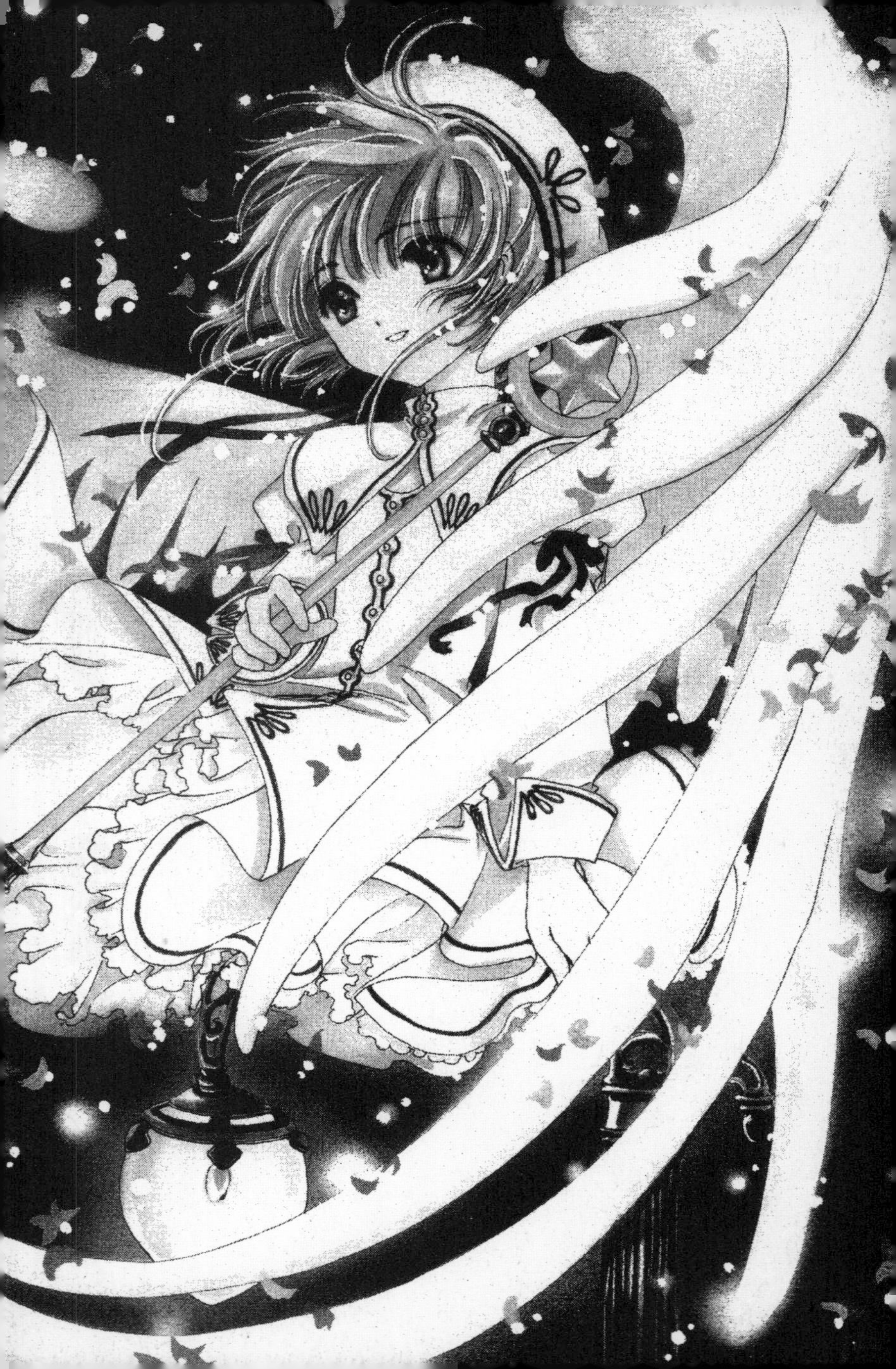

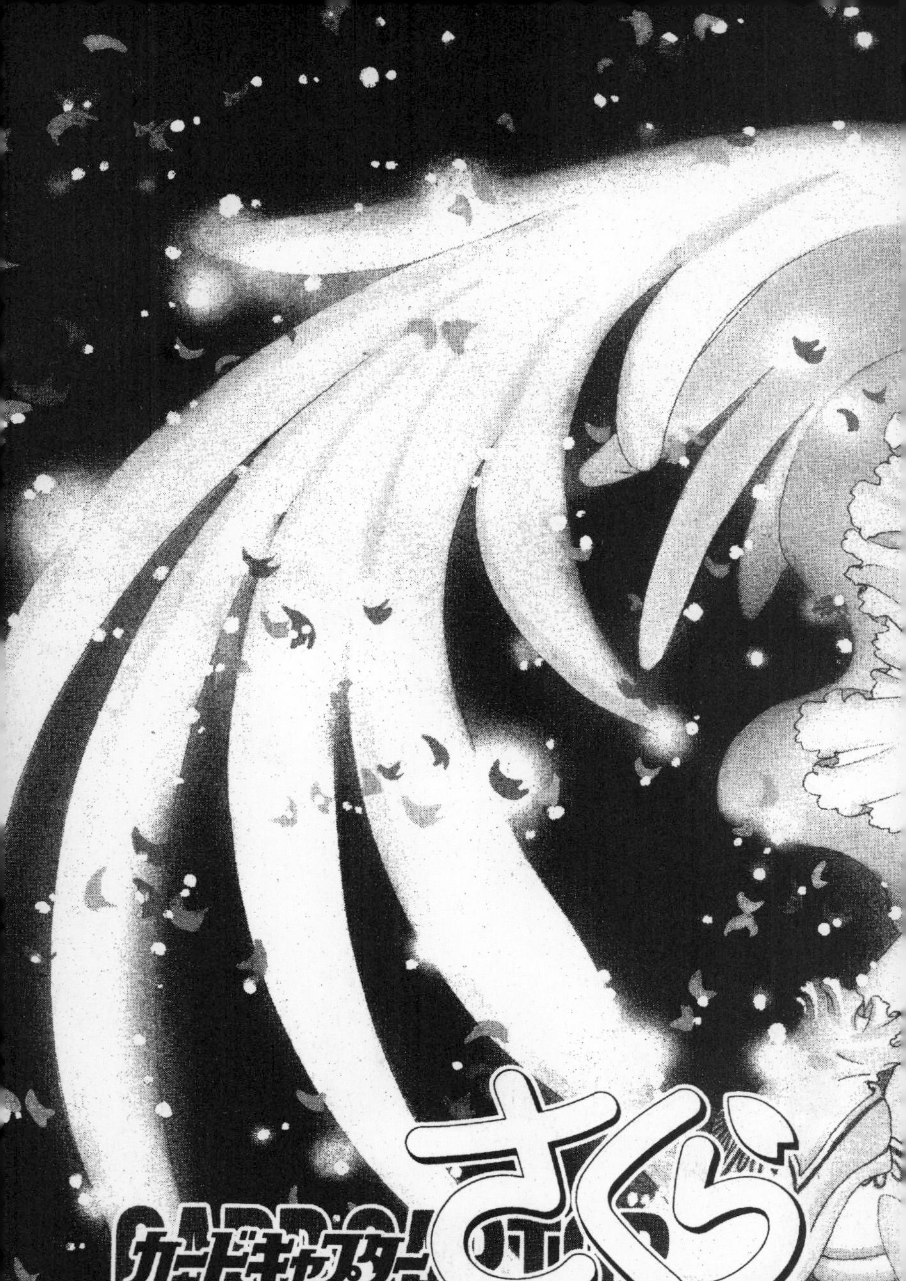
カードキャプター
さくら

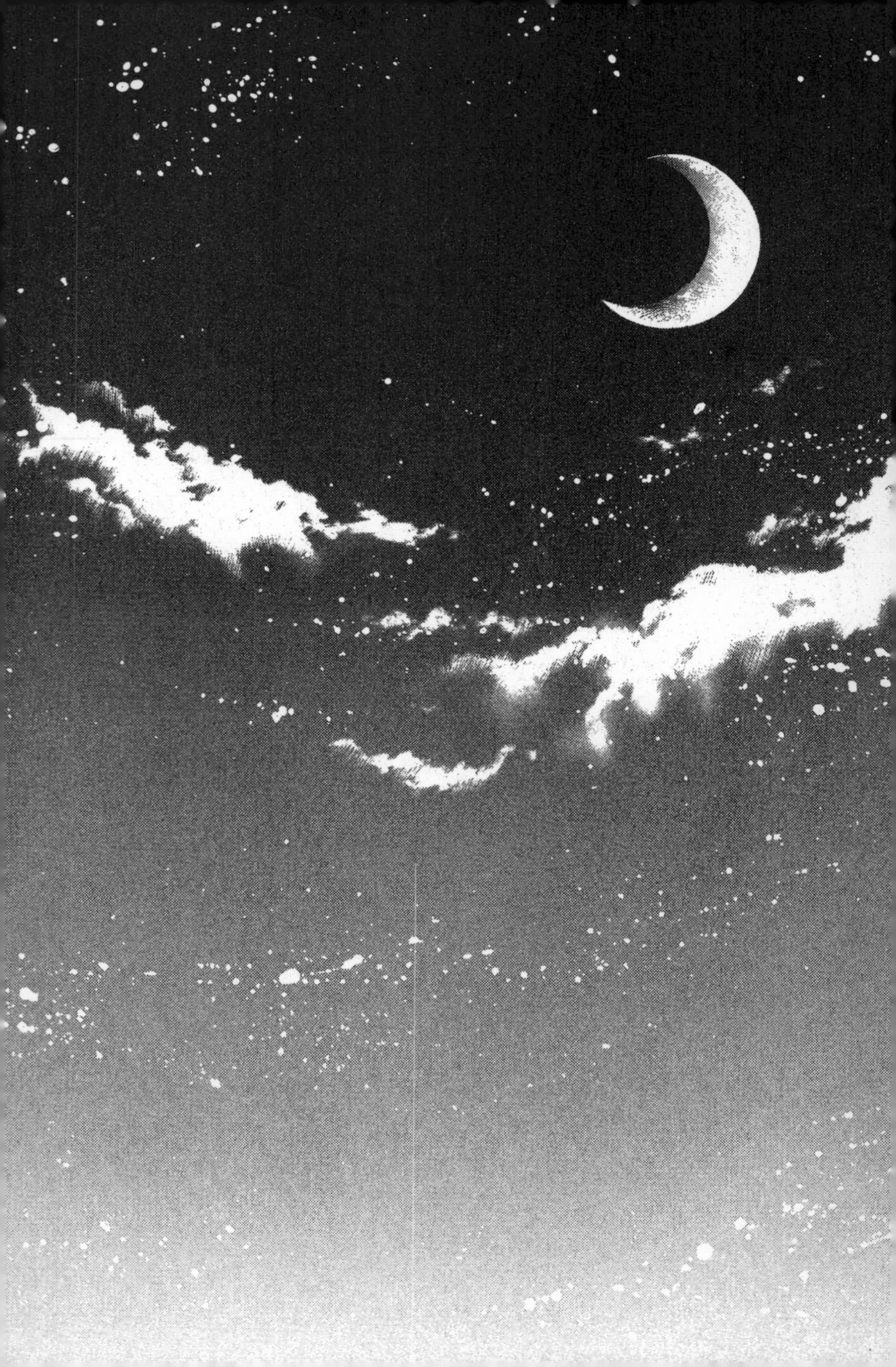

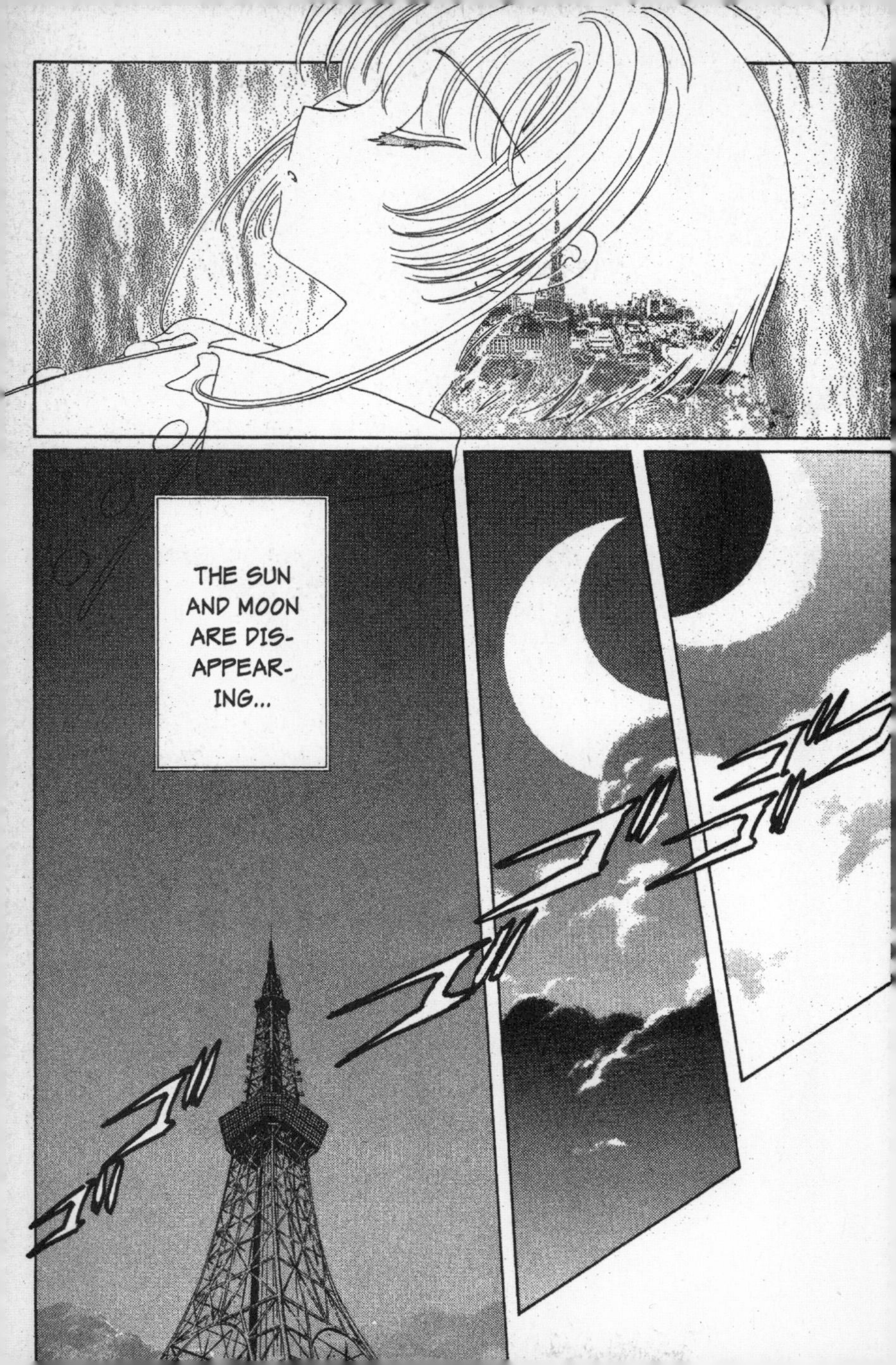
THE SUN AND MOON ARE DIS-APPEAR-ING...

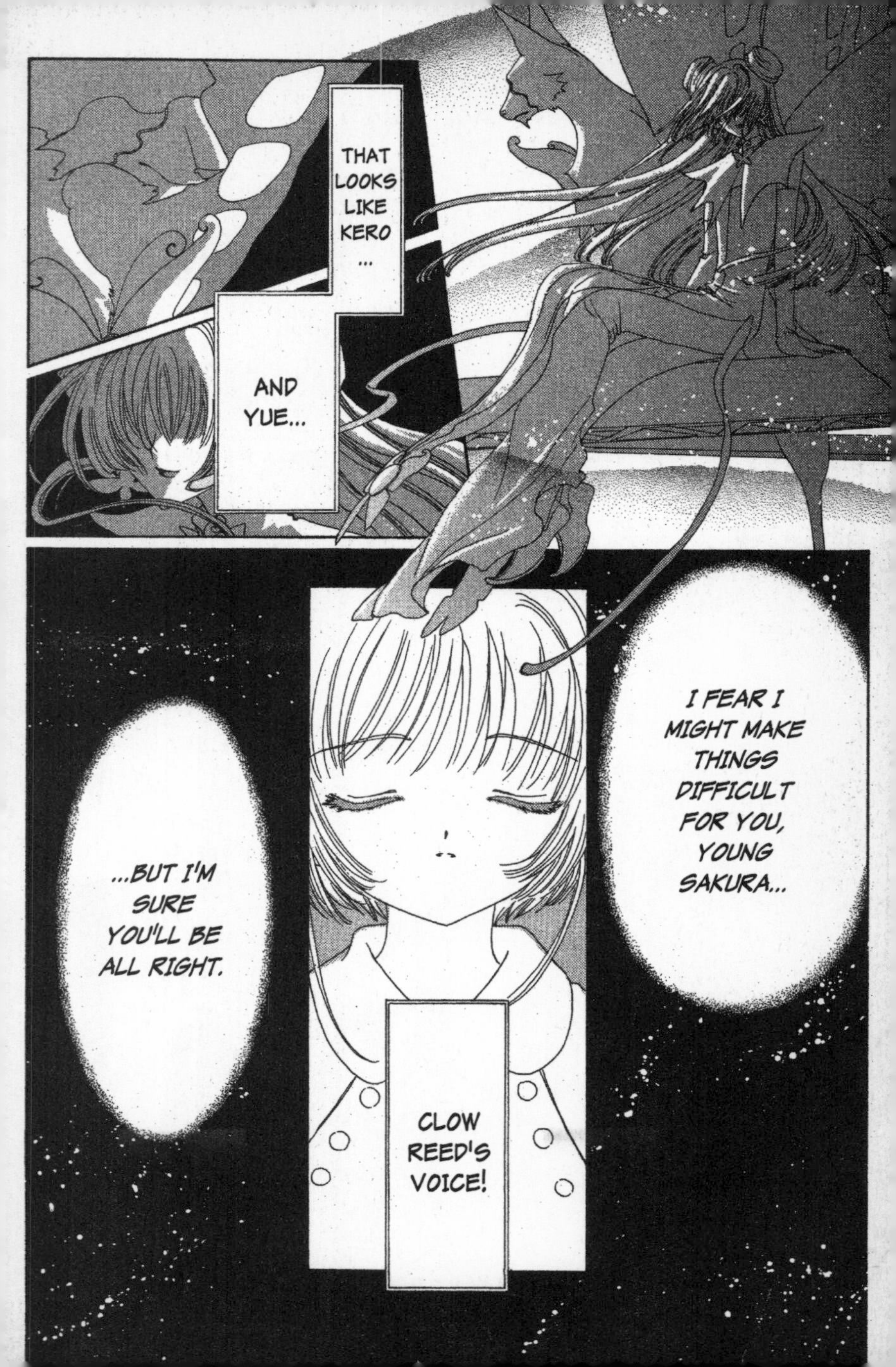
THAT LOOKS LIKE KERO ...
AND YUE...
I FEAR I MIGHT MAKE THINGS DIFFICULT FOR YOU, YOUNG SAKURA...
...BUT I'M SURE YOU'LL BE ALL RIGHT.
CLOW REED'S VOICE!

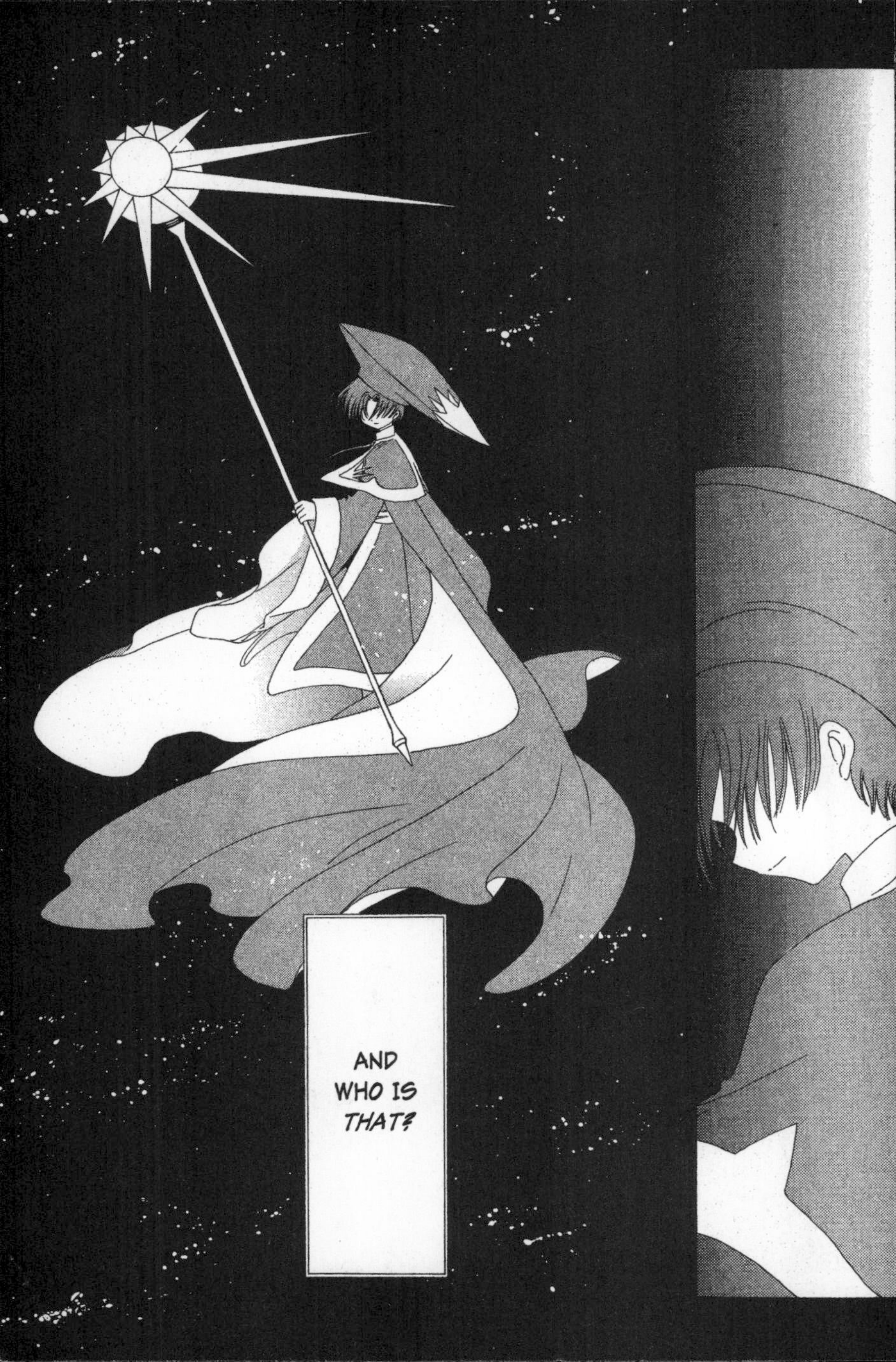
AND WHO IS THAT?

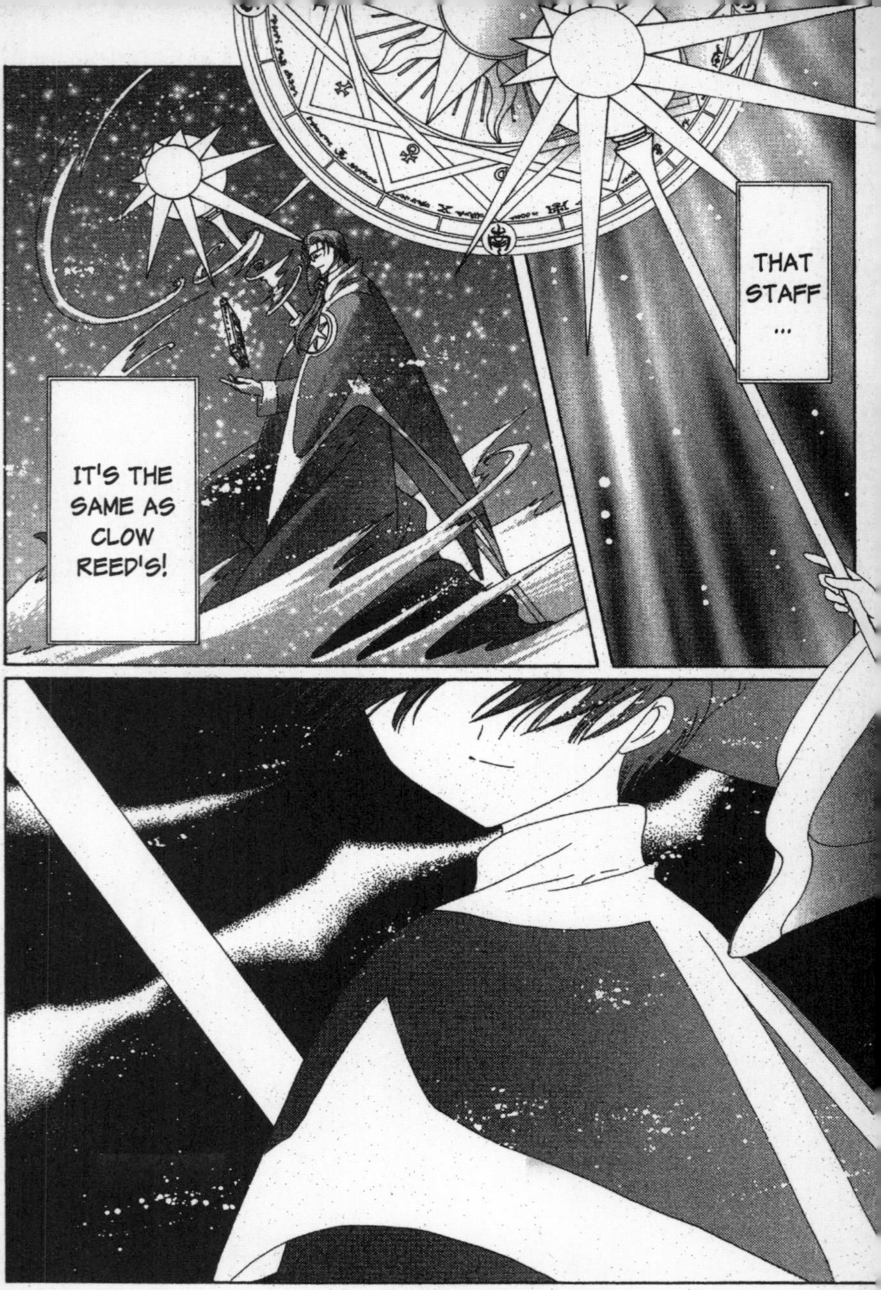
THAT STAFF ...
IT'S THE SAME AS CLOW REED'S!

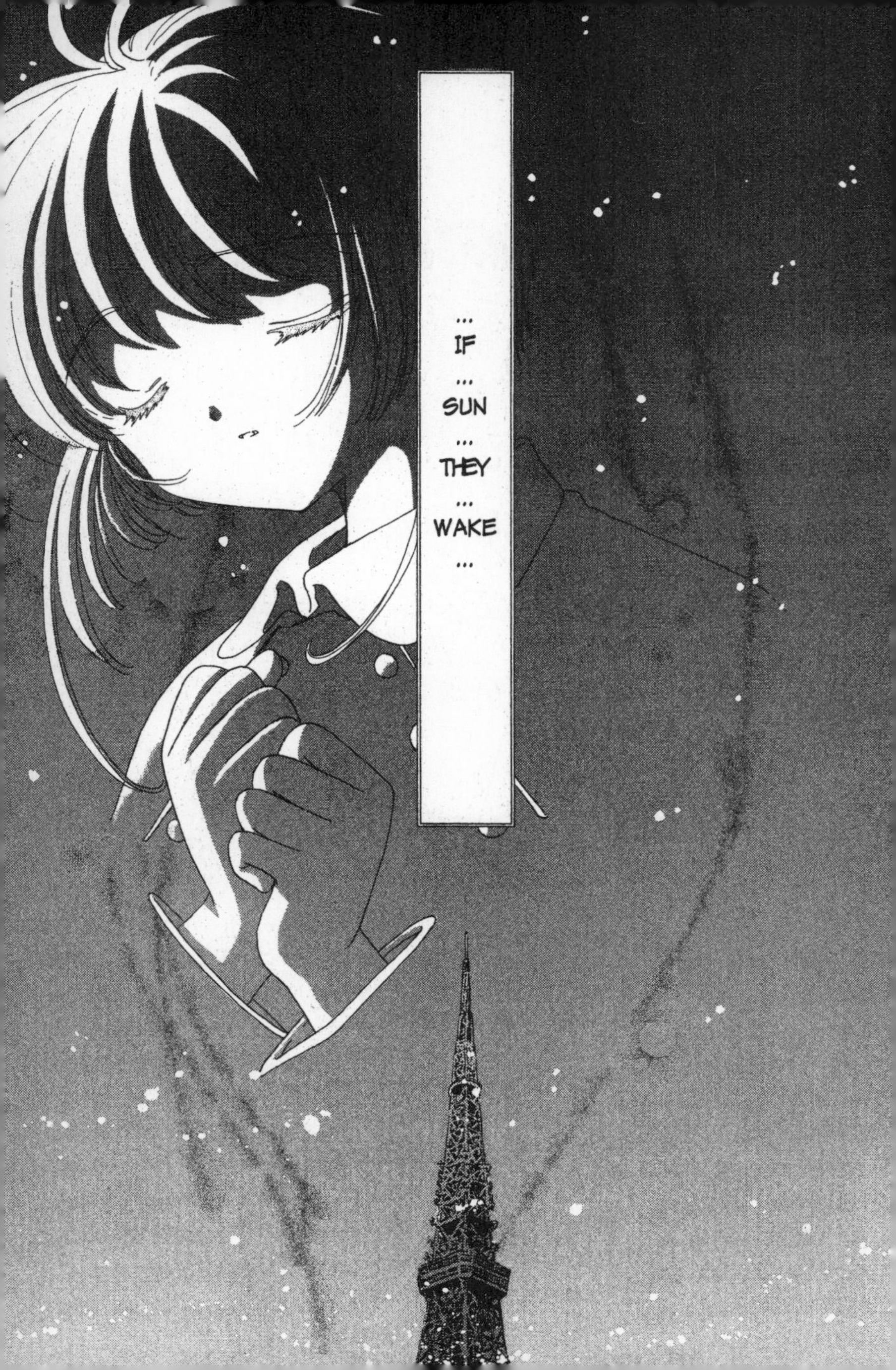
... IF ... SUN ... THEY ... WAKE ...

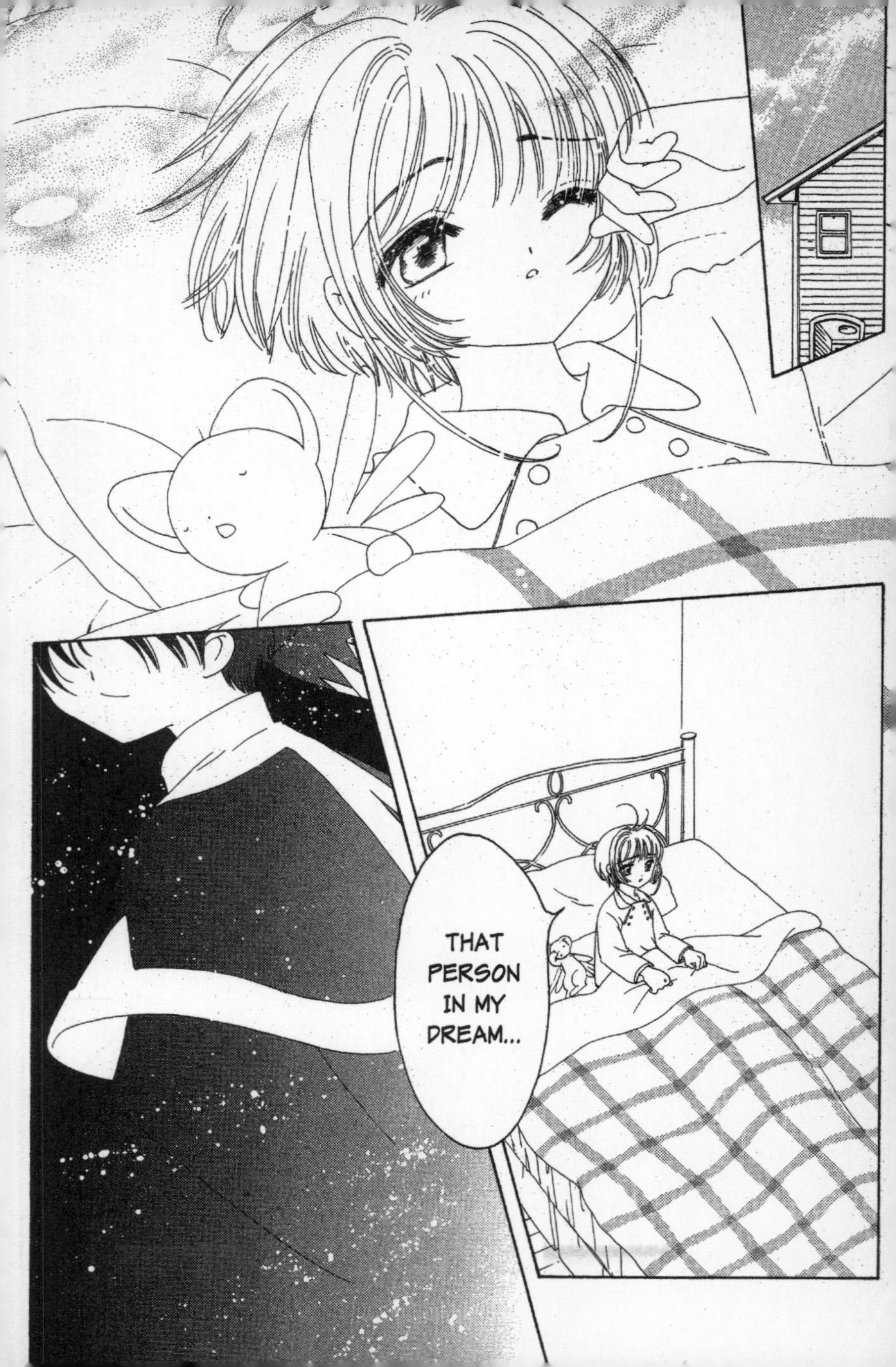
THAT PERSON IN MY DREAM...

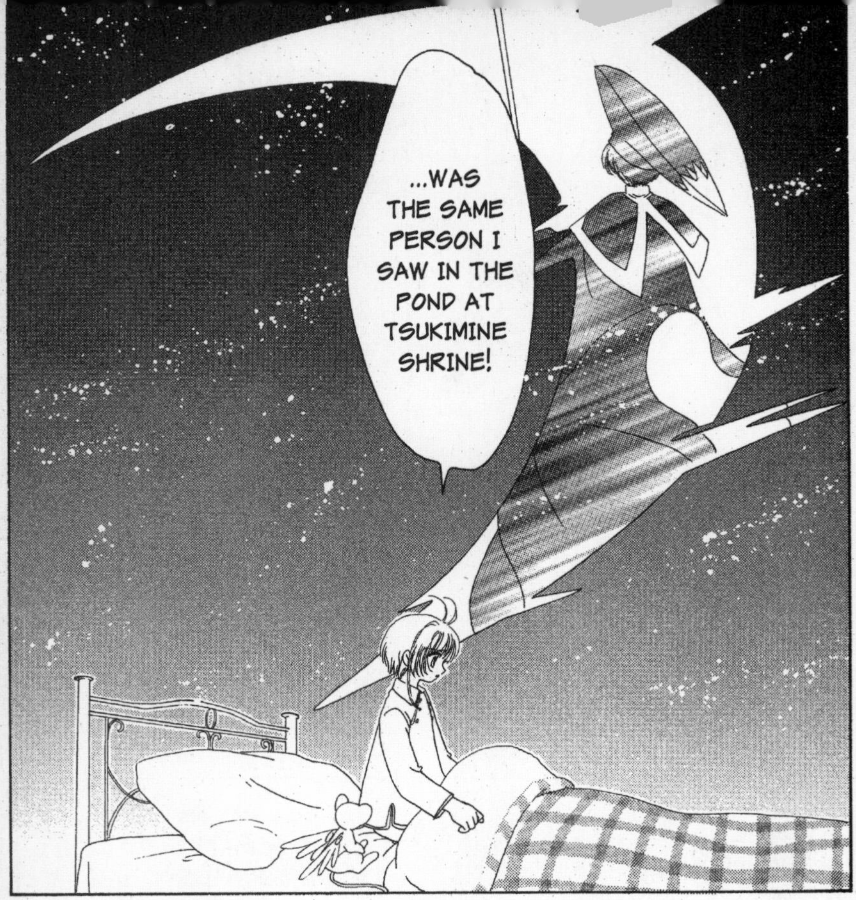
...WAS THE SAME PERSON I SAW IN THE POND AT TSUKIMINE SHRINE!

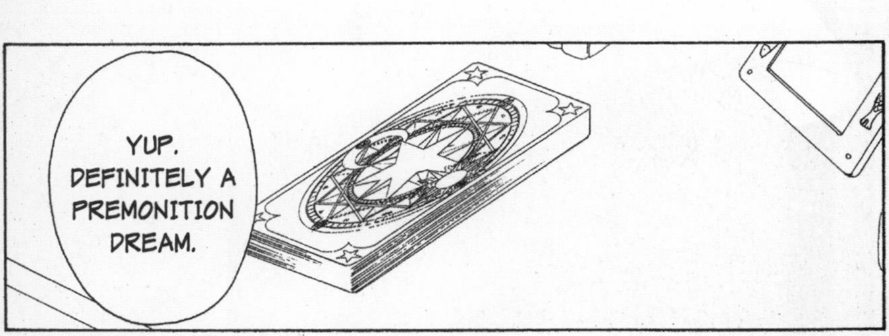
YUP. DEFINITELY A PREMONITION DREAM.

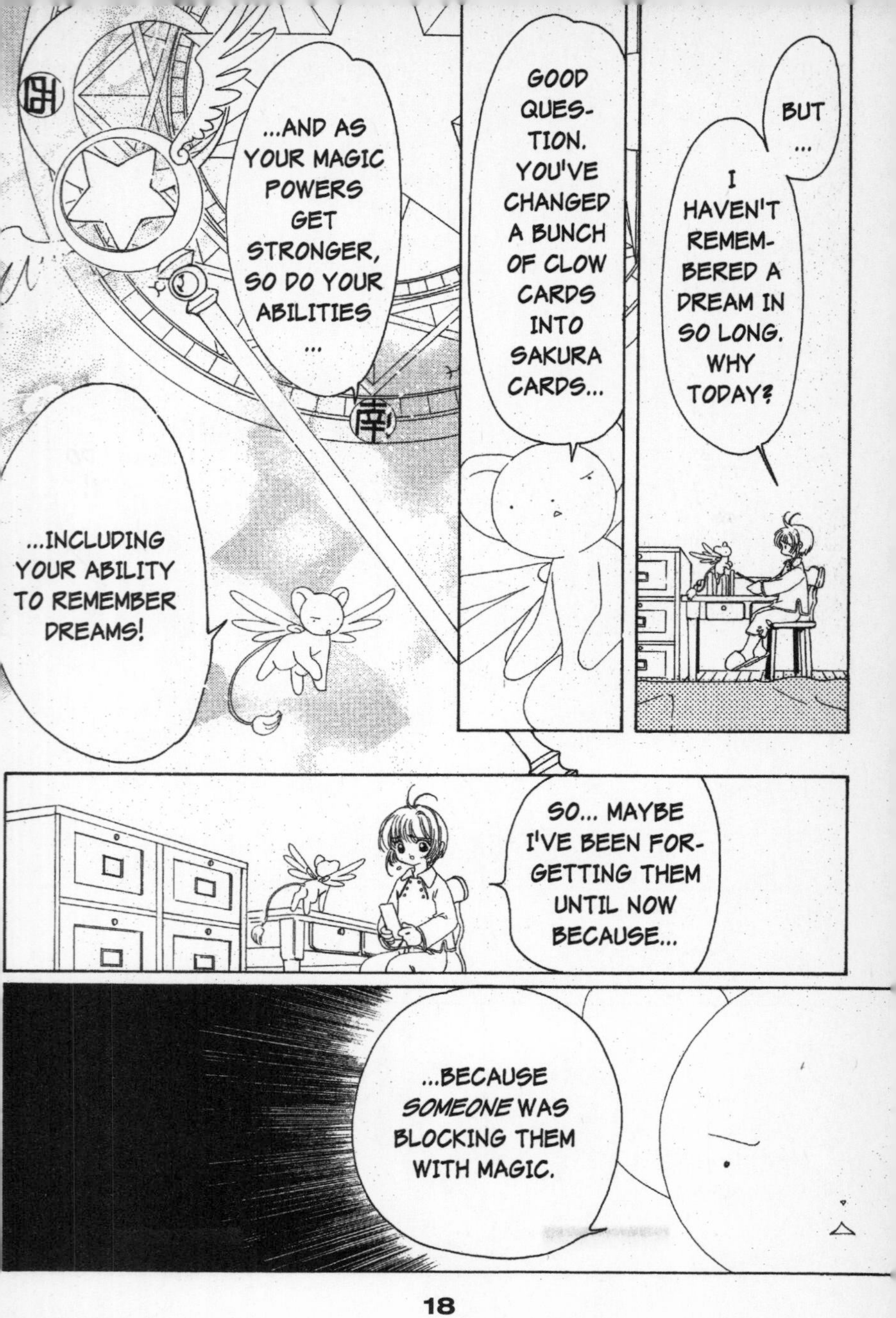
BUT ...
I HAVEN'T REMEMBERED A DREAM IN SO LONG. WHY TODAY?
GOOD QUESTION. YOU'VE CHANGED A BUNCH OF CLOW CARDS INTO SAKURA CARDS...
...AND AS YOUR MAGIC POWERS GET STRONGER, SO DO YOUR ABILITIES ...
...INCLUDING YOUR ABILITY TO REMEMBER DREAMS!
SO... MAYBE I'VE BEEN FORGETTING THEM UNTIL NOW BECAUSE...
...BECAUSE *SOMEONE* WAS BLOCKING THEM WITH MAGIC.

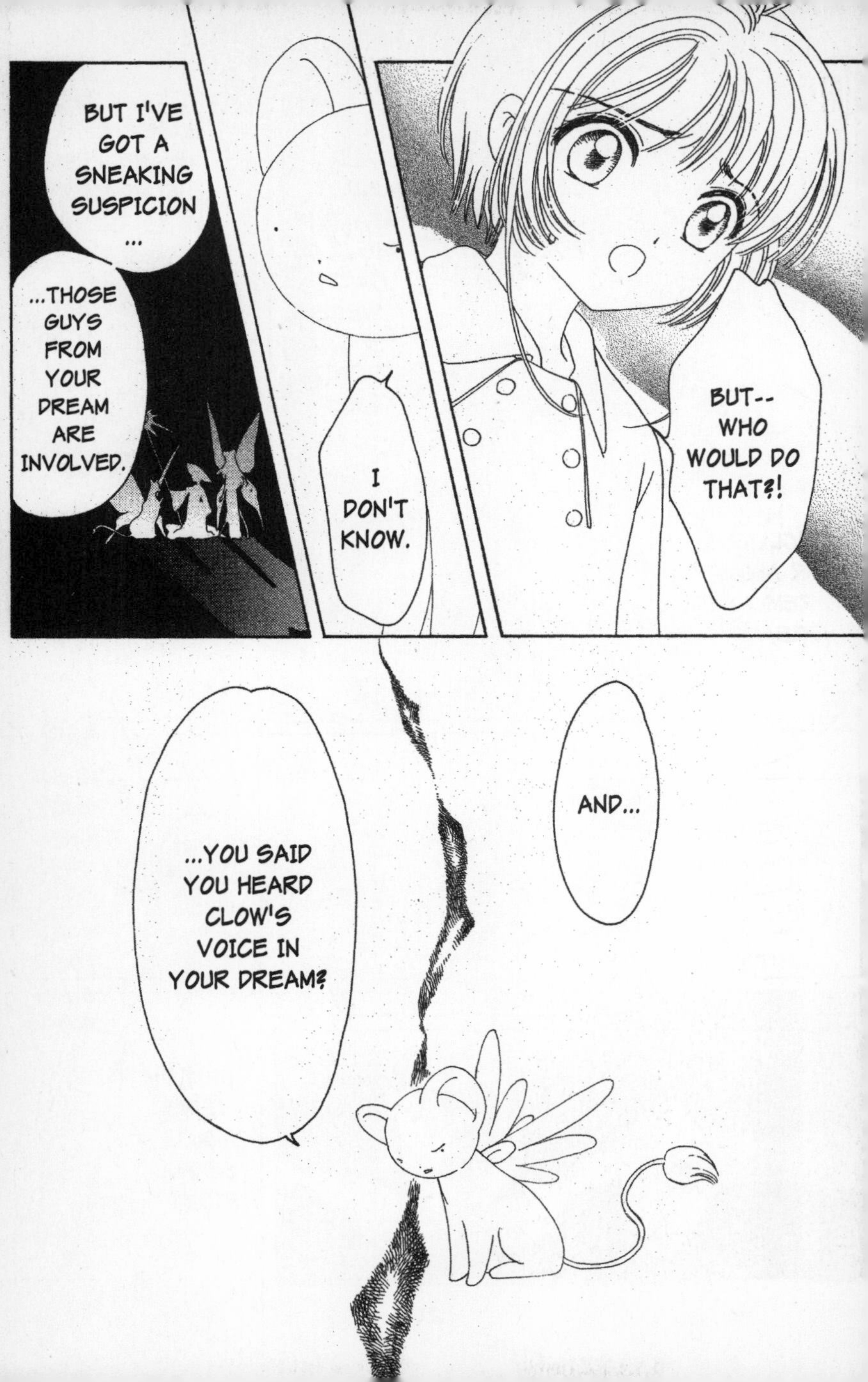
BUT-- WHO WOULD DO THAT?!
I DON'T KNOW.
BUT I'VE GOT A SNEAKING SUSPICION ...
...THOSE GUYS FROM YOUR DREAM ARE INVOLVED.
AND...
...YOU SAID YOU HEARD CLOW'S VOICE IN YOUR DREAM?

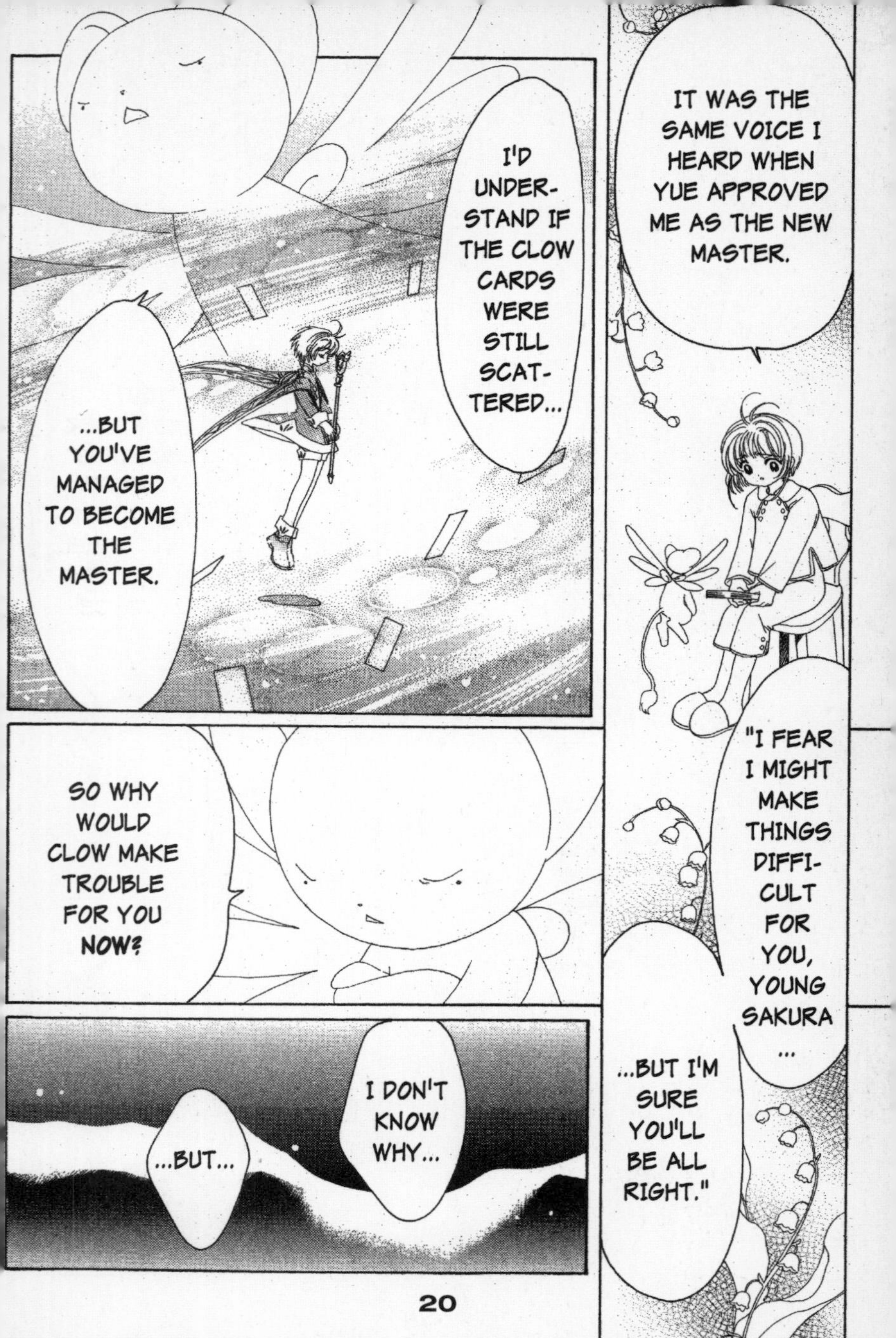
IT WAS THE SAME VOICE I HEARD WHEN YUE APPROVED ME AS THE NEW MASTER.
"I FEAR I MIGHT MAKE THINGS DIFFI-CULT FOR YOU, YOUNG SAKURA ...
...BUT I'M SURE YOU'LL BE ALL RIGHT."
I'D UNDER-STAND IF THE CLOW CARDS WERE STILL SCAT-TERED...
...BUT YOU'VE MANAGED TO BECOME THE MASTER.
SO WHY WOULD CLOW MAKE TROUBLE FOR YOU NOW?
I DON'T KNOW WHY...
...BUT...

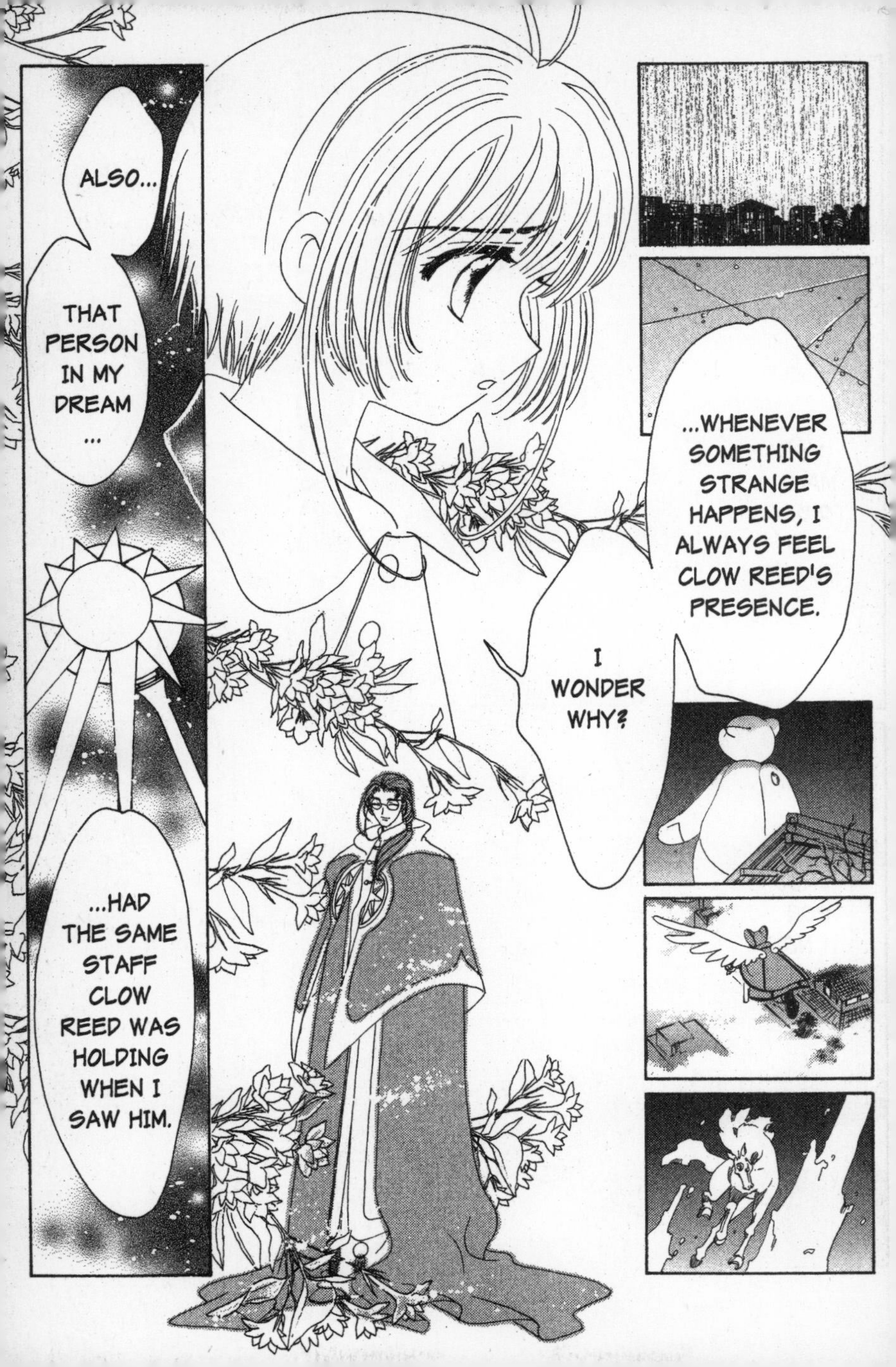
...WHENEVER SOMETHING STRANGE HAPPENS, I ALWAYS FEEL CLOW REED'S PRESENCE.
I WONDER WHY?
ALSO...
THAT PERSON IN MY DREAM ...
...HAD THE SAME STAFF CLOW REED WAS HOLDING WHEN I SAW HIM.

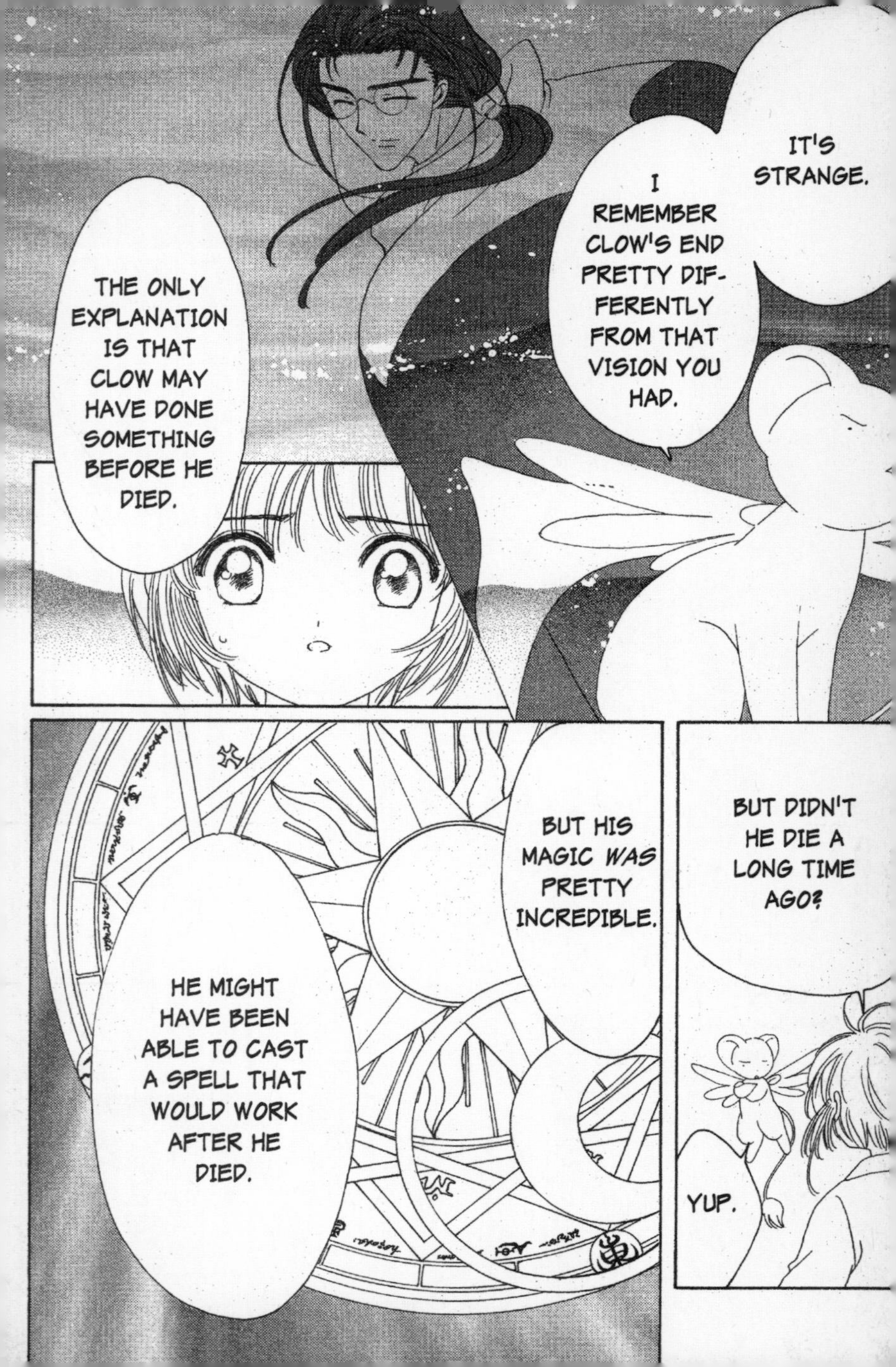
IT'S STRANGE.
I REMEMBER CLOW'S END PRETTY DIF-FERENTLY FROM THAT VISION YOU HAD.
THE ONLY EXPLANATION IS THAT CLOW MAY HAVE DONE SOMETHING BEFORE HE DIED.
BUT DIDN'T HE DIE A LONG TIME AGO?
YUP.
BUT HIS MAGIC *WAS* PRETTY INCREDIBLE.
HE MIGHT HAVE BEEN ABLE TO CAST A SPELL THAT WOULD WORK AFTER HE DIED.

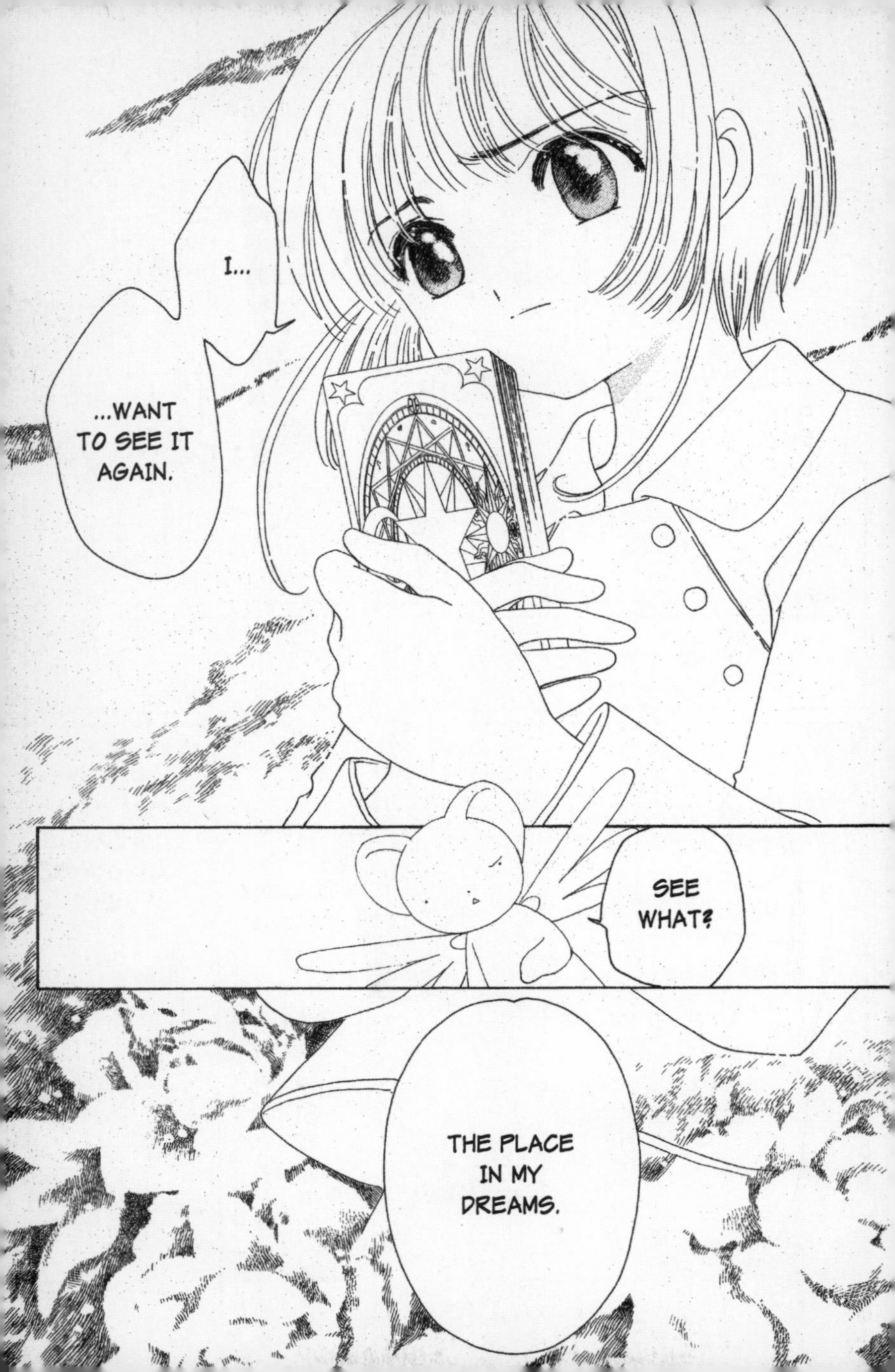
I...
...WANT TO SEE IT AGAIN.
SEE WHAT?
THE PLACE IN MY DREAMS.

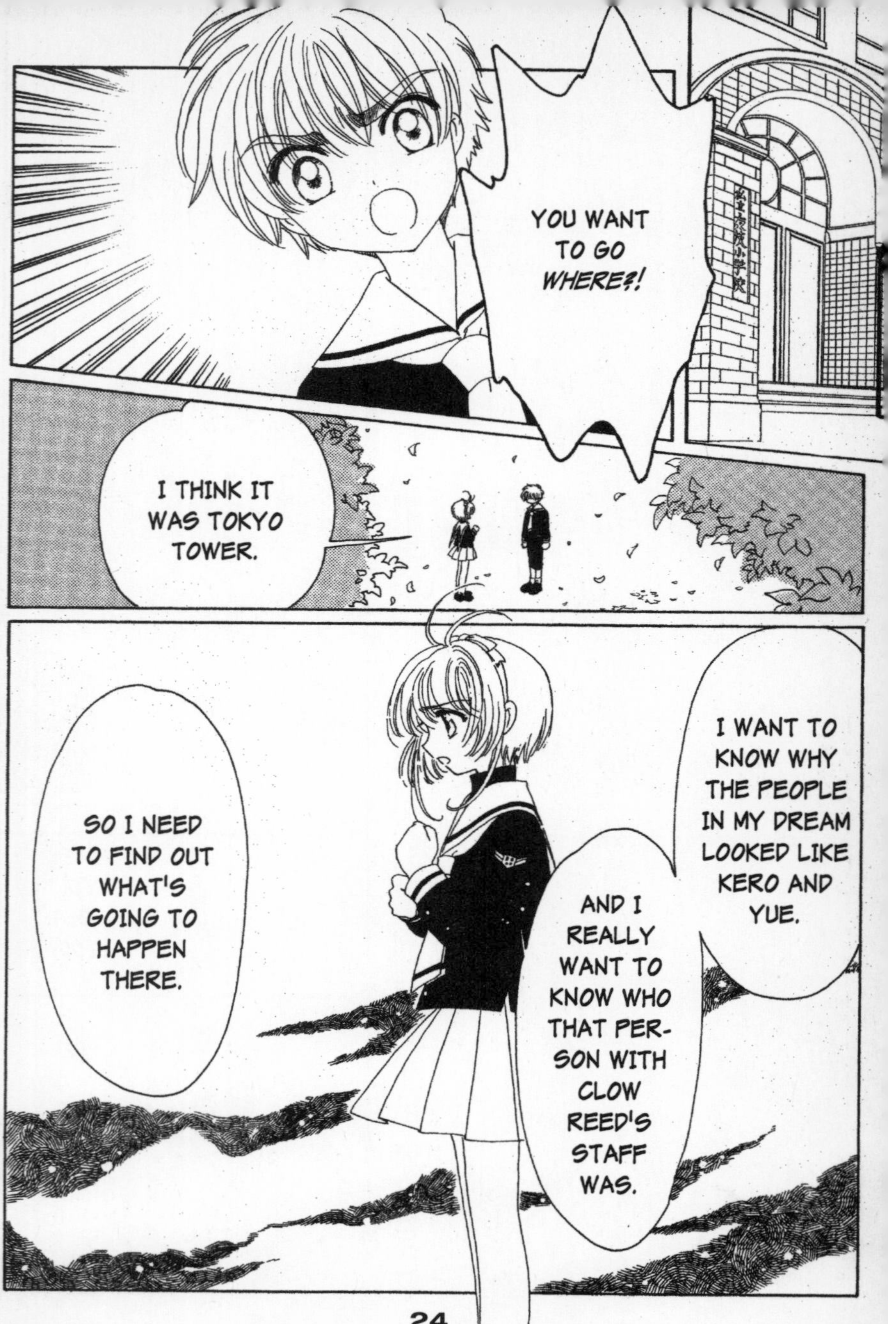
YOU WANT TO GO WHERE?!
I THINK IT WAS TOKYO TOWER.
I WANT TO KNOW WHY THE PEOPLE IN MY DREAM LOOKED LIKE KERO AND YUE.
AND I REALLY WANT TO KNOW WHO THAT PER-SON WITH CLOW REED'S STAFF WAS.
SO I NEED TO FIND OUT WHAT'S GOING TO HAPPEN THERE.

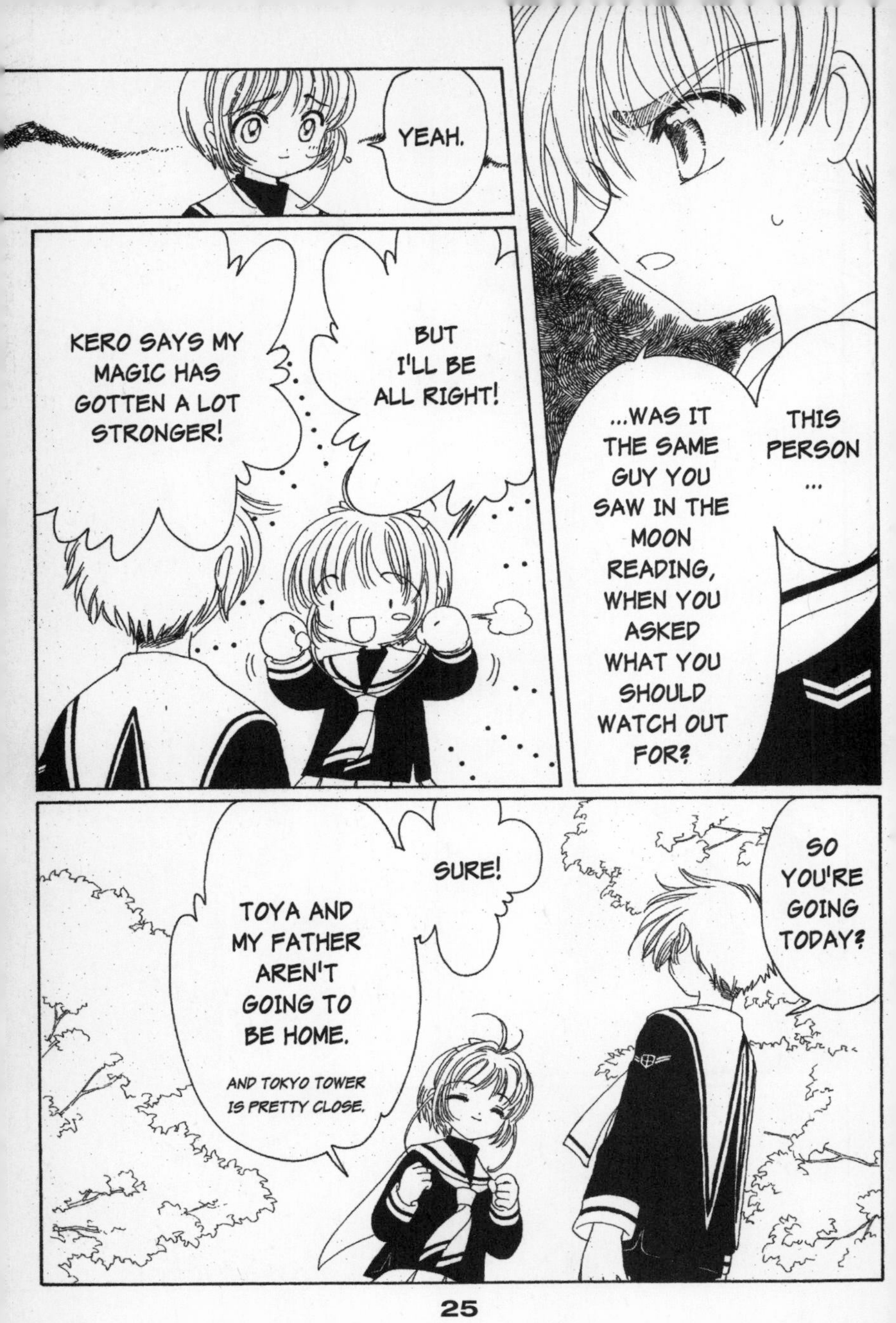
THIS PERSON ...
...WAS IT THE SAME GUY YOU SAW IN THE MOON READING, WHEN YOU ASKED WHAT YOU SHOULD WATCH OUT FOR?
YEAH.
BUT I'LL BE ALL RIGHT!
KERO SAYS MY MAGIC HAS GOTTEN A LOT STRONGER!
SO YOU'RE GOING TODAY?
SURE!
TOYA AND MY FATHER AREN'T GOING TO BE HOME.
AND TOKYO TOWER IS PRETTY CLOSE.

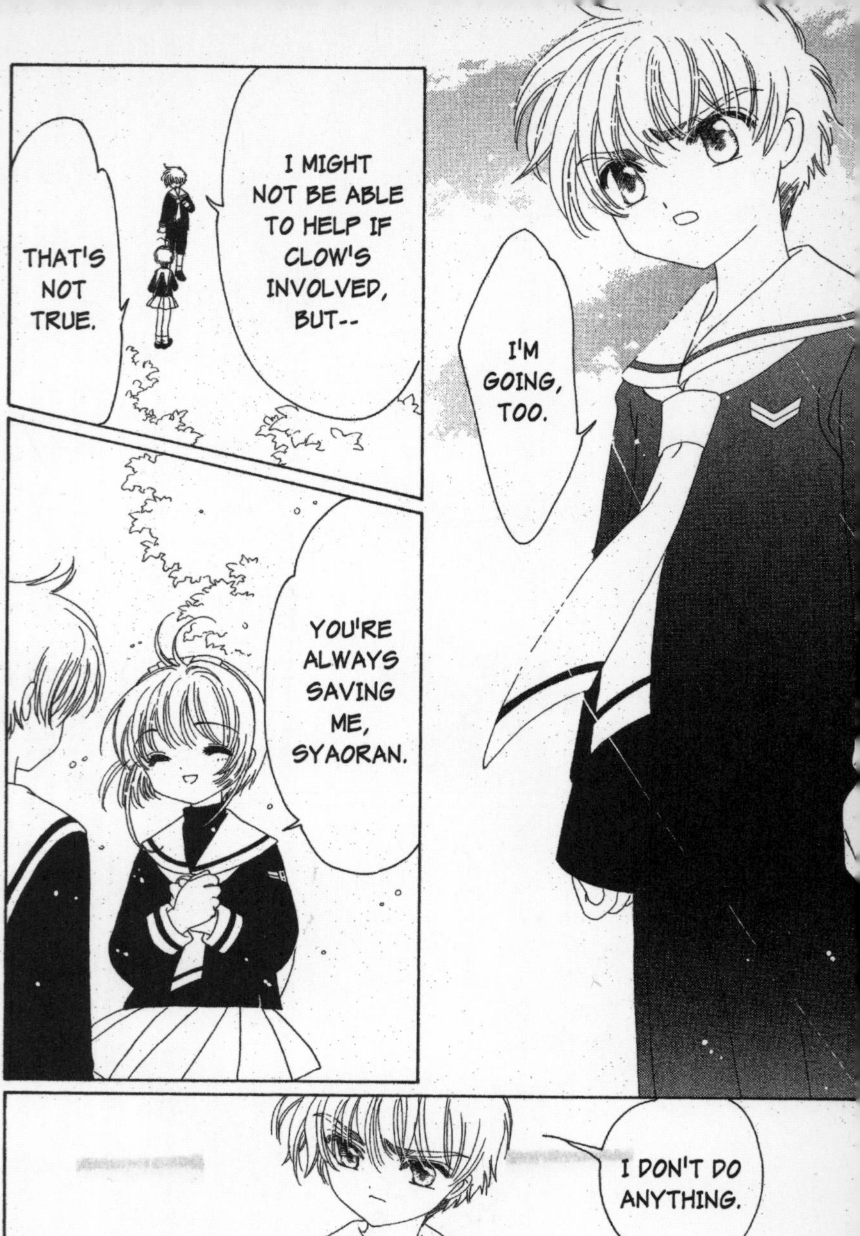
I'M GOING, TOO.
I MIGHT NOT BE ABLE TO HELP IF CLOW'S INVOLVED, BUT--
THAT'S NOT TRUE.
YOU'RE ALWAYS SAVING ME, SYAORAN.
I DON'T DO ANYTHING.

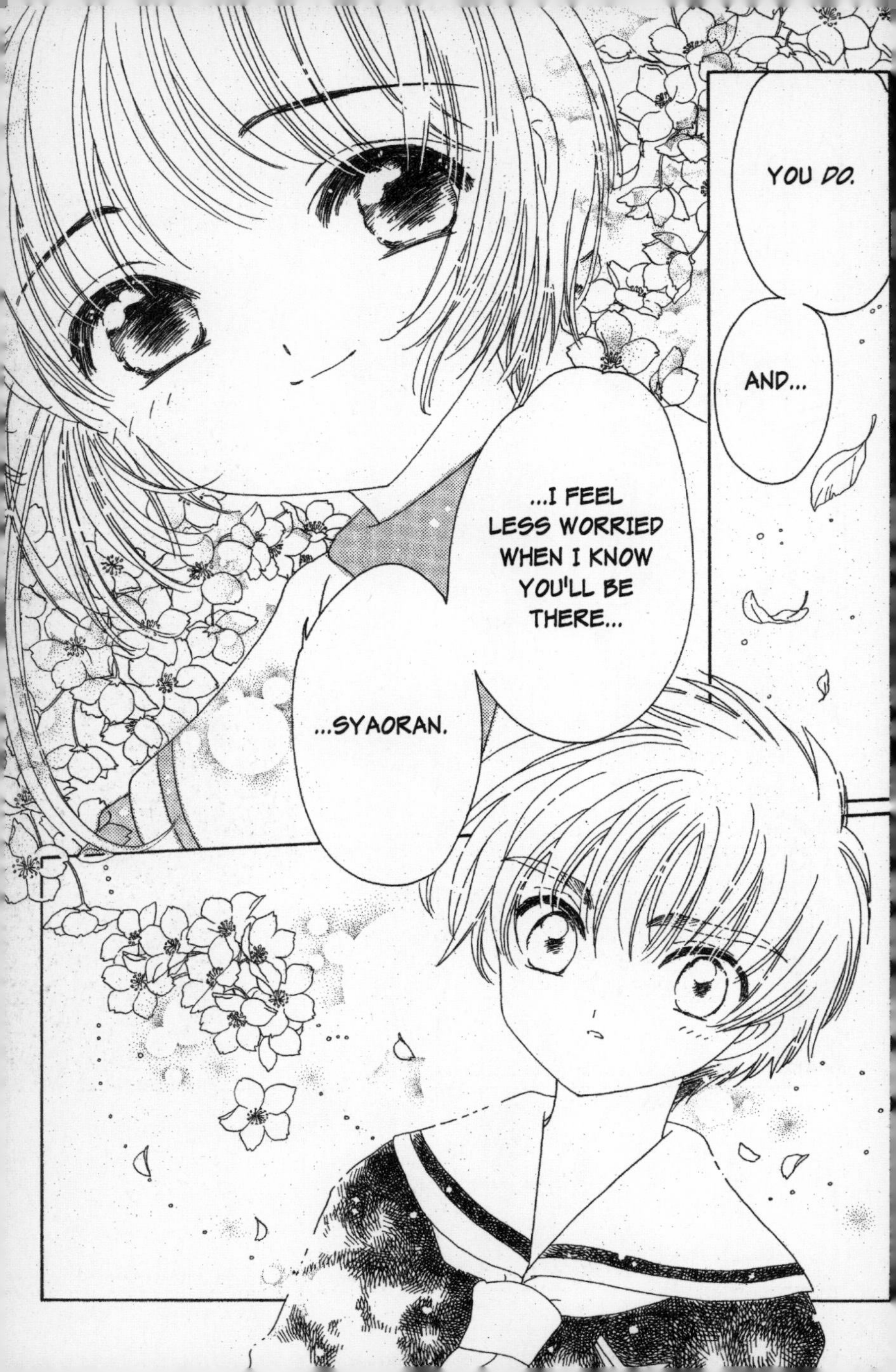
YOU DO.
AND...
...I FEEL LESS WORRIED WHEN I KNOW YOU'LL BE THERE...
...SYAORAN.

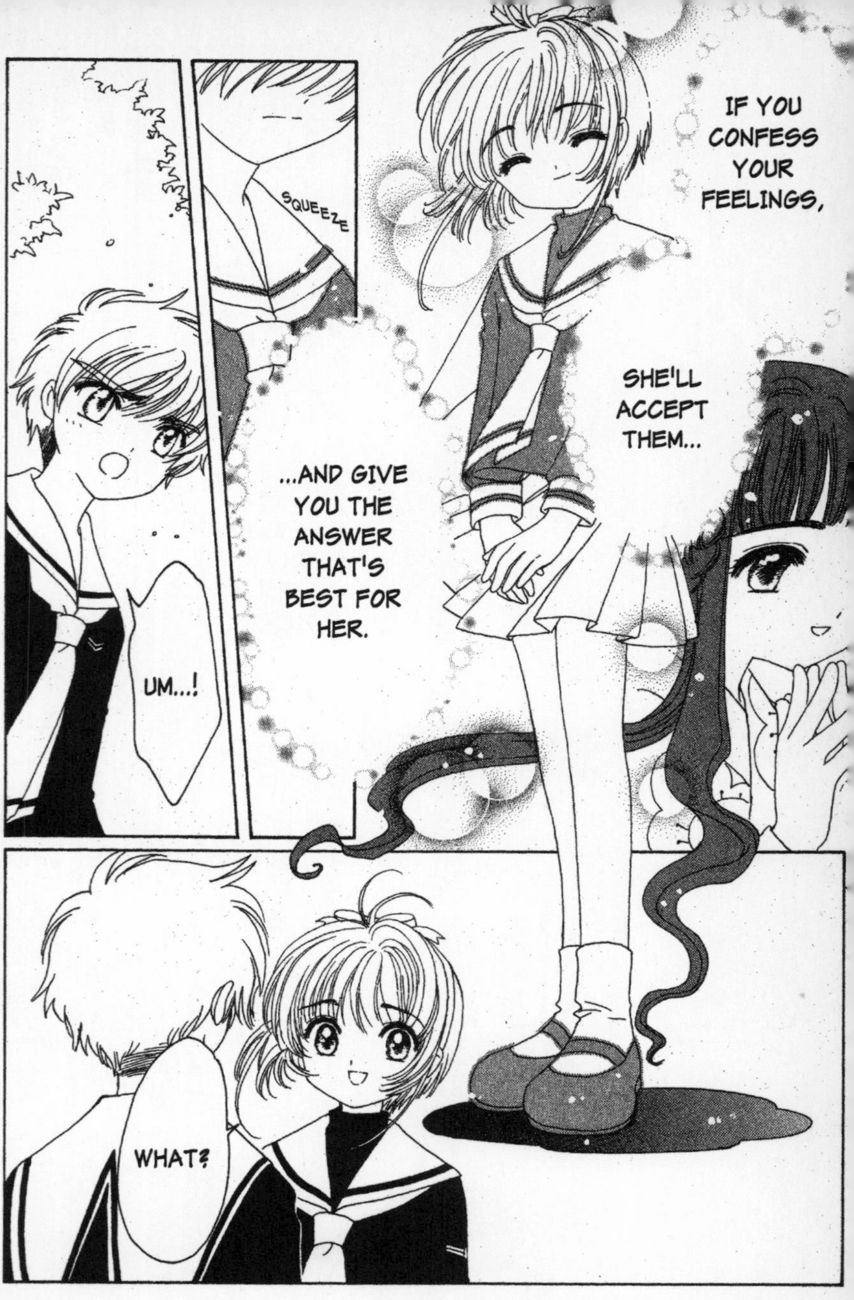
IF YOU CONFESS YOUR FEELINGS,
SHE'LL ACCEPT THEM...
...AND GIVE YOU THE ANSWER THAT'S BEST FOR HER.
SQUEEZE
UM...!
WHAT?

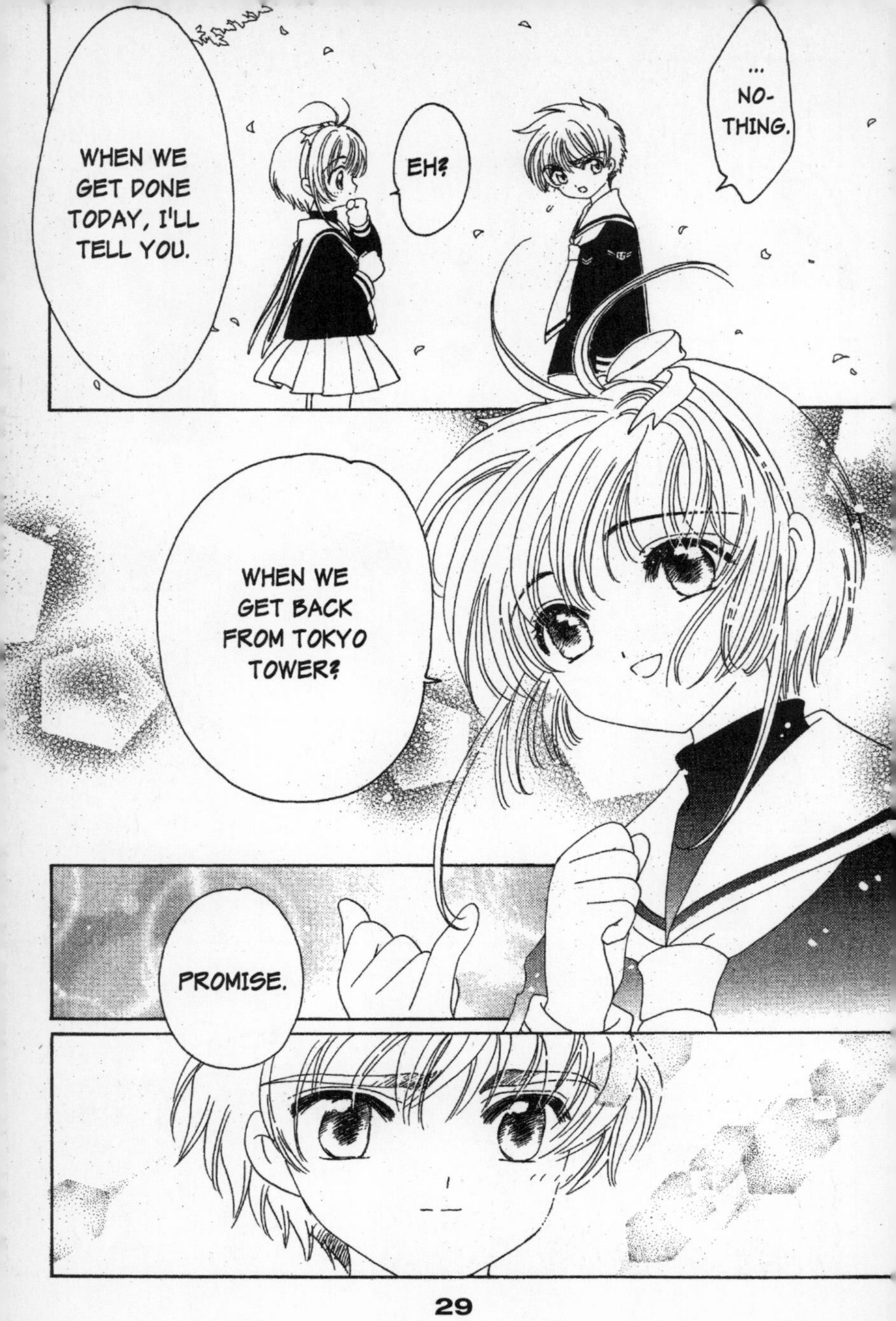
... NO-THING.
EH?
WHEN WE GET DONE TODAY, I'LL TELL YOU.
WHEN WE GET BACK FROM TOKYO TOWER?
PROMISE.

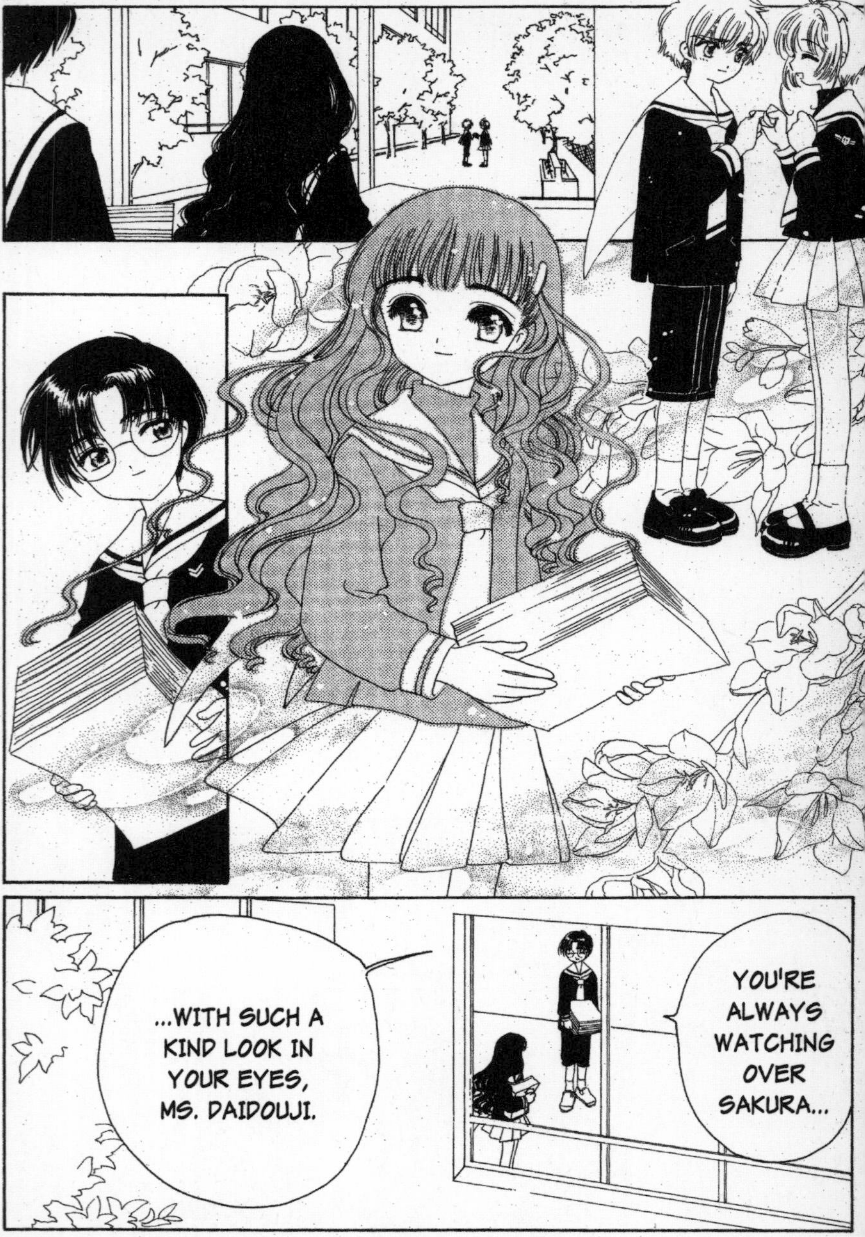
YOU'RE ALWAYS WATCHING OVER SAKURA...
...WITH SUCH A KIND LOOK IN YOUR EYES, MS. DAIDOUJI.

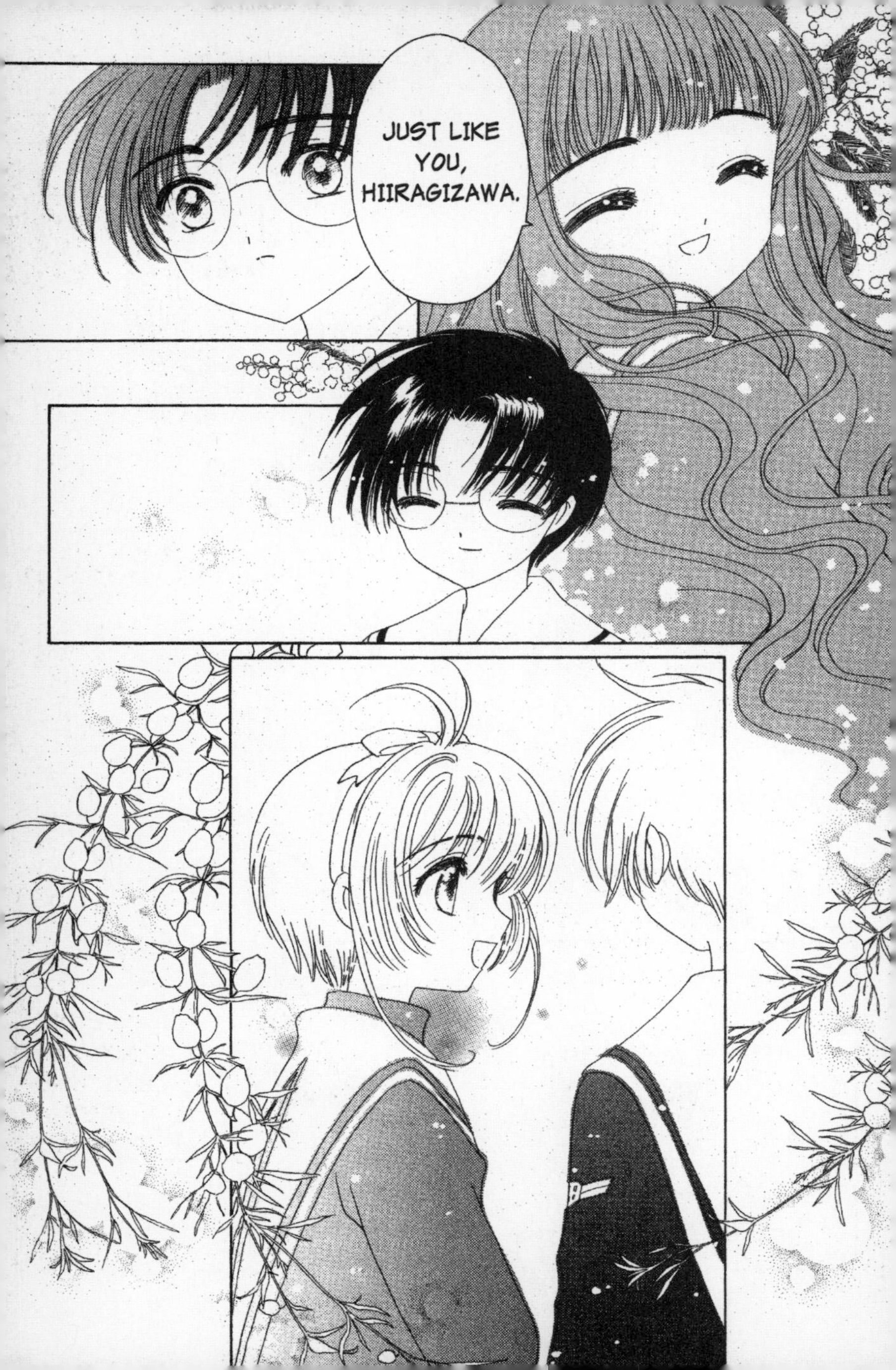
JUST LIKE YOU, HIIRAGIZAWA.

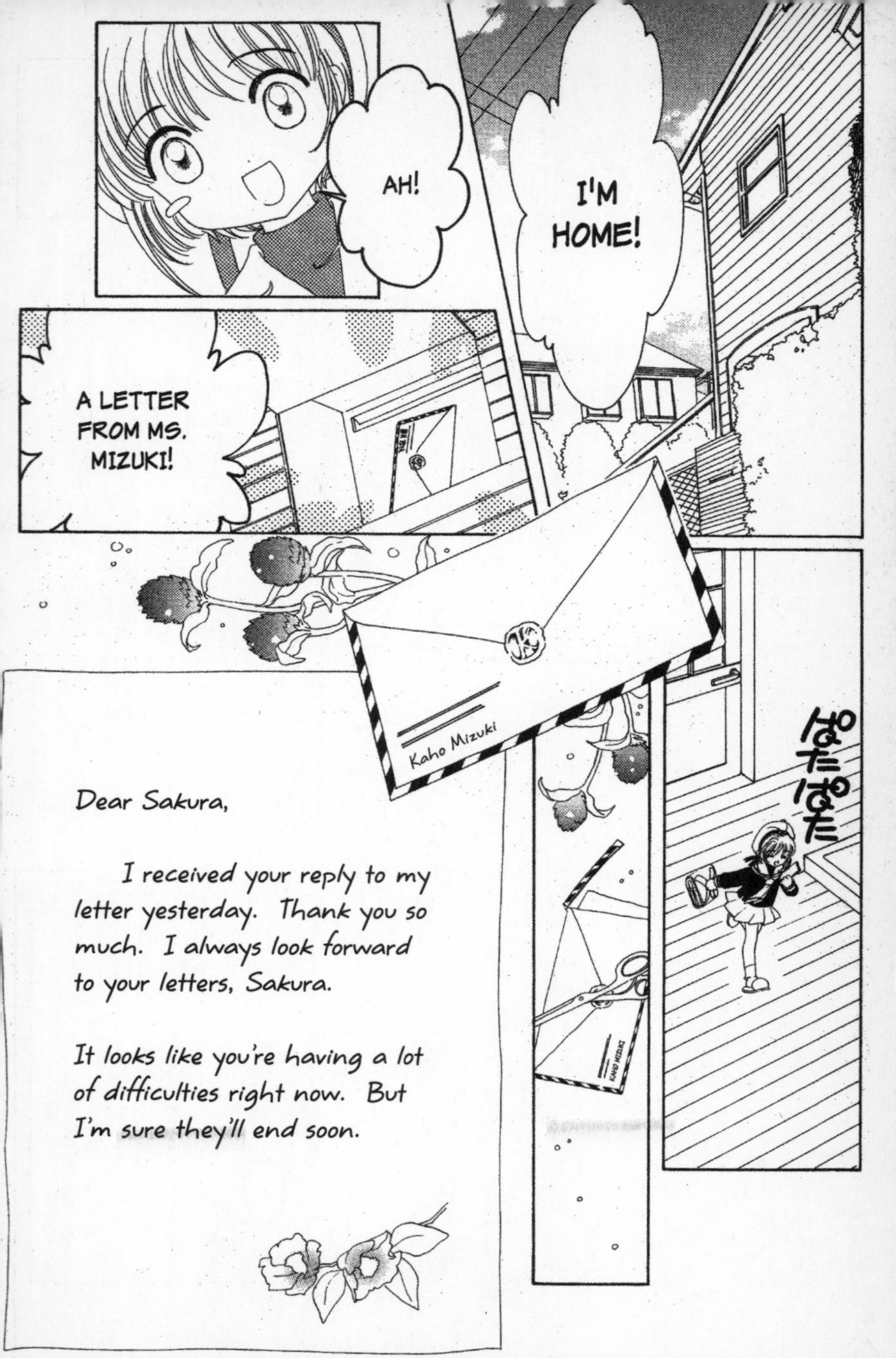
I'M HOME!
AH!
A LETTER FROM MS. MIZUKI!
ぱたぱた
Kaho Mizuki
Dear Sakura,
I received your reply to my letter yesterday. Thank you so much. I always look forward to your letters, Sakura.
It looks like you're having a lot of difficulties right now. But I'm sure they'll end soon.

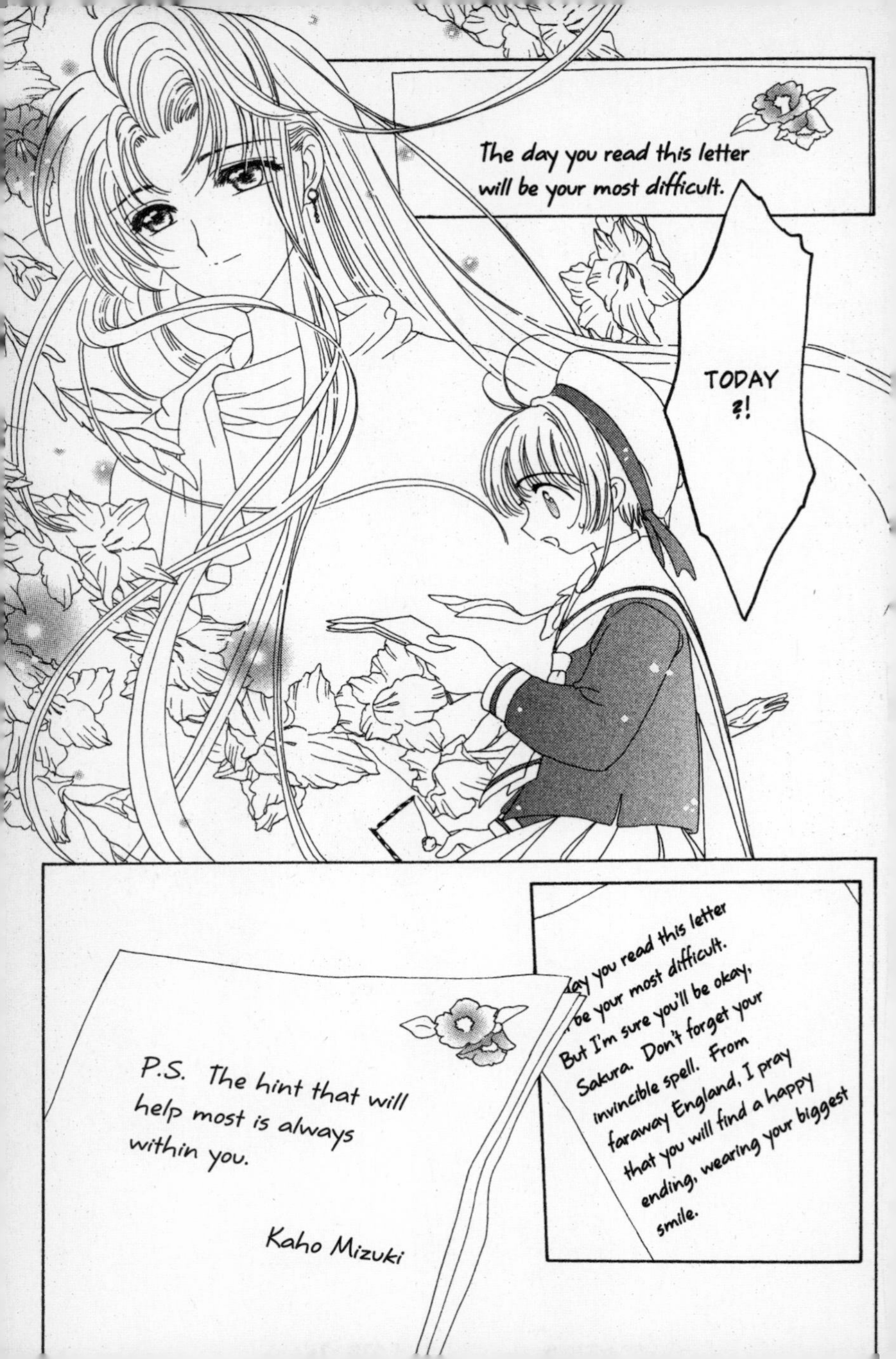
The day you read this letter will be your most difficult.
TODAY ?!
day you read this letter
be your most difficult.
But I'm sure you'll be okay,
Sakura. Don't forget your
invincible spell. From
faraway England, I pray
that you will find a happy
ending, wearing your biggest
smile.
P.S. The hint that will help most is always within you.
Kaho Mizuki

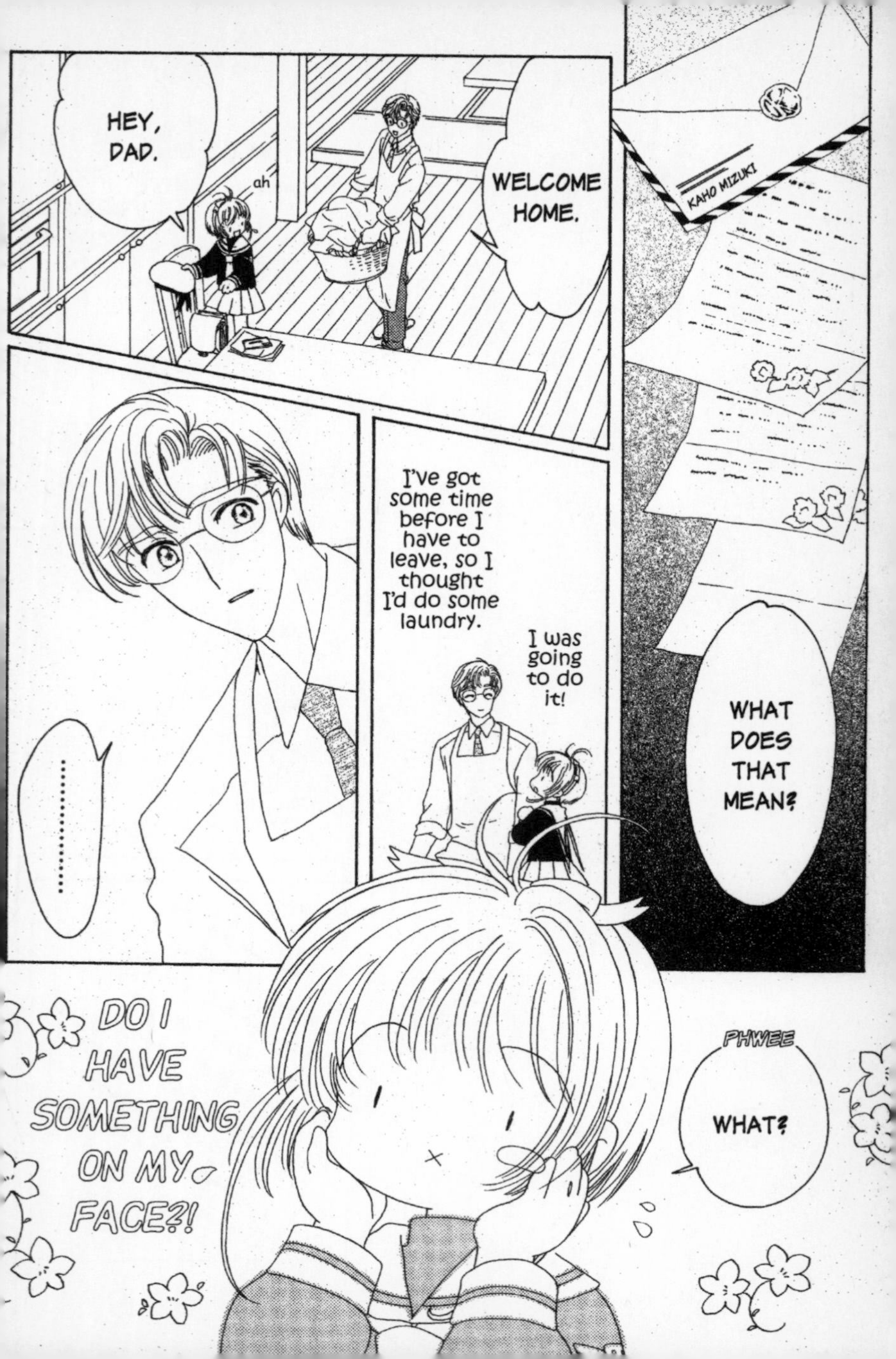
HEY, DAD.
ah
WELCOME HOME.
KAHO MIZUKI
I've got some time before I have to leave, so I thought I'd do some laundry.
I was going to do it!
......
WHAT DOES THAT MEAN?
PHWEE
WHAT?
DO I HAVE SOMETHING ON MY FACE?!

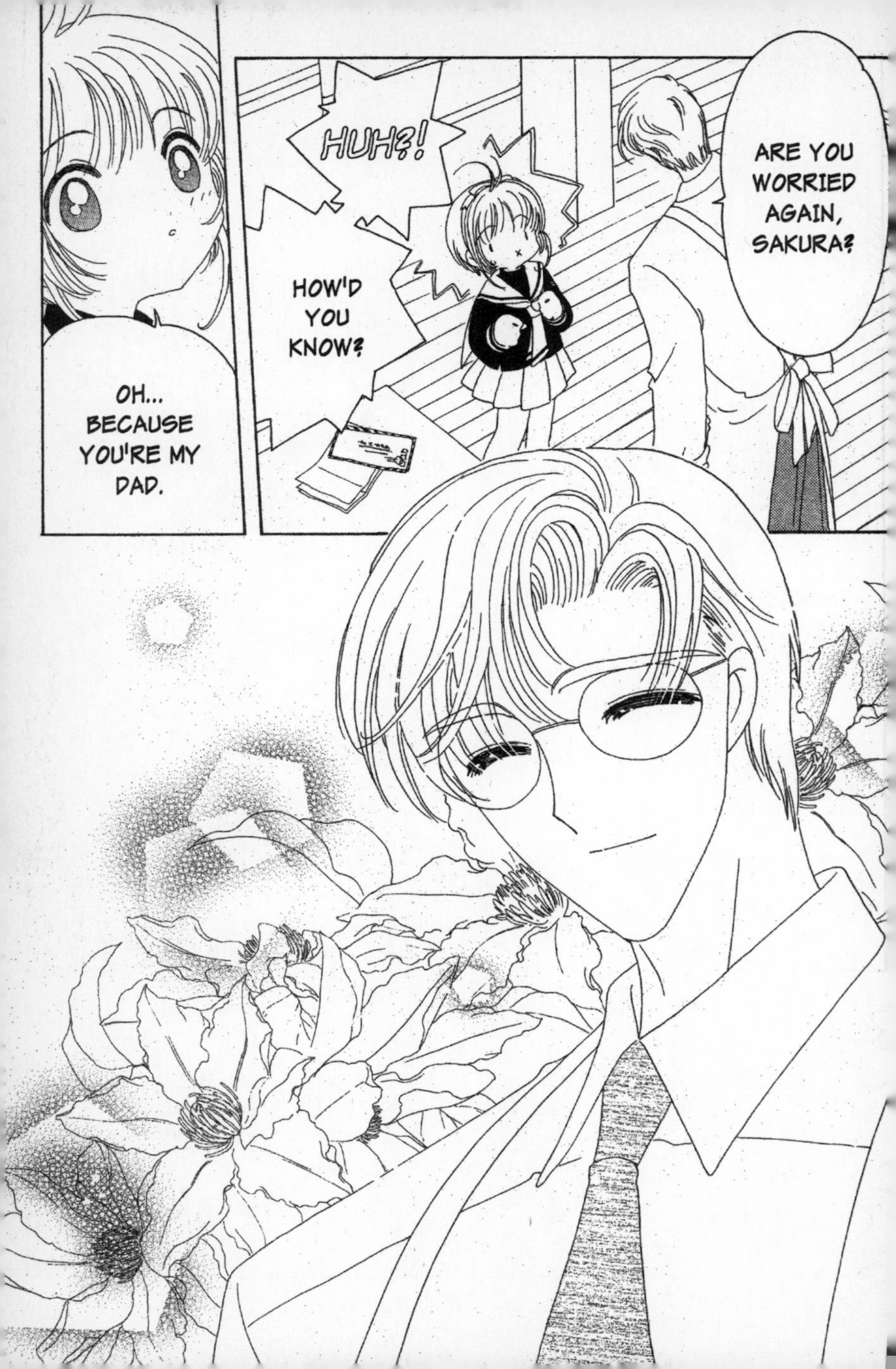
ARE YOU WORRIED AGAIN, SAKURA?
HUH?!
HOW'D YOU KNOW?
OH... BECAUSE YOU'RE MY DAD.

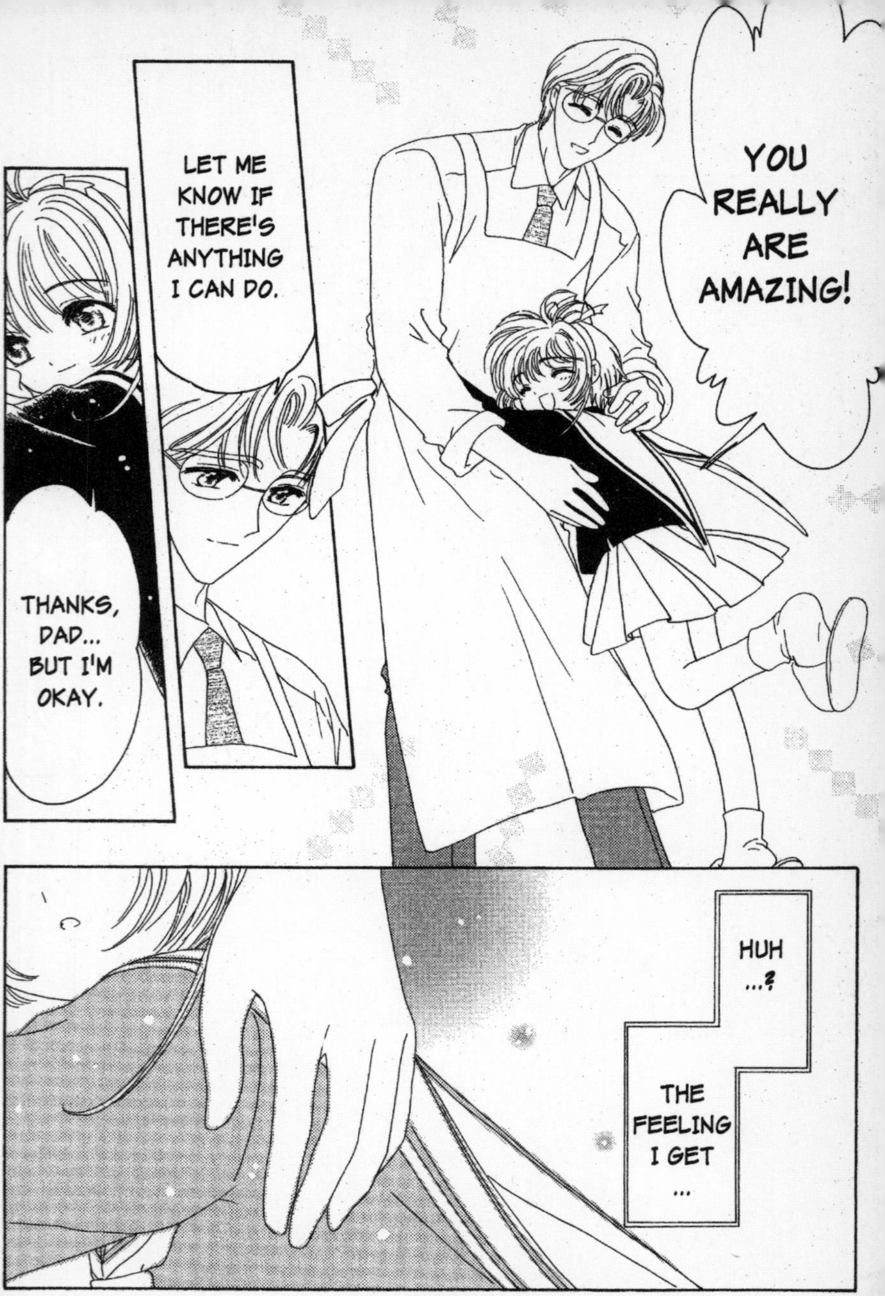
YOU REALLY ARE AMAZING!
LET ME KNOW IF THERE'S ANYTHING I CAN DO.
THANKS, DAD... BUT I'M OKAY.
HUH ...?
THE FEELING I GET ...

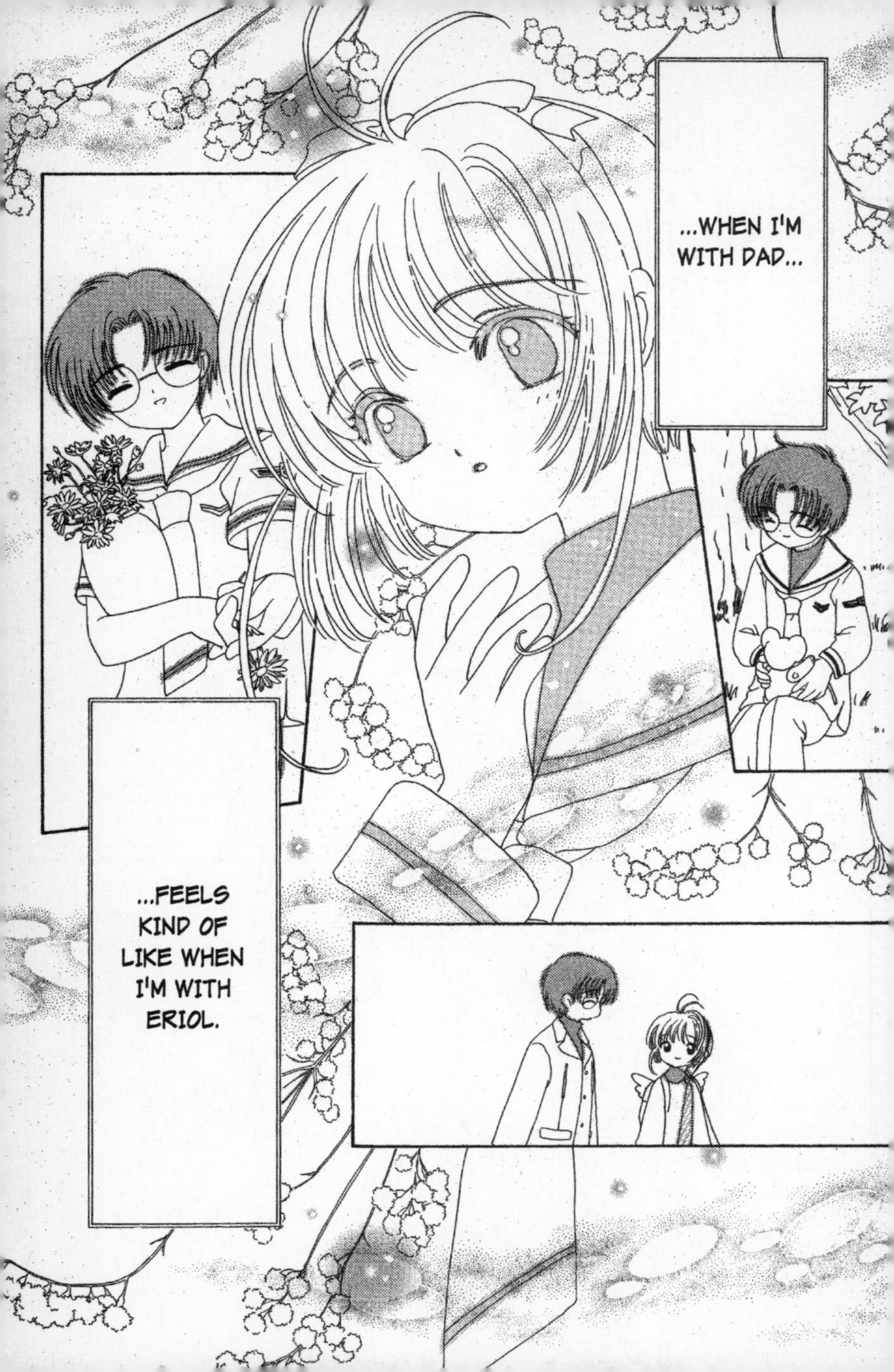
...WHEN I'M WITH DAD...
...FEELS KIND OF LIKE WHEN I'M WITH ERIOL.

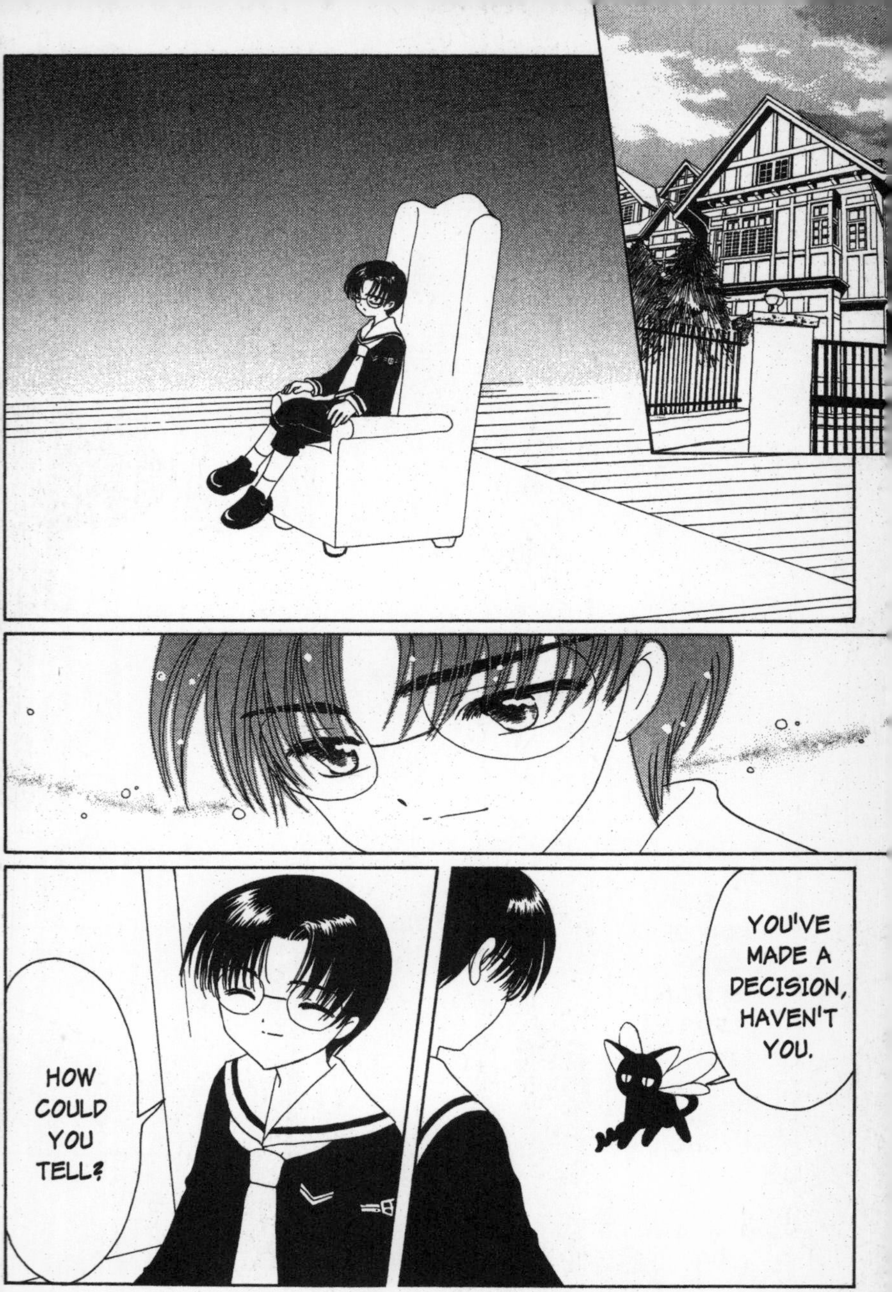
YOU'VE MADE A DECISION, HAVEN'T YOU.
HOW COULD YOU TELL?

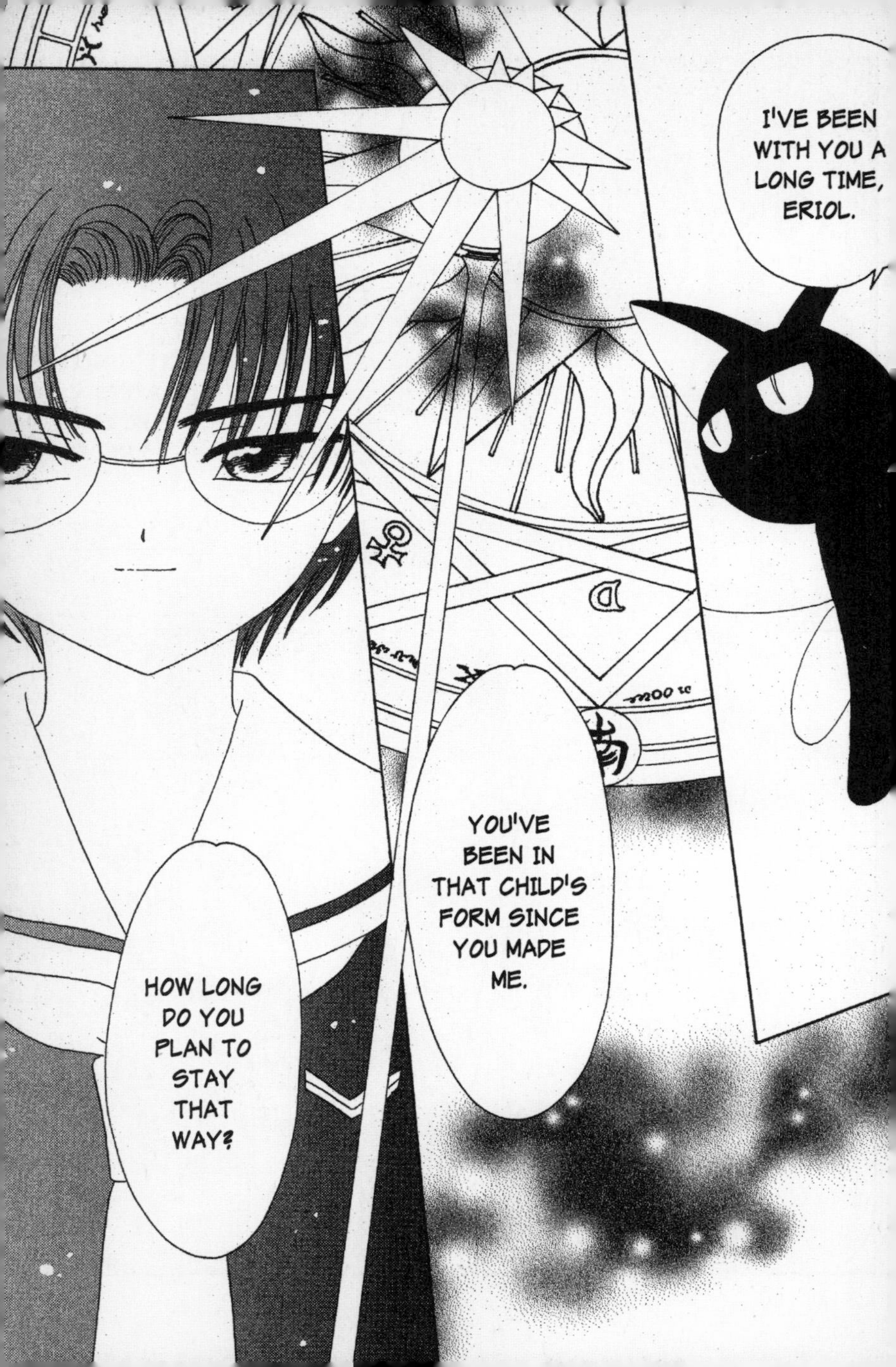
I'VE BEEN WITH YOU A LONG TIME, ERIOL.
YOU'VE BEEN IN THAT CHILD'S FORM SINCE YOU MADE ME.
HOW LONG DO YOU PLAN TO STAY THAT WAY?

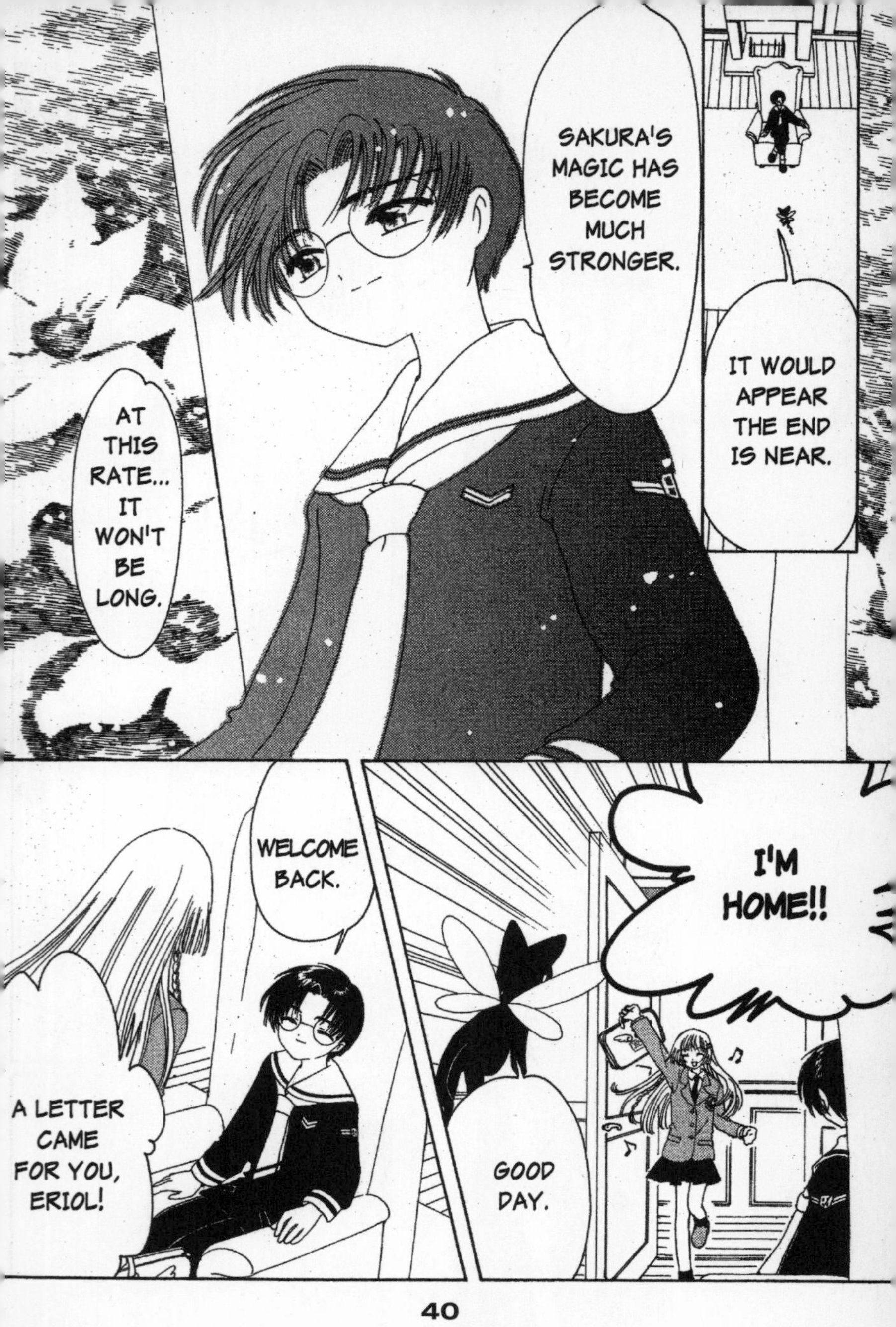
IT WOULD APPEAR THE END IS NEAR.
SAKURA'S MAGIC HAS BECOME MUCH STRONGER.
AT THIS RATE... IT WON'T BE LONG.
I'M HOME!!
GOOD DAY.
WELCOME BACK.
A LETTER CAME FOR YOU, ERIOL!

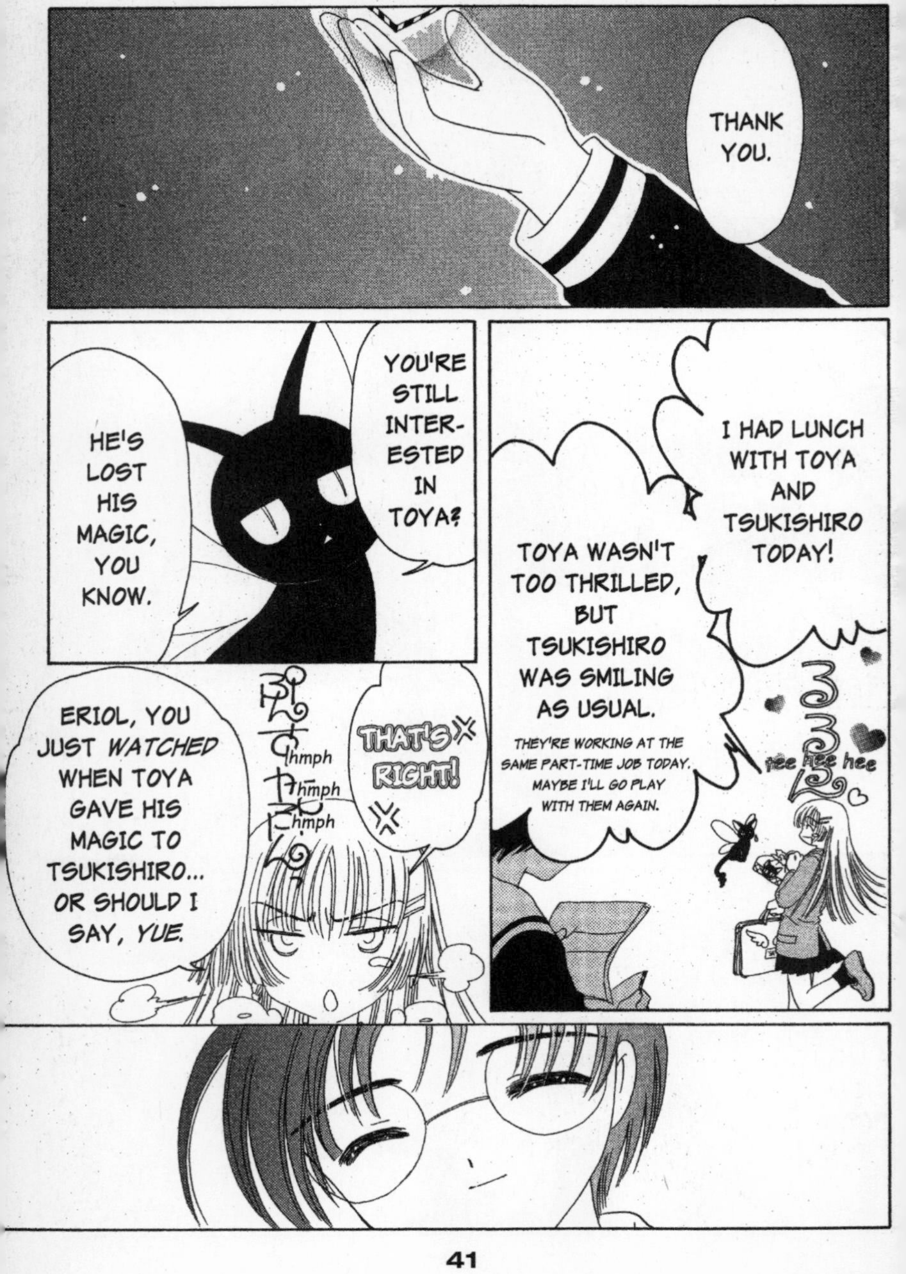
THANK YOU.
I HAD LUNCH WITH TOYA AND TSUKISHIRO TODAY!
TOYA WASN'T TOO THRILLED, BUT TSUKISHIRO WAS SMILING AS USUAL.
THEY'RE WORKING AT THE SAME PART-TIME JOB TODAY. MAYBE I'LL GO PLAY WITH THEM AGAIN.
tee hee hee
YOU'RE STILL INTER-ESTED IN TOYA?
HE'S LOST HIS MAGIC, YOU KNOW.
THAT'S RIGHT!
hmph
hmph
hmph
ERIOL, YOU JUST *WATCHED* WHEN TOYA GAVE HIS MAGIC TO TSUKISHIRO... OR SHOULD I SAY, *YUE*.

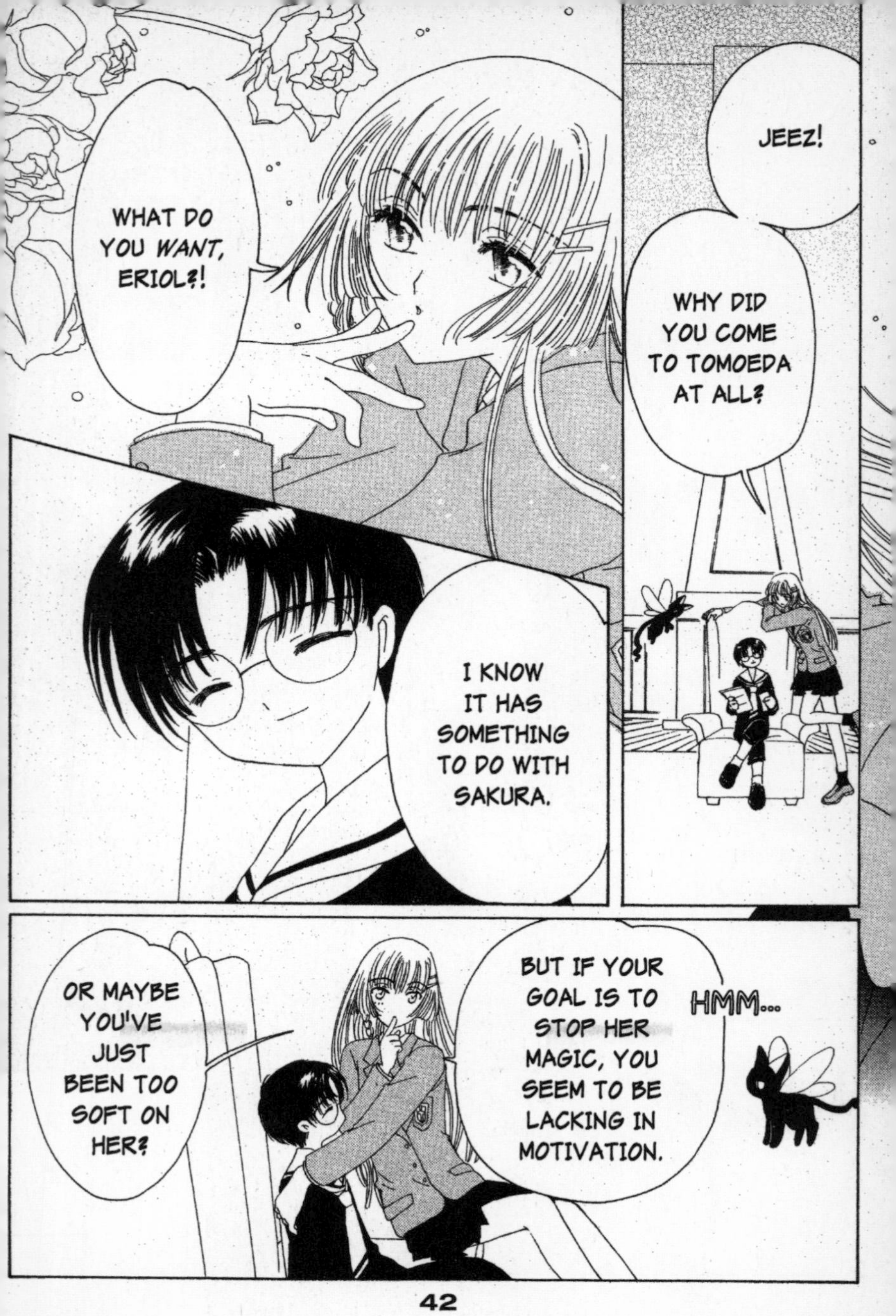
JEEZ!
WHY DID YOU COME TO TOMOEDA AT ALL?
WHAT DO YOU *WANT*, ERIOL?!
I KNOW IT HAS SOMETHING TO DO WITH SAKURA.
HMM...
BUT IF YOUR GOAL IS TO STOP HER MAGIC, YOU SEEM TO BE LACKING IN MOTIVATION.
OR MAYBE YOU'VE JUST BEEN TOO SOFT ON HER?

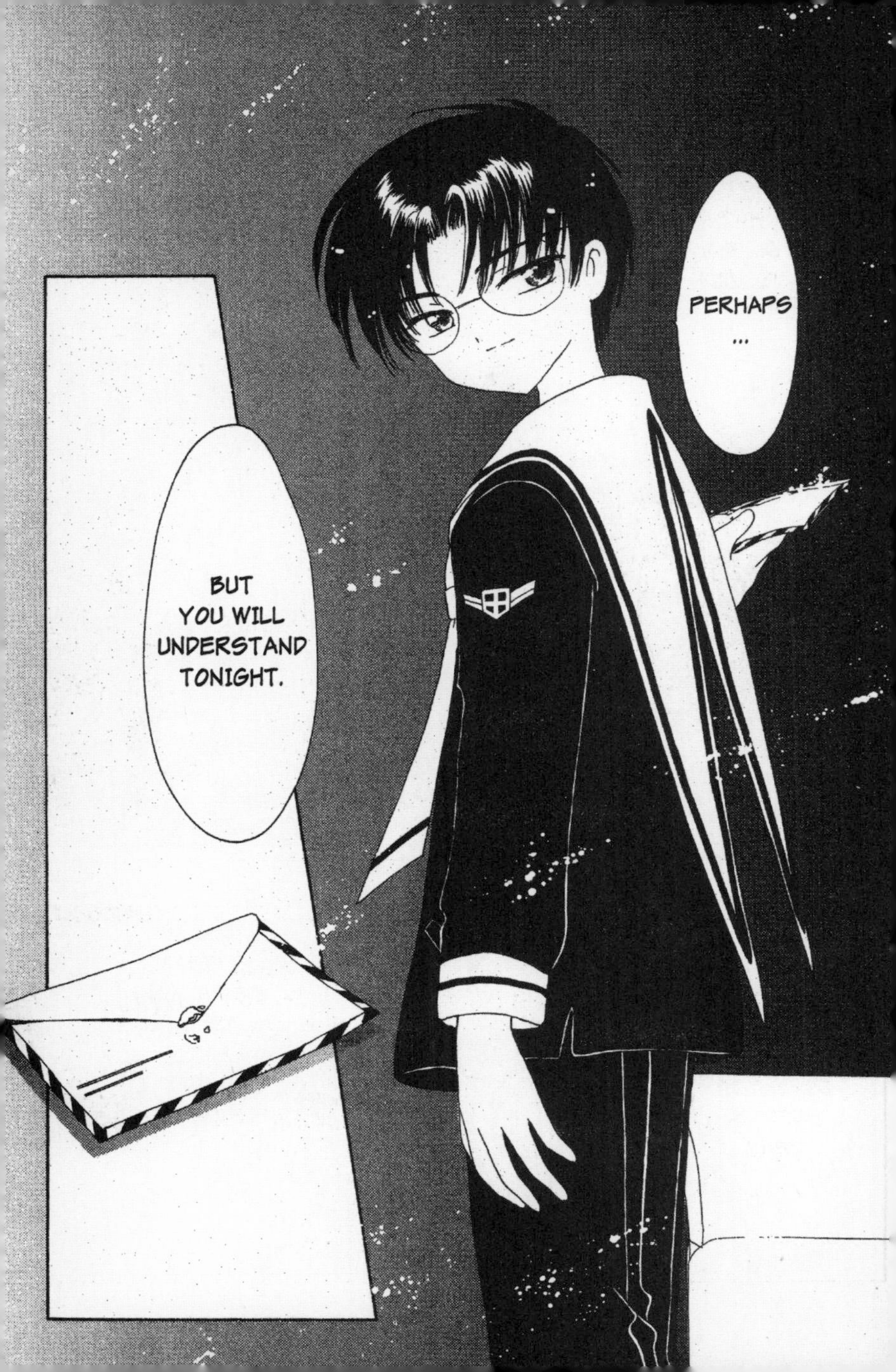
PERHAPS ...
BUT YOU WILL UNDERSTAND TONIGHT.

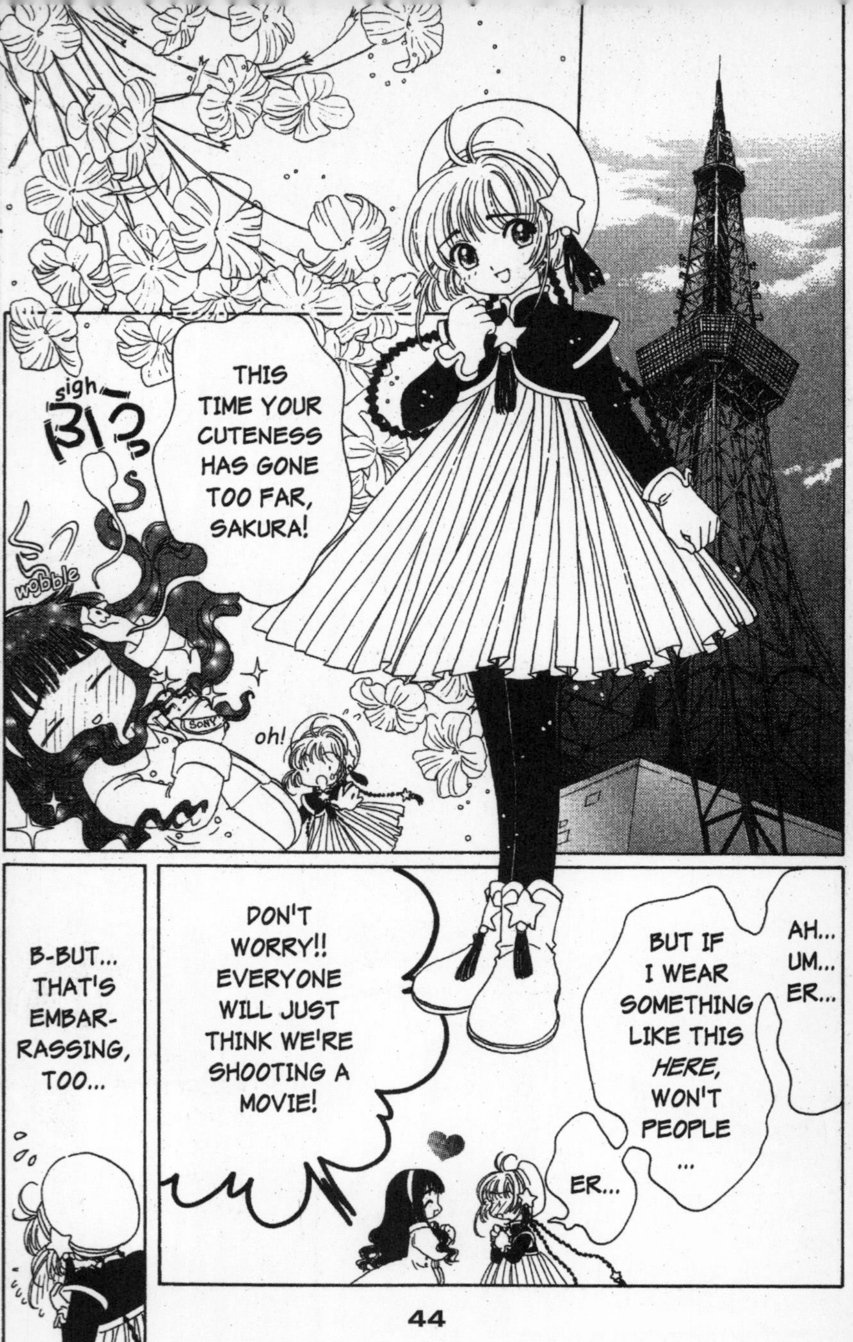
THIS TIME YOUR CUTENESS HAS GONE TOO FAR, SAKURA!
sigh
wobble
SONY
oh!
AH... UM... ER...
BUT IF I WEAR SOMETHING LIKE THIS *HERE*, WON'T PEOPLE ...
ER...
DON'T WORRY!! EVERYONE WILL JUST THINK WE'RE SHOOTING A MOVIE!
B-BUT... THAT'S EMBAR-RASSING, TOO...

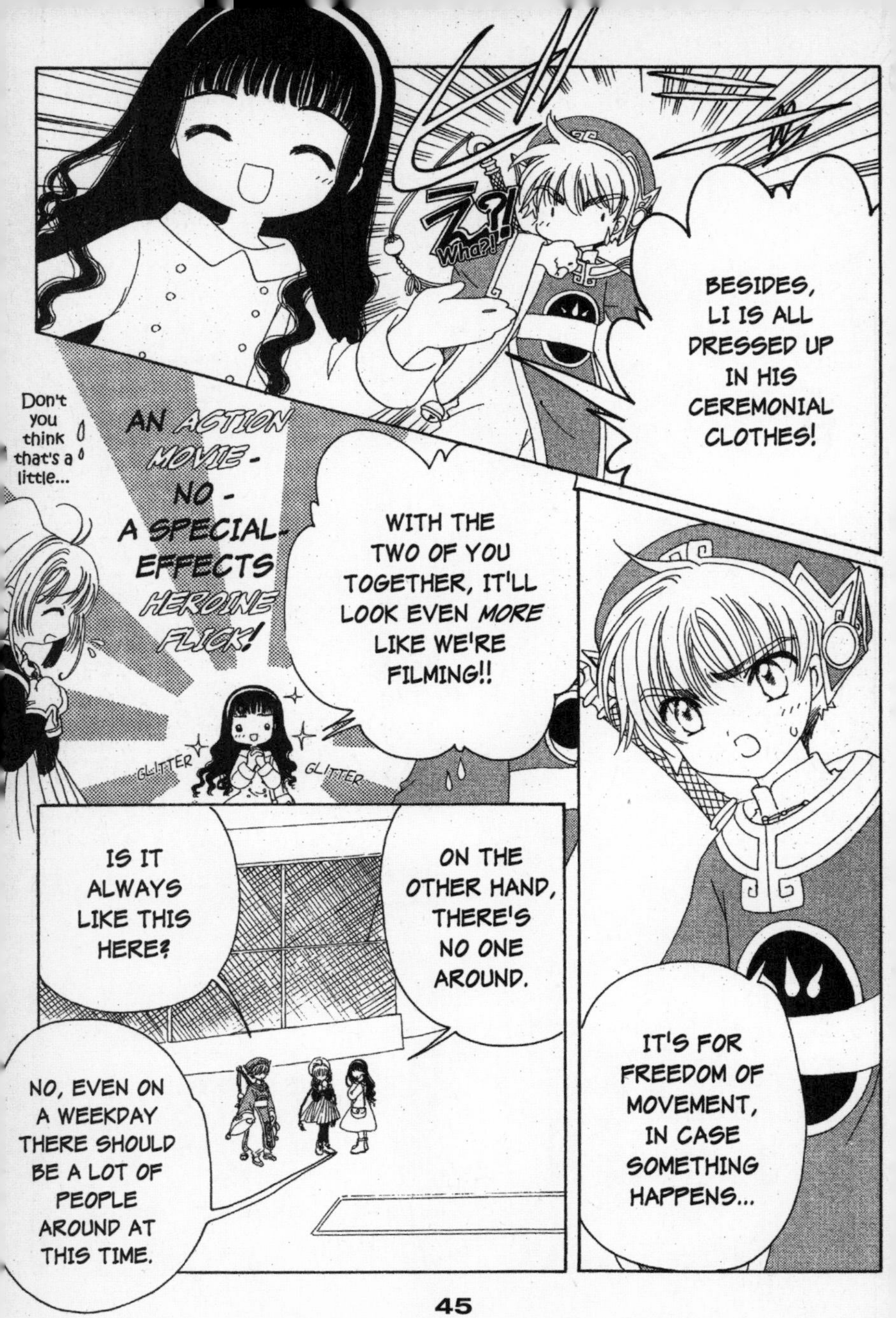
Z?! Wha?!
BESIDES, LI IS ALL DRESSED UP IN HIS CEREMONIAL CLOTHES!
IT'S FOR FREEDOM OF MOVEMENT, IN CASE SOMETHING HAPPENS...
WITH THE TWO OF YOU TOGETHER, IT'LL LOOK EVEN MORE LIKE WE'RE FILMING!!
AN ACTION MOVIE - NO - A SPECIAL-EFFECTS HEROINE FLICK!
GLITTER GLITTER
Don't you think that's a little...
ON THE OTHER HAND, THERE'S NO ONE AROUND.
IS IT ALWAYS LIKE THIS HERE?
NO, EVEN ON A WEEKDAY THERE SHOULD BE A LOT OF PEOPLE AROUND AT THIS TIME.

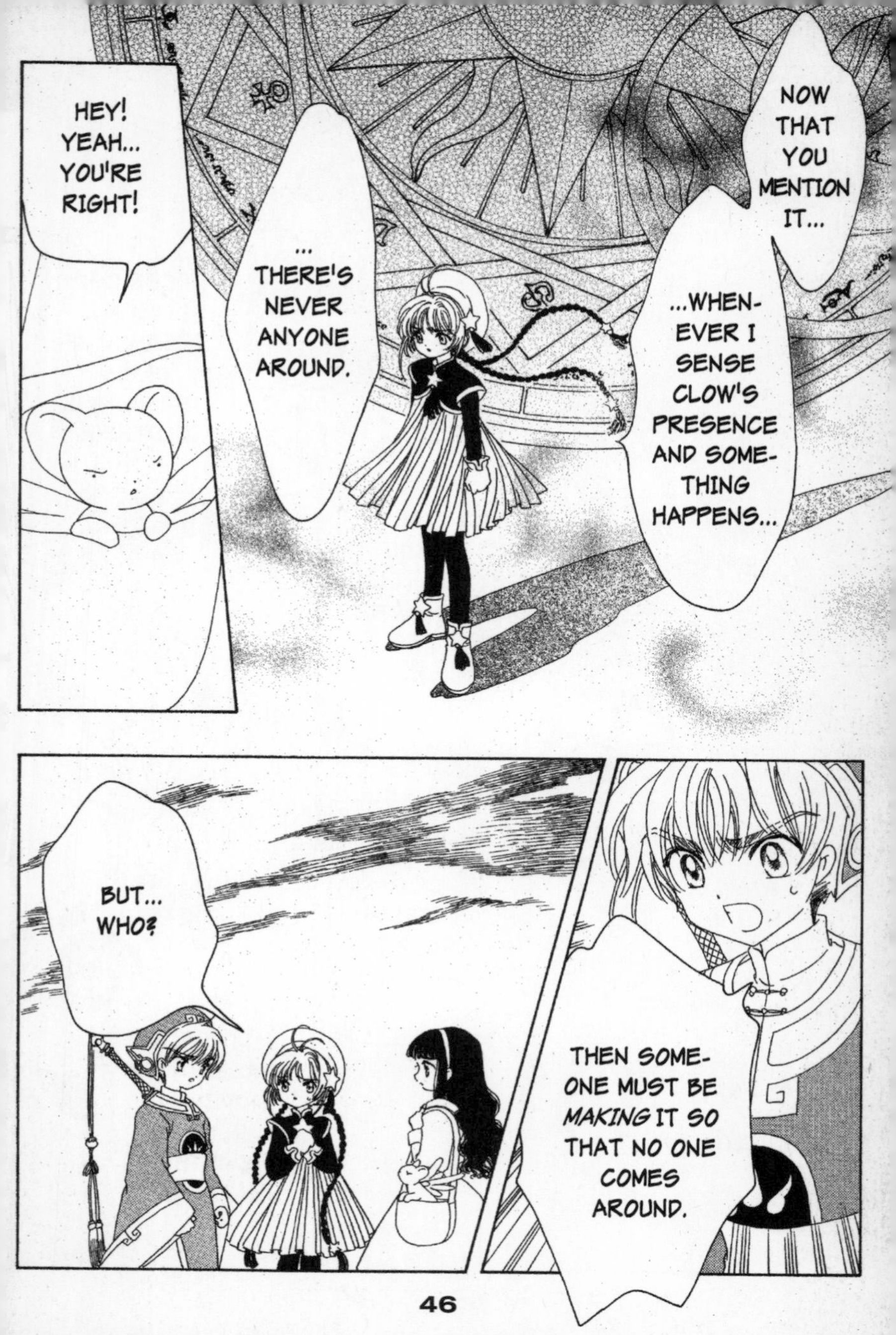
NOW THAT YOU MENTION IT...
...WHEN-EVER I SENSE CLOW'S PRESENCE AND SOME-THING HAPPENS...
... THERE'S NEVER ANYONE AROUND.
HEY! YEAH... YOU'RE RIGHT!
THEN SOME-ONE MUST BE *MAKING* IT SO THAT NO ONE COMES AROUND.
BUT... WHO?

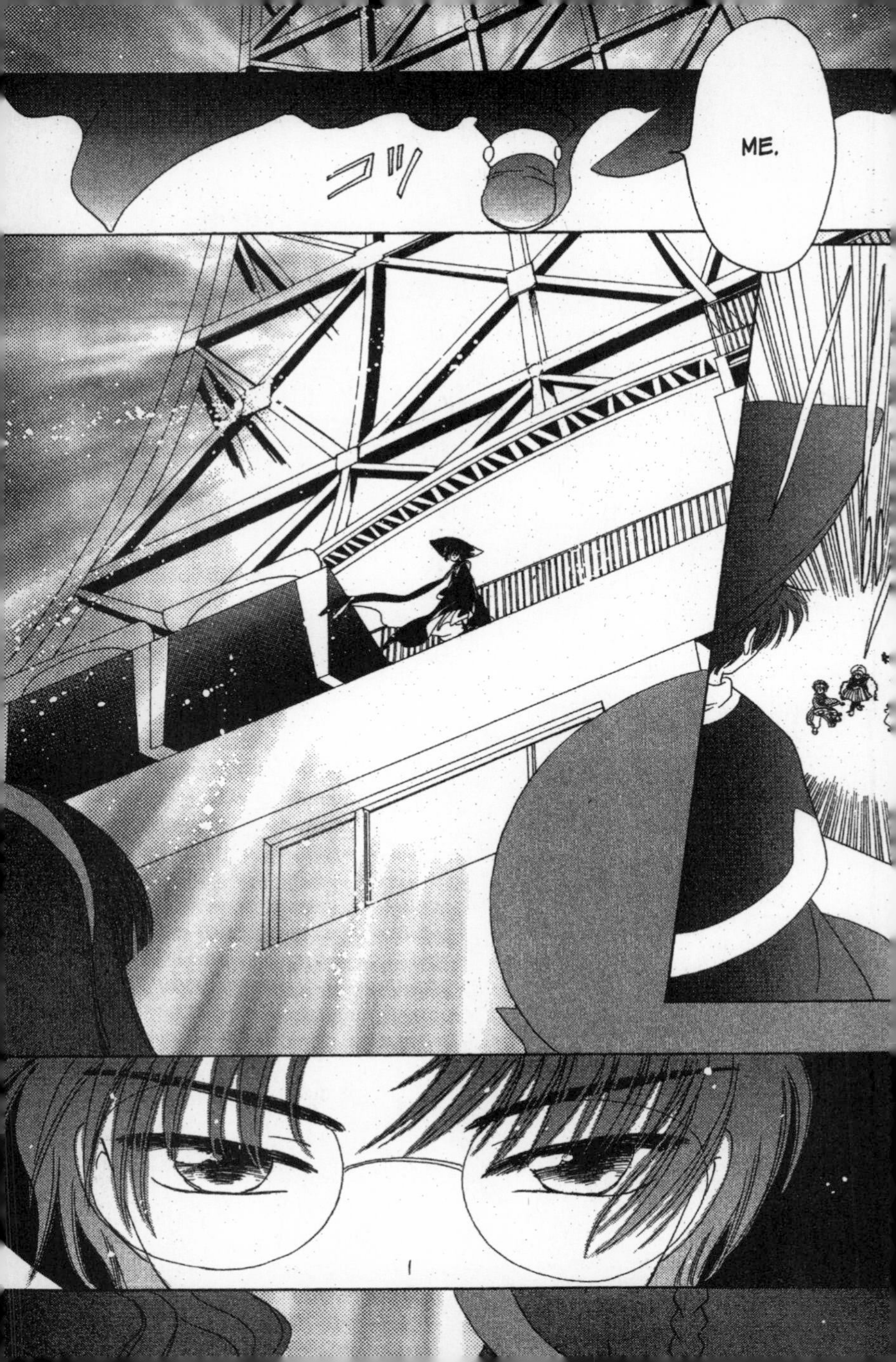
ME.
コツ

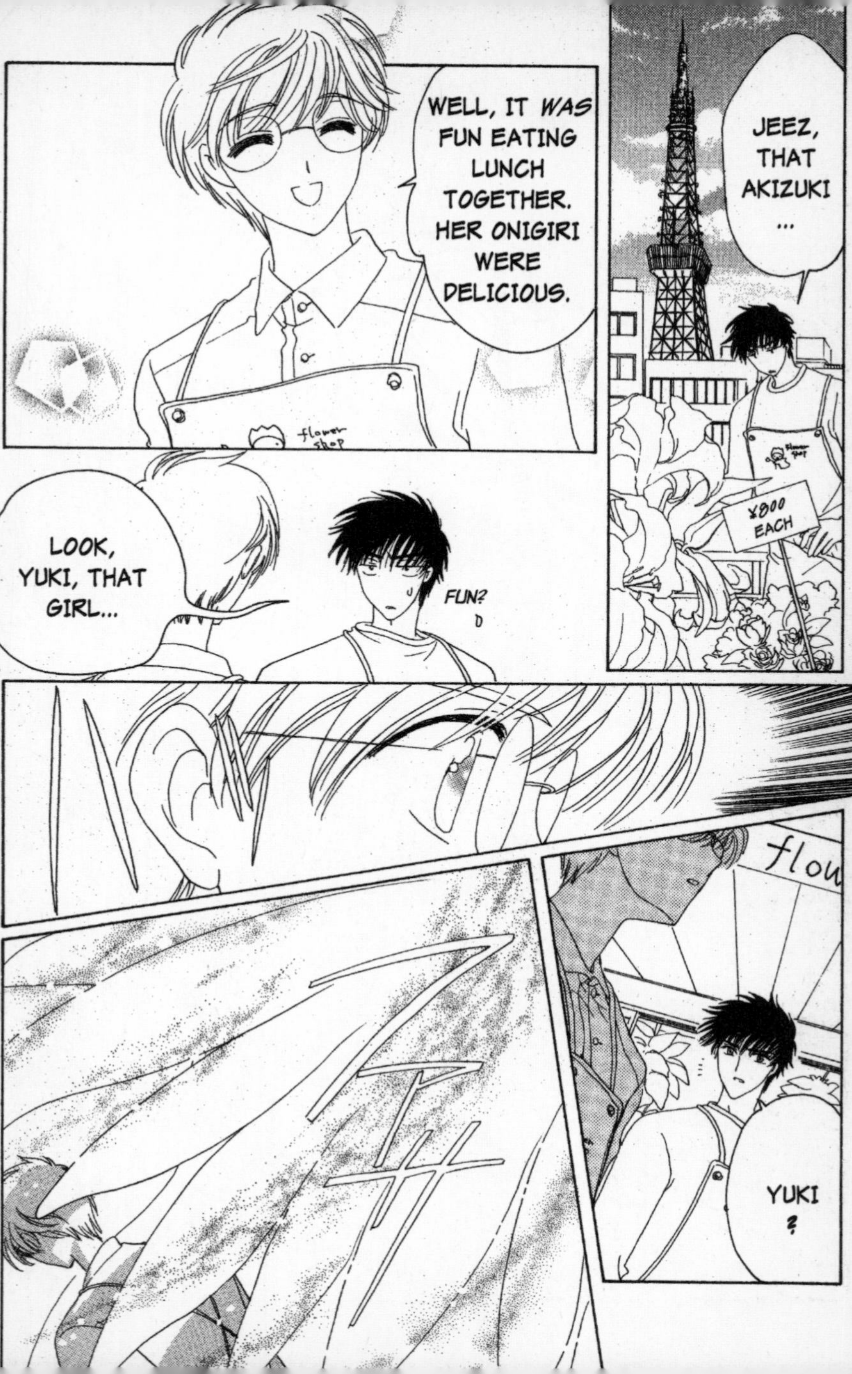
JEEZ, THAT AKIZUKI ...
¥800 EACH
WELL, IT *WAS* FUN EATING LUNCH TOGETHER. HER ONIGIRI WERE DELICIOUS.
flower shop
FUN?
LOOK, YUKI, THAT GIRL...
flow
YUKI?

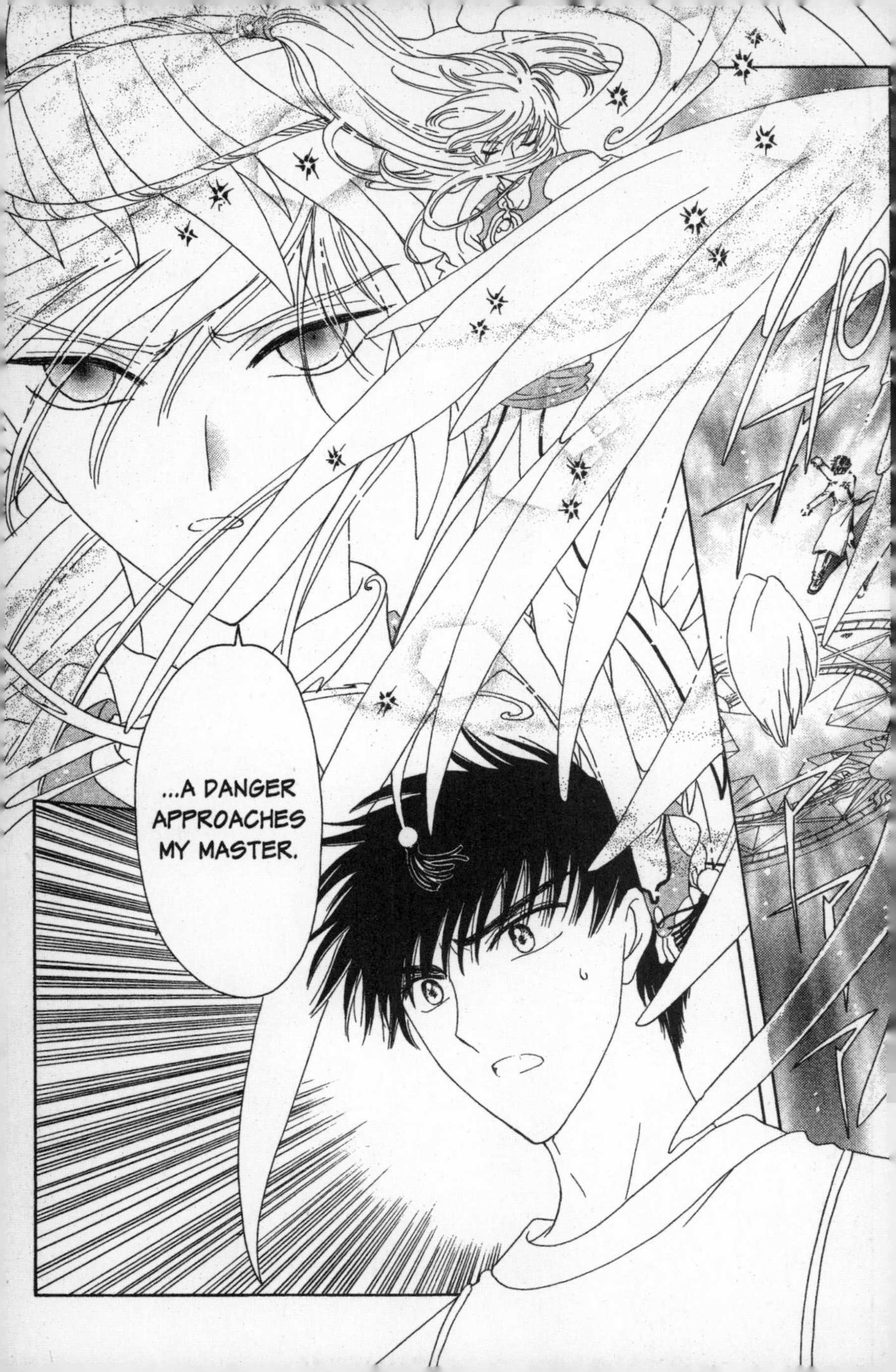
...A DANGER APPROACHES MY MASTER.

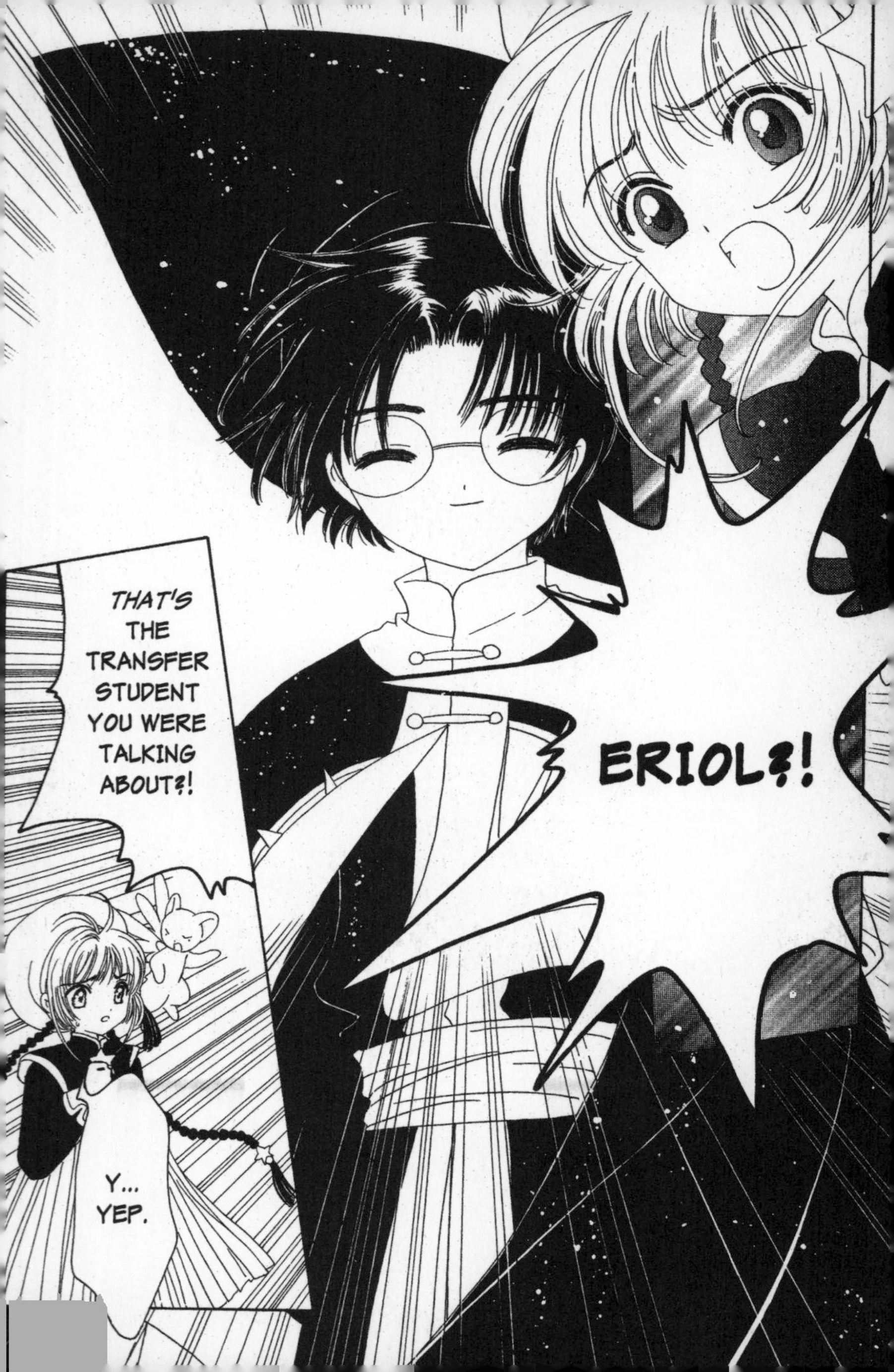
ERIOL?!
THAT'S THE TRANSFER STUDENT YOU WERE TALKING ABOUT?!
Y... YEP.

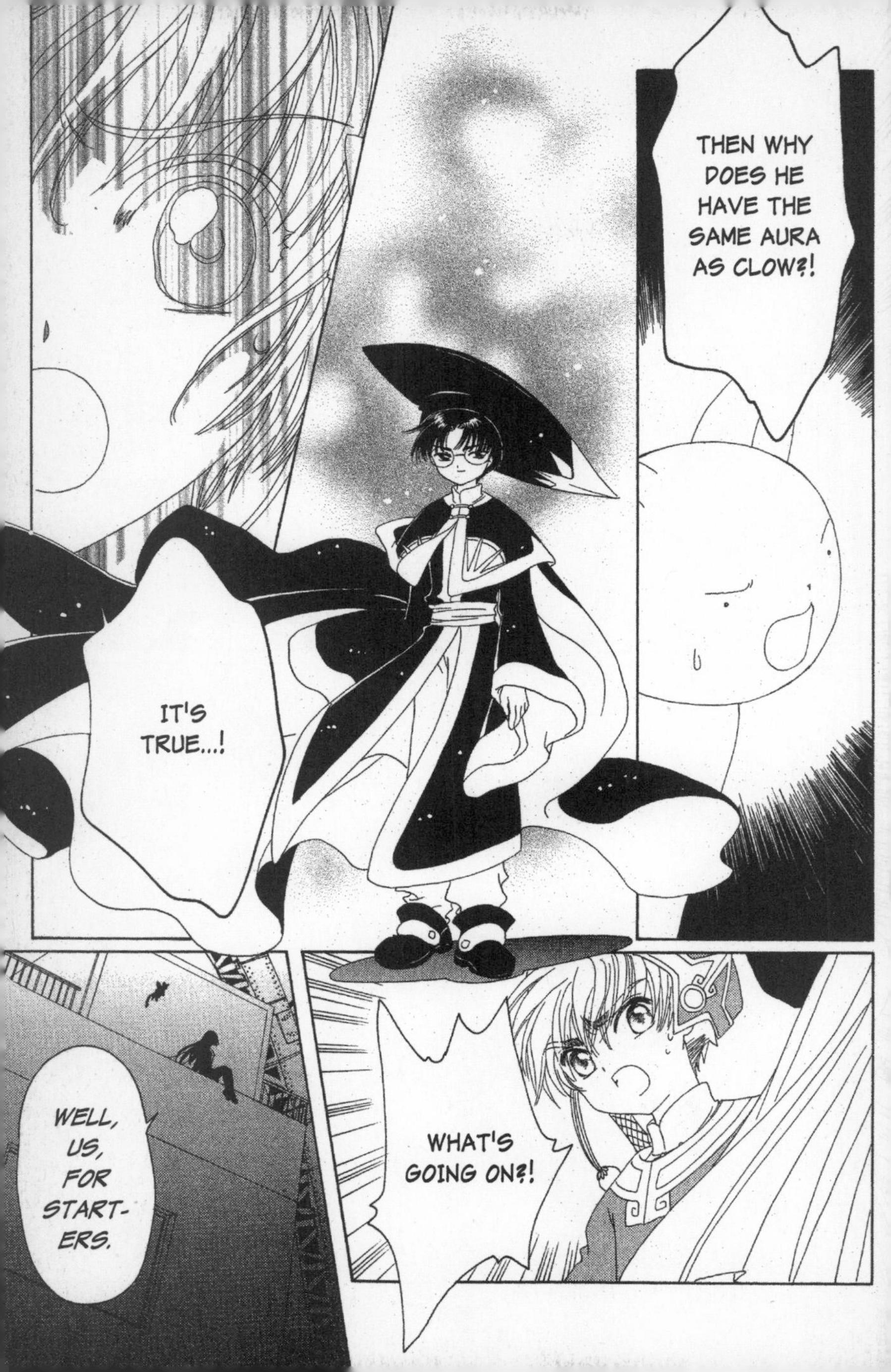
THEN WHY DOES HE HAVE THE SAME AURA AS CLOW?!
IT'S TRUE...!
WHAT'S GOING ON?!
WELL, US, FOR START-ERS.

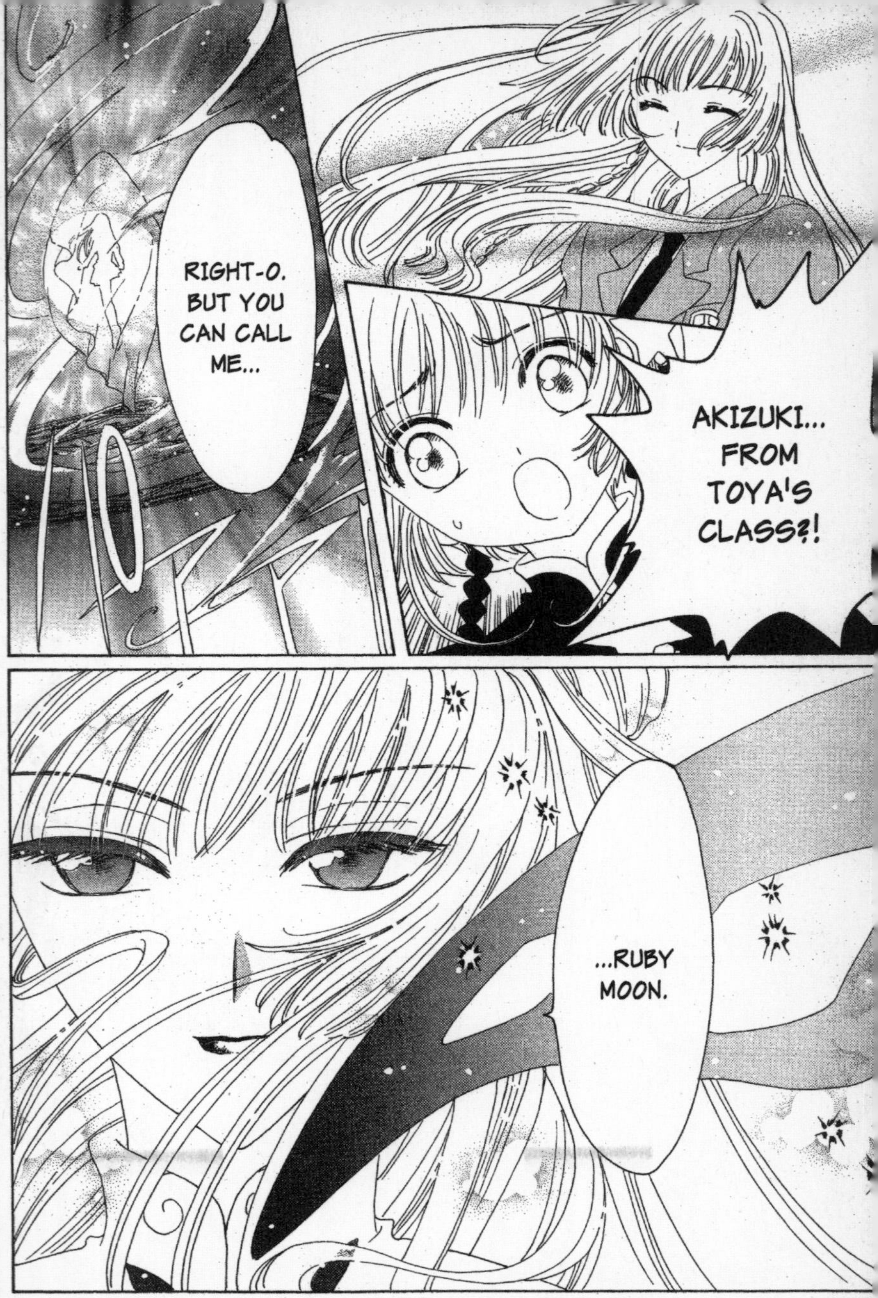
AKIZUKI... FROM TOYA'S CLASS?!
RIGHT-O. BUT YOU CAN CALL ME...
...RUBY MOON.

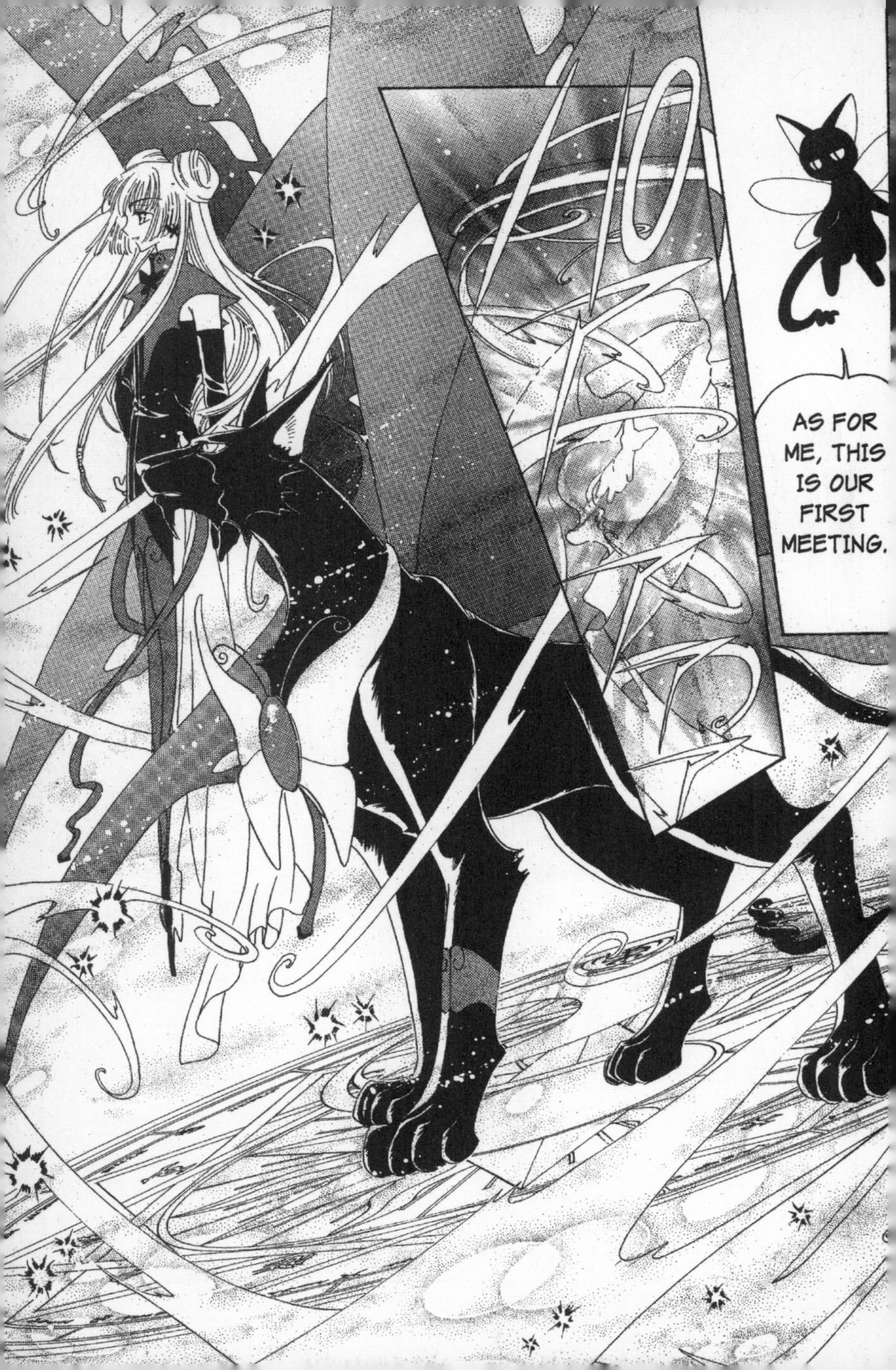
AS FOR ME, THIS IS OUR FIRST MEETING.

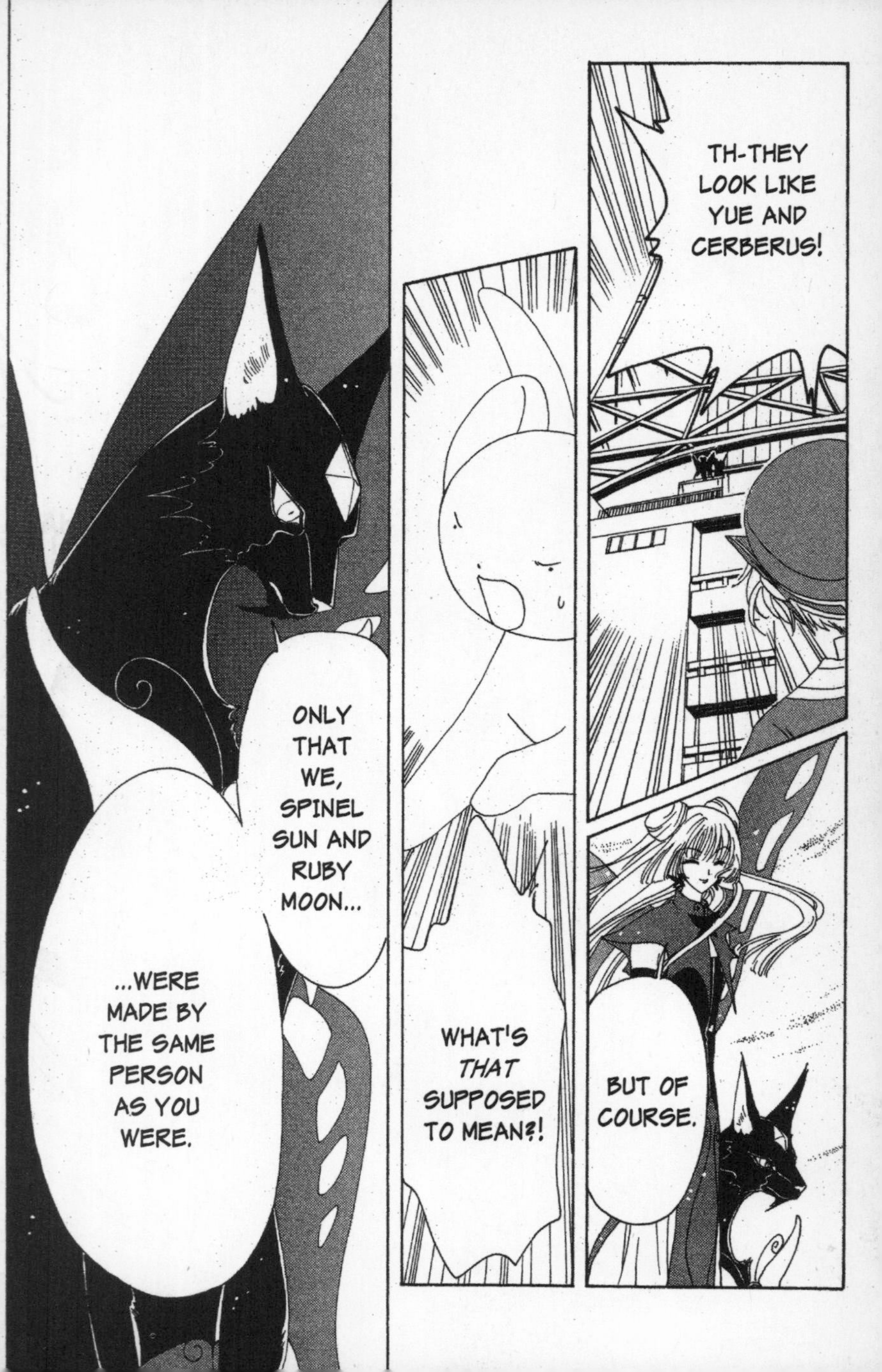
TH-THEY LOOK LIKE YUE AND CERBERUS!
BUT OF COURSE.
WHAT'S *THAT* SUPPOSED TO MEAN?!
ONLY THAT WE, SPINEL SUN AND RUBY MOON...
...WERE MADE BY THE SAME PERSON AS YOU WERE.

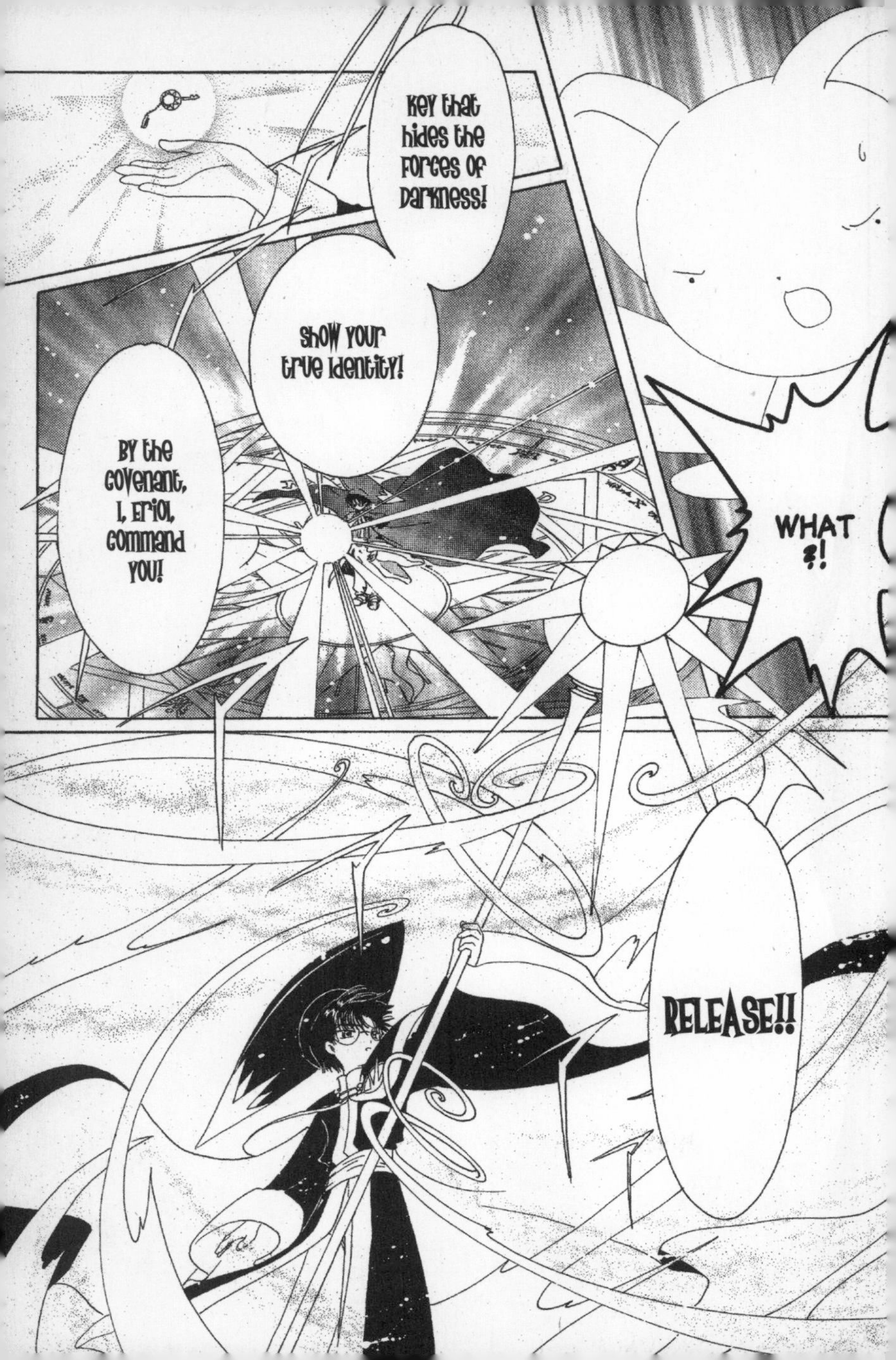

Key that hides the forces of darkness!
Show your true identity!
By the covenant, I, Eriol, command you!
WHAT ?!
RELEASE!!

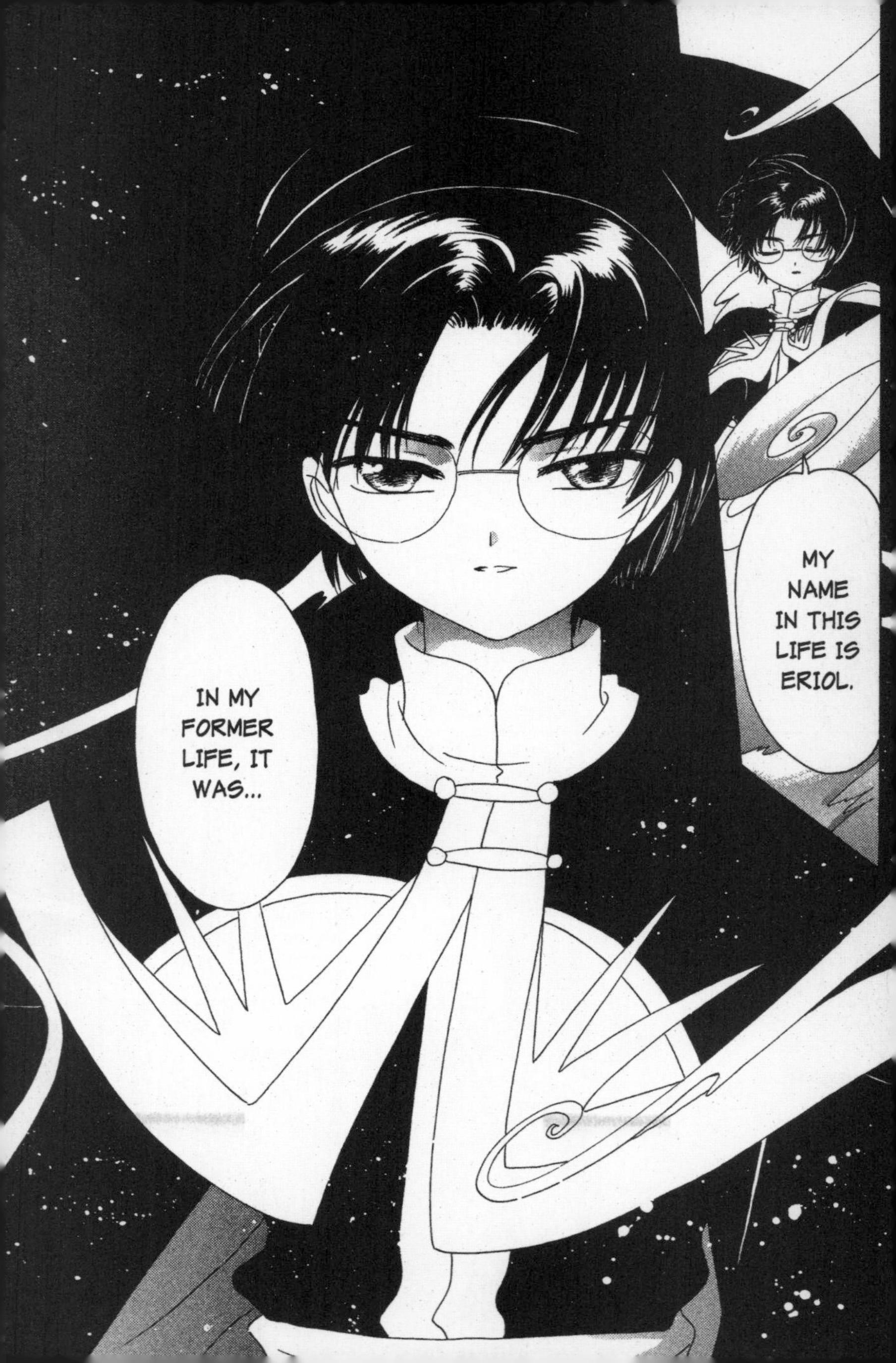
MY NAME IN THIS LIFE IS ERIOL.
IN MY FORMER LIFE, IT WAS...

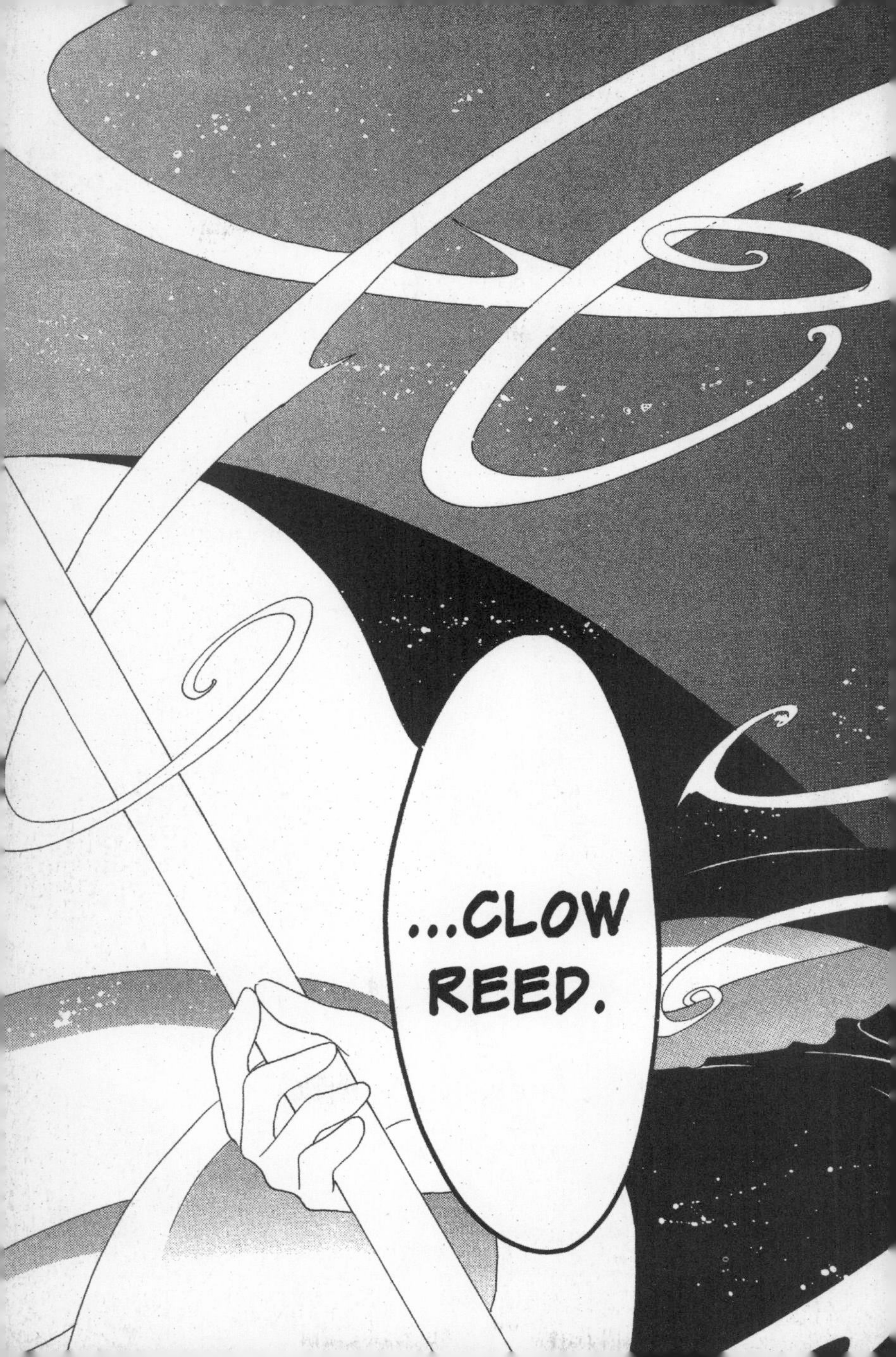
...CLOW REED.

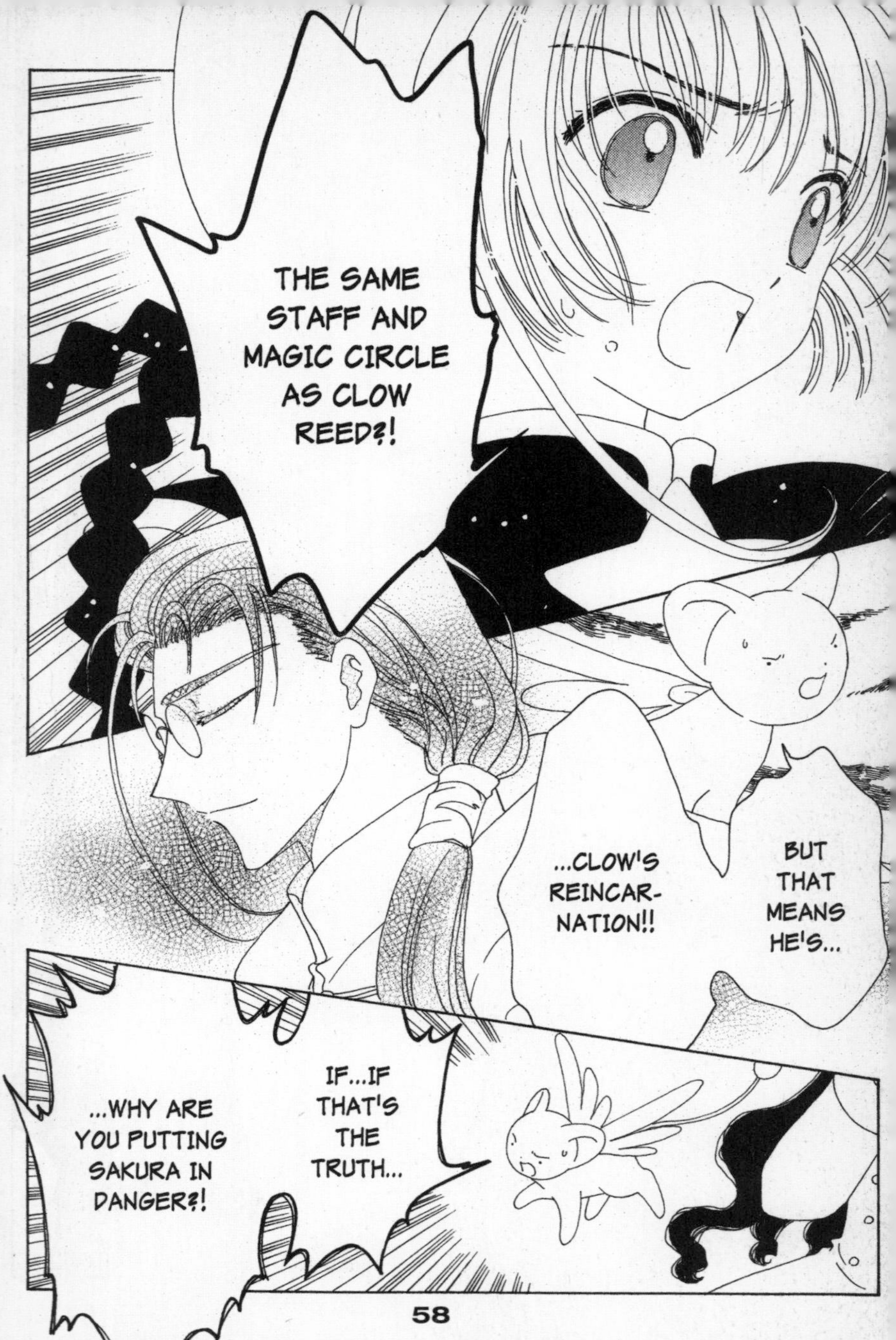
THE SAME STAFF AND MAGIC CIRCLE AS CLOW REED?!
BUT THAT MEANS HE'S...
...CLOW'S REINCAR-NATION!!
IF...IF THAT'S THE TRUTH...
...WHY ARE YOU PUTTING SAKURA IN DANGER?!

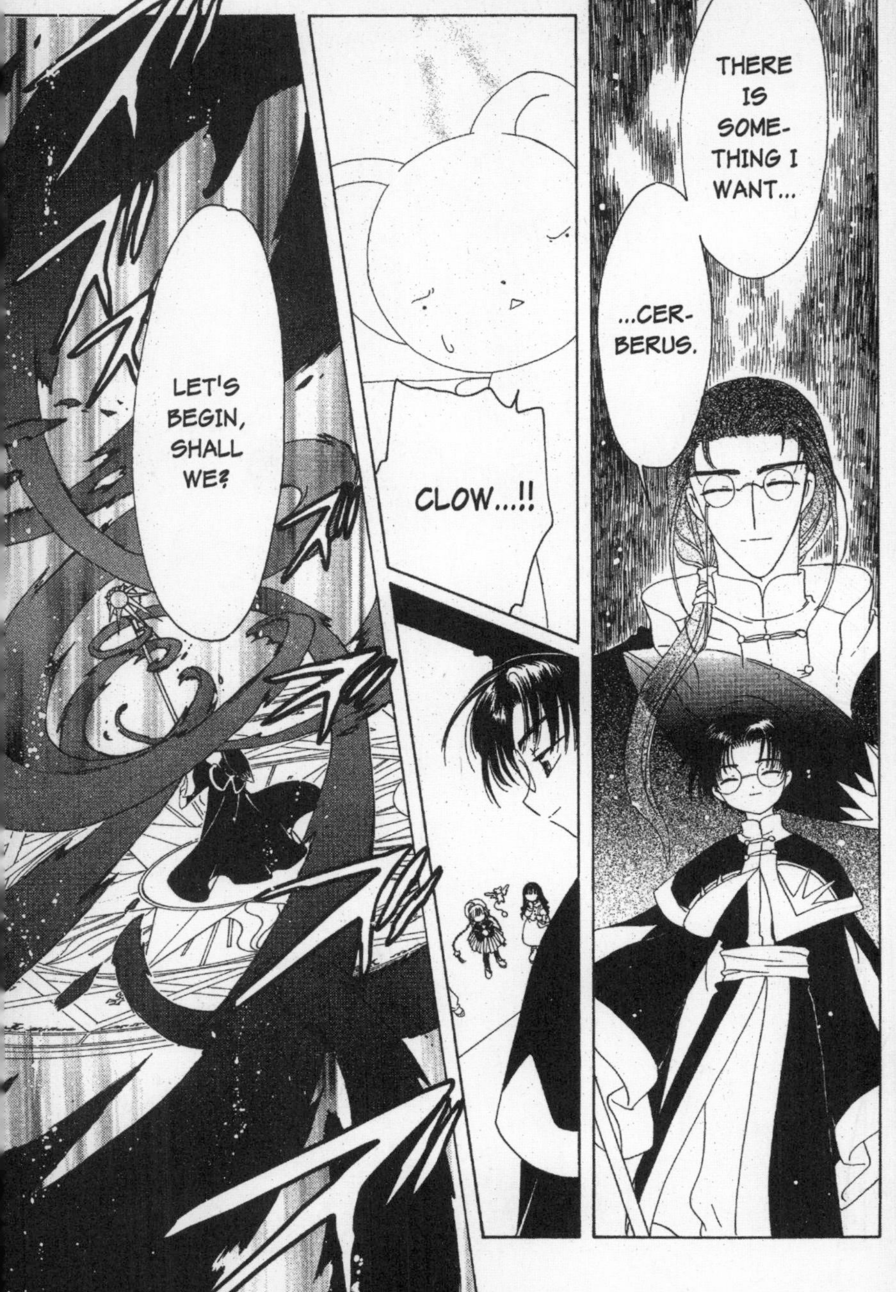
THERE IS SOME-THING I WANT...
...CER-BERUS.
CLOW...!!
LET'S BEGIN, SHALL WE?

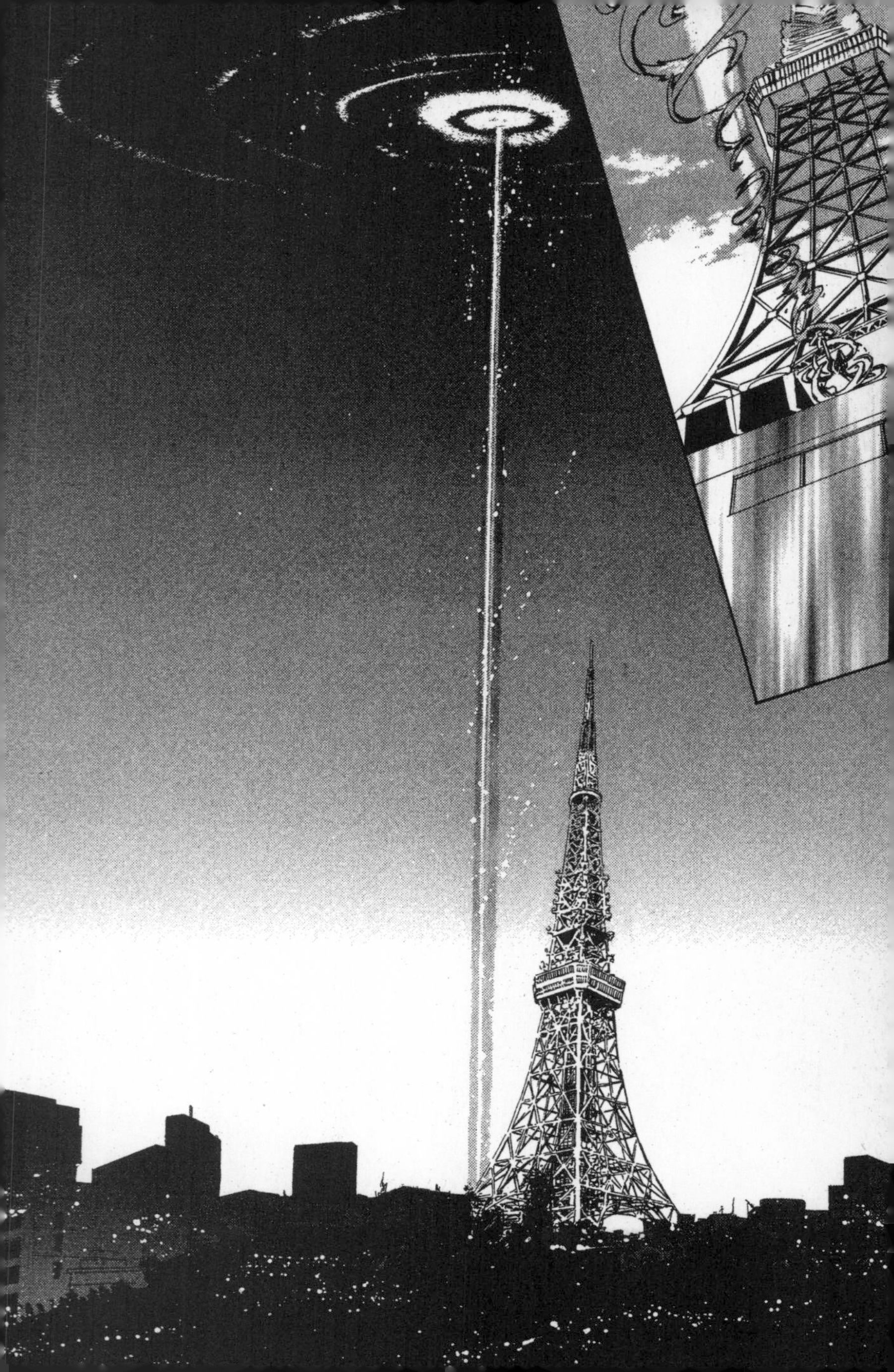

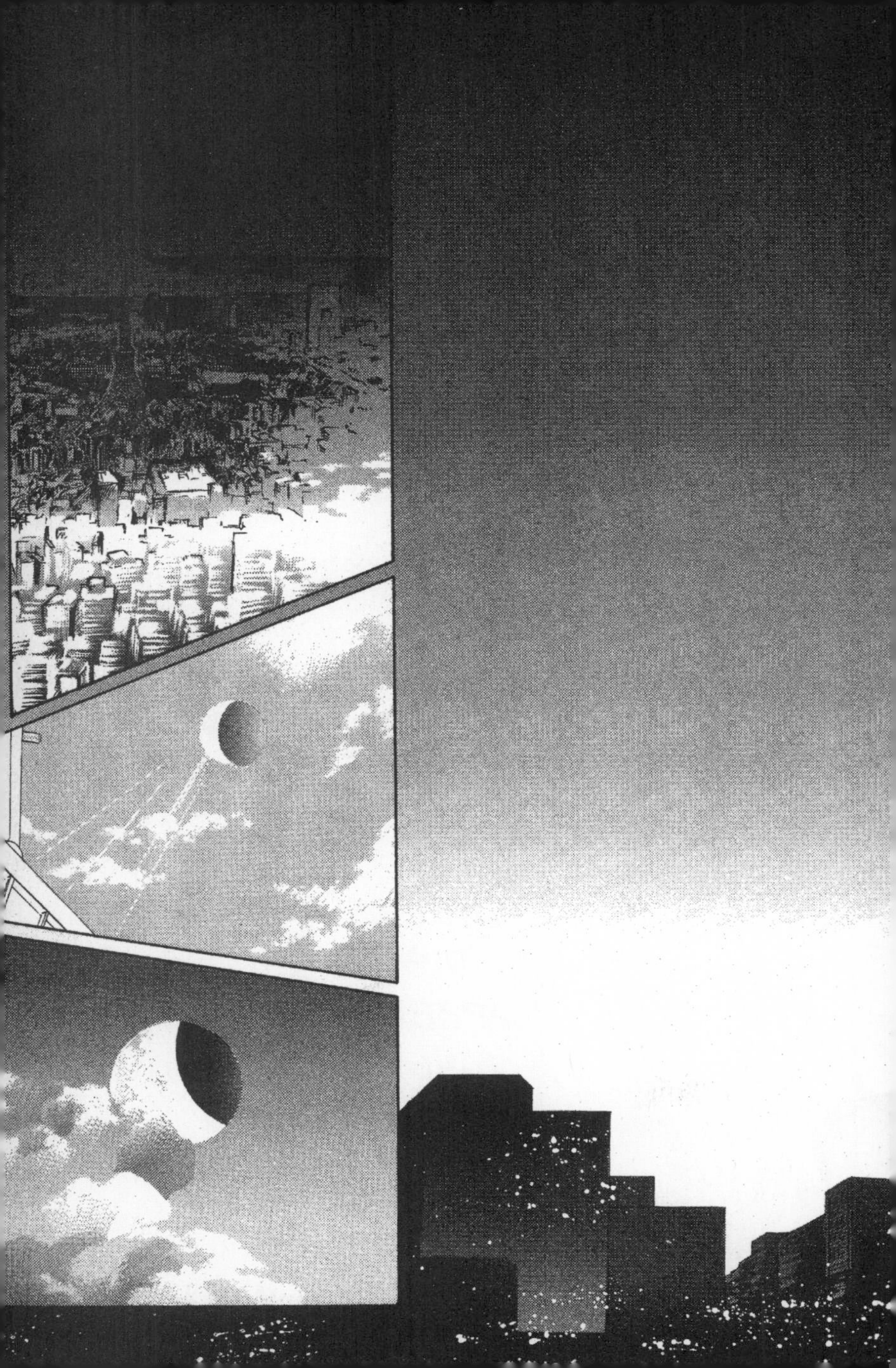

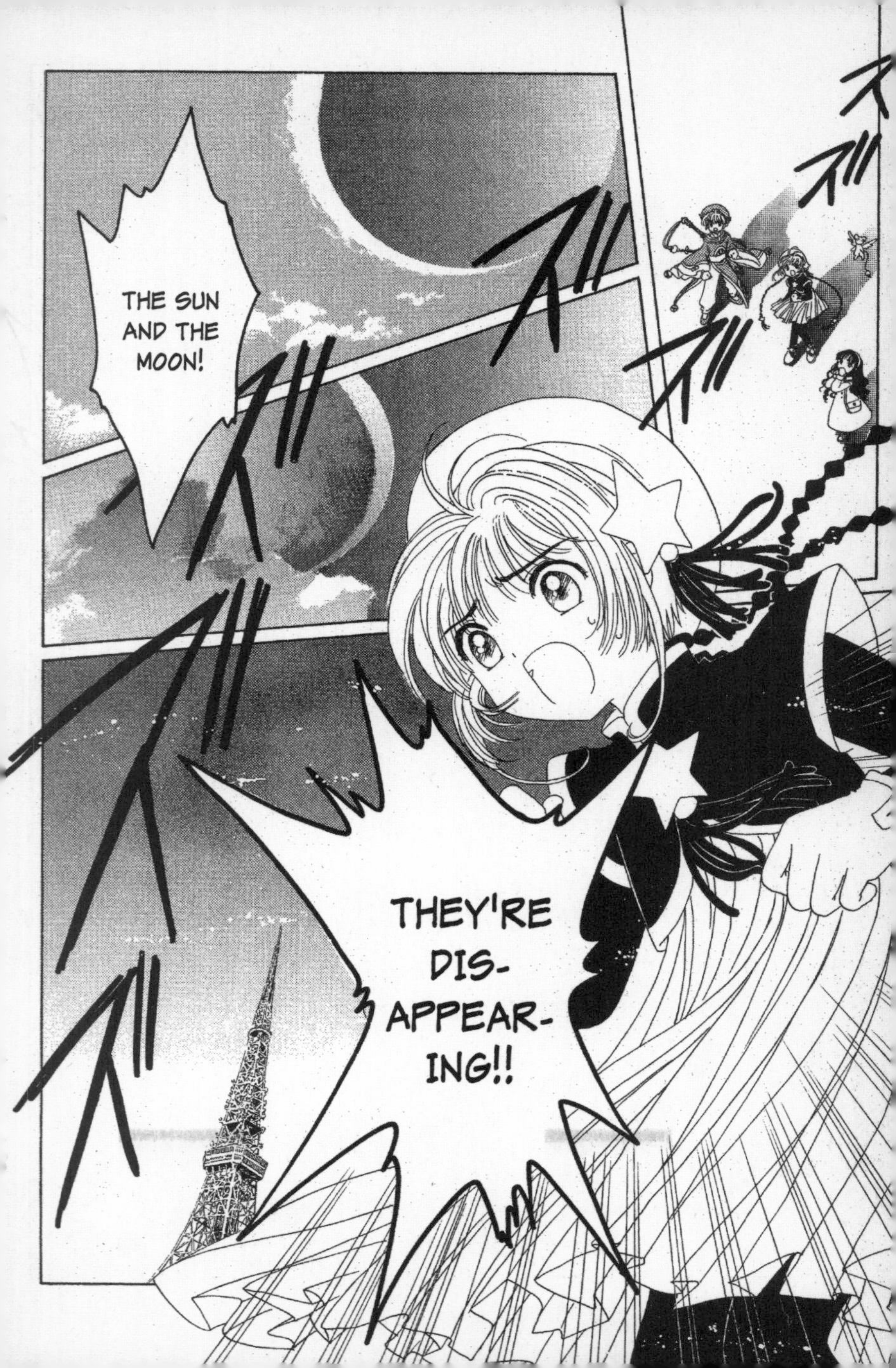
THE SUN AND THE MOON!
THEY'RE DIS-APPEAR-ING!!

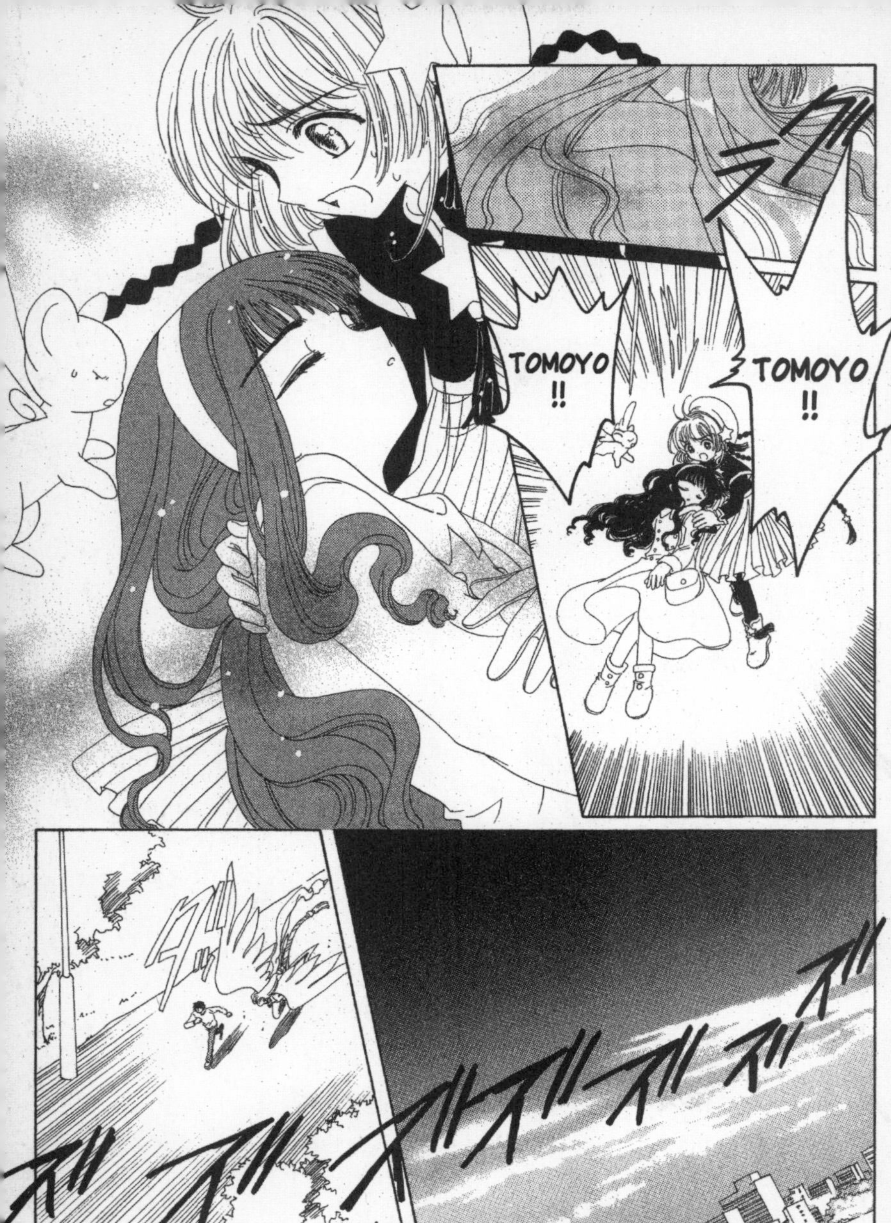
TOMOYO !!
TOMOYO !!

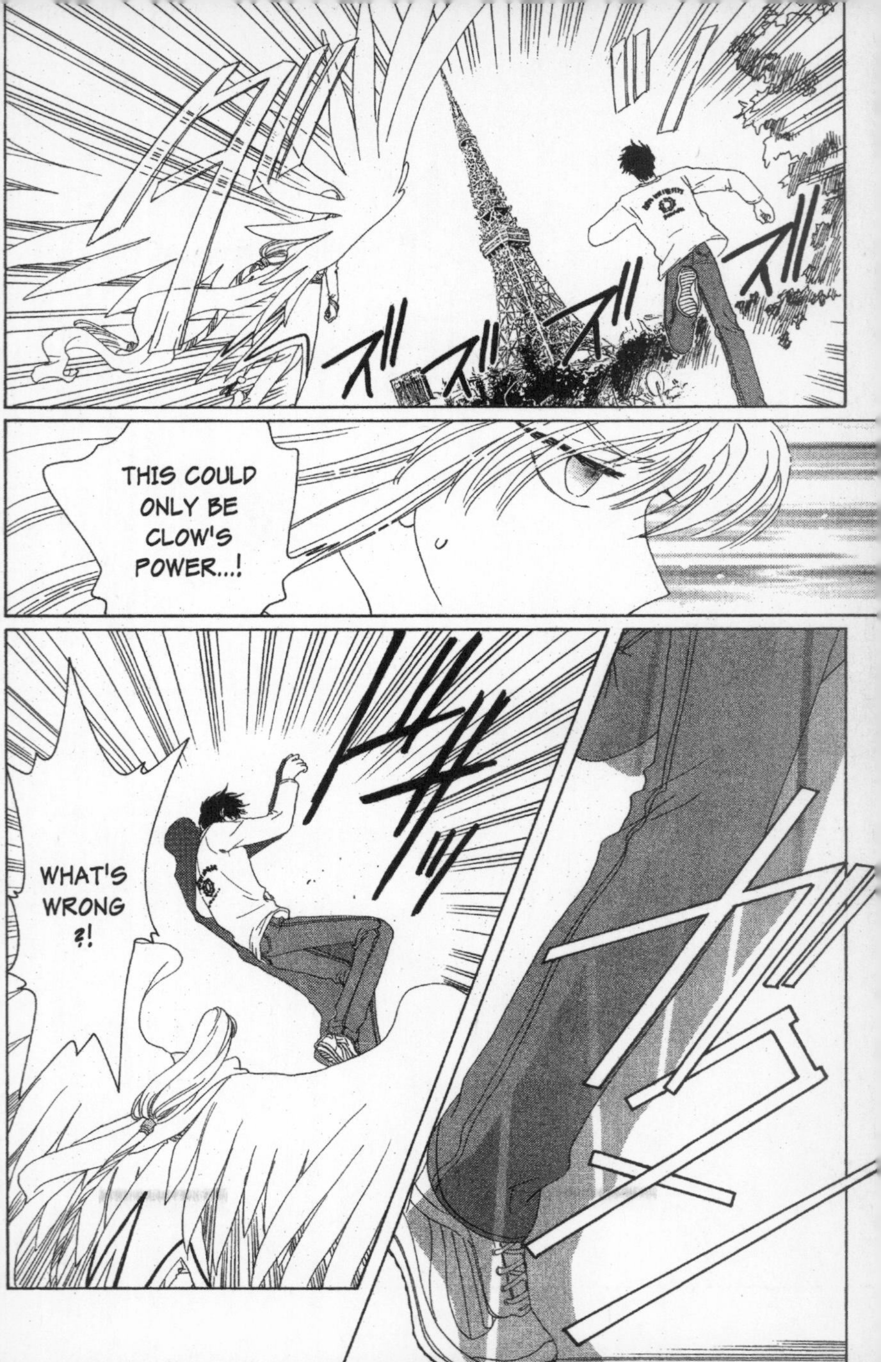
THIS COULD ONLY BE CLOW'S POWER...!
WHAT'S WRONG ?!

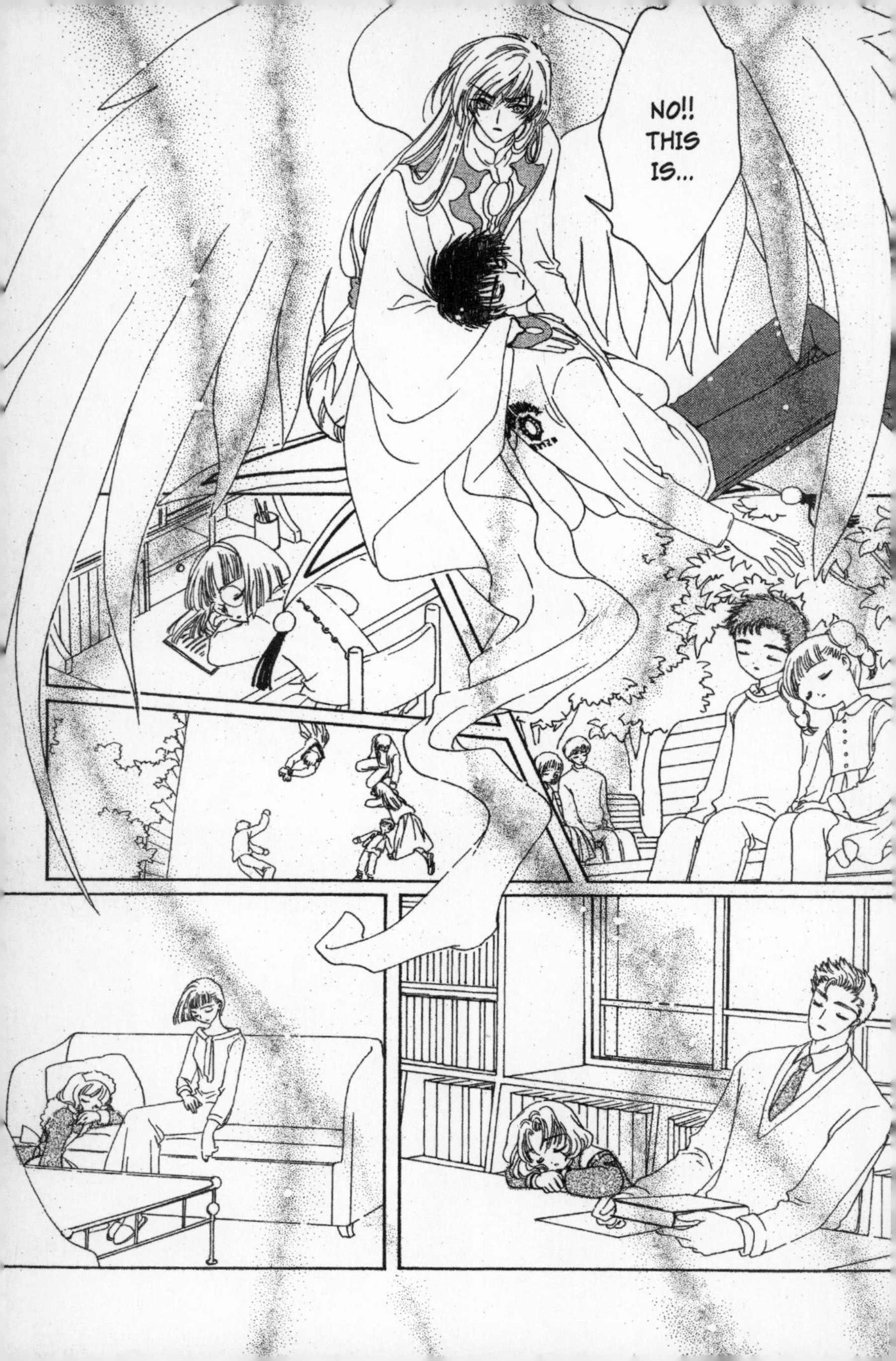
NO!! THIS IS...

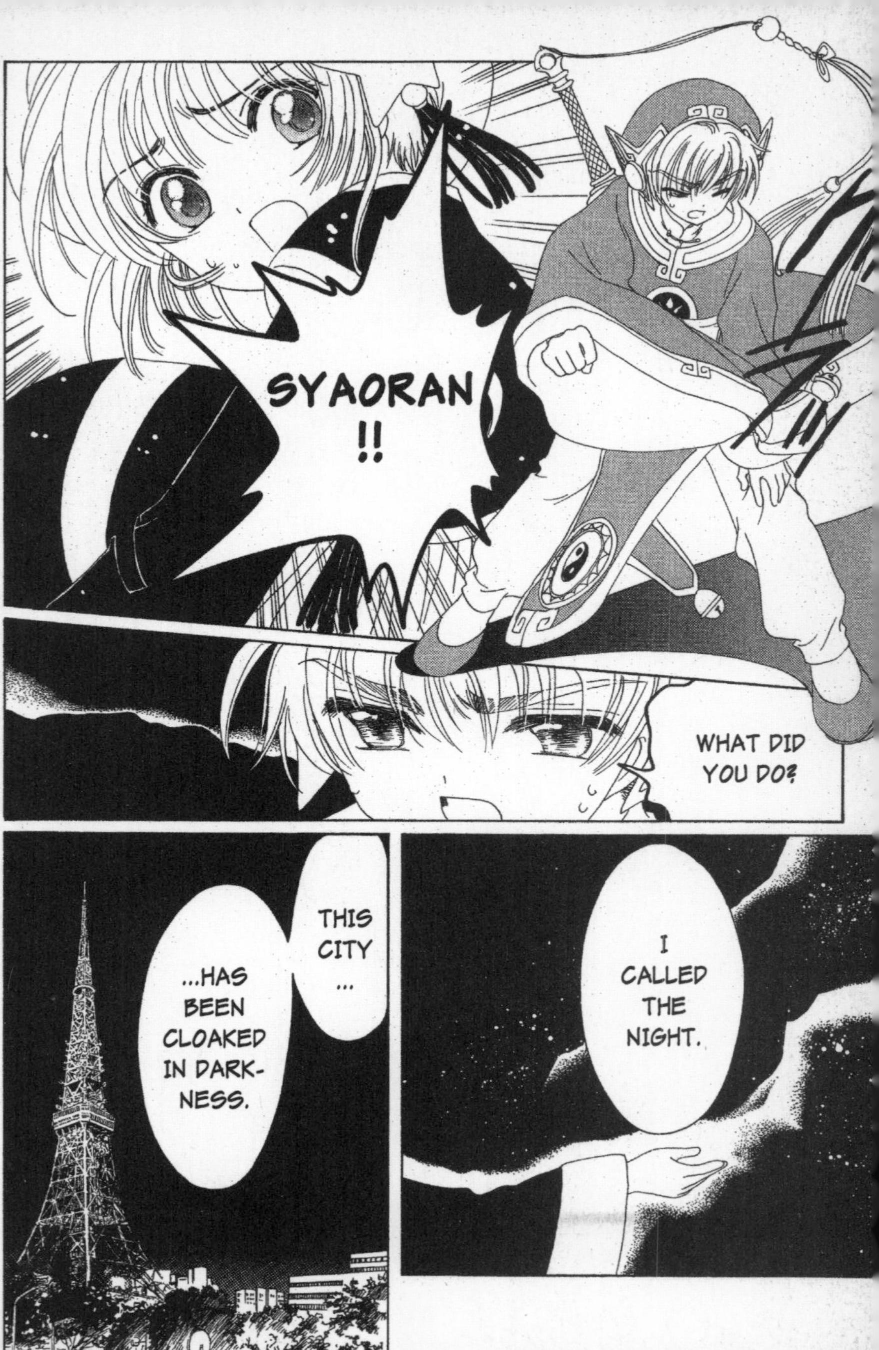
SYAORAN !!
WHAT DID YOU DO?
I CALLED THE NIGHT.
THIS CITY ...
...HAS BEEN CLOAKED IN DARK-NESS.

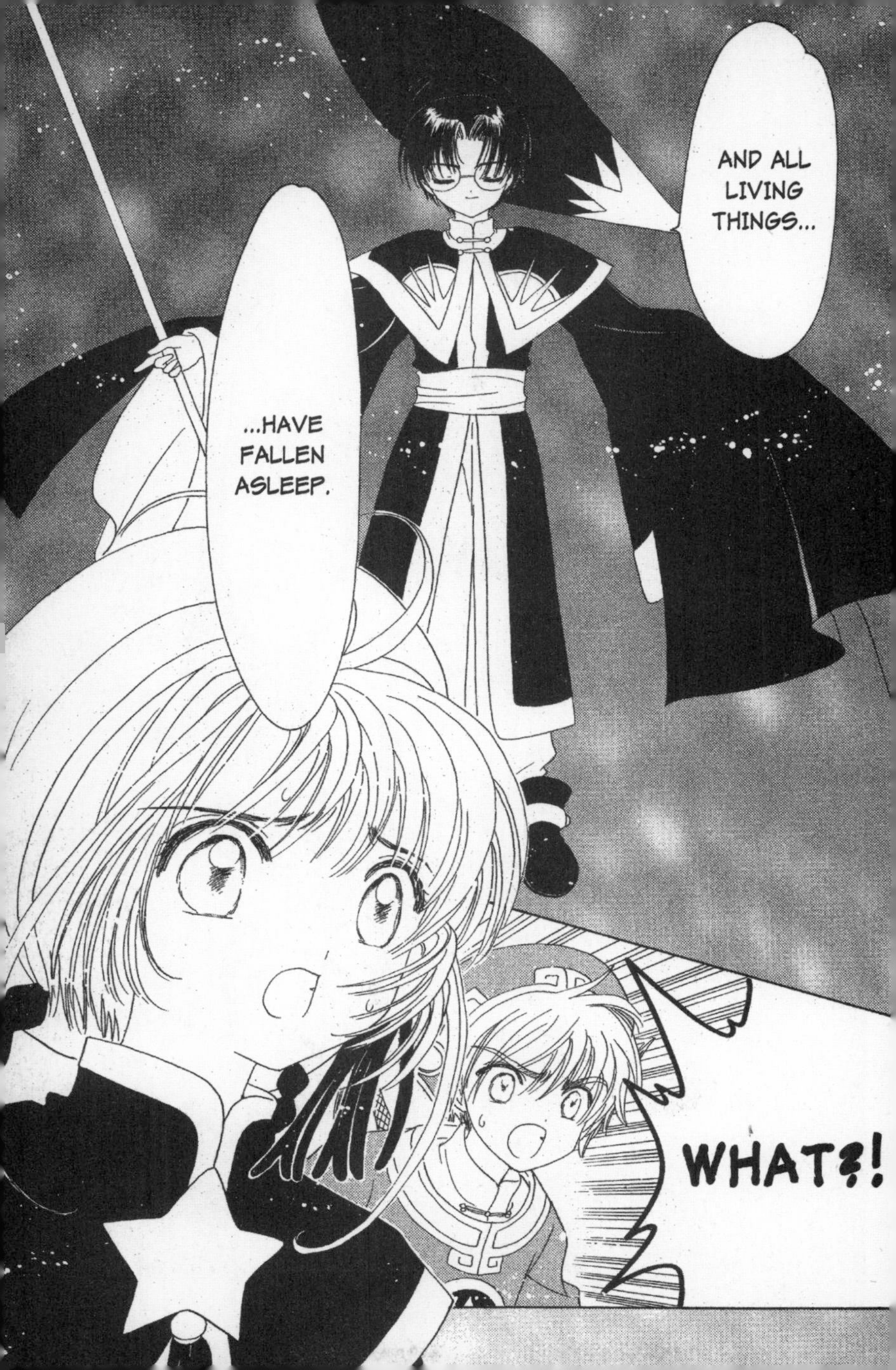
AND ALL LIVING THINGS...
...HAVE FALLEN ASLEEP.
WHAT?!

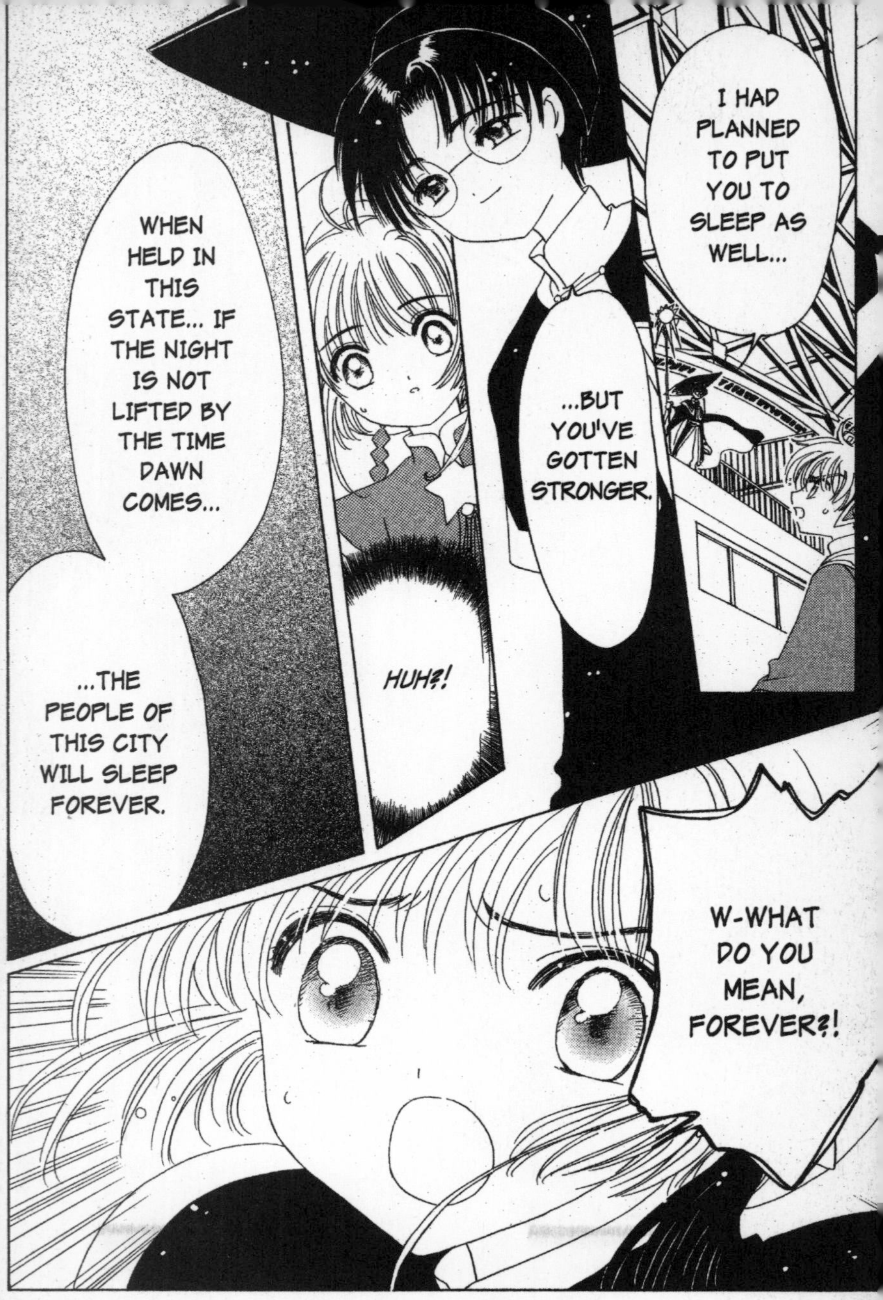
I HAD PLANNED TO PUT YOU TO SLEEP AS WELL...
...BUT YOU'VE GOTTEN STRONGER.
HUH?!
WHEN HELD IN THIS STATE... IF THE NIGHT IS NOT LIFTED BY THE TIME DAWN COMES...
...THE PEOPLE OF THIS CITY WILL SLEEP FOREVER.
W-WHAT DO YOU MEAN, FOREVER?!

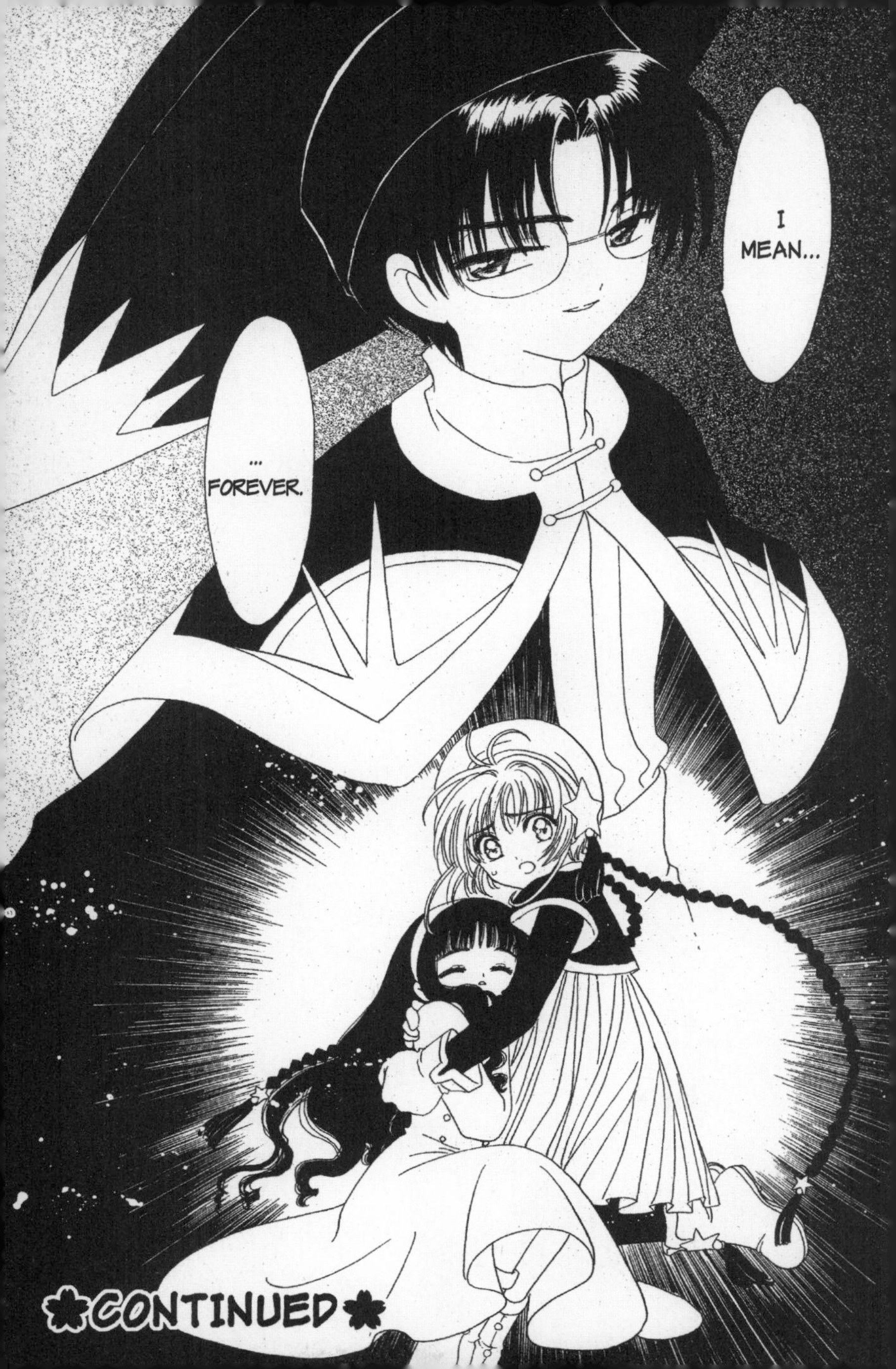
I MEAN...
... FOREVER.
CONTINUED

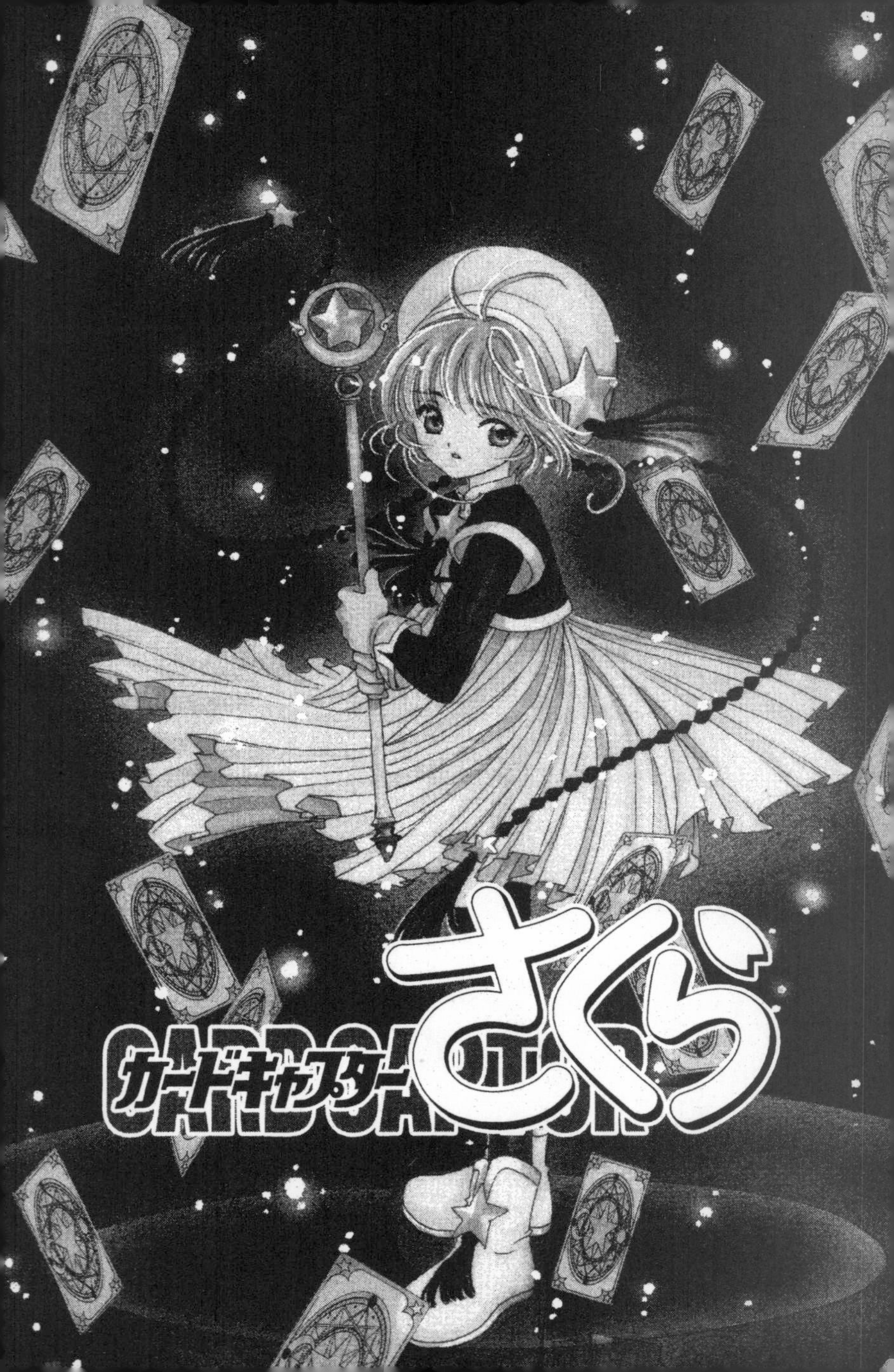
カードキャプターさくら

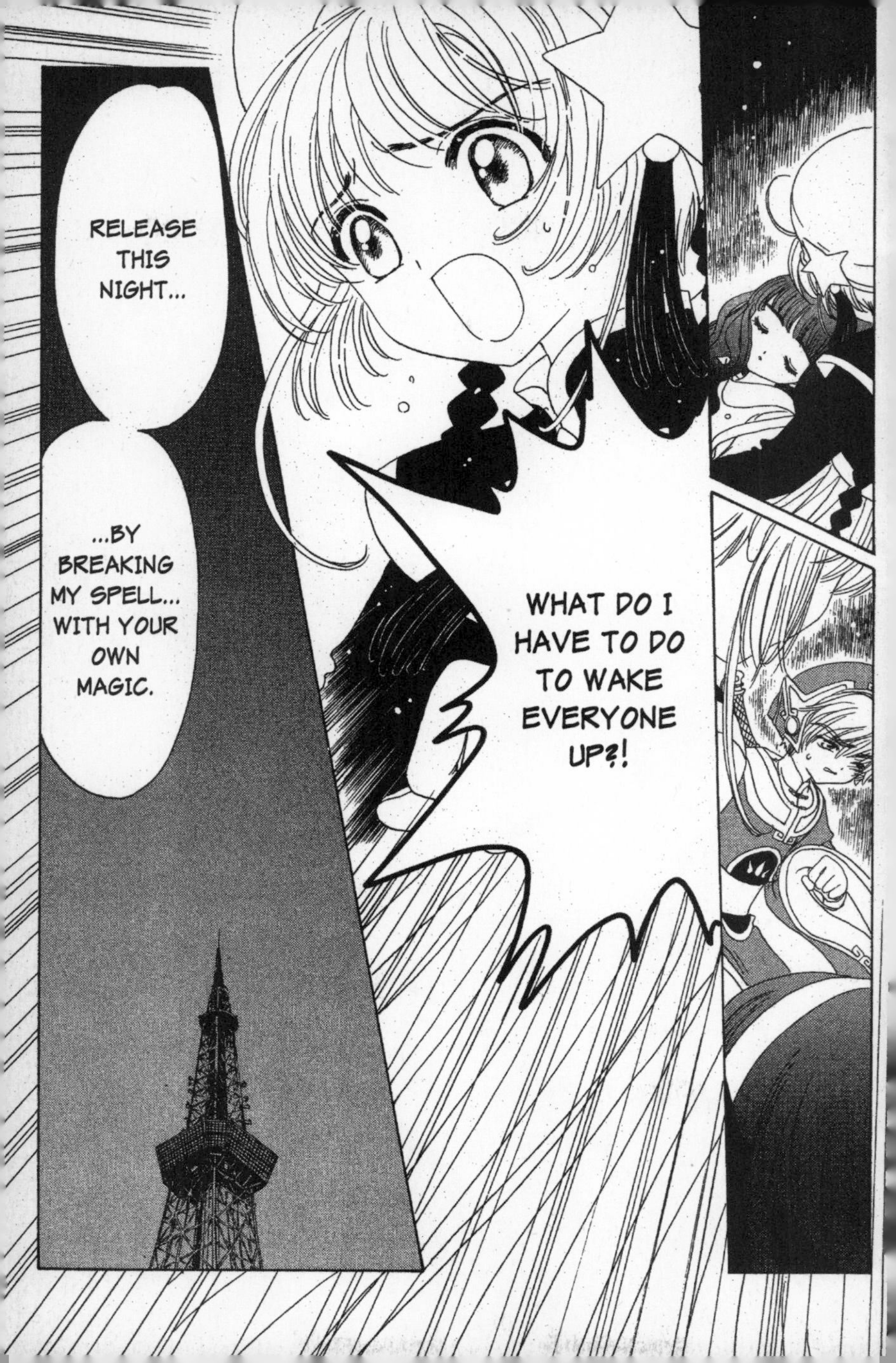
WHAT DO I HAVE TO DO TO WAKE EVERYONE UP?!
RELEASE THIS NIGHT...
...BY BREAKING MY SPELL... WITH YOUR OWN MAGIC.

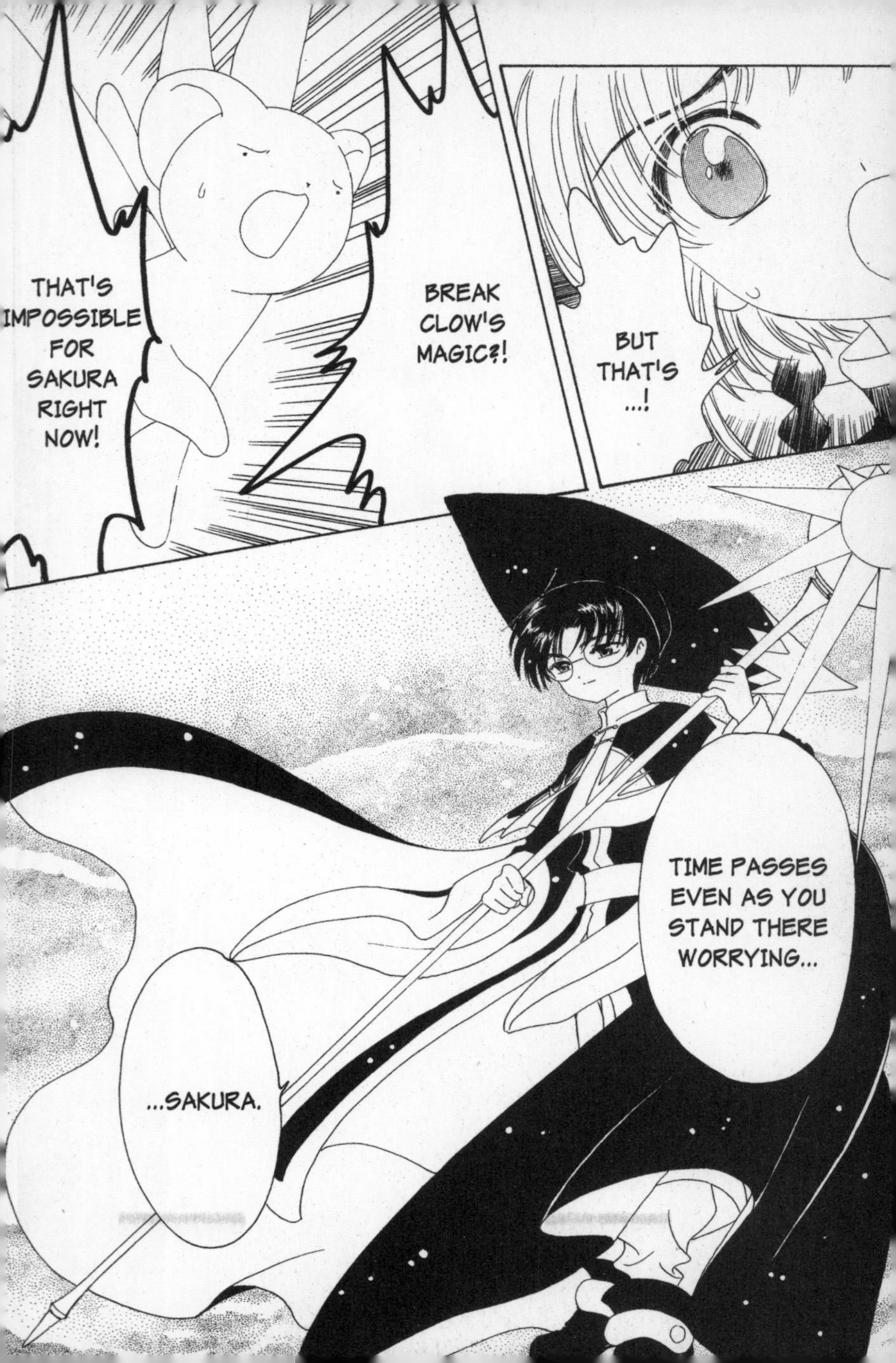
BUT THAT'S ...!
BREAK CLOW'S MAGIC?!
THAT'S IMPOSSIBLE FOR SAKURA RIGHT NOW!
TIME PASSES EVEN AS YOU STAND THERE WORRYING...
...SAKURA.

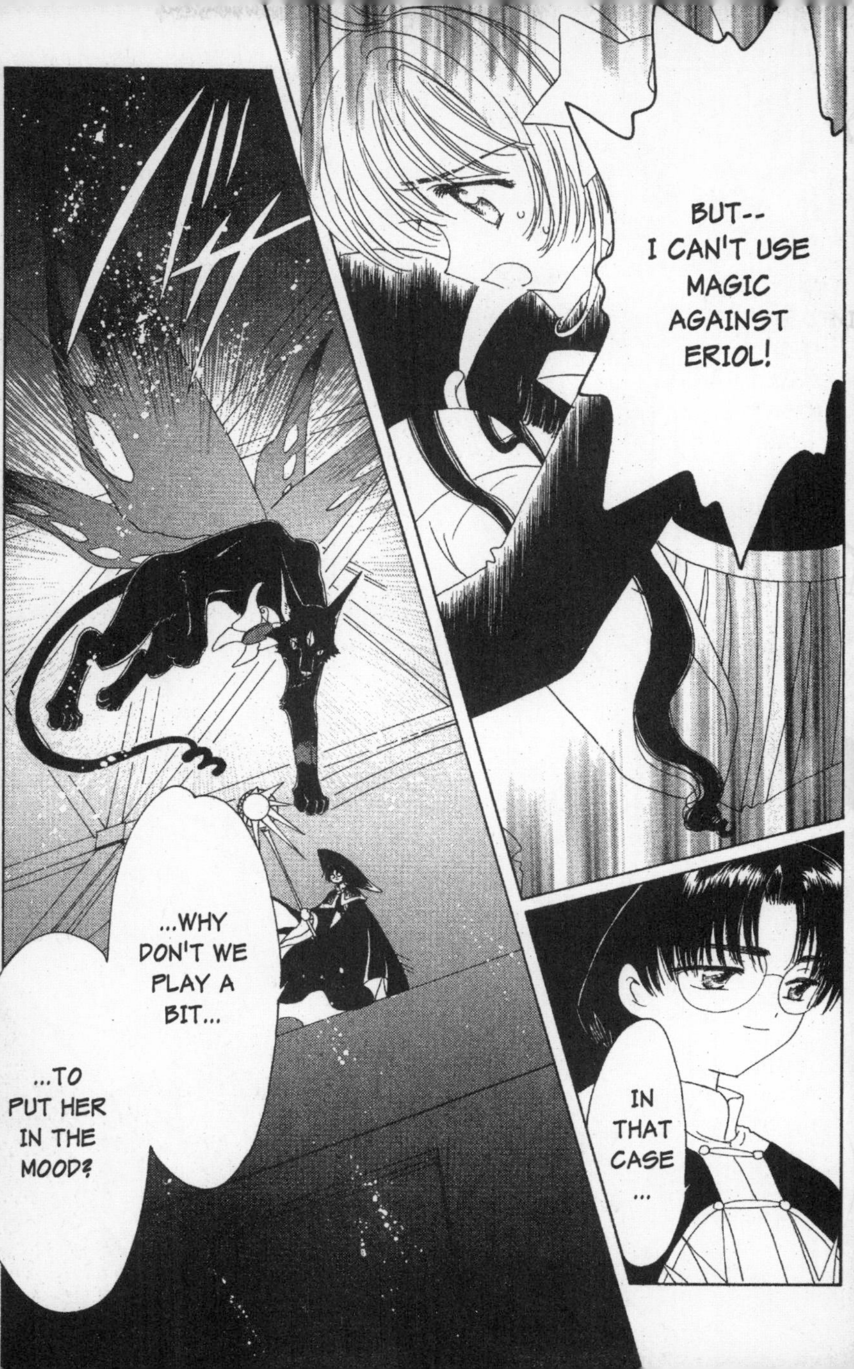
BUT-- I CAN'T USE MAGIC AGAINST ERIOL!
IN THAT CASE ...
...WHY DON'T WE PLAY A BIT...
...TO PUT HER IN THE MOOD?

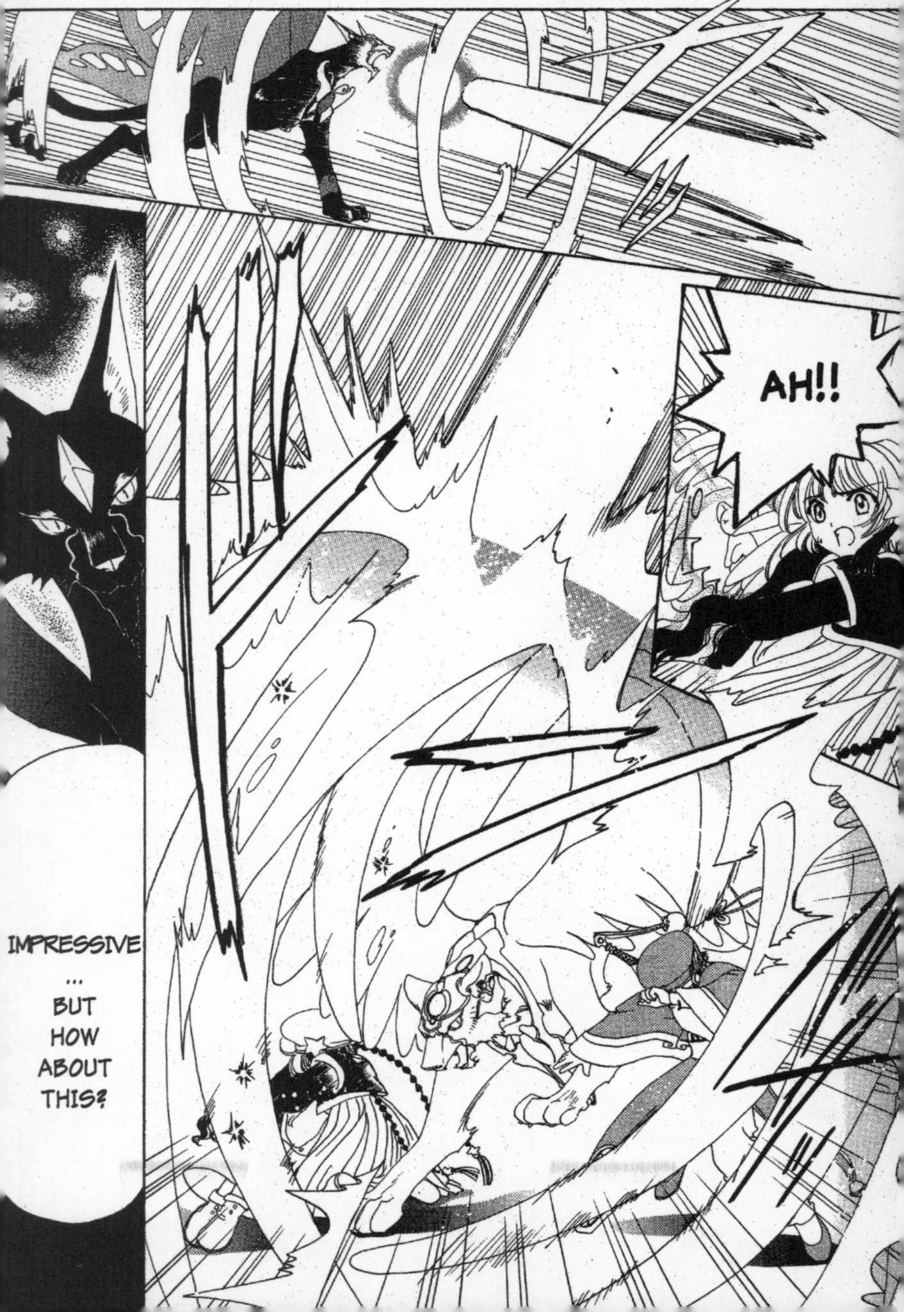
AH!!
IMPRESSIVE ... BUT HOW ABOUT THIS?

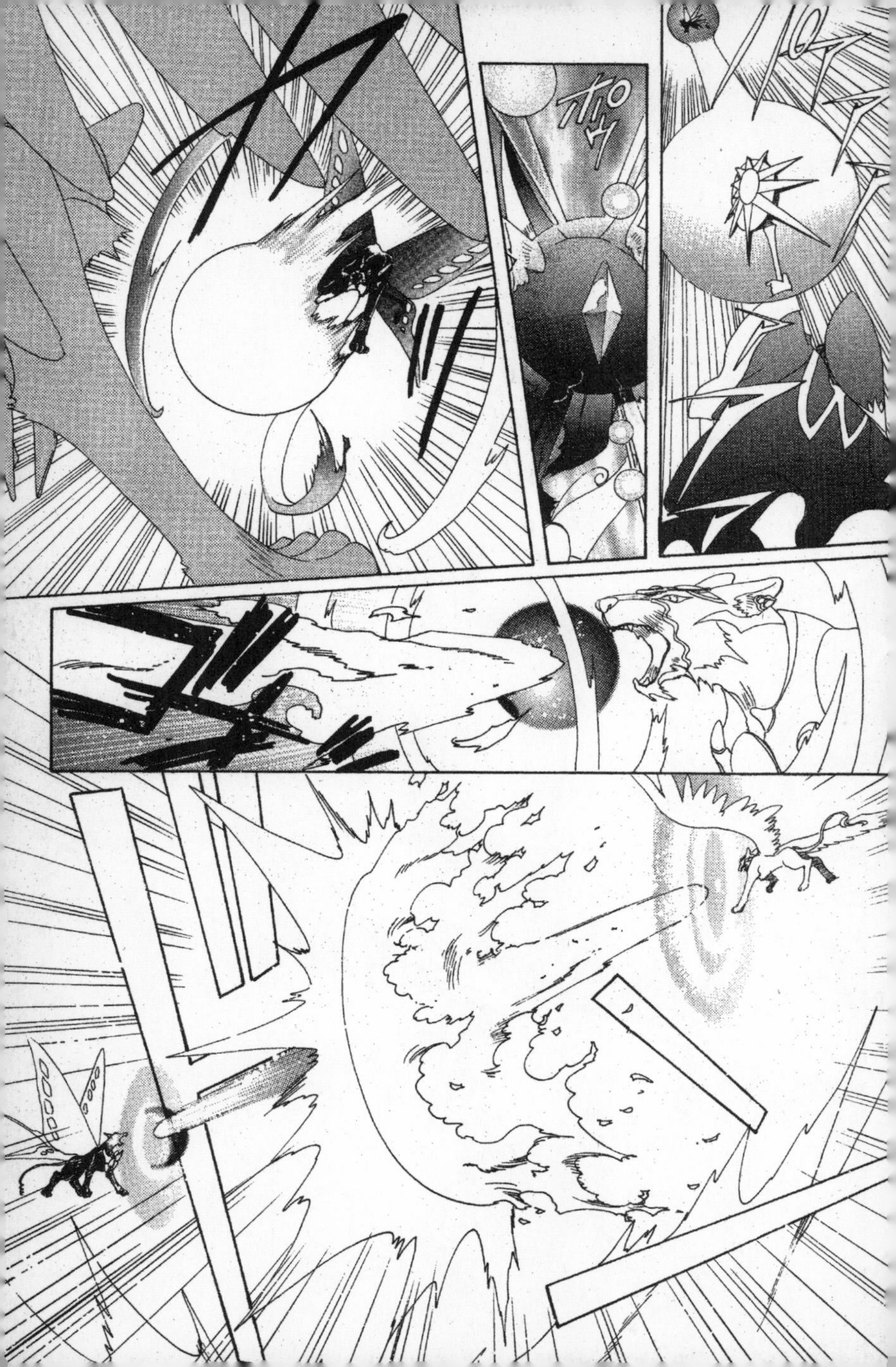

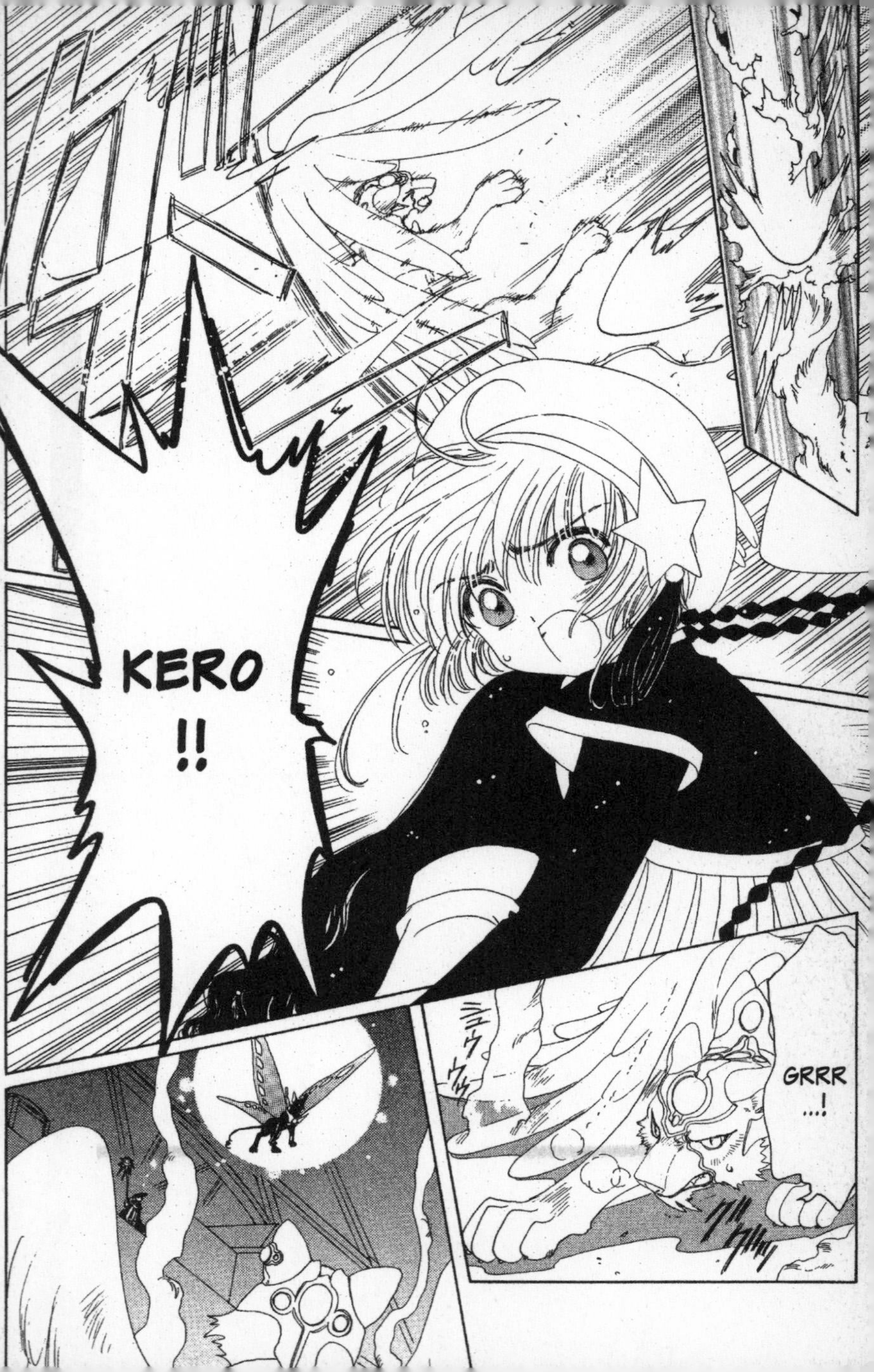
KERO
!!
GRRR
...!

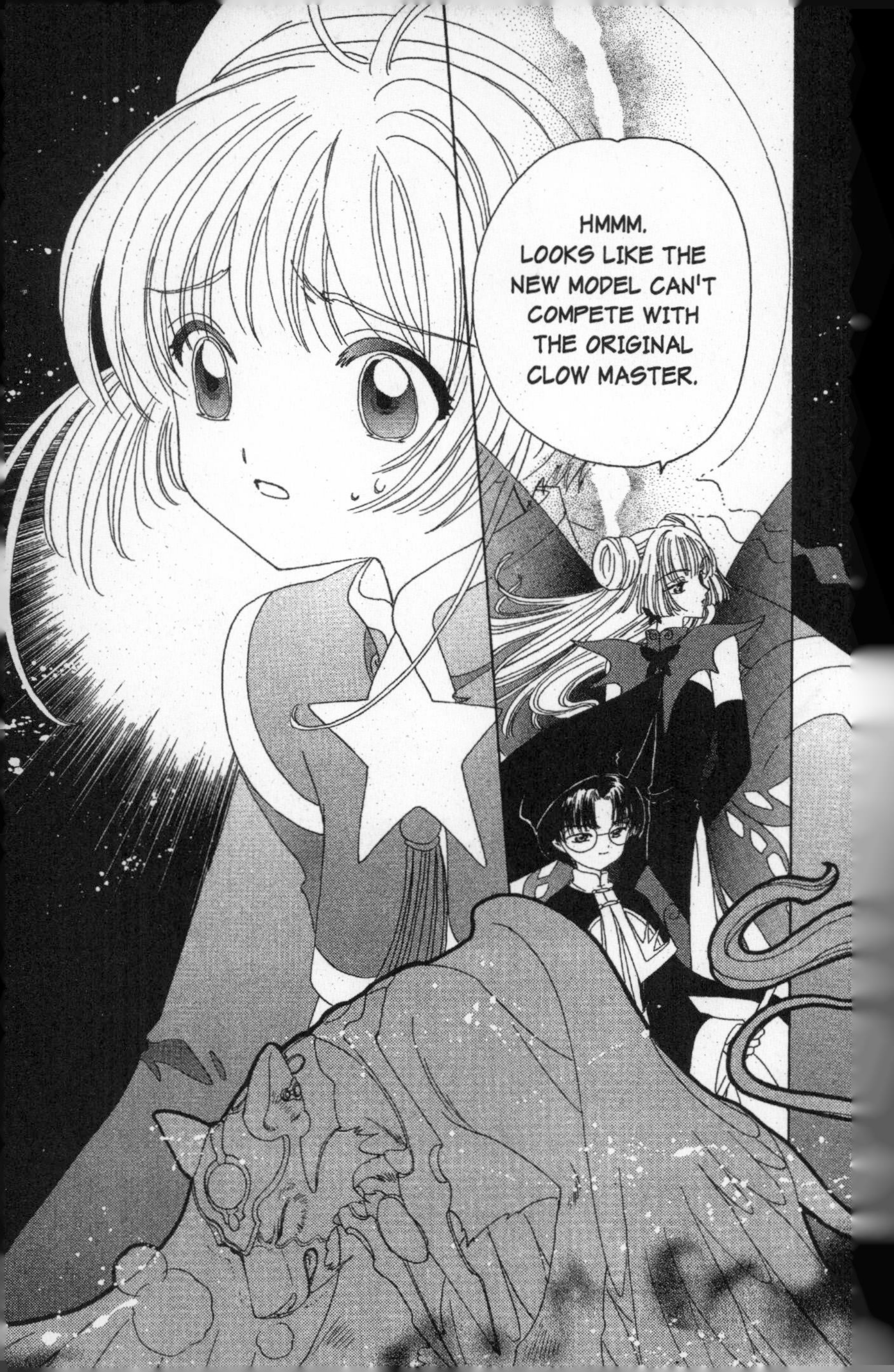
HMMM. LOOKS LIKE THE NEW MODEL CAN'T COMPETE WITH THE ORIGINAL CLOW MASTER.

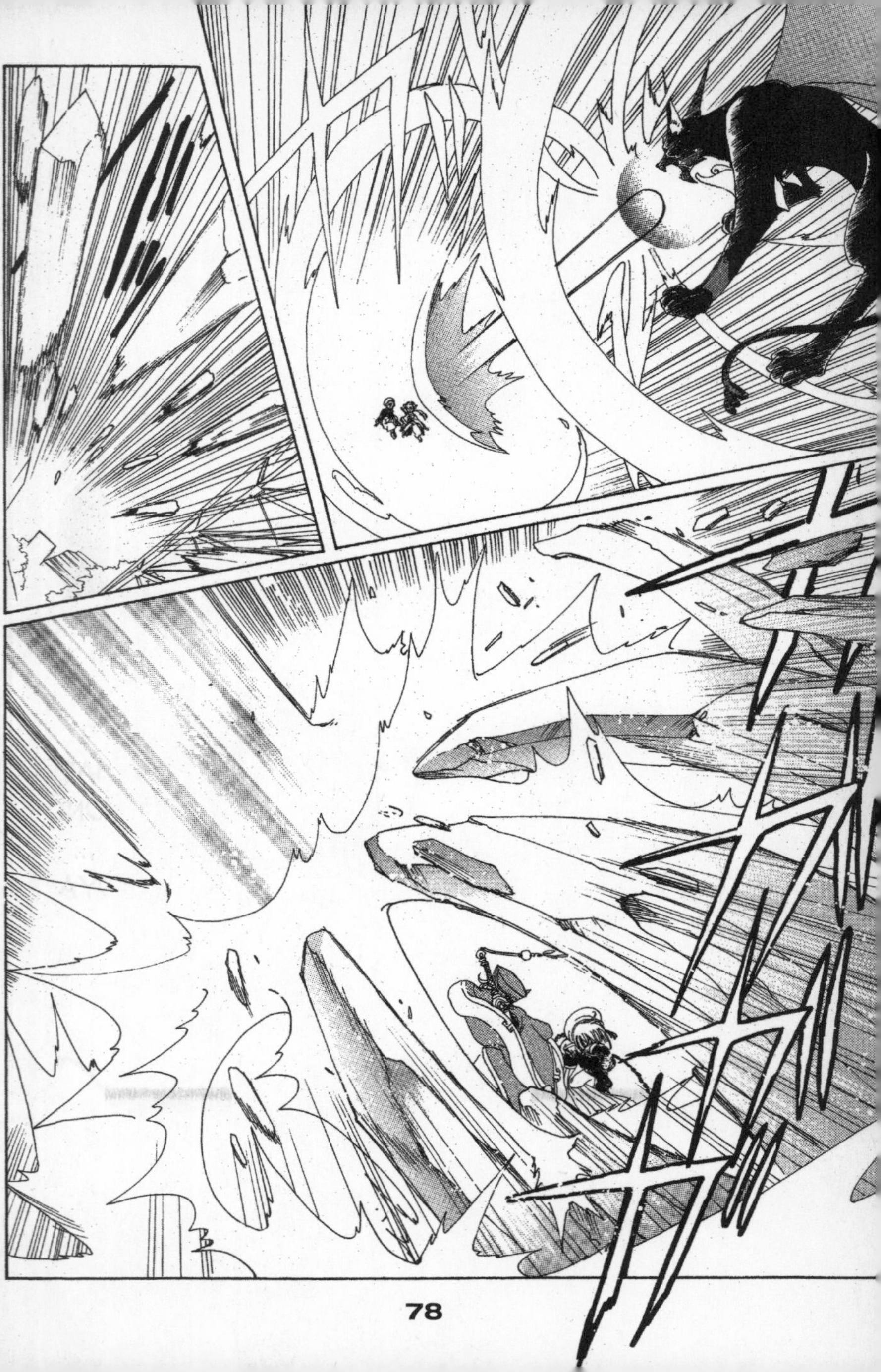

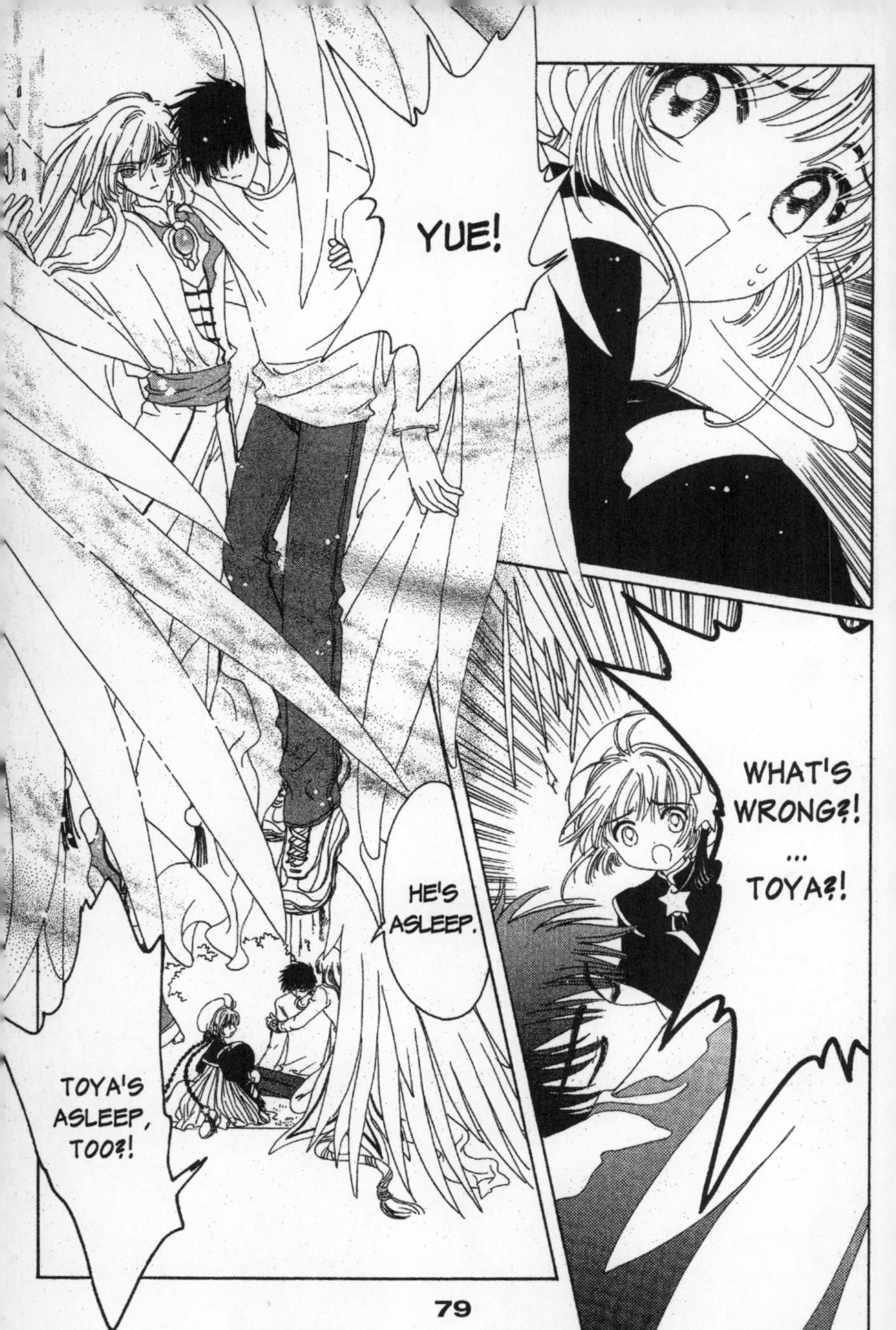
YUE!
WHAT'S WRONG?! ... TOYA?!
HE'S ASLEEP.
TOYA'S ASLEEP, TOO?!

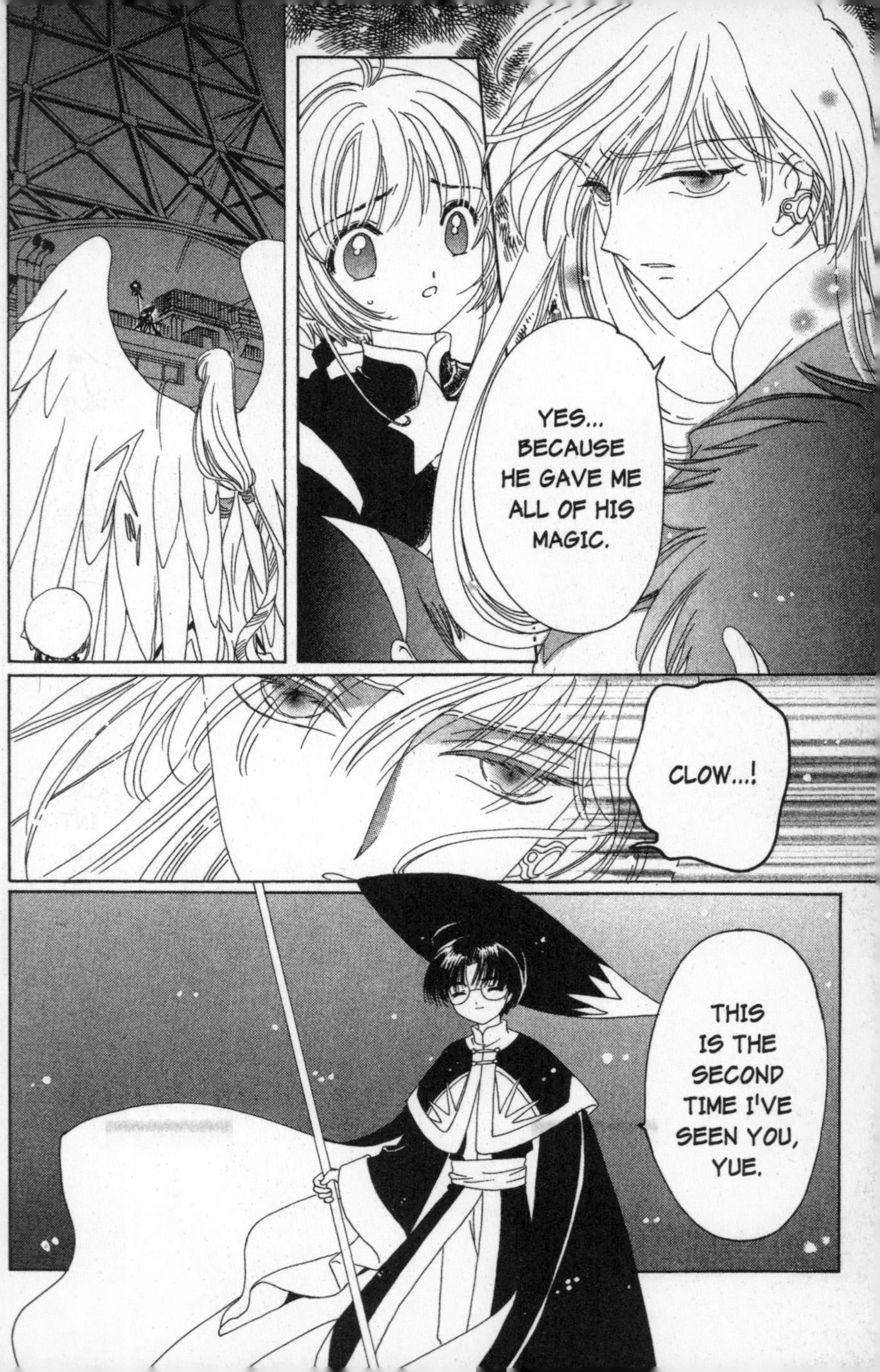
YES... BECAUSE HE GAVE ME ALL OF HIS MAGIC.
CLOW...!
THIS IS THE SECOND TIME I'VE SEEN YOU, YUE.

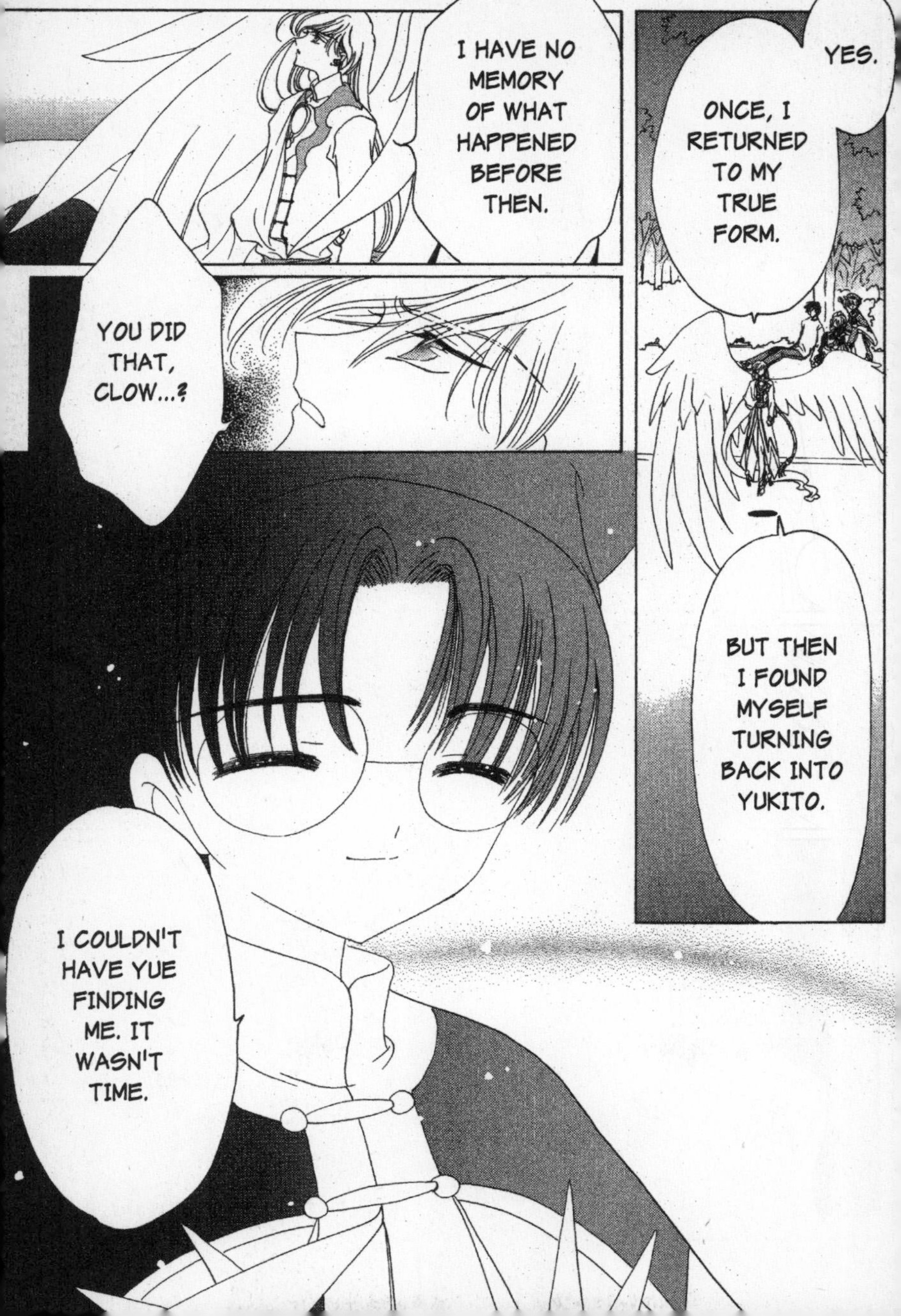
YES.
ONCE, I RETURNED TO MY TRUE FORM.
BUT THEN I FOUND MYSELF TURNING BACK INTO YUKITO.
I HAVE NO MEMORY OF WHAT HAPPENED BEFORE THEN.
YOU DID THAT, CLOW...?
I COULDN'T HAVE YUE FINDING ME. IT WASN'T TIME.

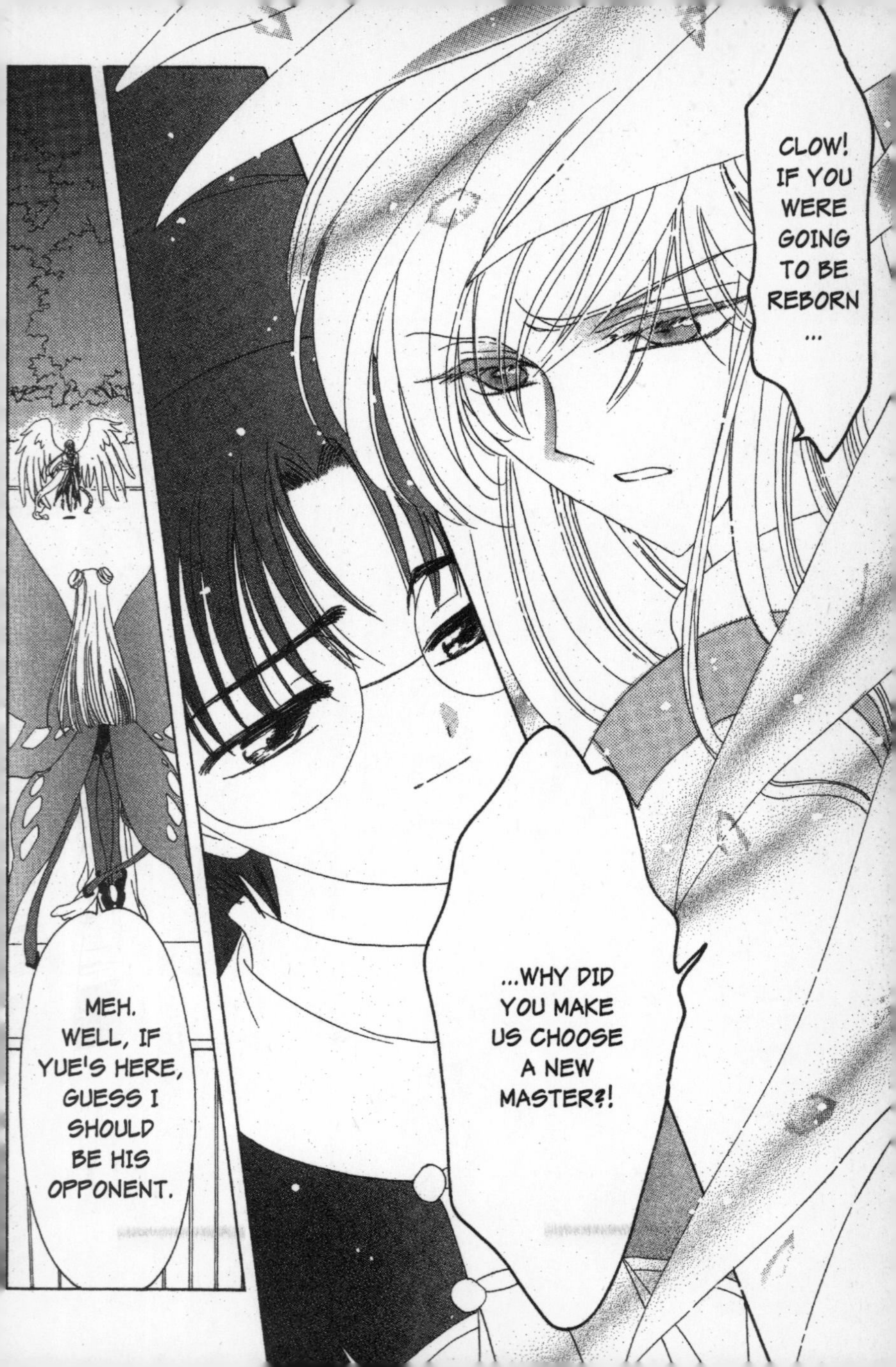
CLOW! IF YOU WERE GOING TO BE REBORN ...
...WHY DID YOU MAKE US CHOOSE A NEW MASTER?!
MEH. WELL, IF YUE'S HERE, GUESS I SHOULD BE HIS OPPONENT.

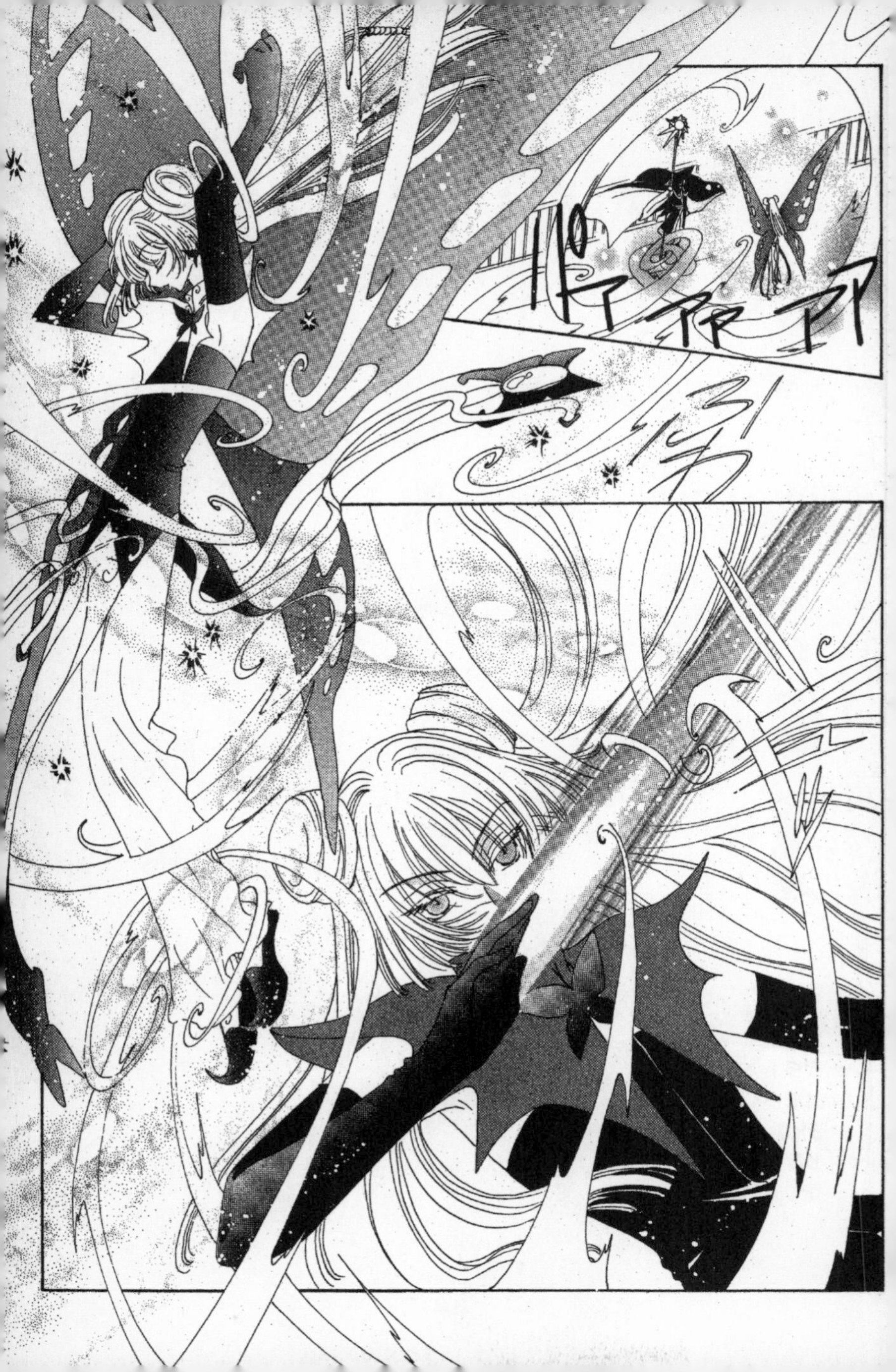
パアァァア

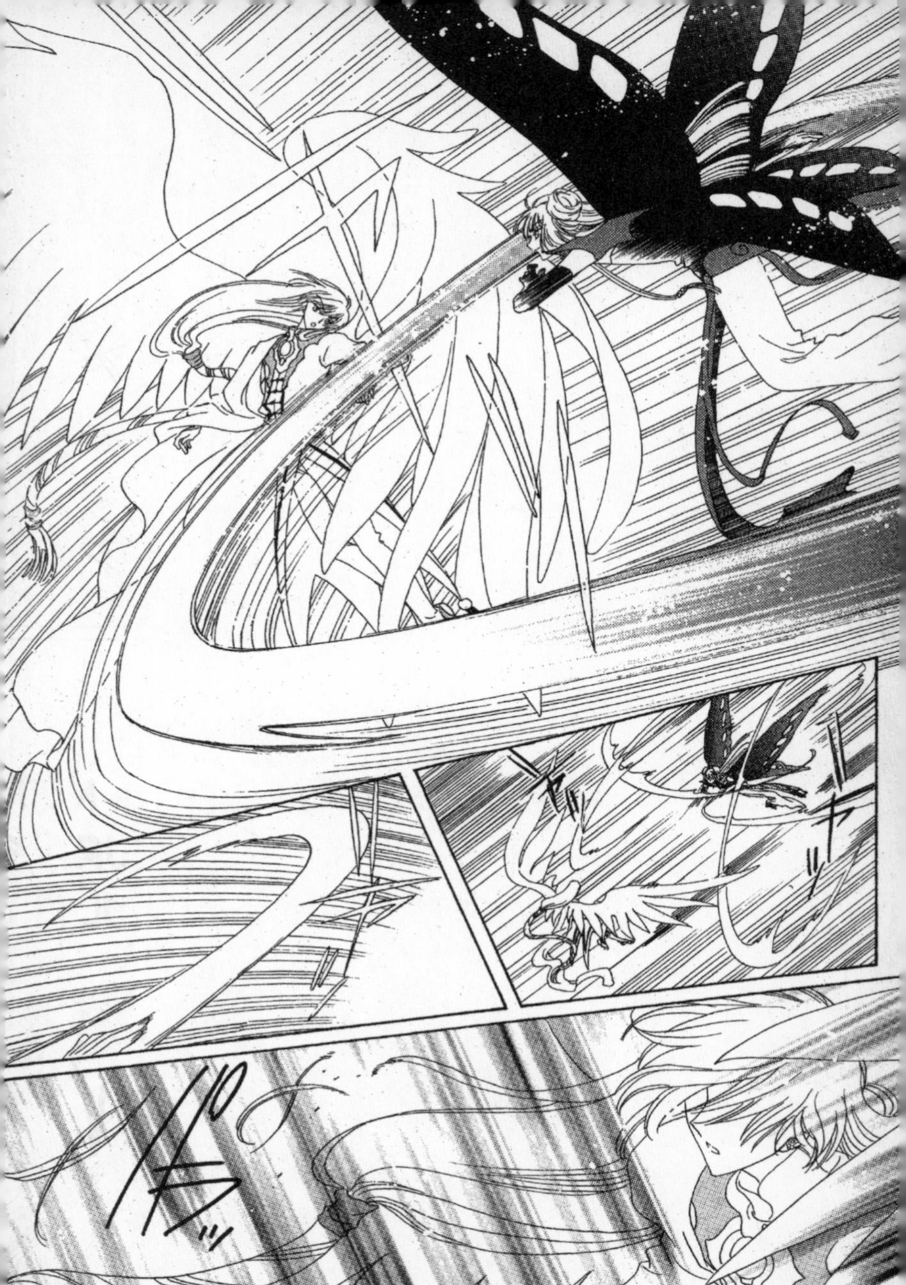

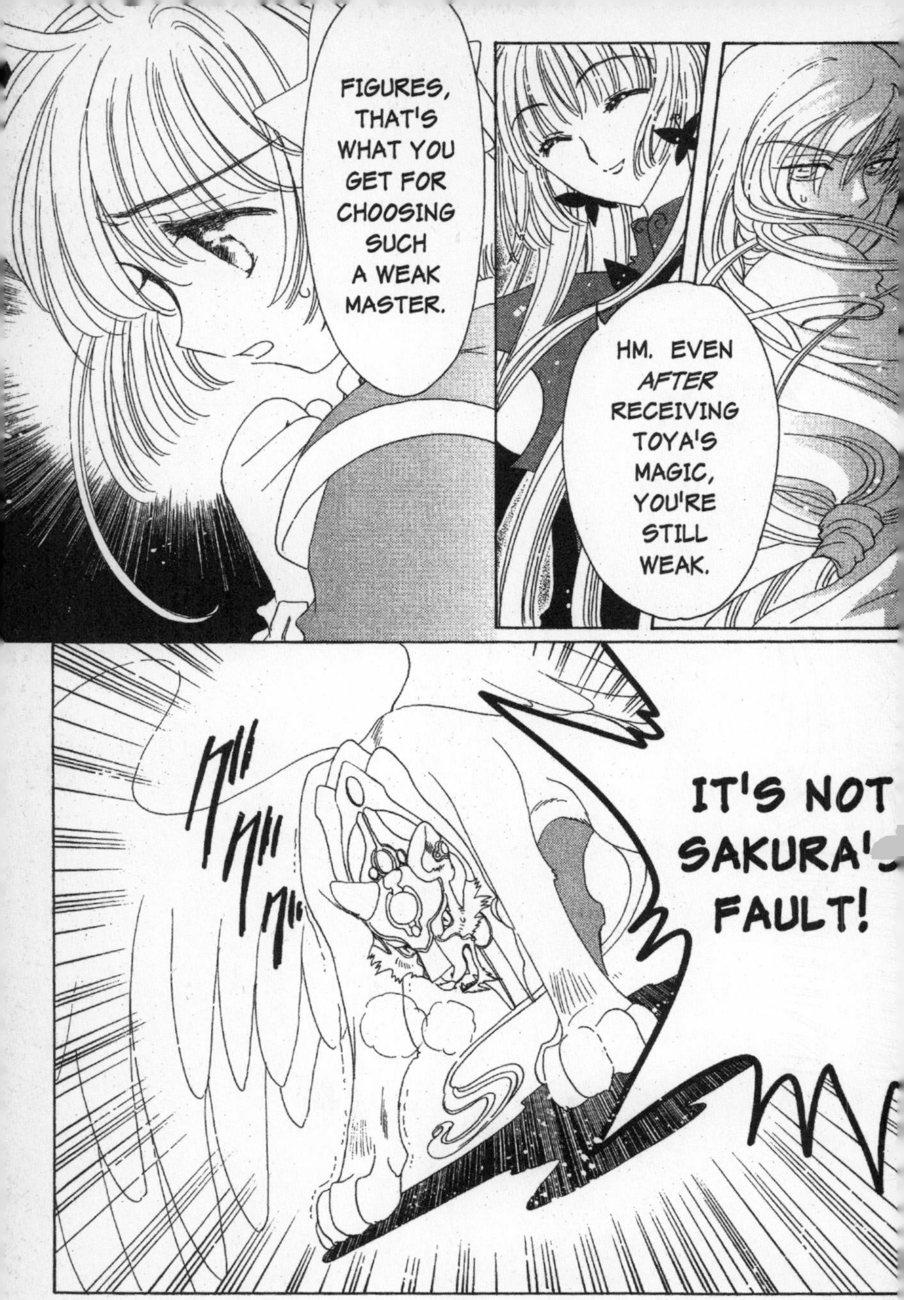
HM. EVEN *AFTER* RECEIVING TOYA'S MAGIC, YOU'RE STILL WEAK.
FIGURES, THAT'S WHAT YOU GET FOR CHOOSING SUCH A WEAK MASTER.
IT'S NOT SAKURA'S FAULT!

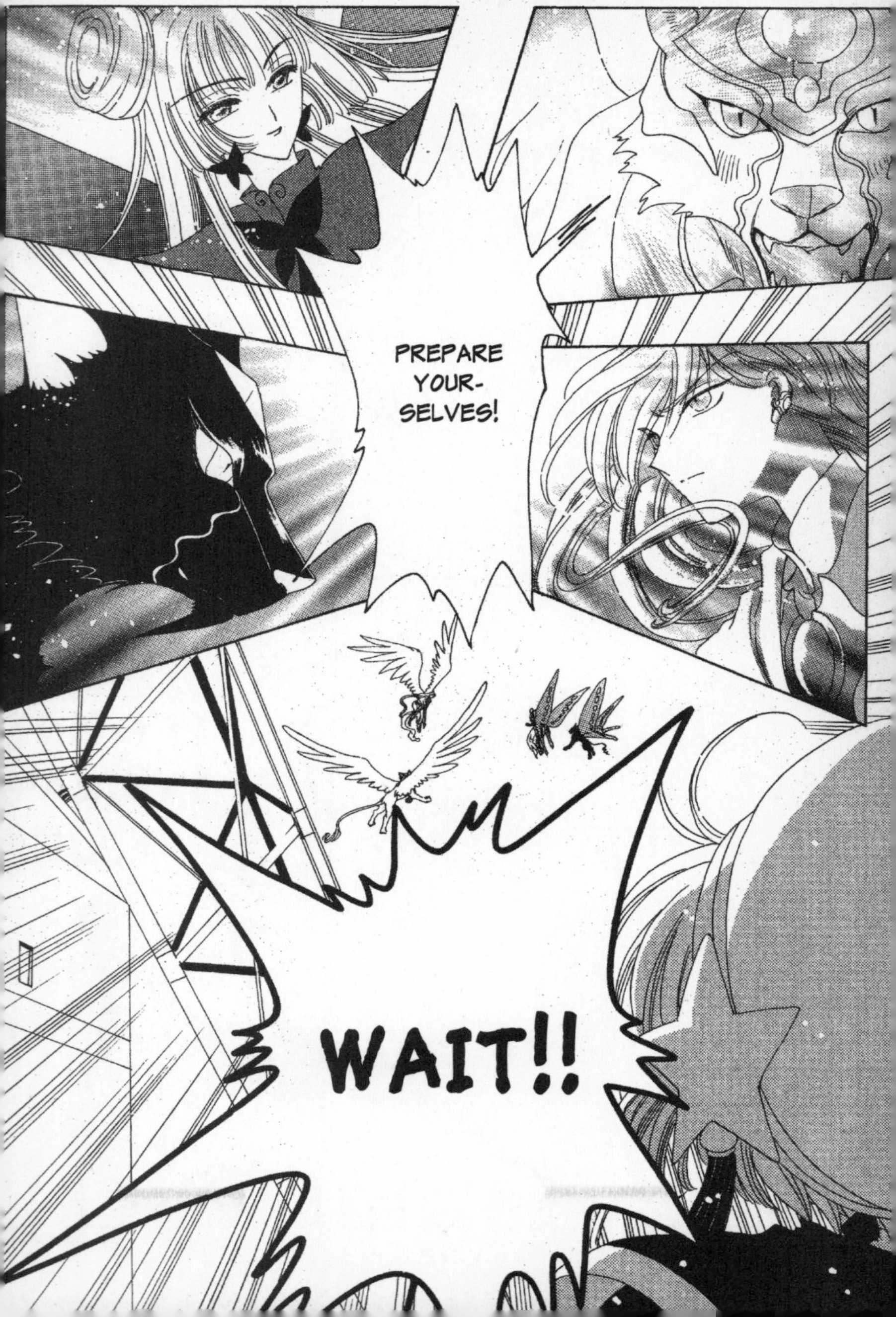
PREPARE YOUR-SELVES!
WAIT!!

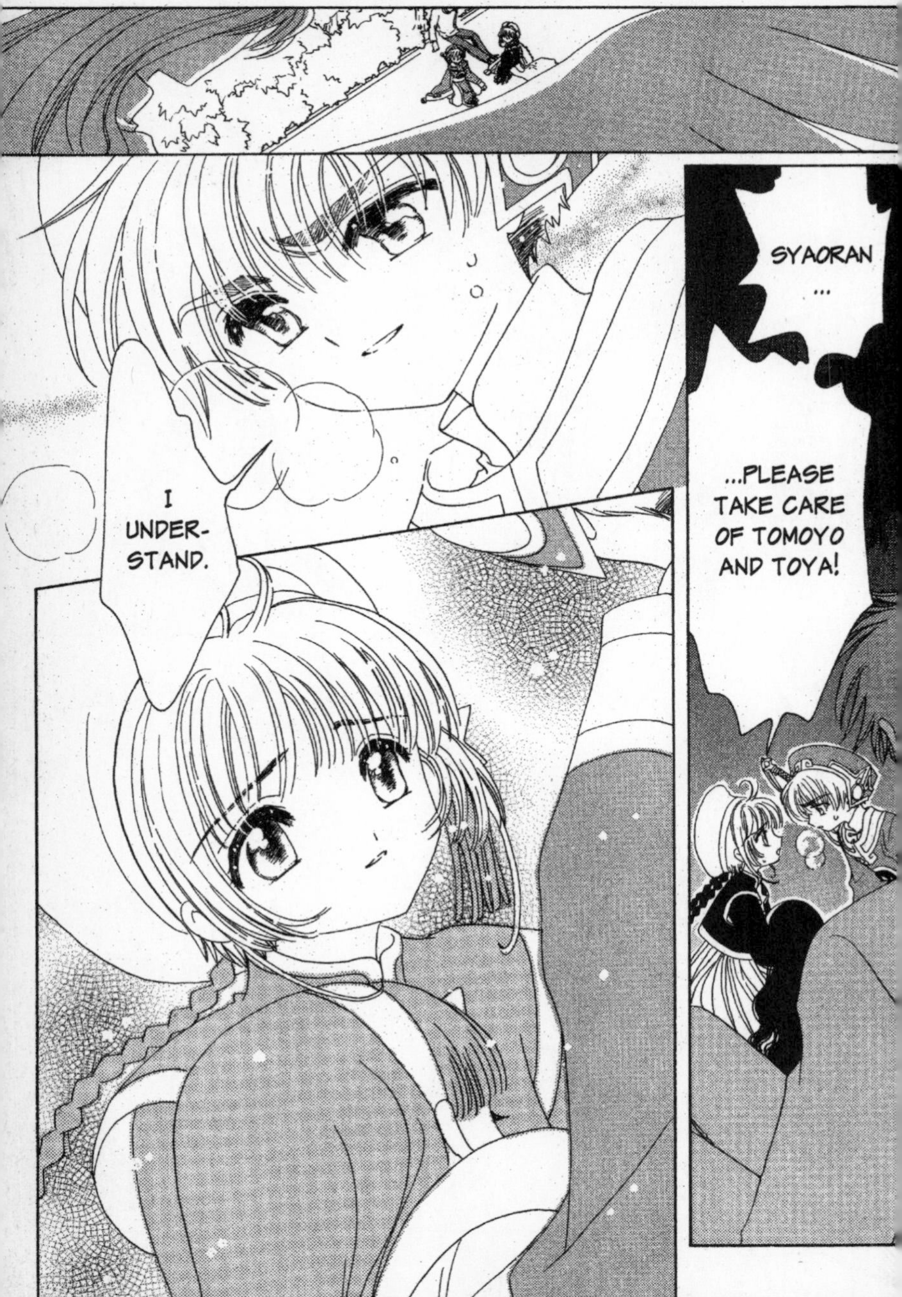
SYAORAN ...
...PLEASE TAKE CARE OF TOMOYO AND TOYA!
I UNDER-STAND.

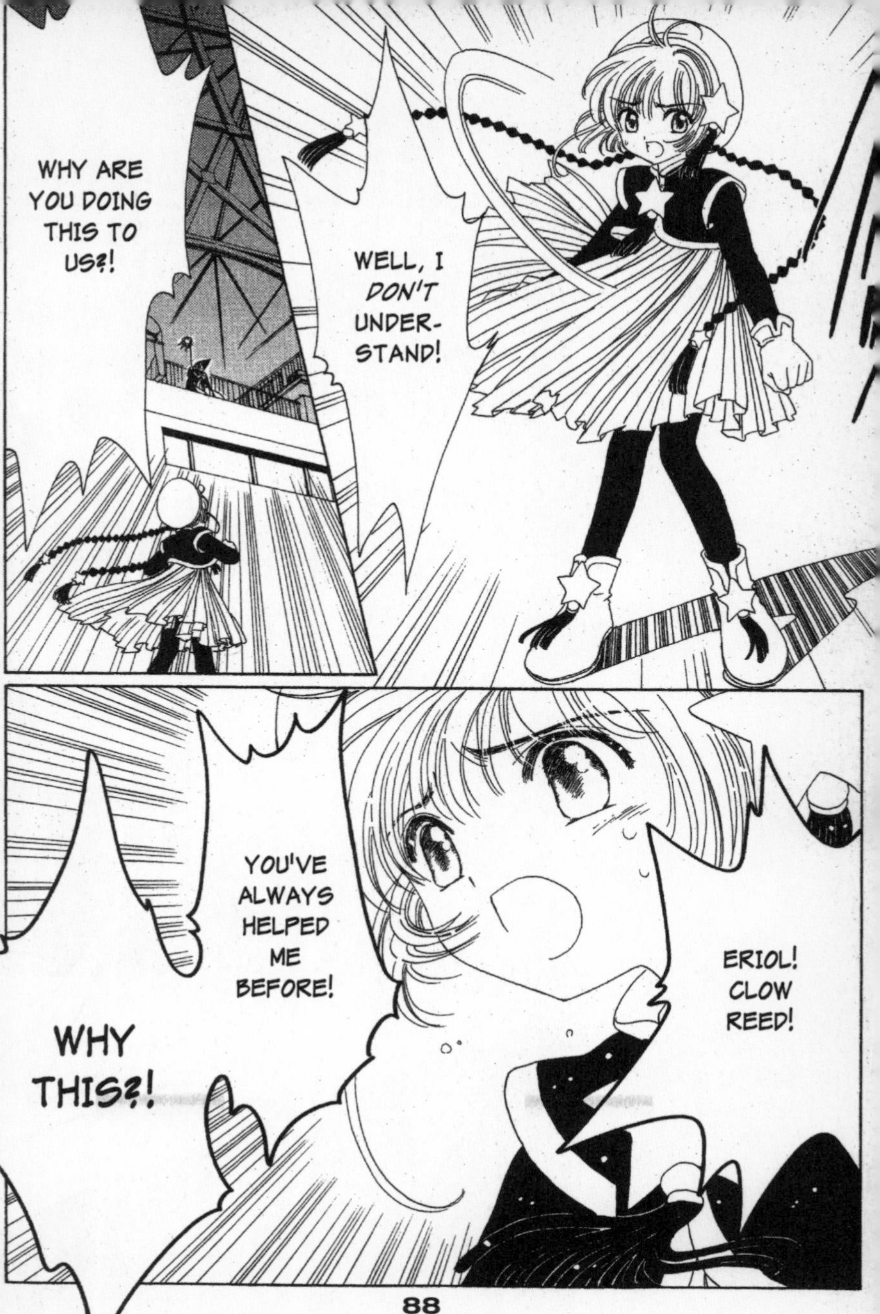
WELL, I DON'T UNDERSTAND!
WHY ARE YOU DOING THIS TO US?!
ERIOL! CLOW REED!
YOU'VE ALWAYS HELPED ME BEFORE!
WHY THIS?!

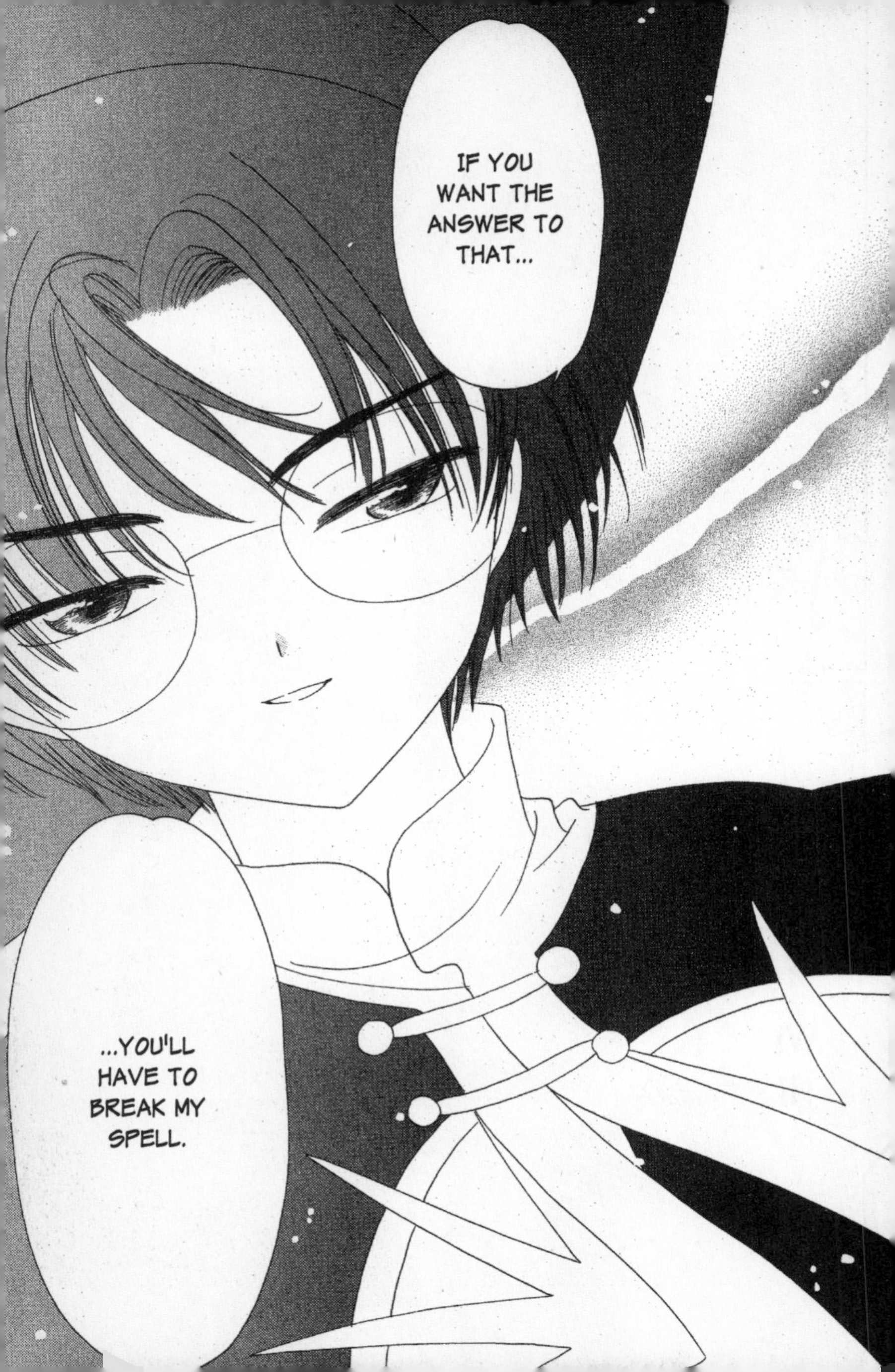
IF YOU WANT THE ANSWER TO THAT...
...YOU'LL HAVE TO BREAK MY SPELL.

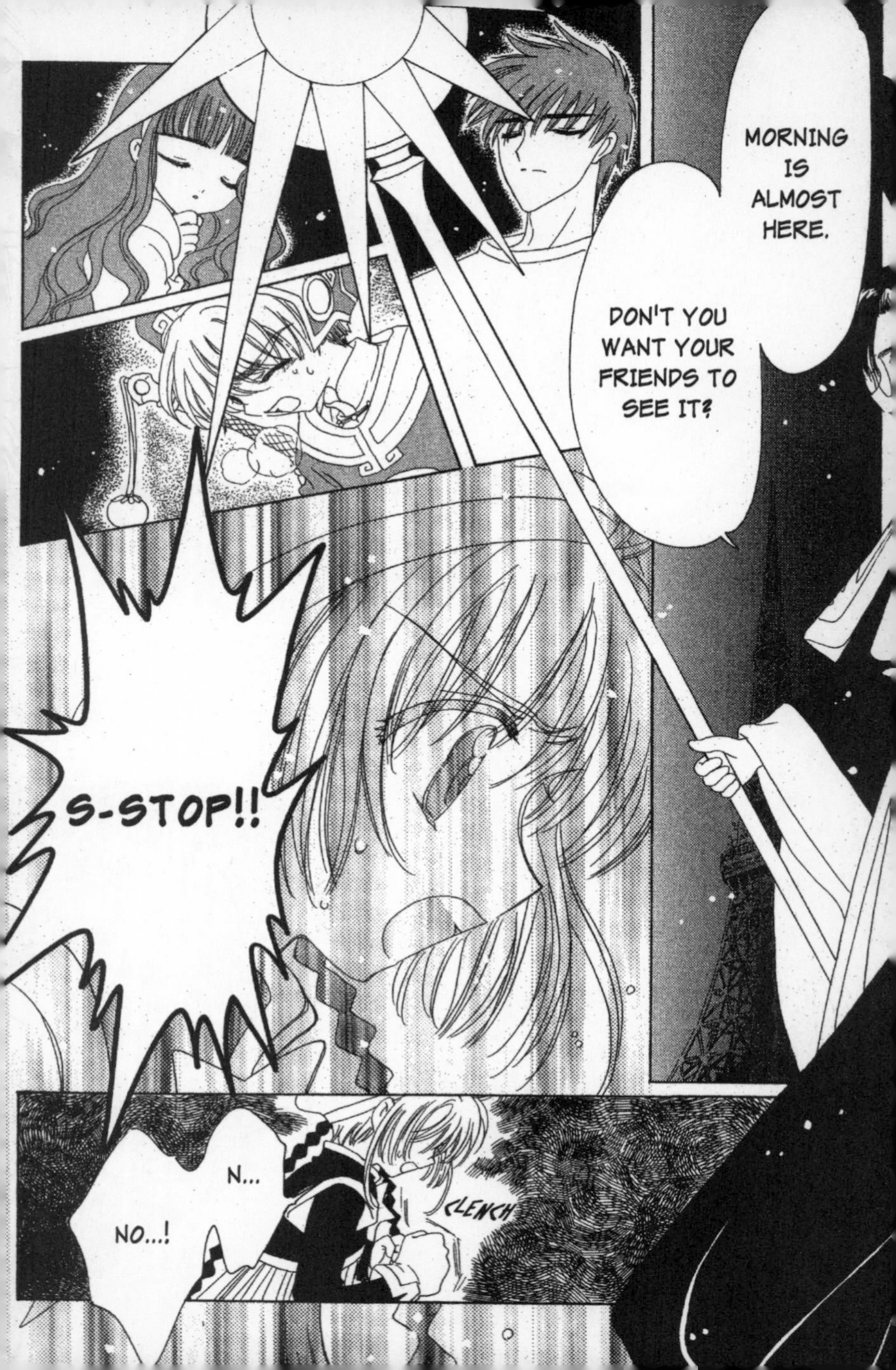
MORNING IS ALMOST HERE.
DON'T YOU WANT YOUR FRIENDS TO SEE IT?
S-STOP!!
CLENCH
N...
NO...!

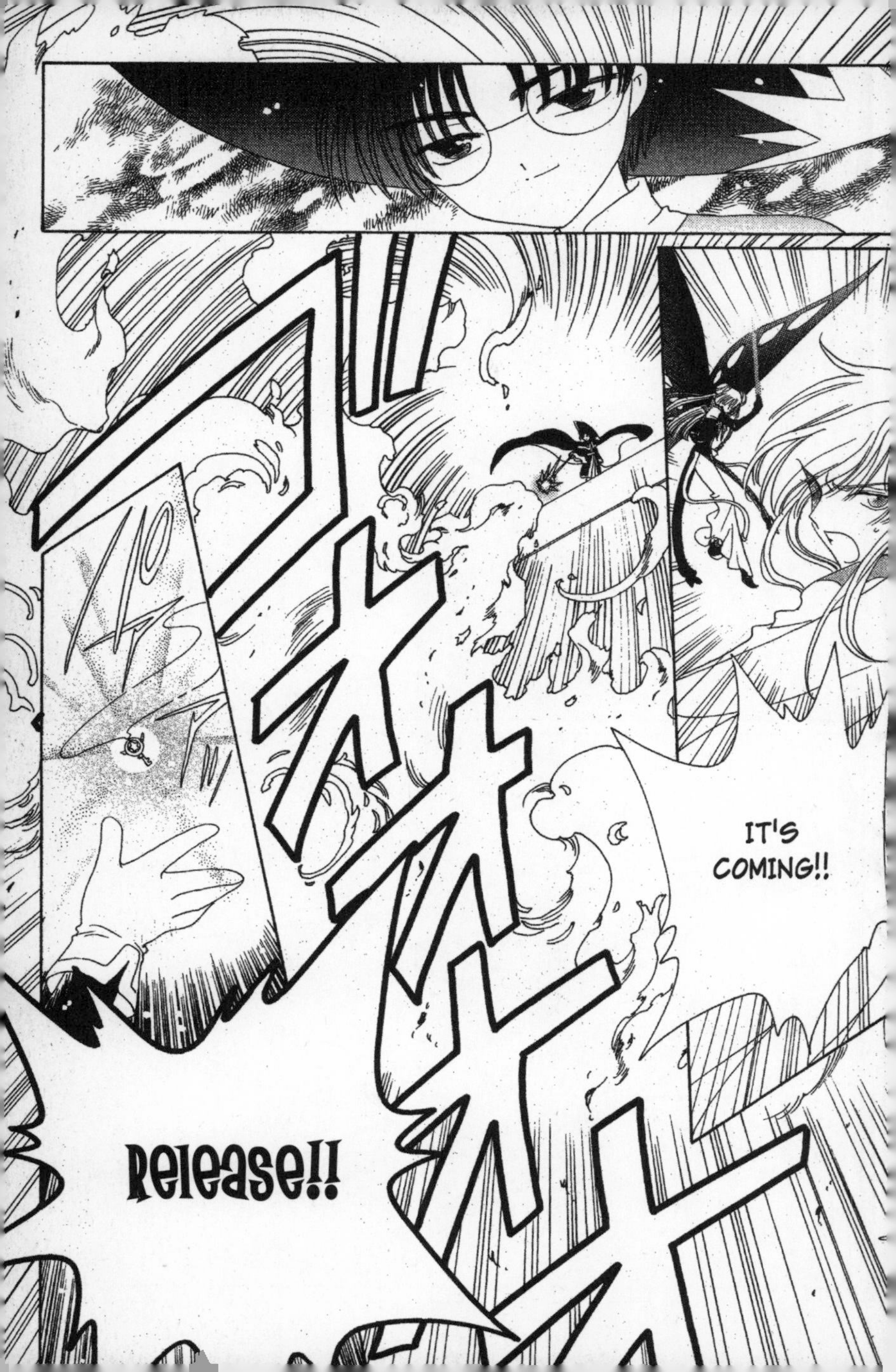
IT'S COMING!!
Release!!

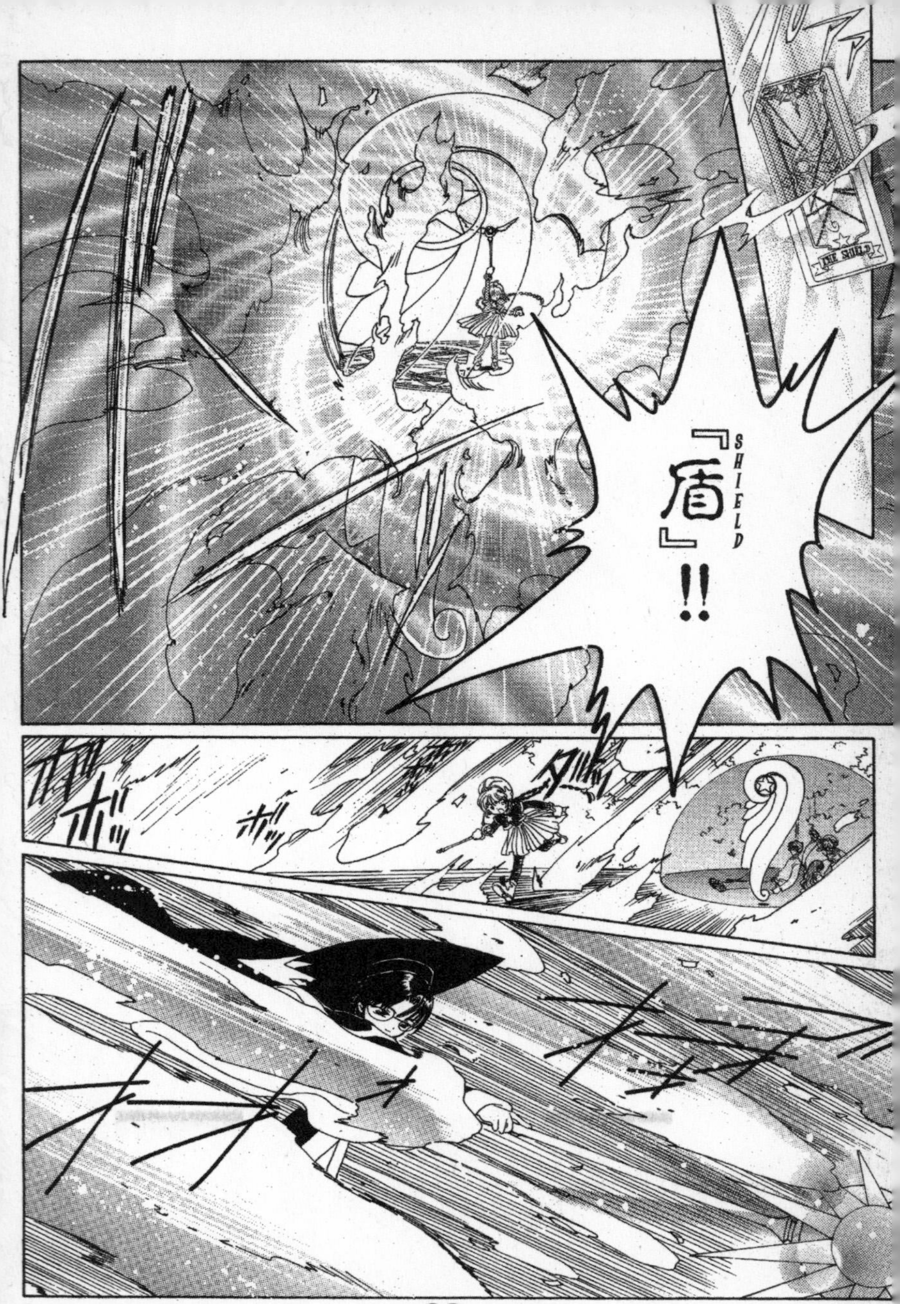
THE SHIELD
『盾(SHIELD)』!!

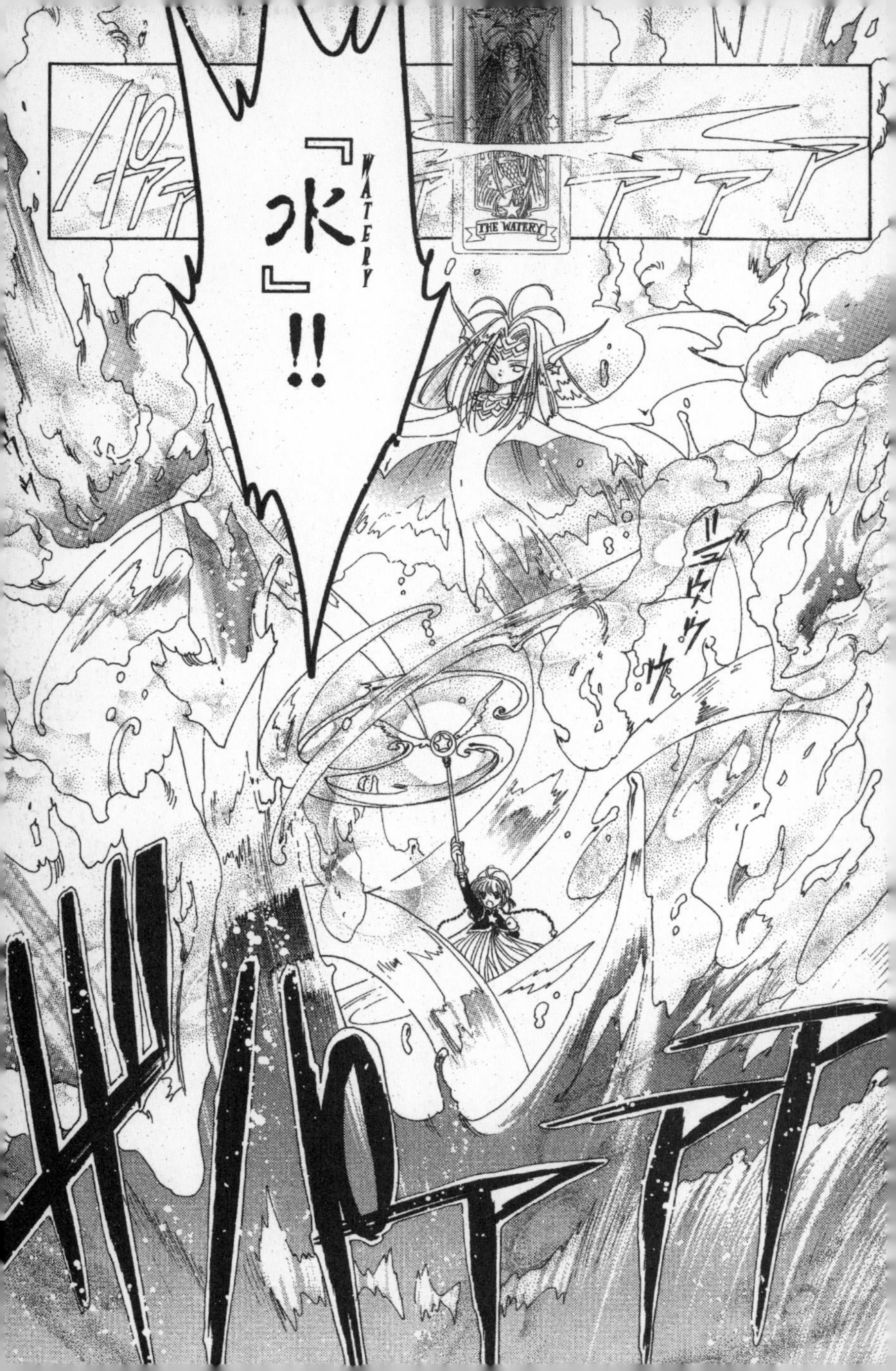
パァァァァァァァ
THE WATERY
「水」!!
WATERY
ザパァァァ

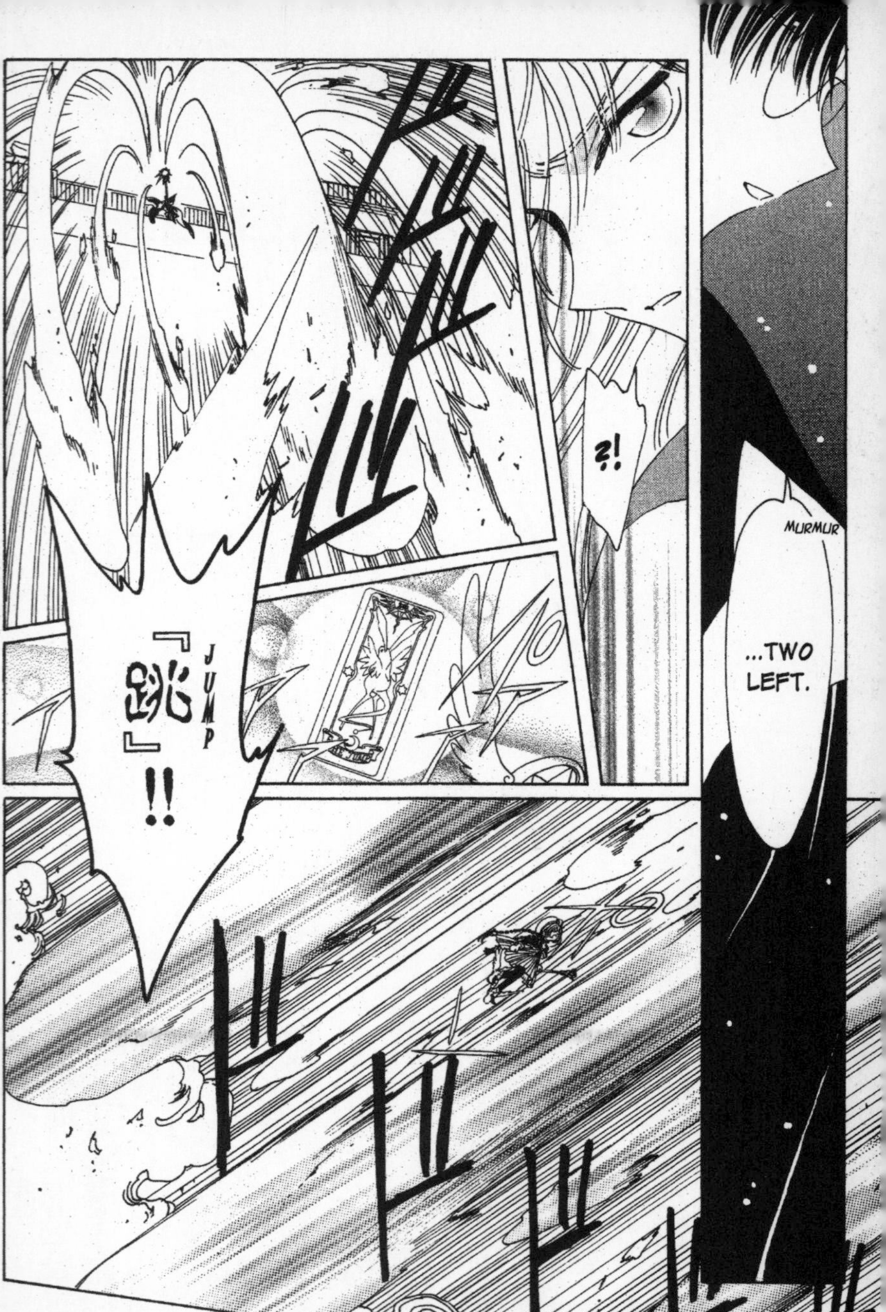

MURMUR
...TWO LEFT.
?!
「跳」!!
JUMP

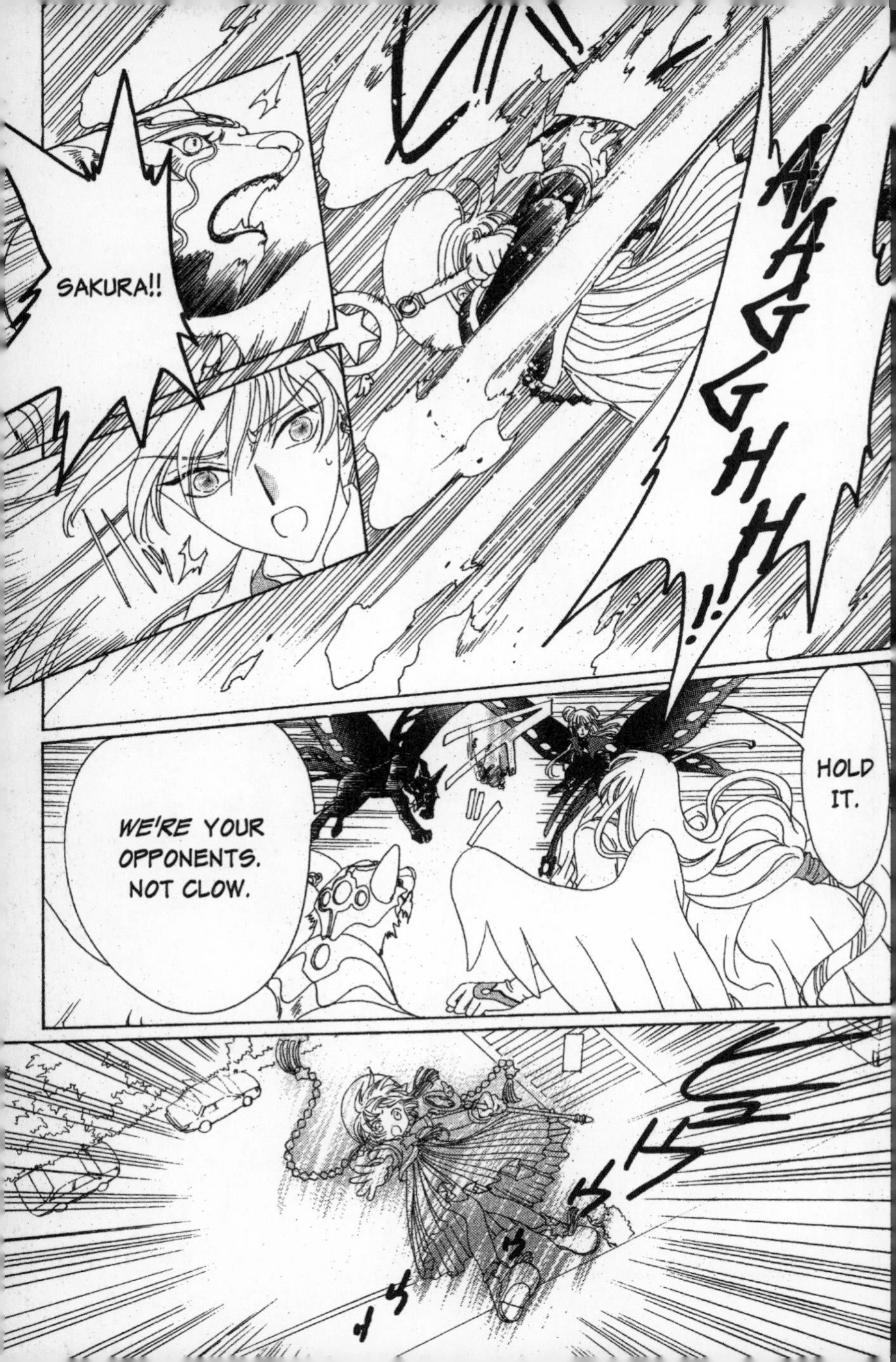
AAGGHH!!
SAKURA!!
HOLD IT.
WE'RE YOUR OPPONENTS. NOT CLOW.

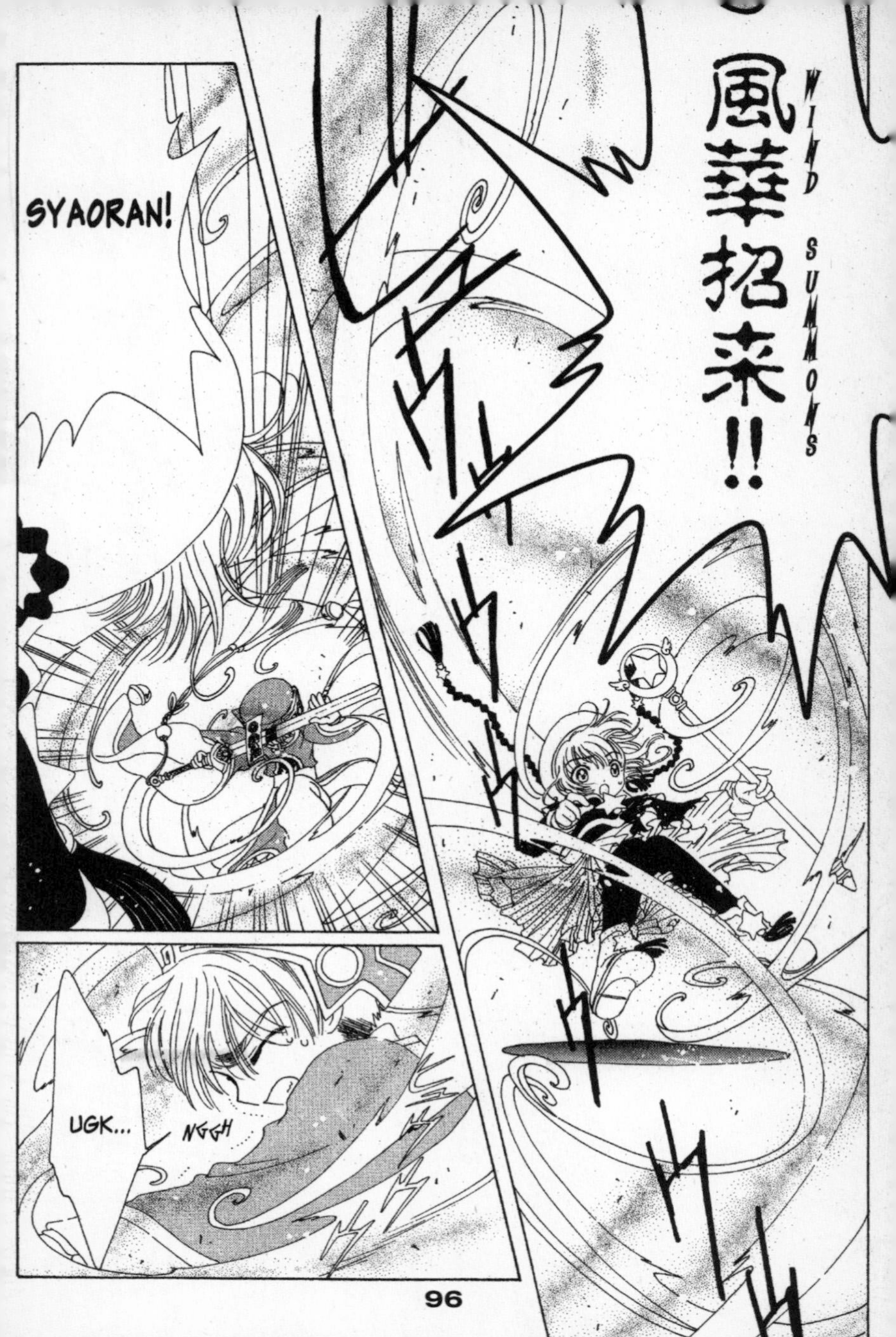
風華招来!!
WIND SUMMONS
SYAORAN!
UGK...
NGGH

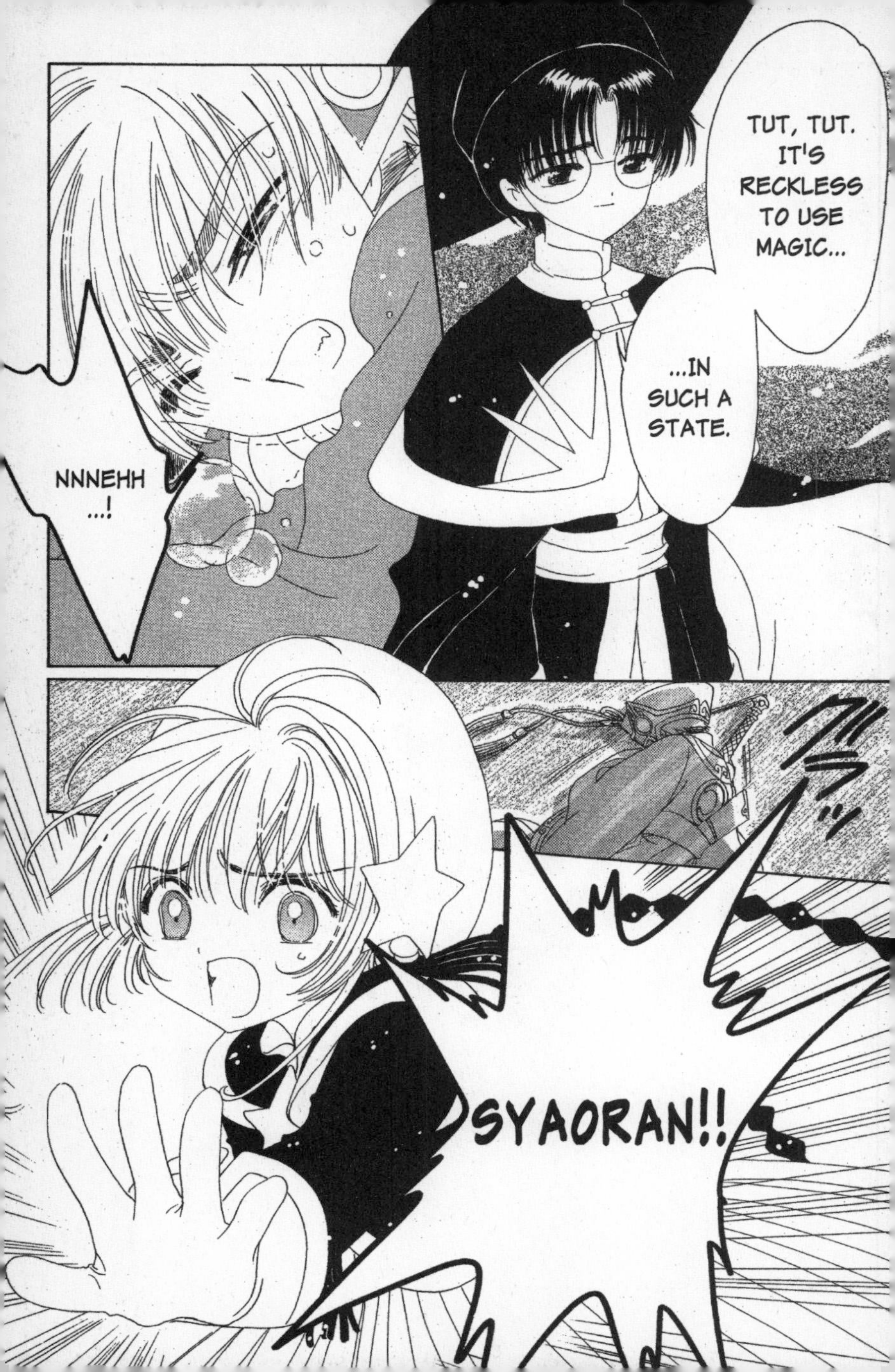
TUT, TUT. IT'S RECKLESS TO USE MAGIC...
...IN SUCH A STATE.
NNNEHH ...!
SYAORAN!!

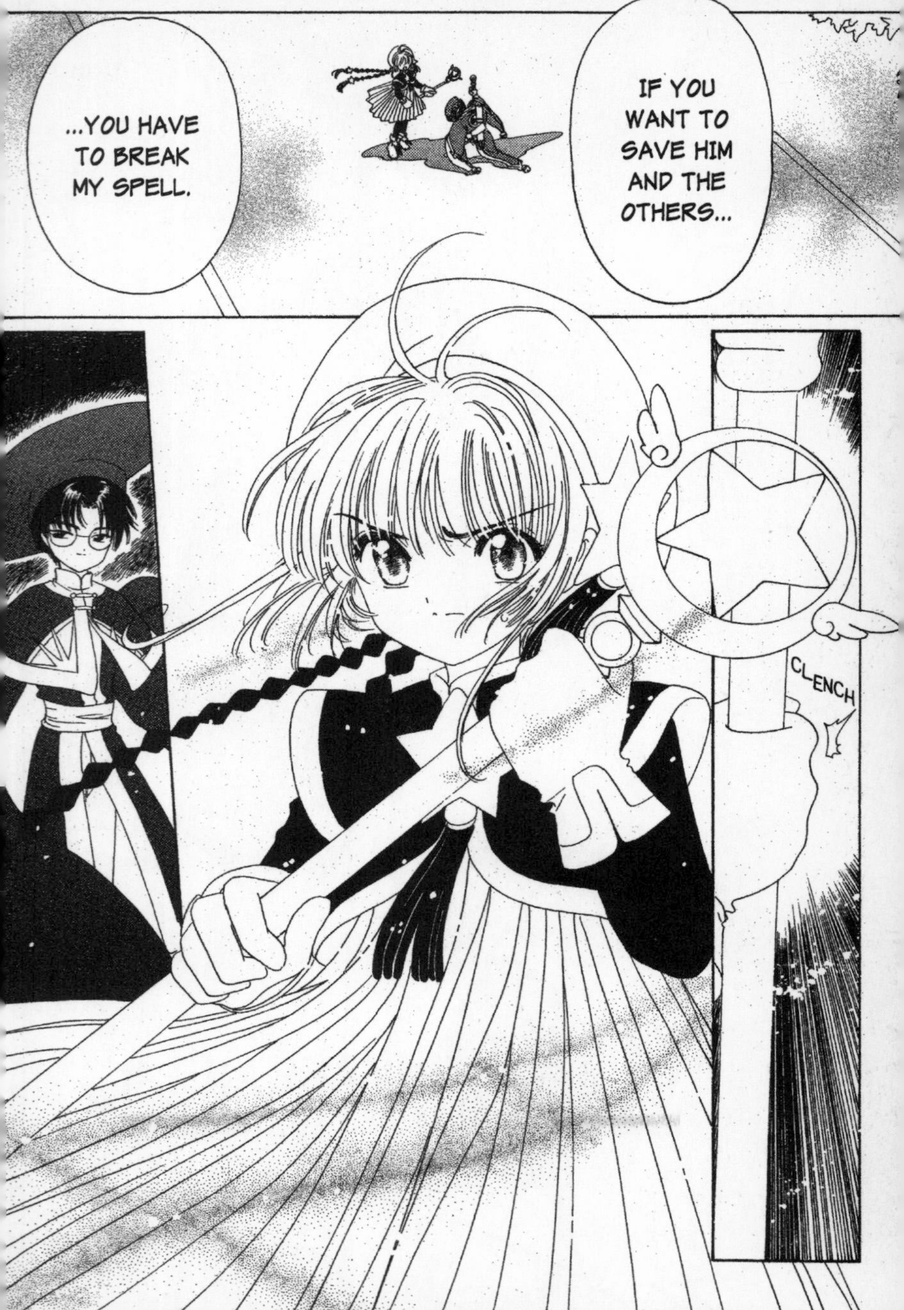
IF YOU WANT TO SAVE HIM AND THE OTHERS...
...YOU HAVE TO BREAK MY SPELL.
CLENCH

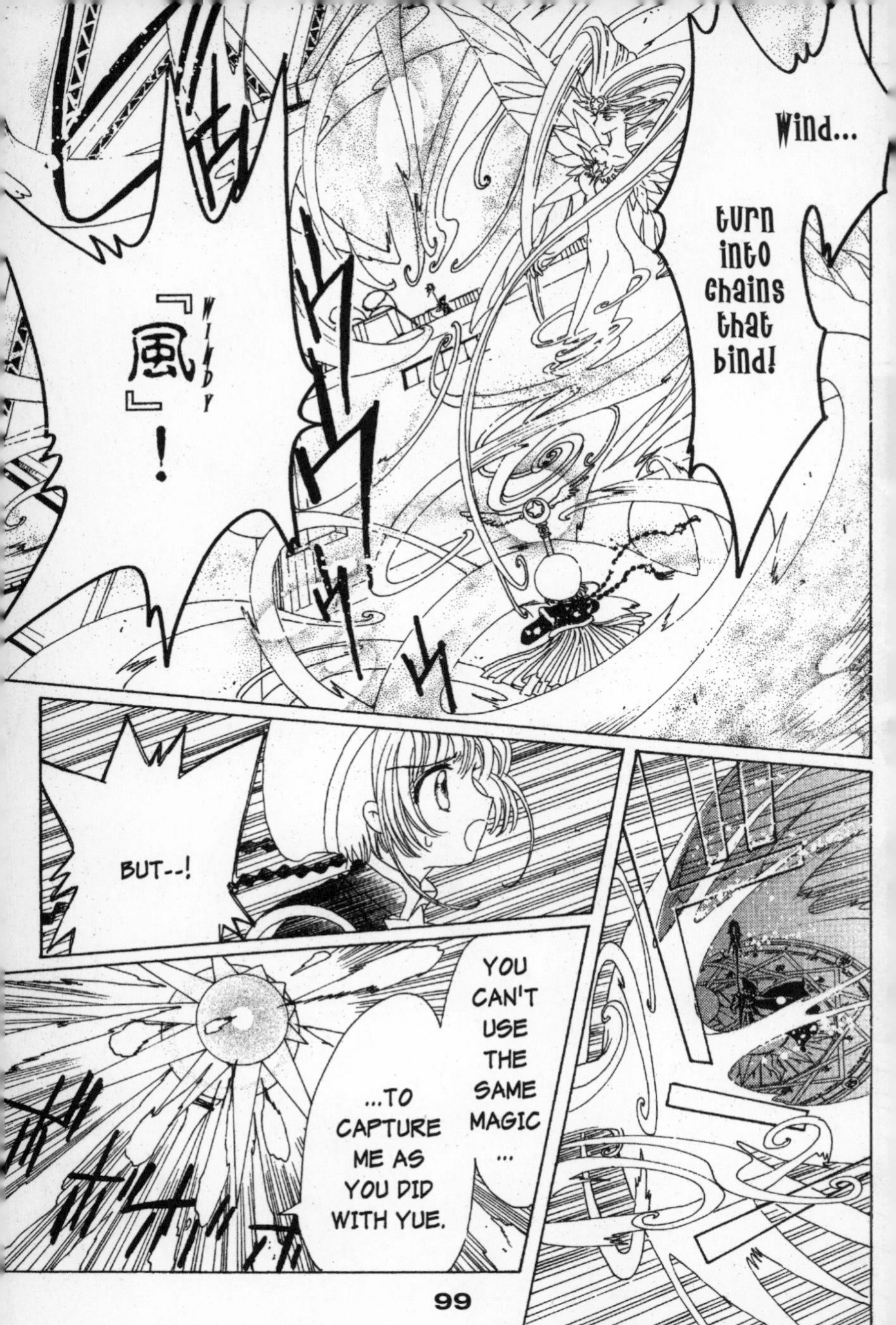

Wind...
turn into chains that bind!
『風』! WINDY
BUT--!
YOU CAN'T USE THE SAME MAGIC ...
...TO CAPTURE ME AS YOU DID WITH YUE.

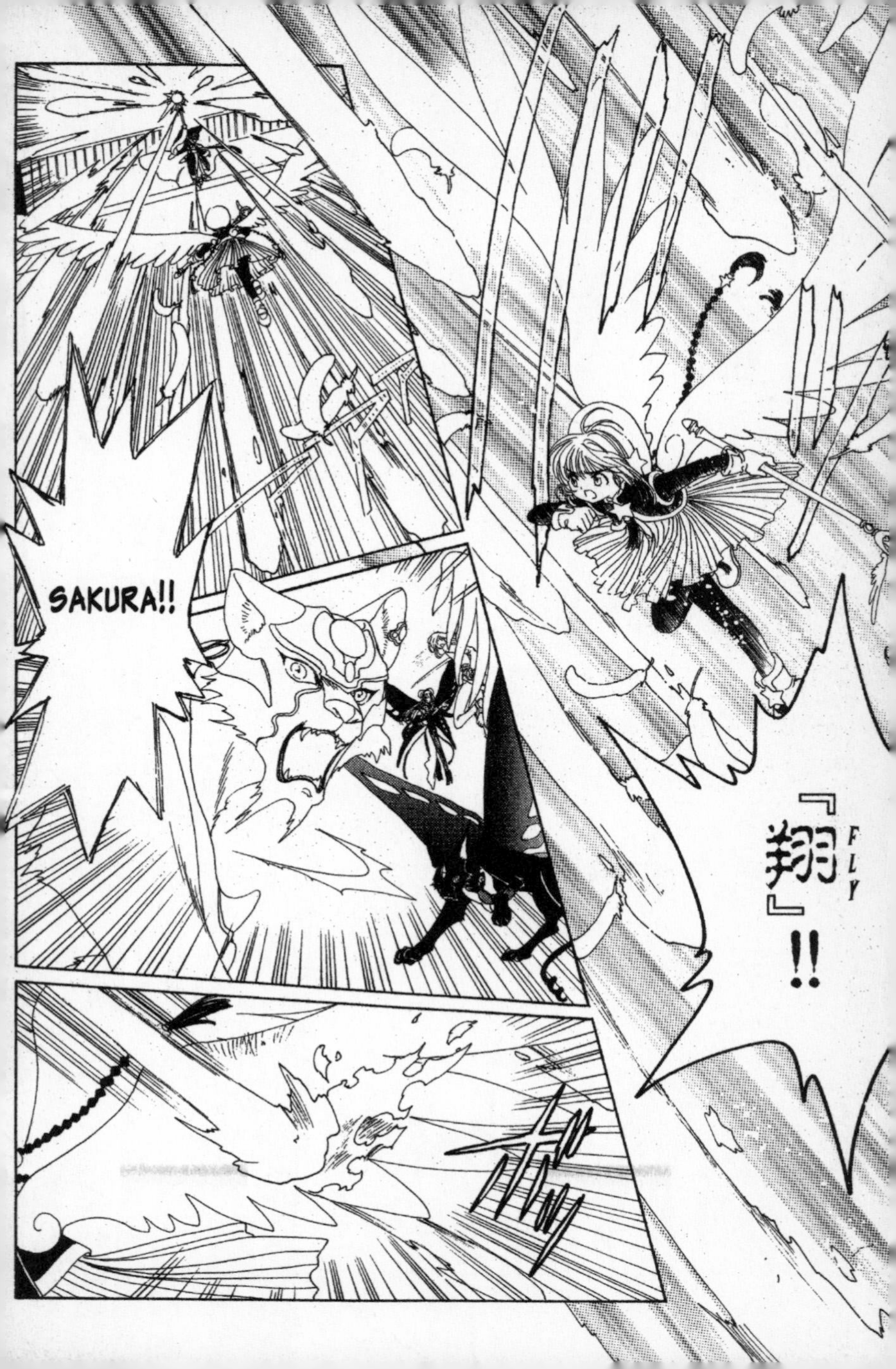
『翔』!!
FLY
SAKURA!!

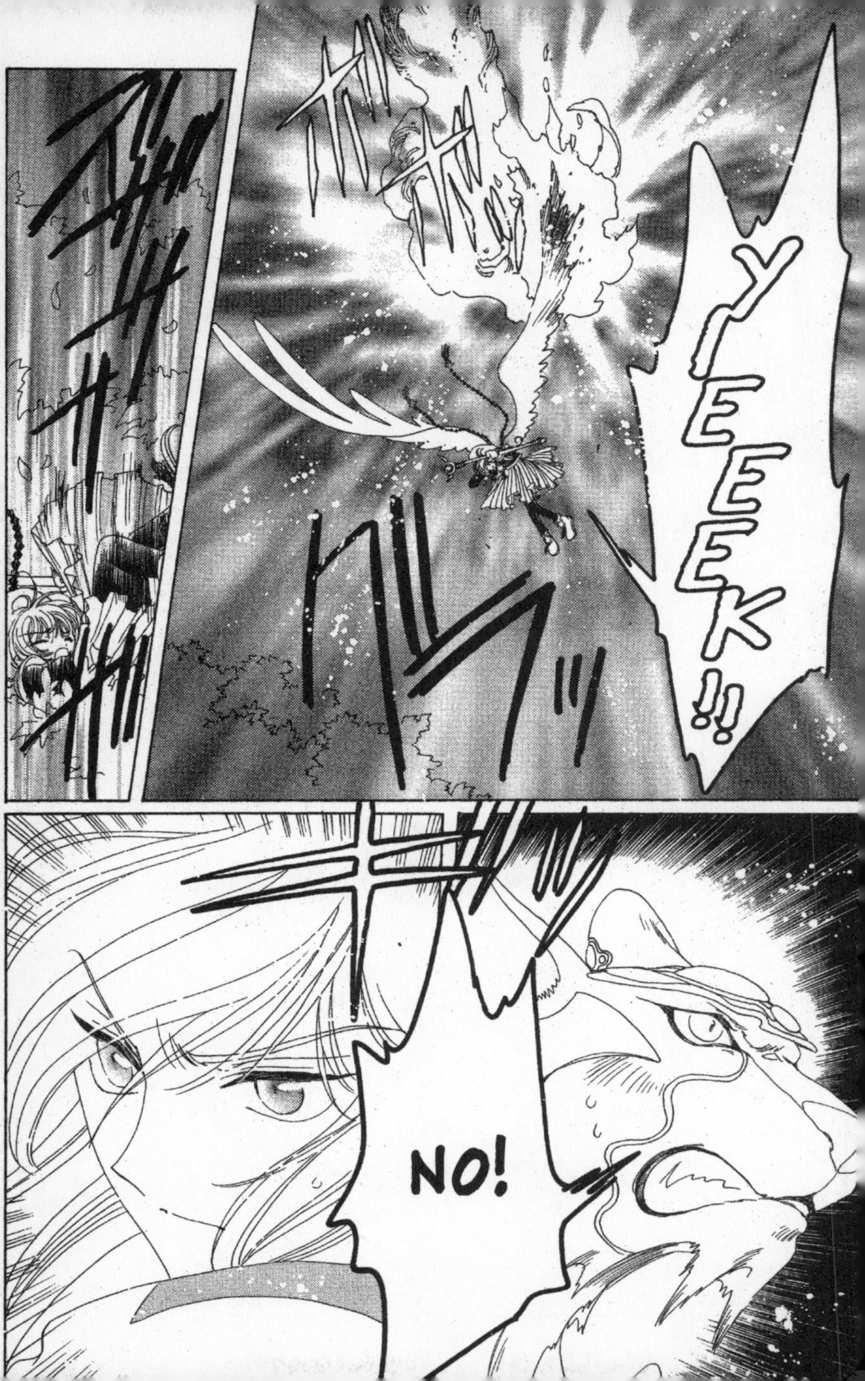
YIEEEEK!!
NO!

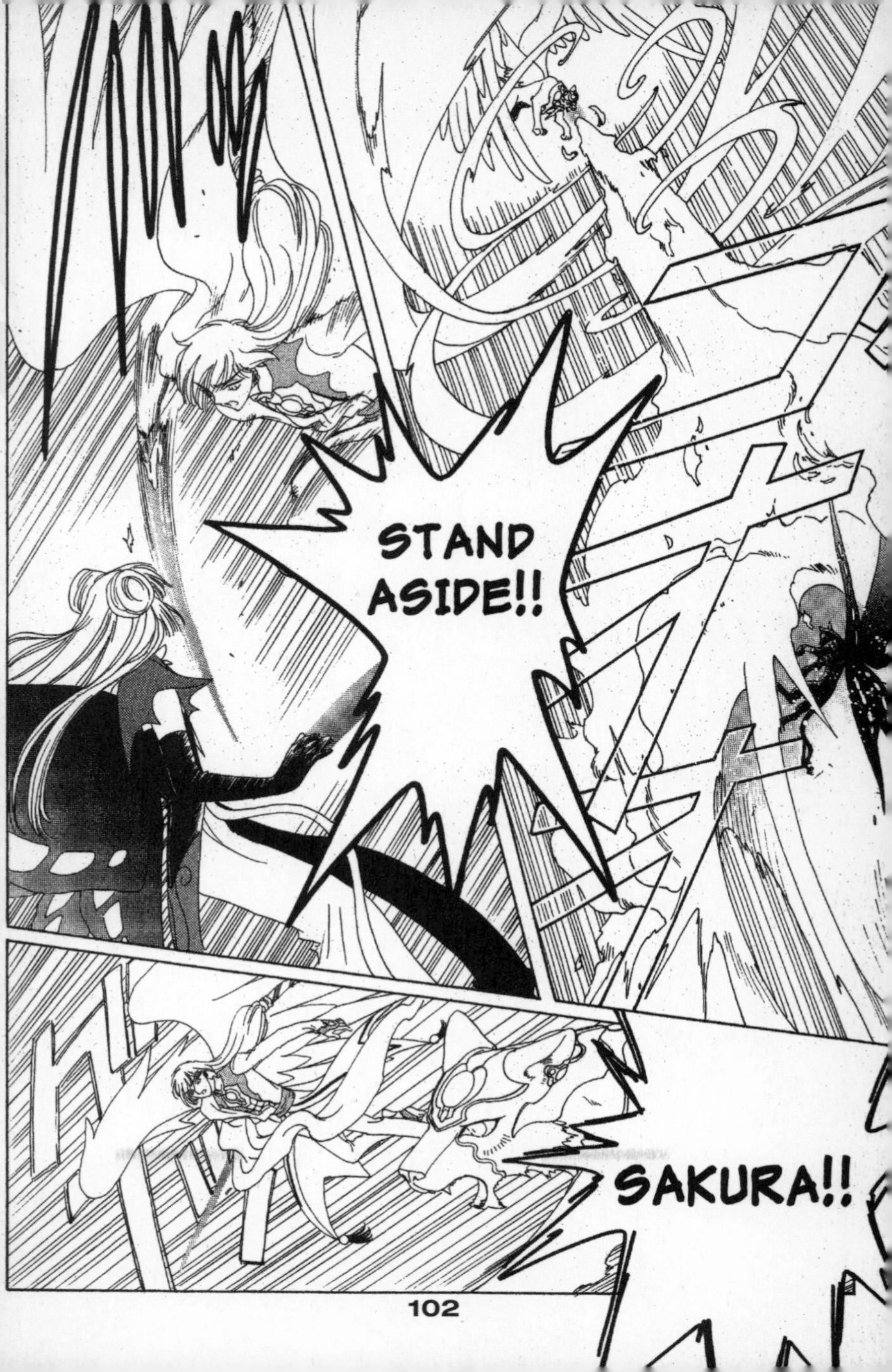
STAND ASIDE!!
SAKURA!!

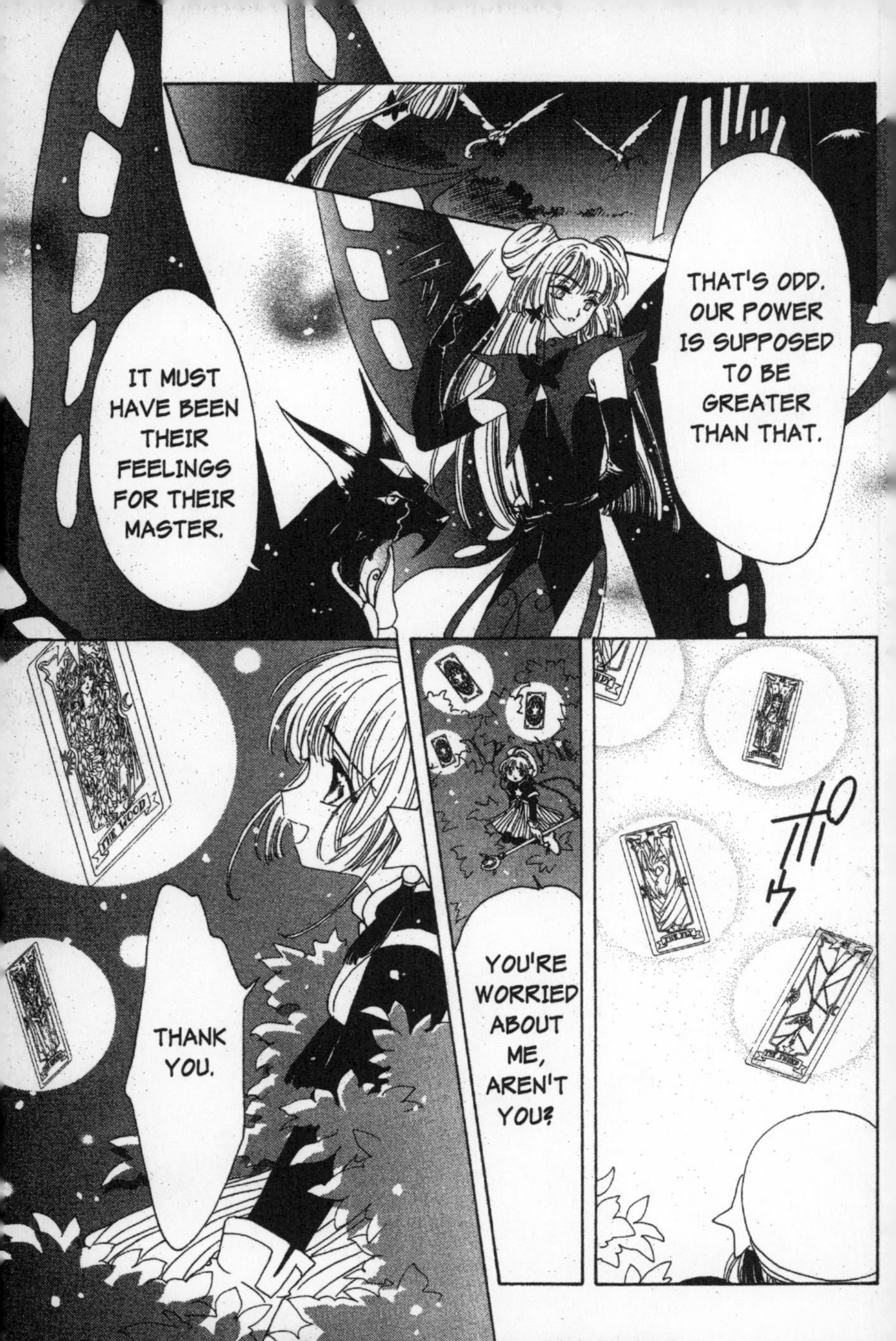
THAT'S ODD. OUR POWER IS SUPPOSED TO BE GREATER THAN THAT.
IT MUST HAVE BEEN THEIR FEELINGS FOR THEIR MASTER.
YOU'RE WORRIED ABOUT ME, AREN'T YOU?
THANK YOU.

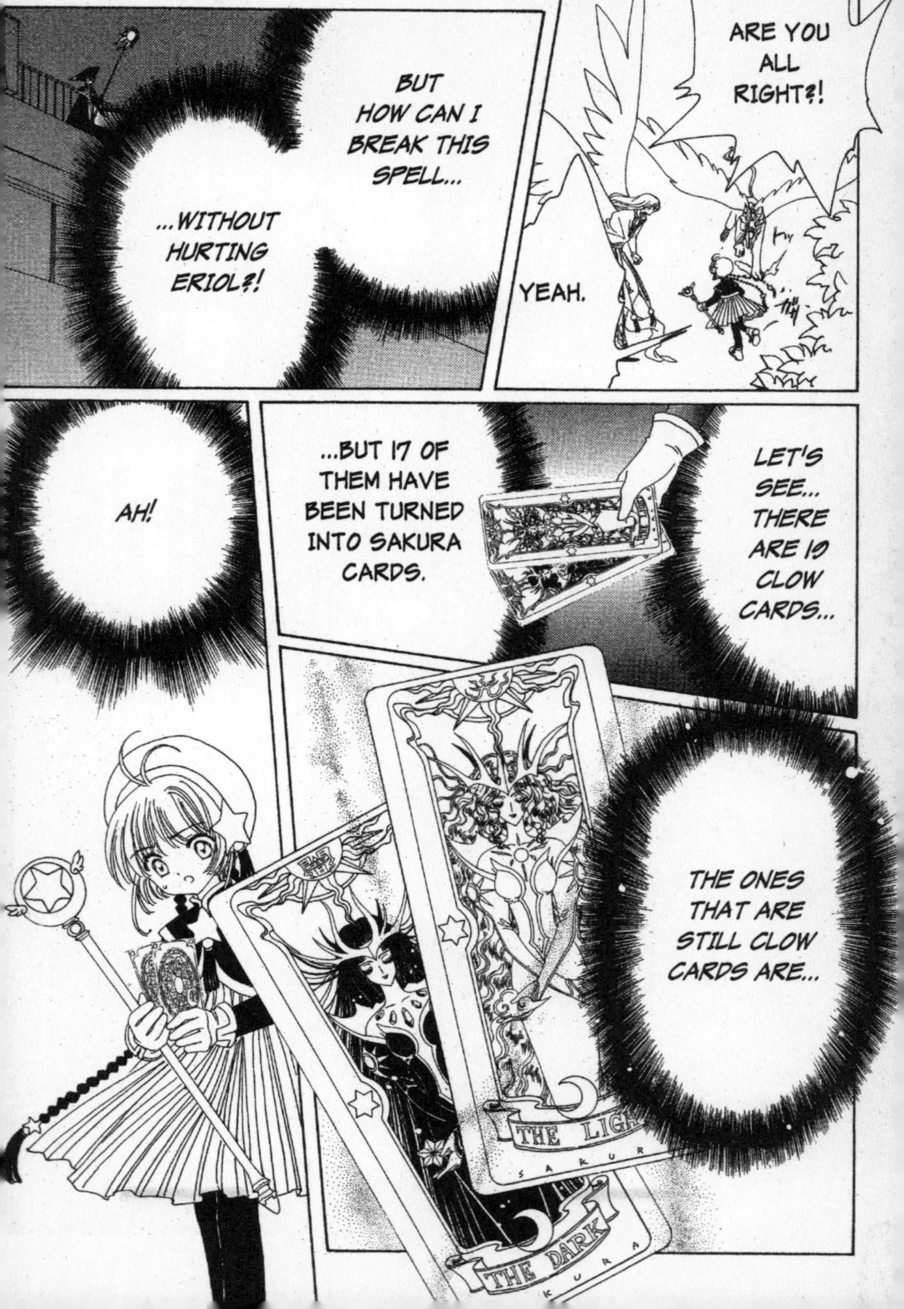

ARE YOU ALL RIGHT?!
YEAH.
BUT HOW CAN I BREAK THIS SPELL...
...WITHOUT HURTING ERIOL?!
LET'S SEE... THERE ARE 19 CLOW CARDS...
...BUT 17 OF THEM HAVE BEEN TURNED INTO SAKURA CARDS.
AH!
THE ONES THAT ARE STILL CLOW CARDS ARE...
THE DARK

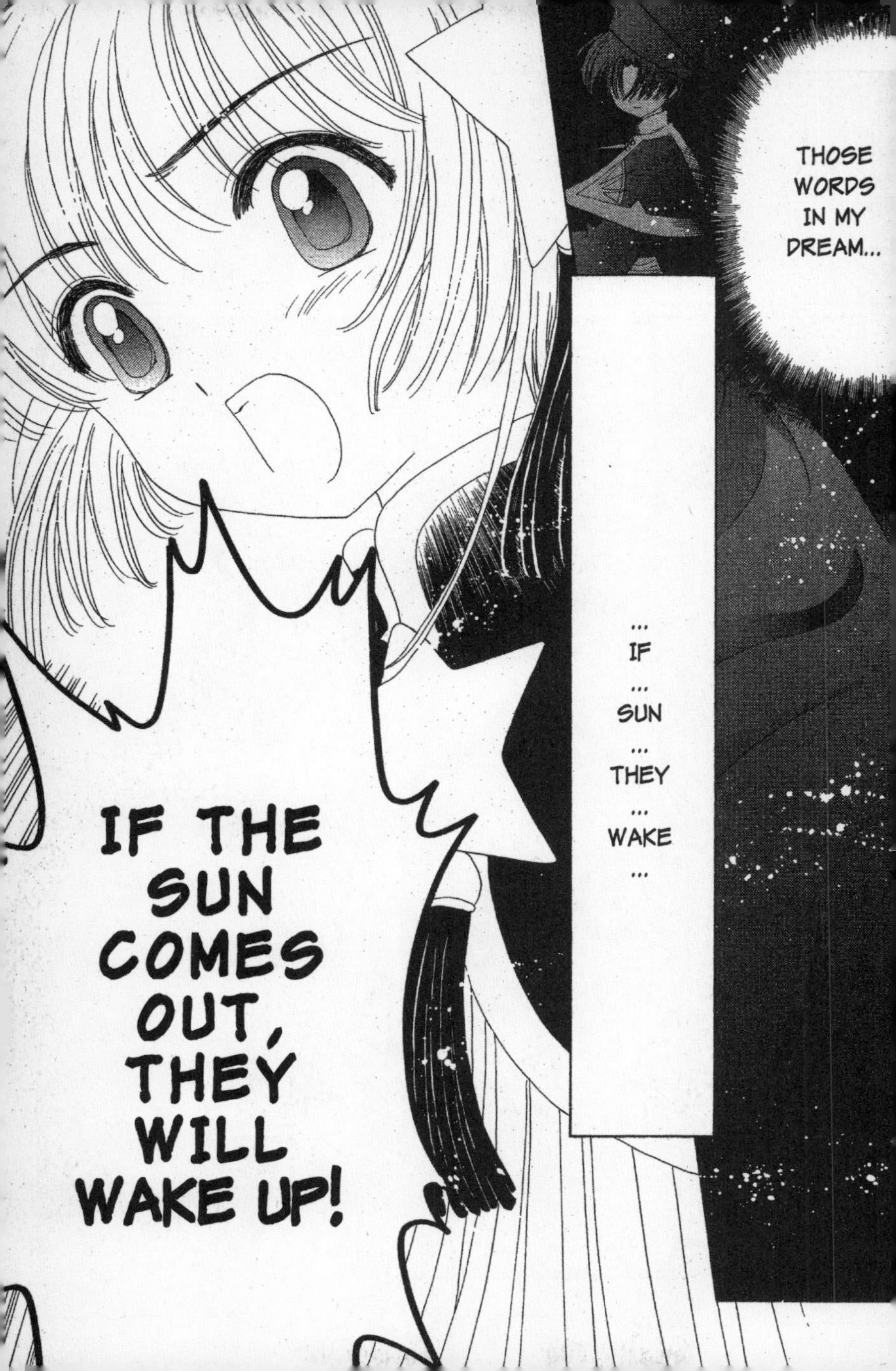
THOSE WORDS IN MY DREAM...
... IF ... SUN ... THEY ... WAKE ...
IF THE SUN COMES OUT, THEY WILL WAKE UP!

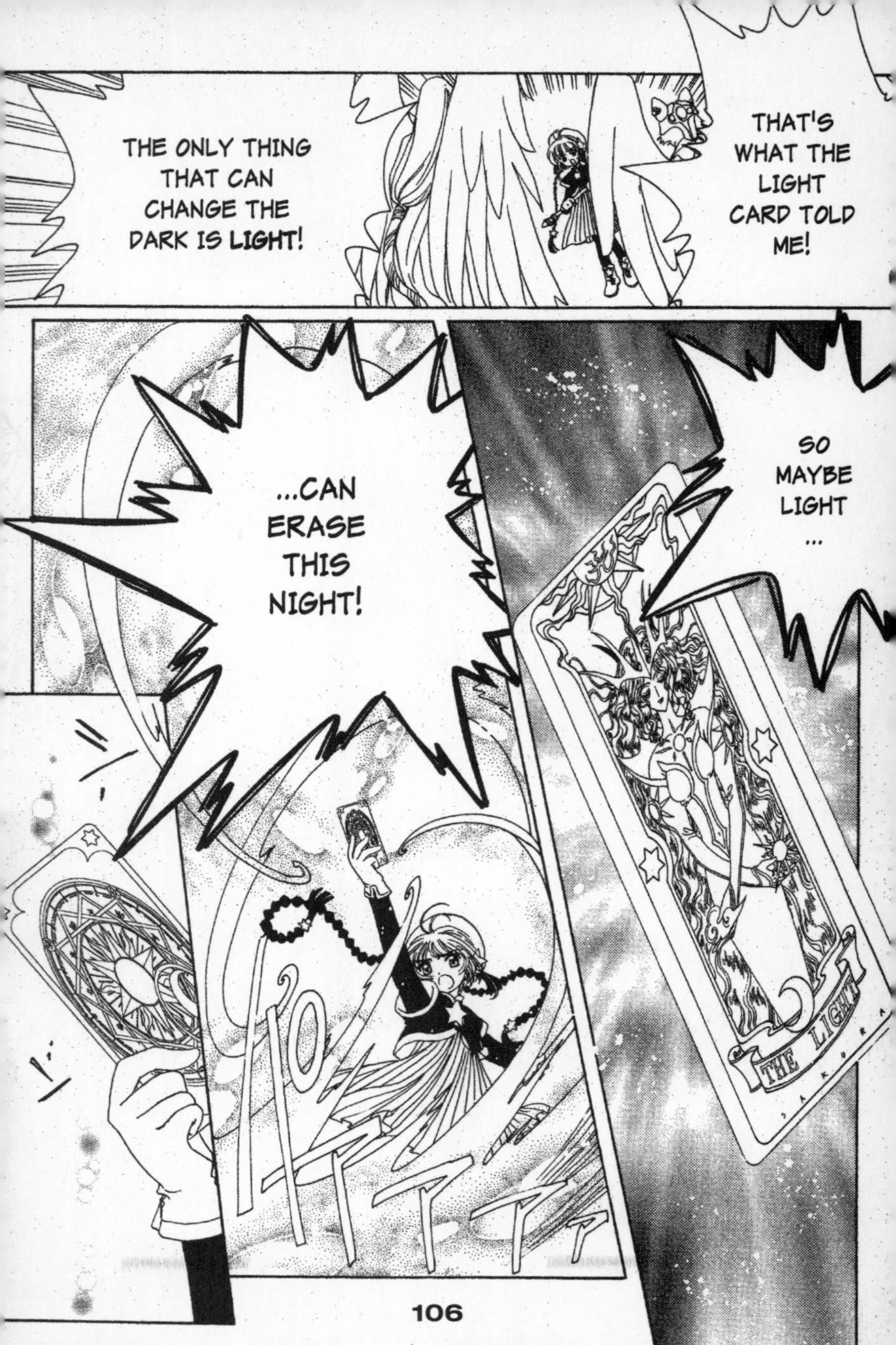
THE ONLY THING THAT CAN CHANGE THE DARK IS LIGHT!
THAT'S WHAT THE LIGHT CARD TOLD ME!
SO MAYBE LIGHT ...
...CAN ERASE THIS NIGHT!
THE LIGHT
SAKURA

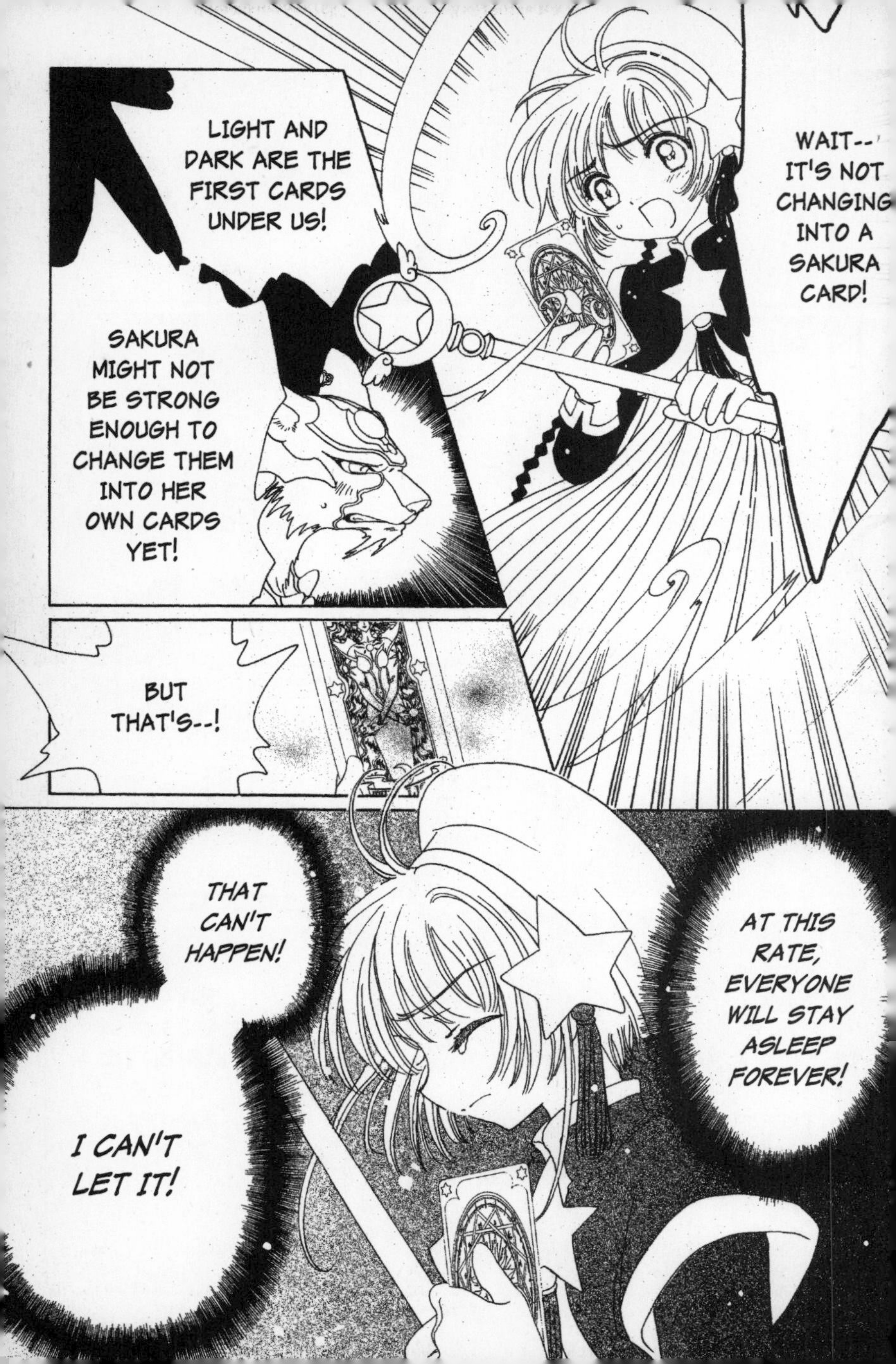
WAIT-- IT'S NOT CHANGING INTO A SAKURA CARD!
LIGHT AND DARK ARE THE FIRST CARDS UNDER US!
SAKURA MIGHT NOT BE STRONG ENOUGH TO CHANGE THEM INTO HER OWN CARDS YET!
BUT THAT'S--!
AT THIS RATE, EVERYONE WILL STAY ASLEEP FOREVER!
THAT CAN'T HAPPEN!
I CAN'T LET IT!

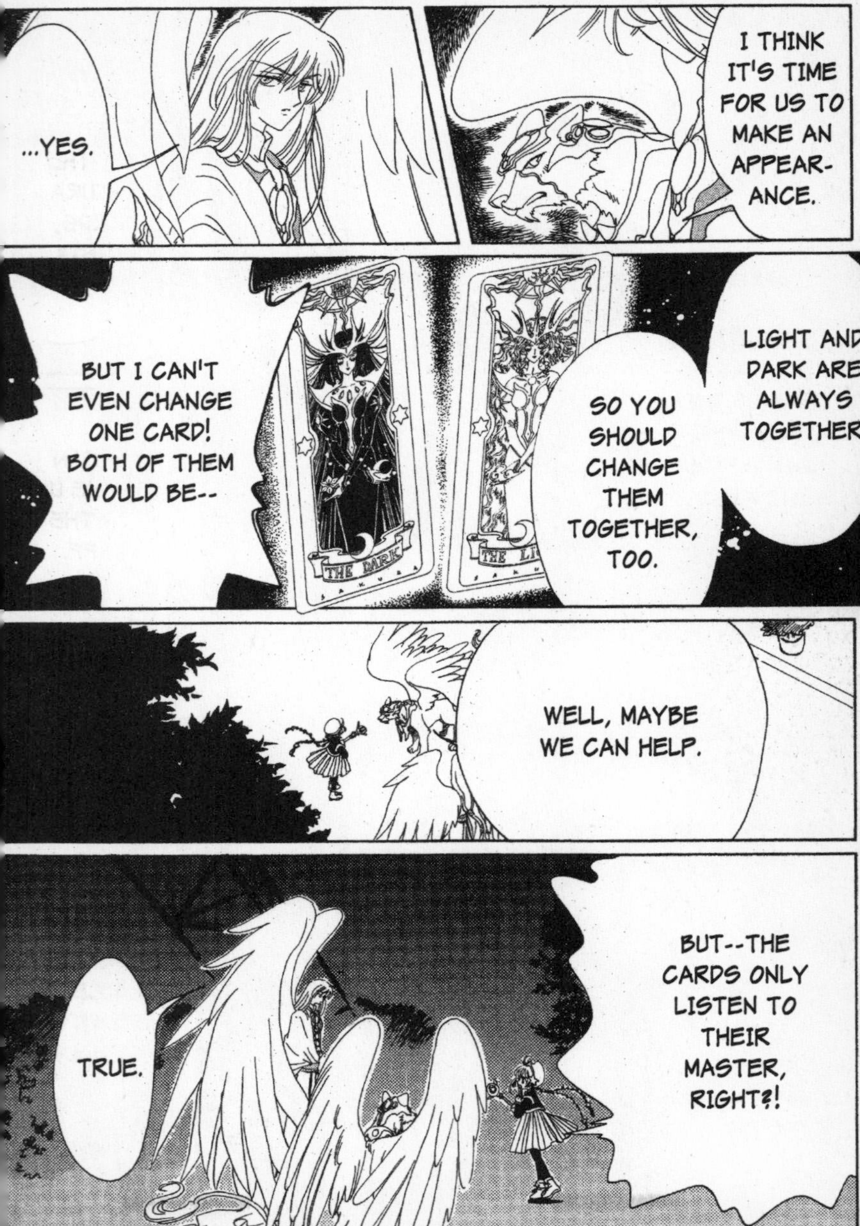
I THINK IT'S TIME FOR US TO MAKE AN APPEAR-ANCE.
...YES.
LIGHT AND DARK ARE ALWAYS TOGETHER.
SO YOU SHOULD CHANGE THEM TOGETHER, TOO.
THE DARK
BUT I CAN'T EVEN CHANGE ONE CARD! BOTH OF THEM WOULD BE--
WELL, MAYBE WE CAN HELP.
BUT--THE CARDS ONLY LISTEN TO THEIR MASTER, RIGHT?!
TRUE.

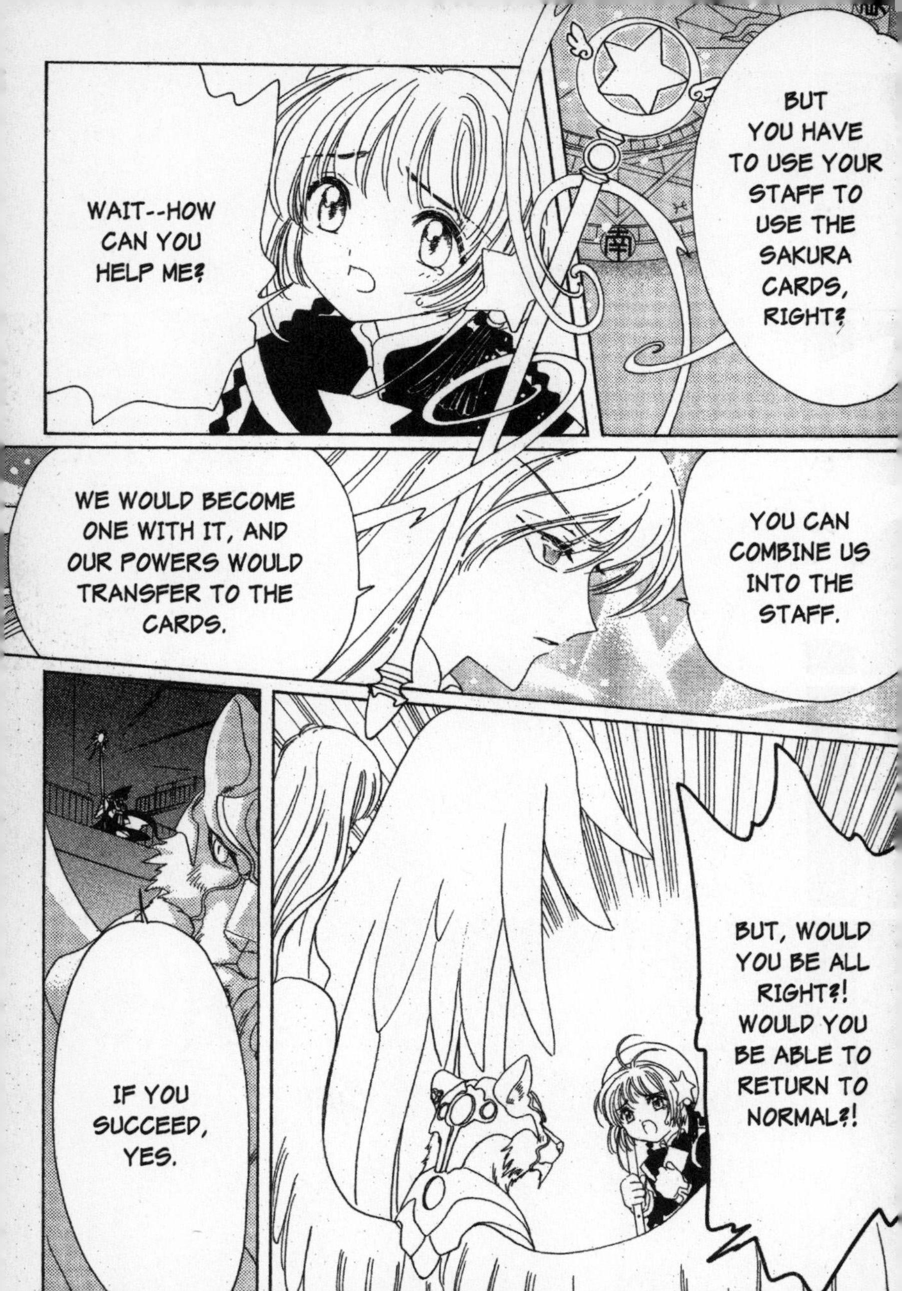
BUT YOU HAVE TO USE YOUR STAFF TO USE THE SAKURA CARDS, RIGHT?
WAIT--HOW CAN YOU HELP ME?
YOU CAN COMBINE US INTO THE STAFF.
WE WOULD BECOME ONE WITH IT, AND OUR POWERS WOULD TRANSFER TO THE CARDS.
BUT, WOULD YOU BE ALL RIGHT?! WOULD YOU BE ABLE TO RETURN TO NORMAL?!
IF YOU SUCCEED, YES.

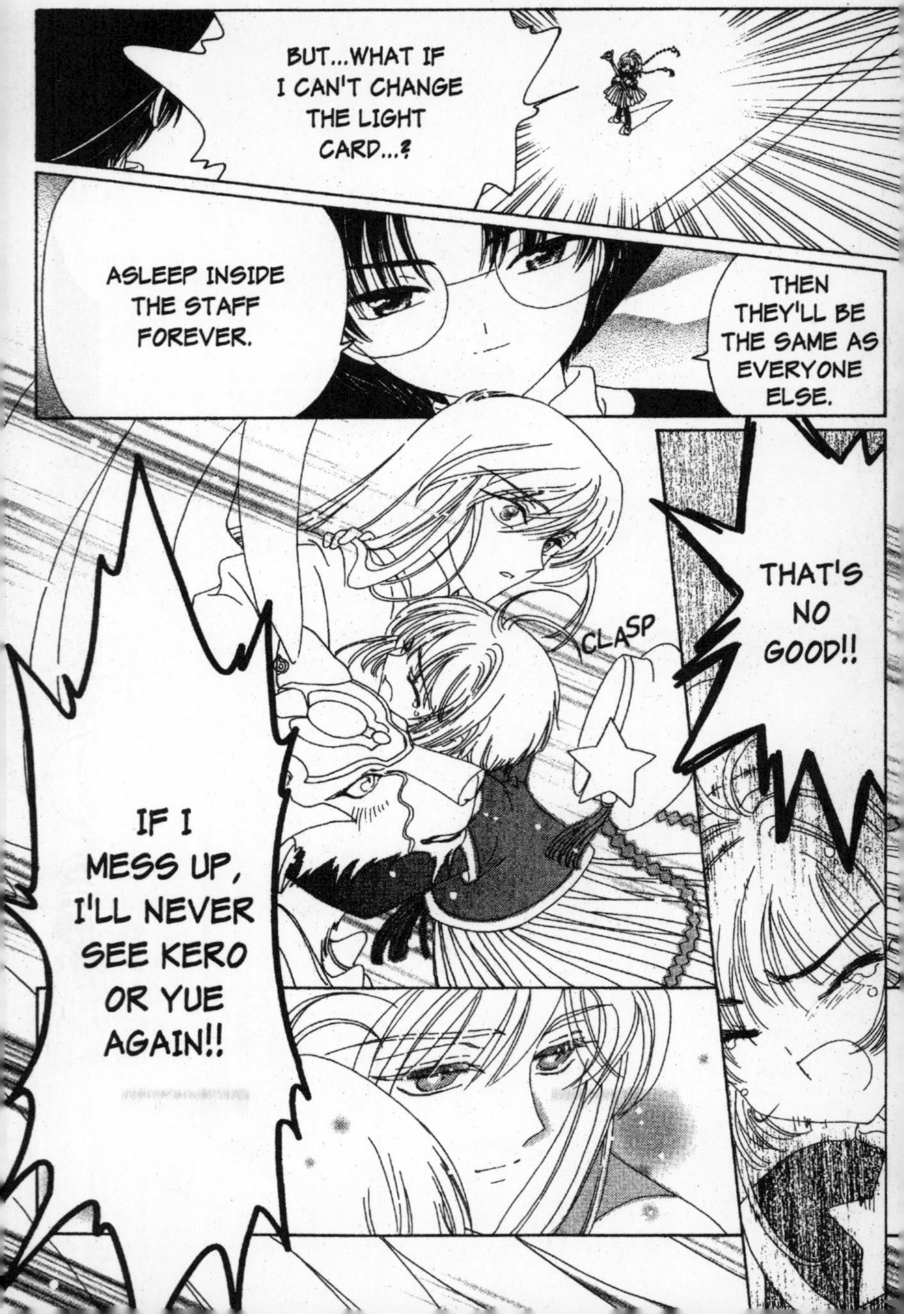
BUT...WHAT IF I CAN'T CHANGE THE LIGHT CARD...?
THEN THEY'LL BE THE SAME AS EVERYONE ELSE.
ASLEEP INSIDE THE STAFF FOREVER.
THAT'S NO GOOD!!
CLASP
IF I MESS UP, I'LL NEVER SEE KERO OR YUE AGAIN!!

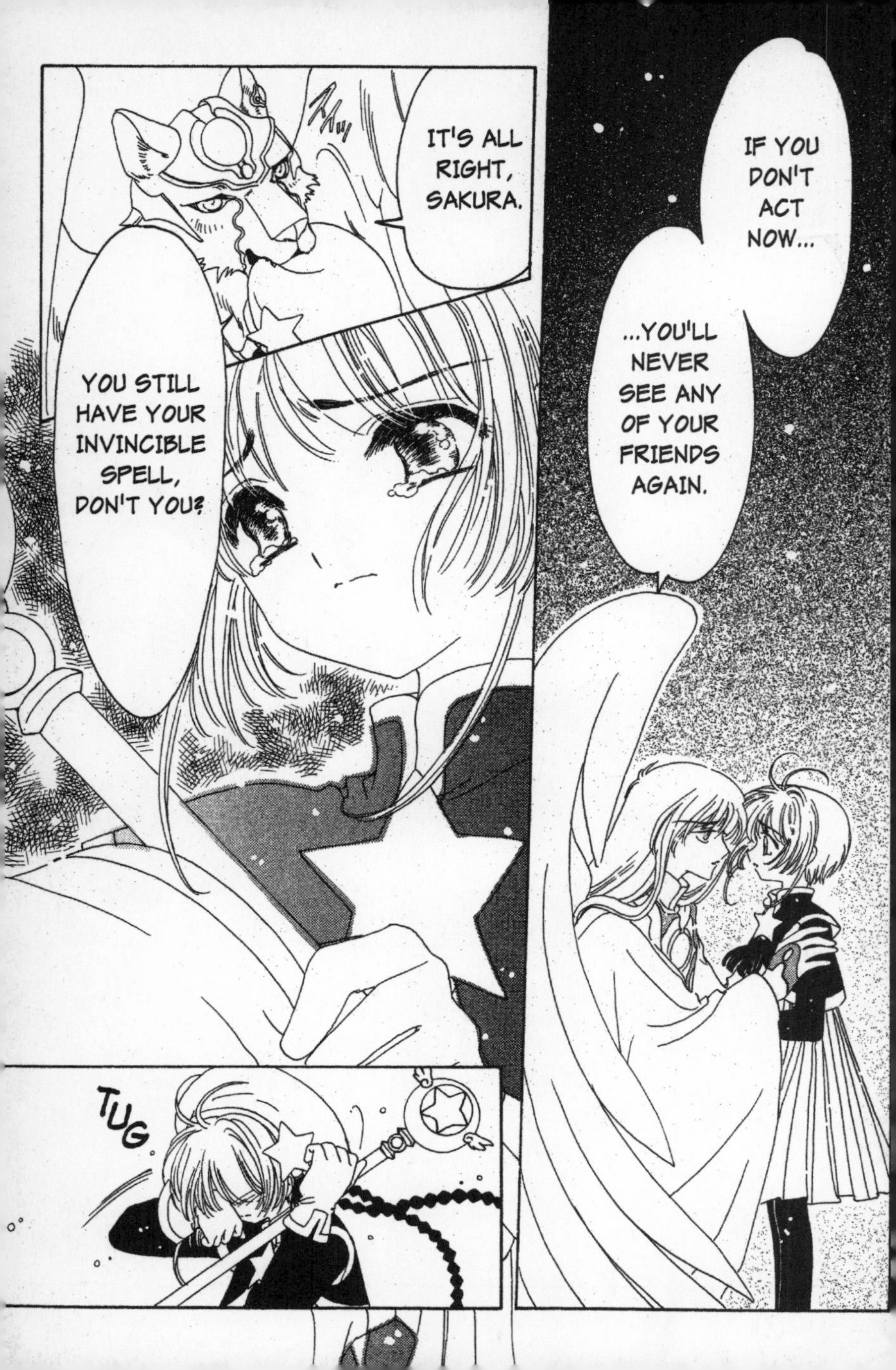
IF YOU DON'T ACT NOW...
...YOU'LL NEVER SEE ANY OF YOUR FRIENDS AGAIN.
IT'S ALL RIGHT, SAKURA.
YOU STILL HAVE YOUR INVINCIBLE SPELL, DON'T YOU?
TUG

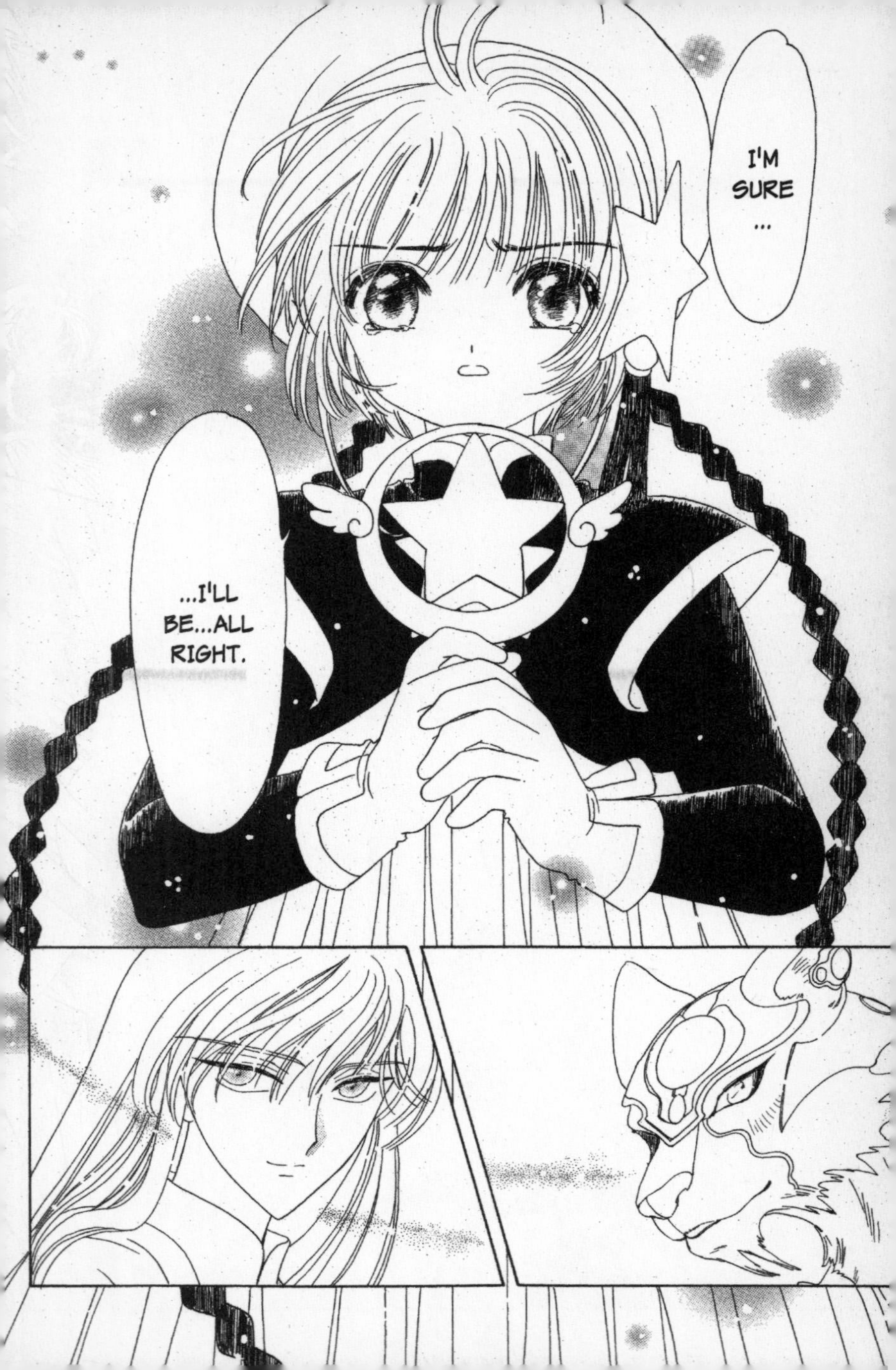
I'M SURE ...
...I'LL BE...ALL RIGHT.

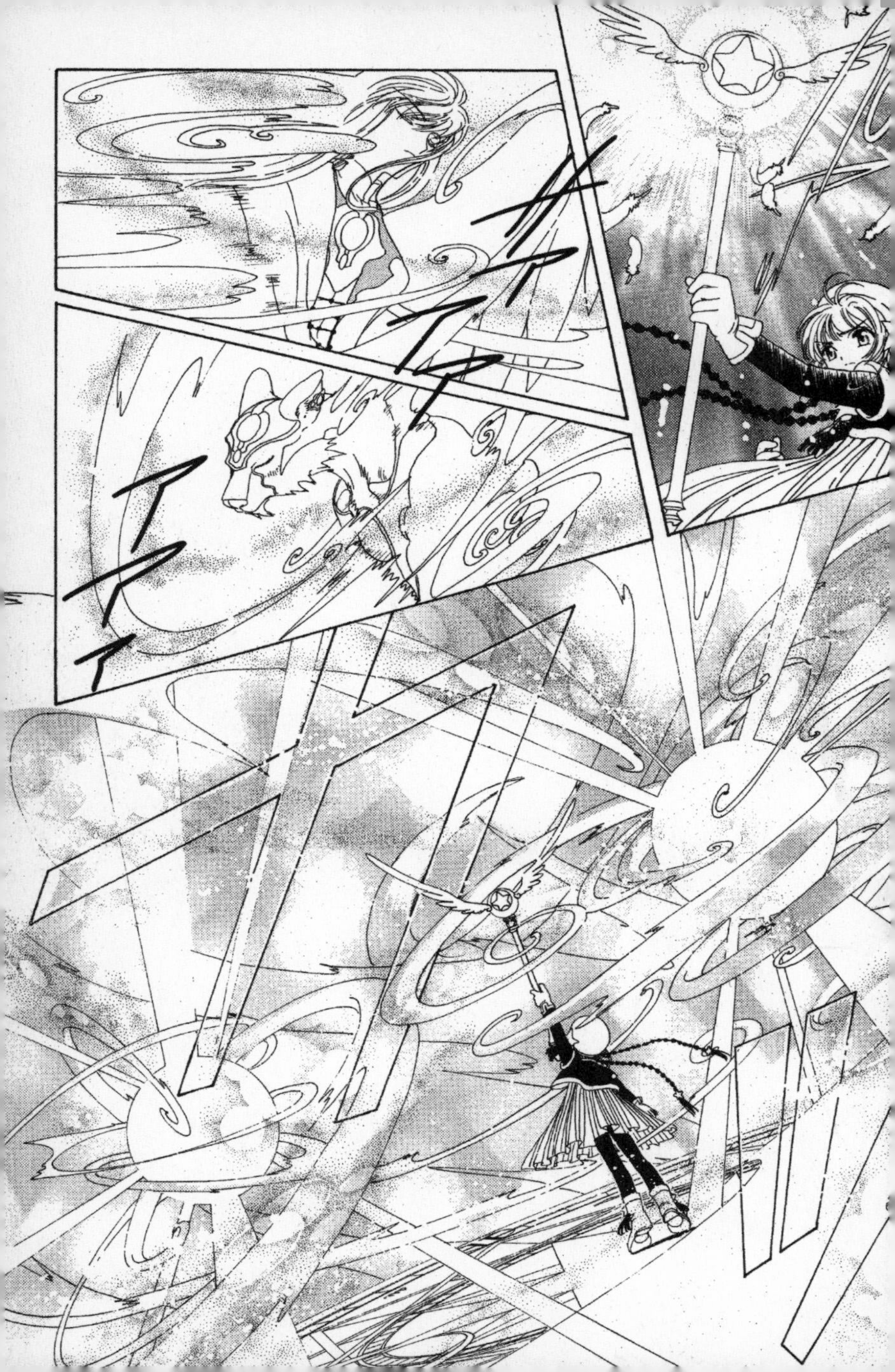
!
サアアア
アアアア

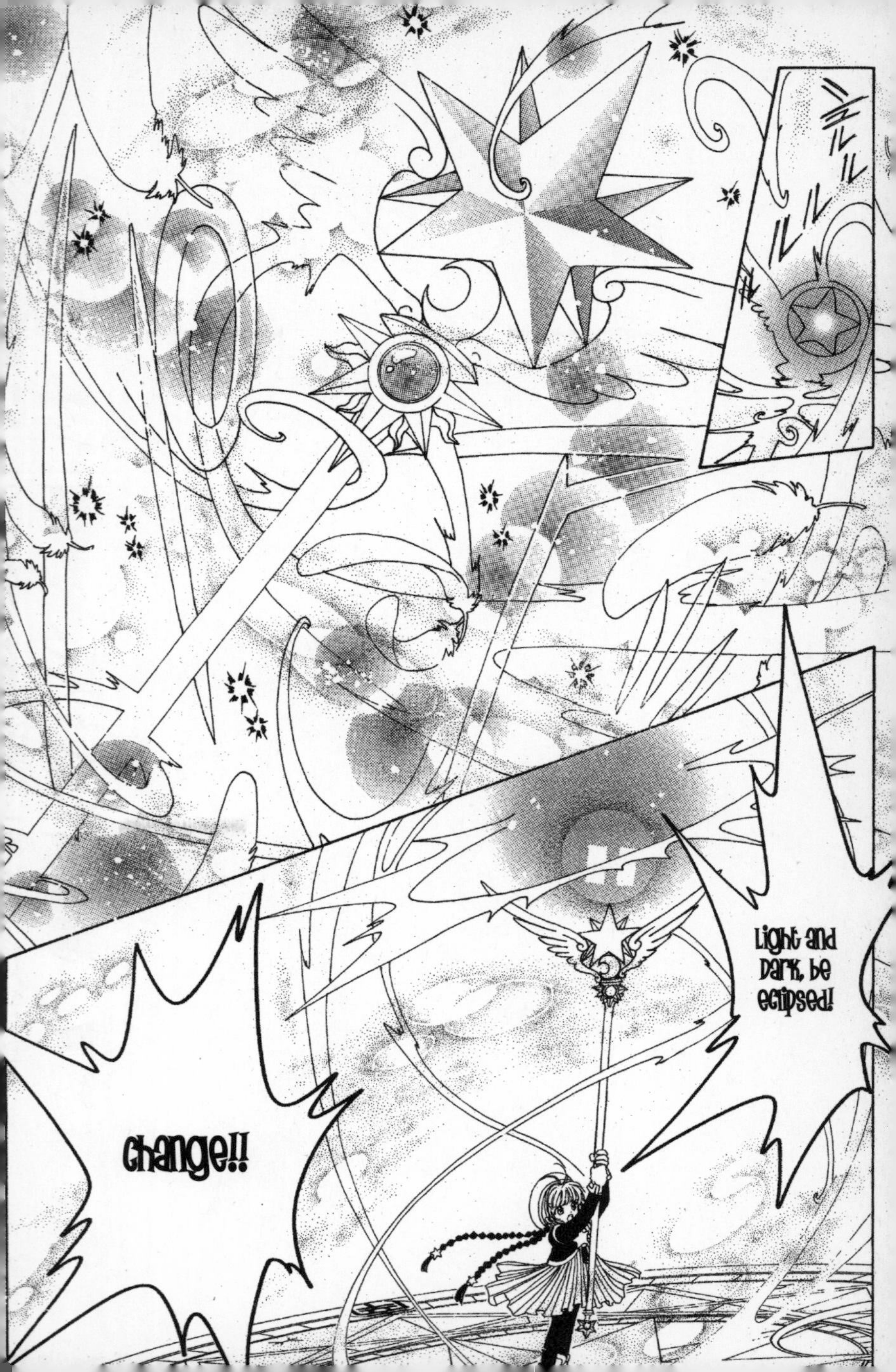
Light and Dark, be eclipsed!
Change!!

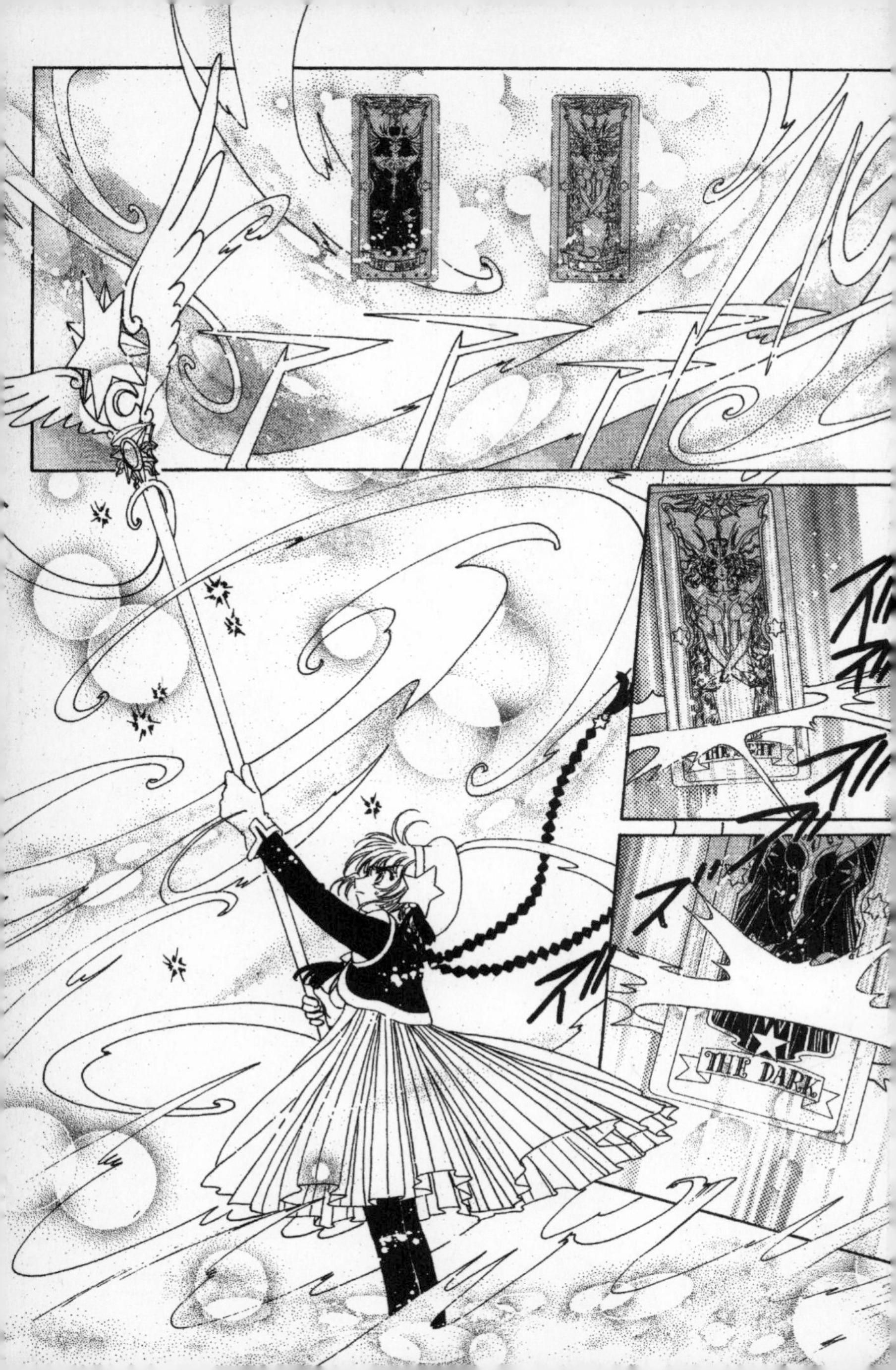
THE DARK.

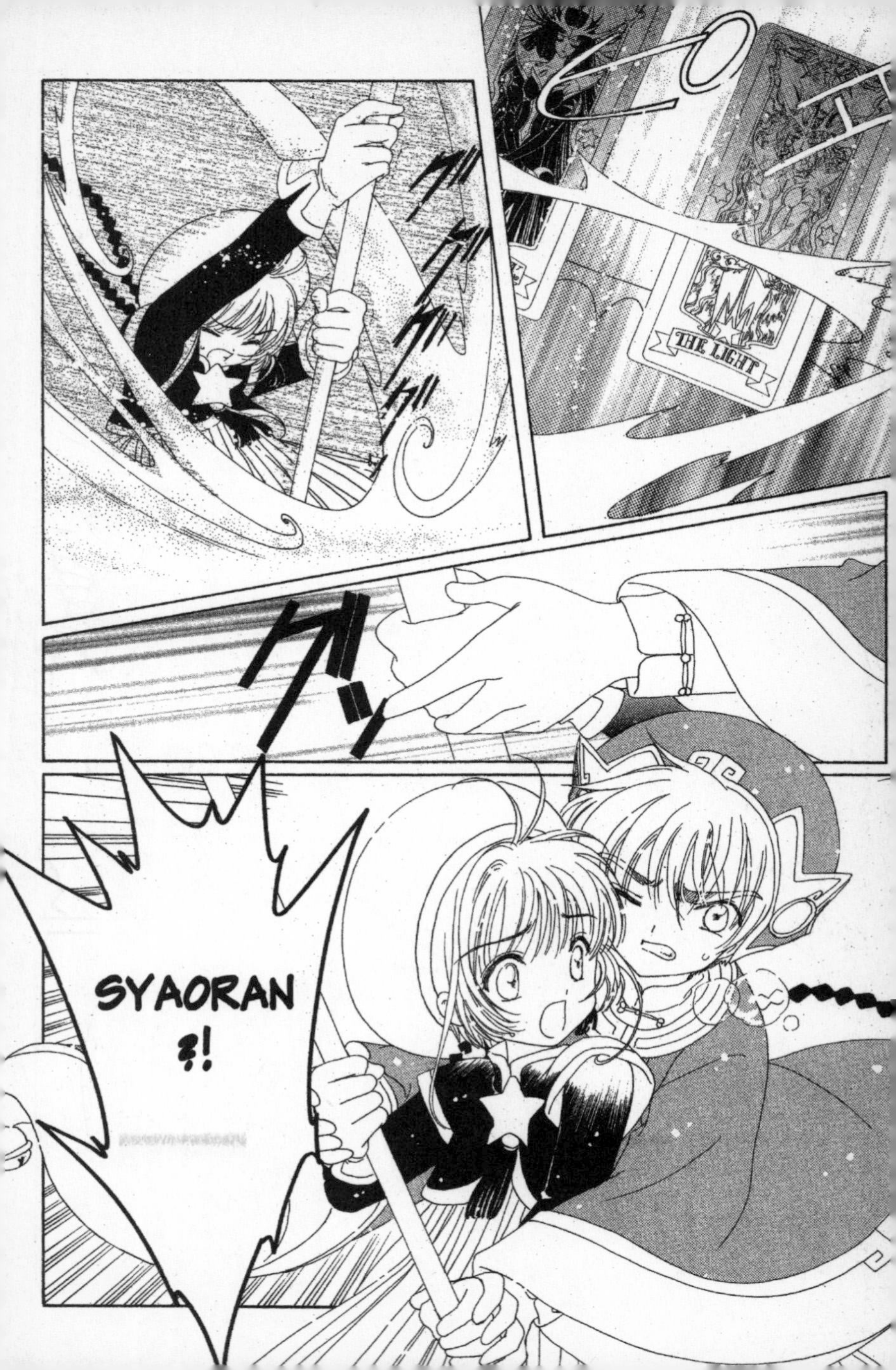
THE LIGHT
SYAORAN ?!

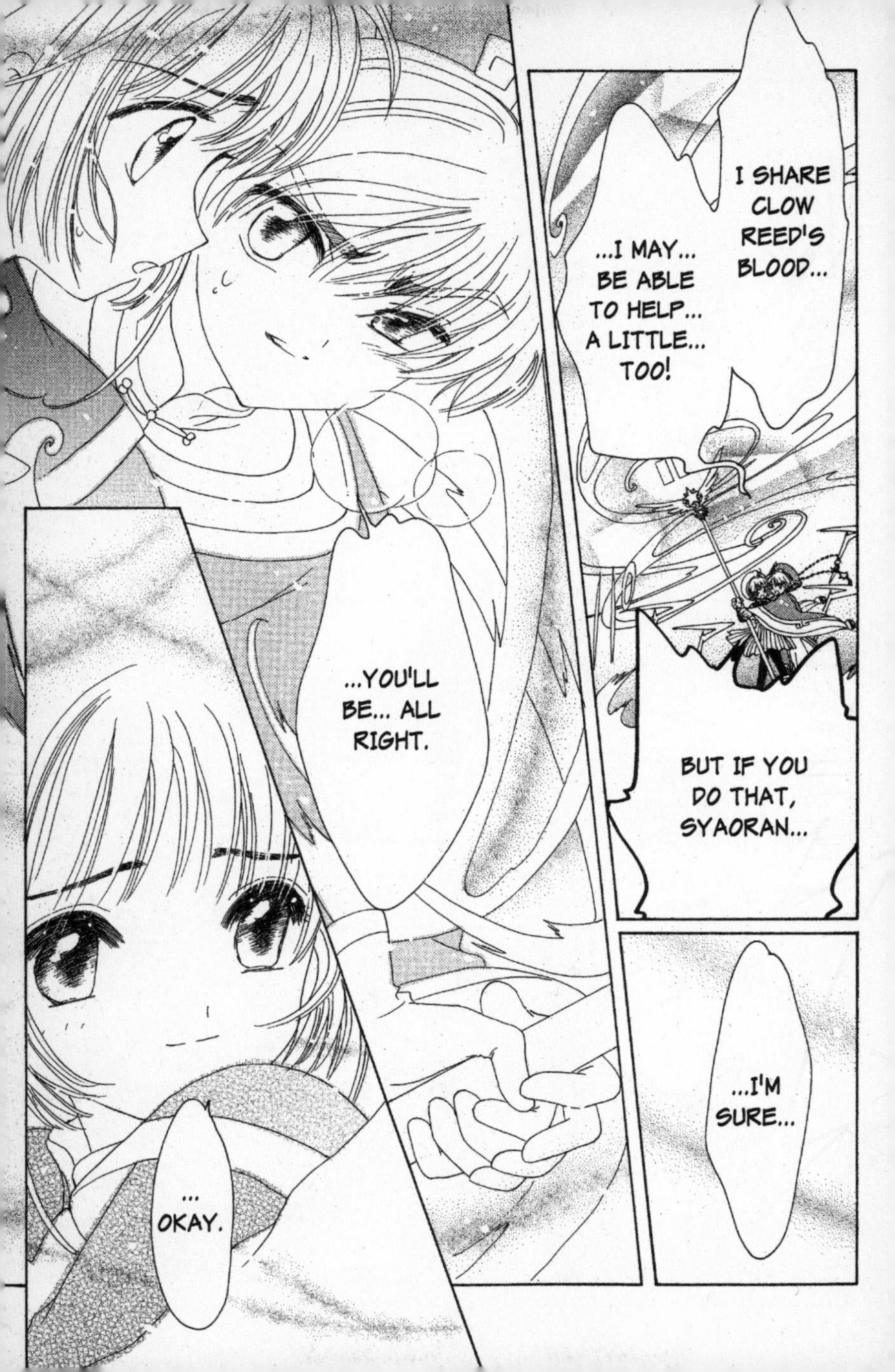
I SHARE CLOW REED'S BLOOD...
...I MAY... BE ABLE TO HELP... A LITTLE... TOO!
BUT IF YOU DO THAT, SYAORAN...
...I'M SURE...
...YOU'LL BE... ALL RIGHT.
... OKAY.

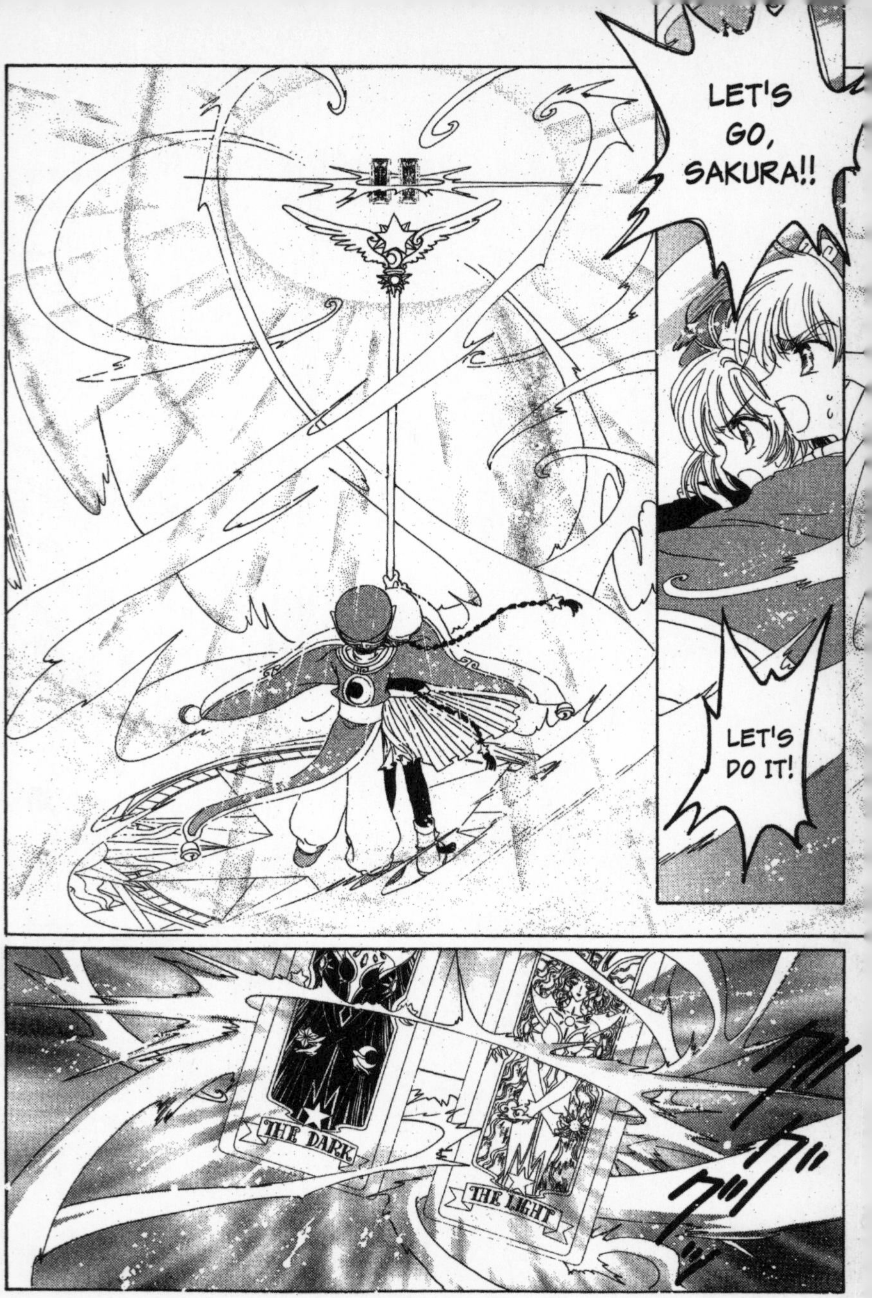
LET'S GO, SAKURA!!
LET'S DO IT!
THE DARK
THE LIGHT

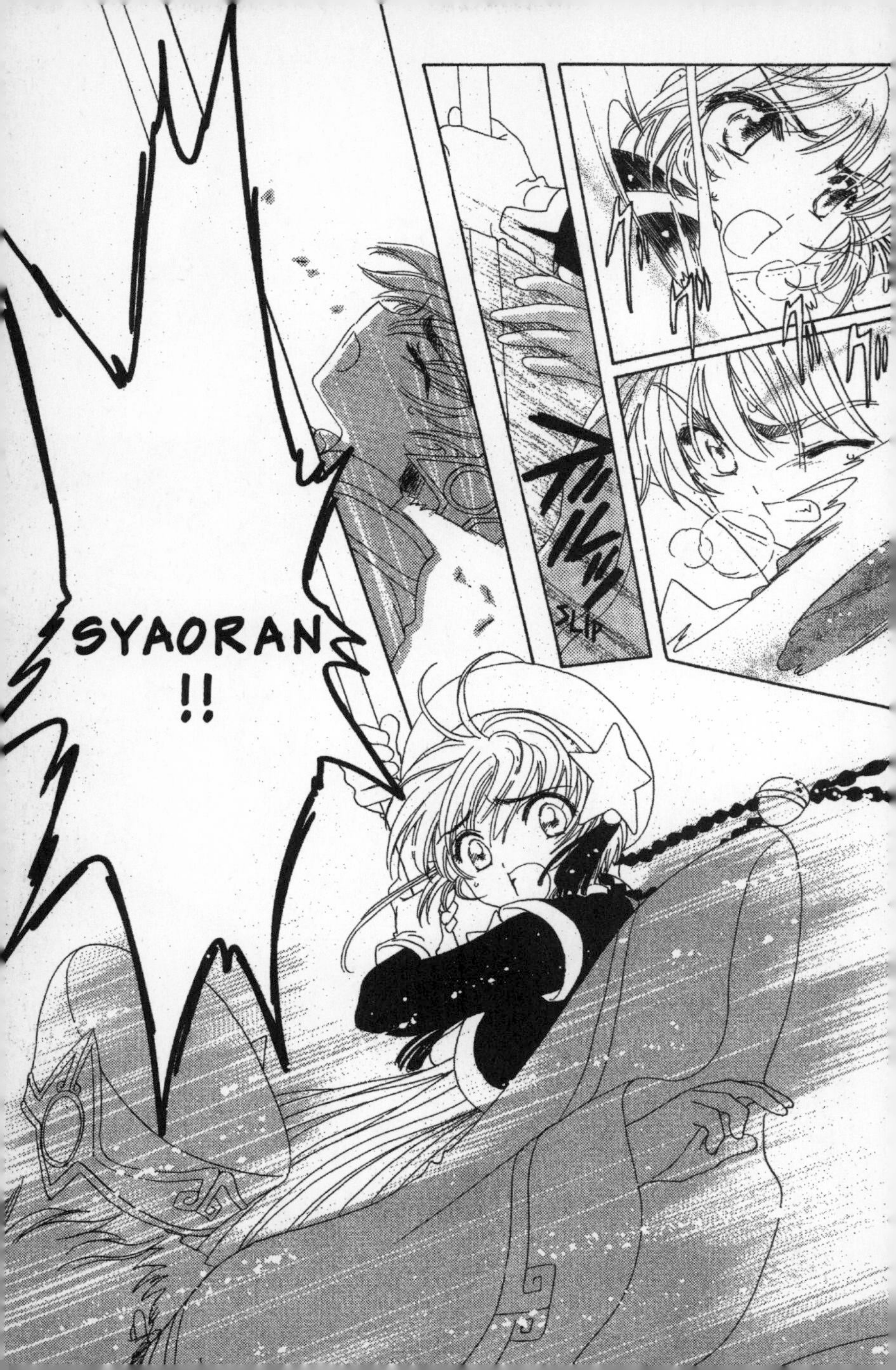
SLIP
SYAORAN
!!

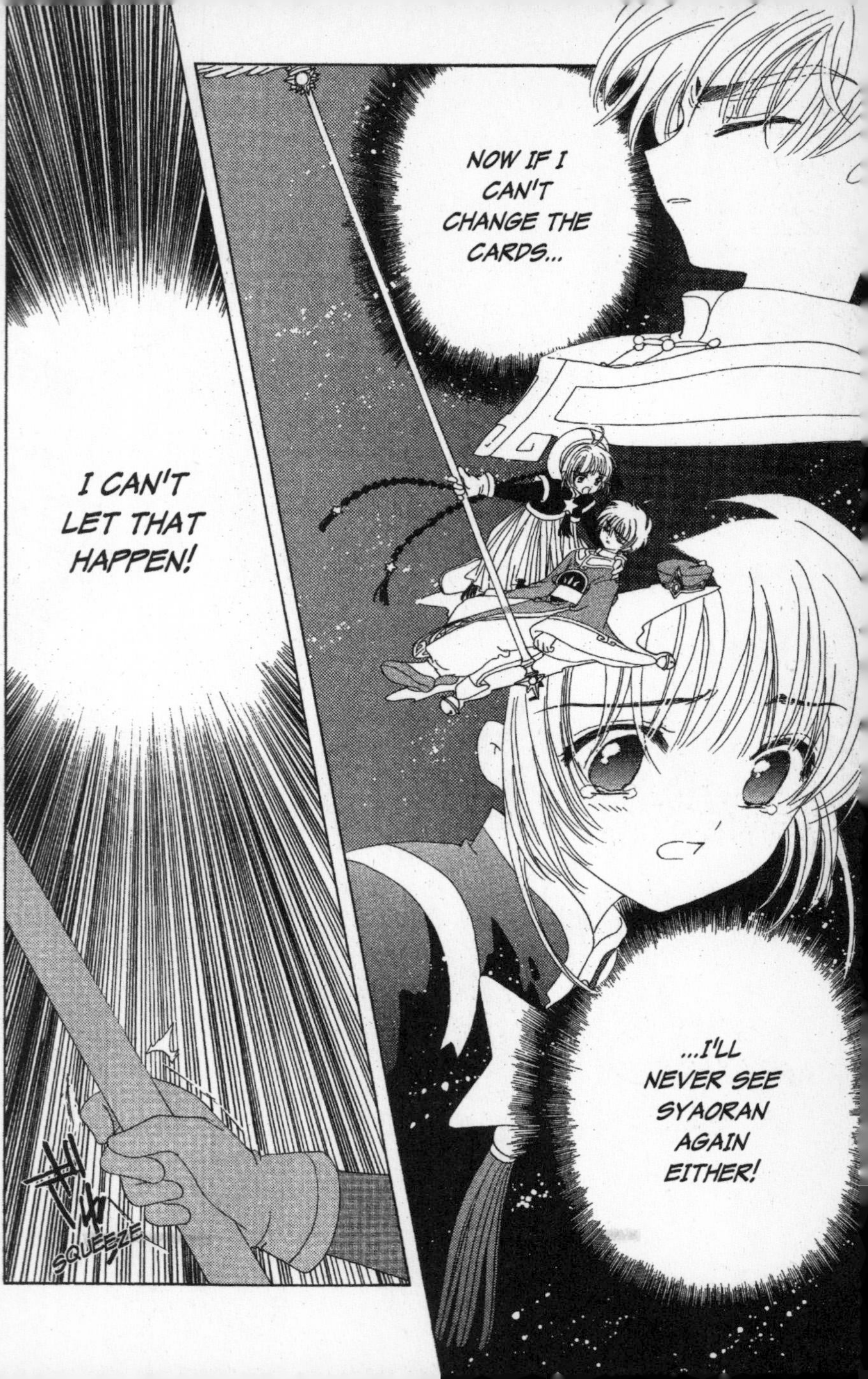
NOW IF I CAN'T CHANGE THE CARDS...
...I'LL NEVER SEE SYAORAN AGAIN EITHER!
I CAN'T LET THAT HAPPEN!
SQUEEZE

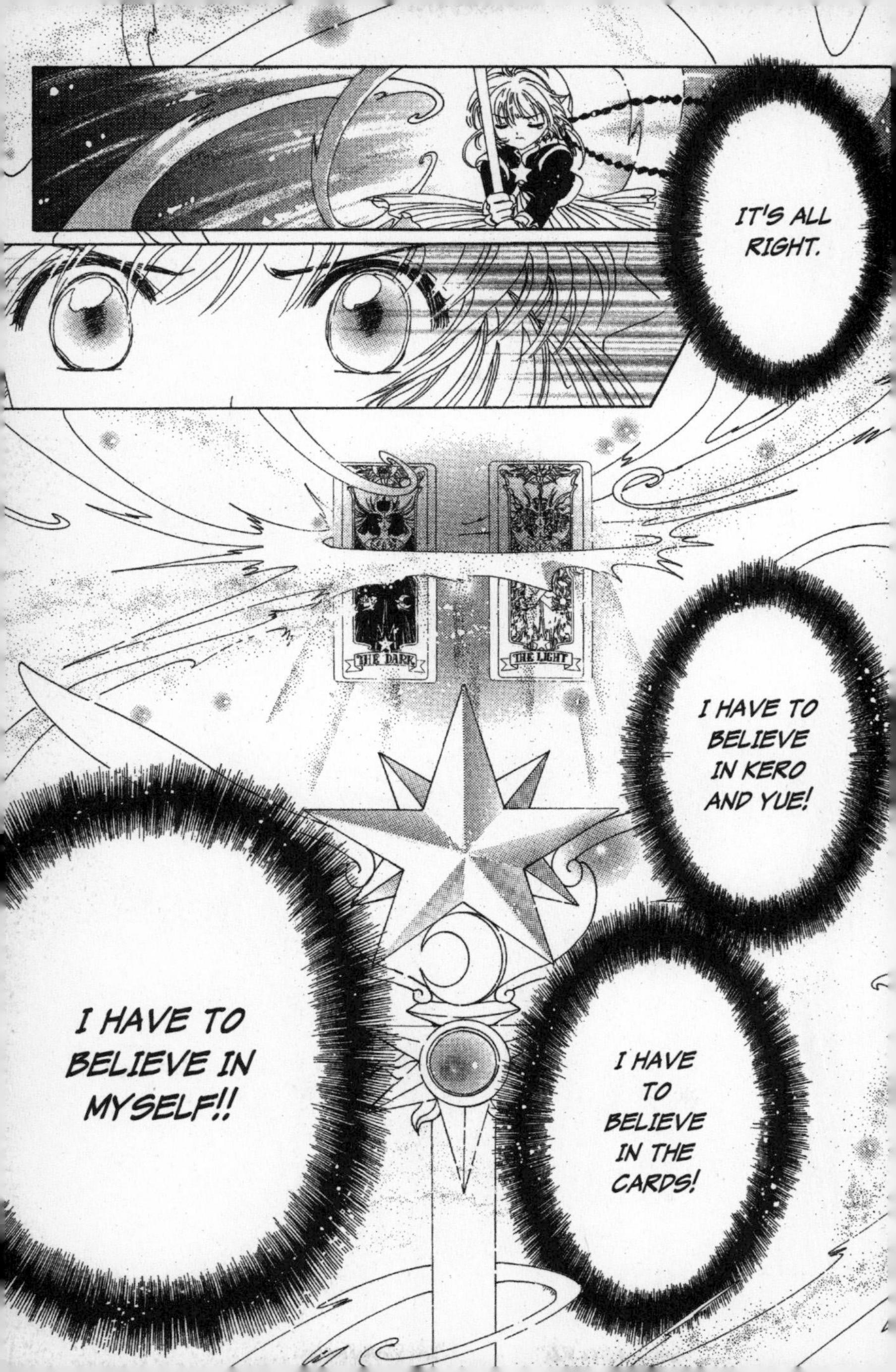

IT'S ALL RIGHT.
I HAVE TO BELIEVE IN KERO AND YUE!
THE DARK
THE LIGHT
I HAVE TO BELIEVE IN THE CARDS!
I HAVE TO BELIEVE IN MYSELF!!

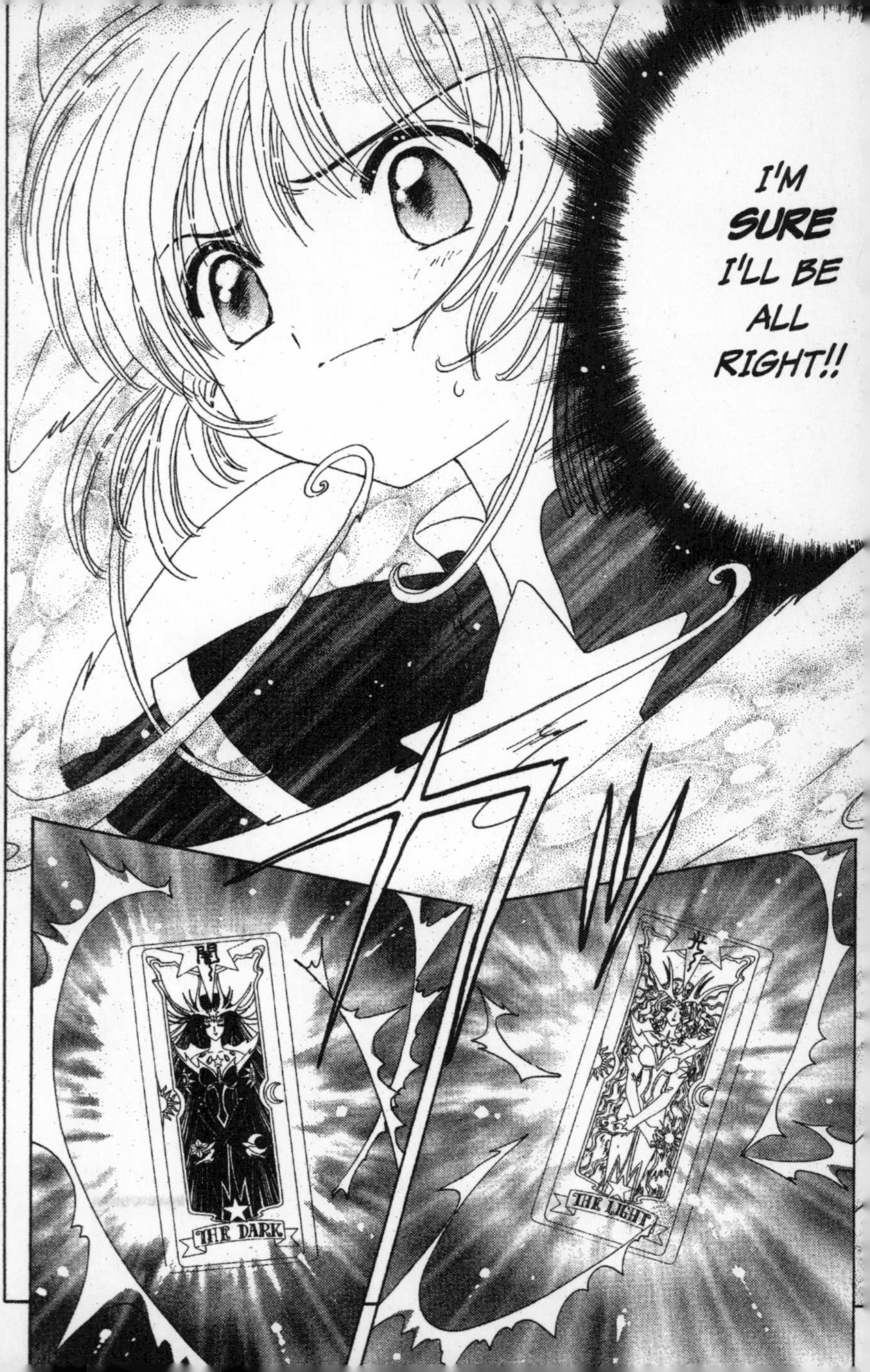
I'M SURE I'LL BE ALL RIGHT!!
THE LIGHT
THE DARK

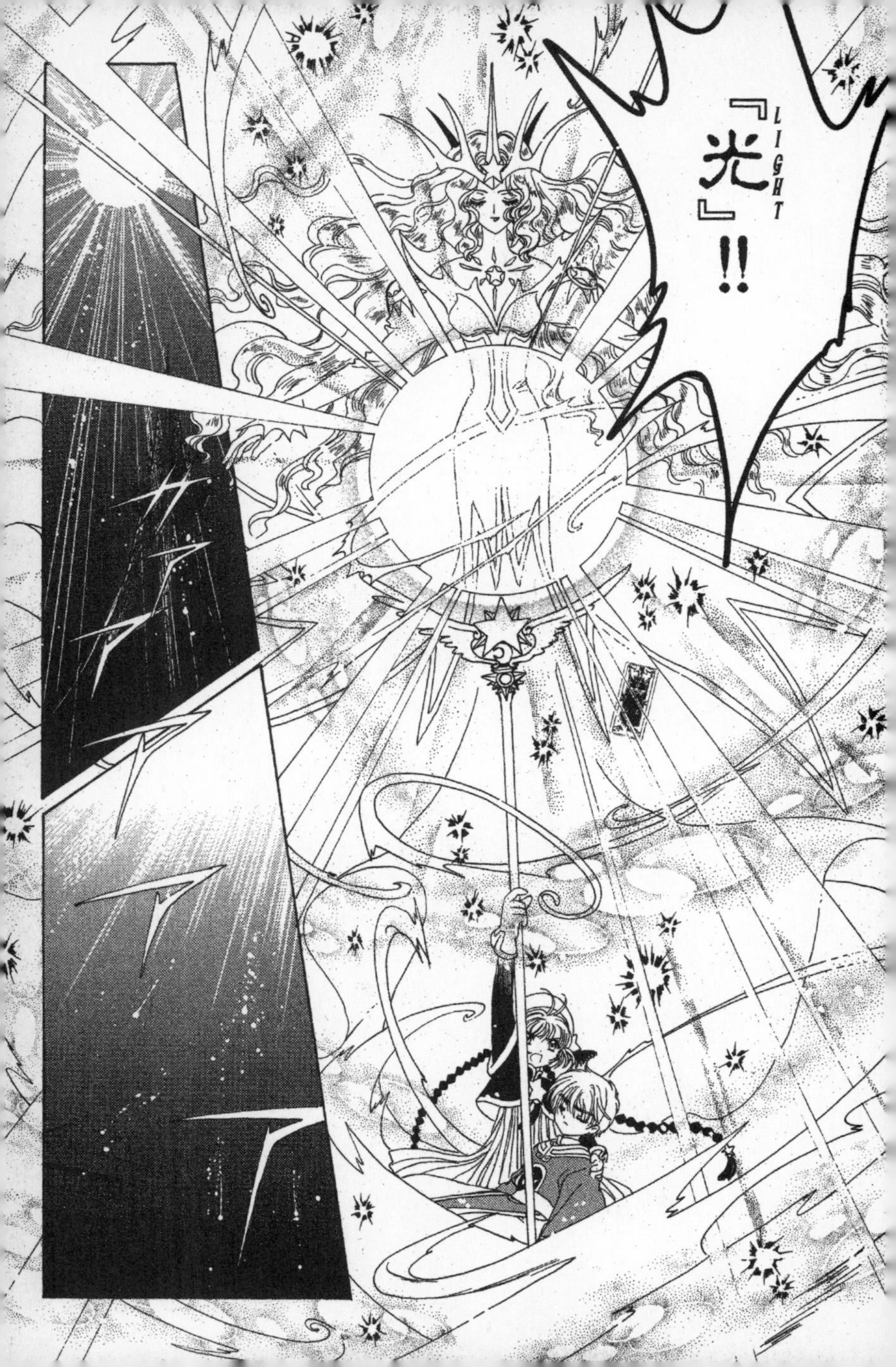
『光』!!
LIGHT

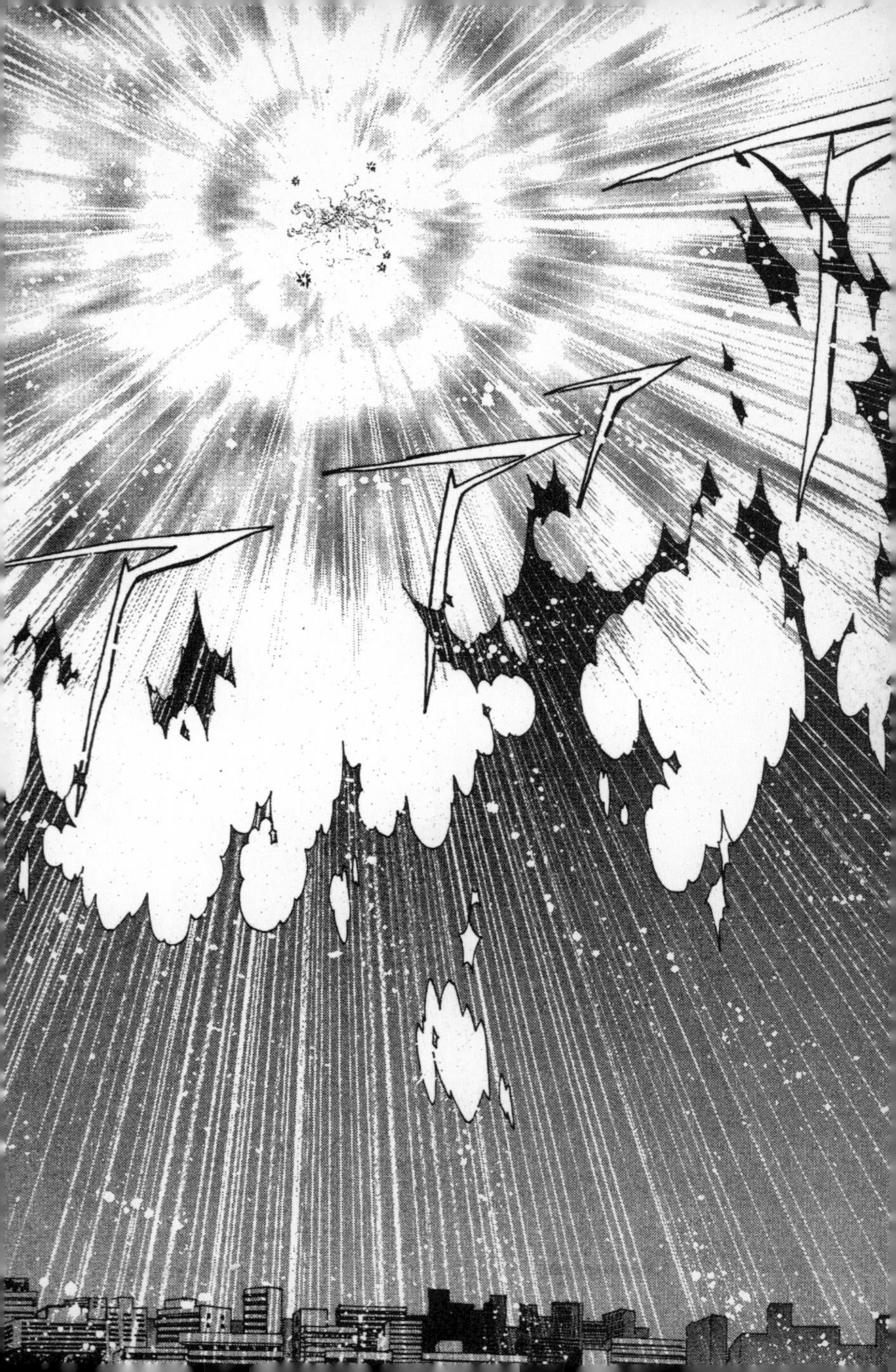

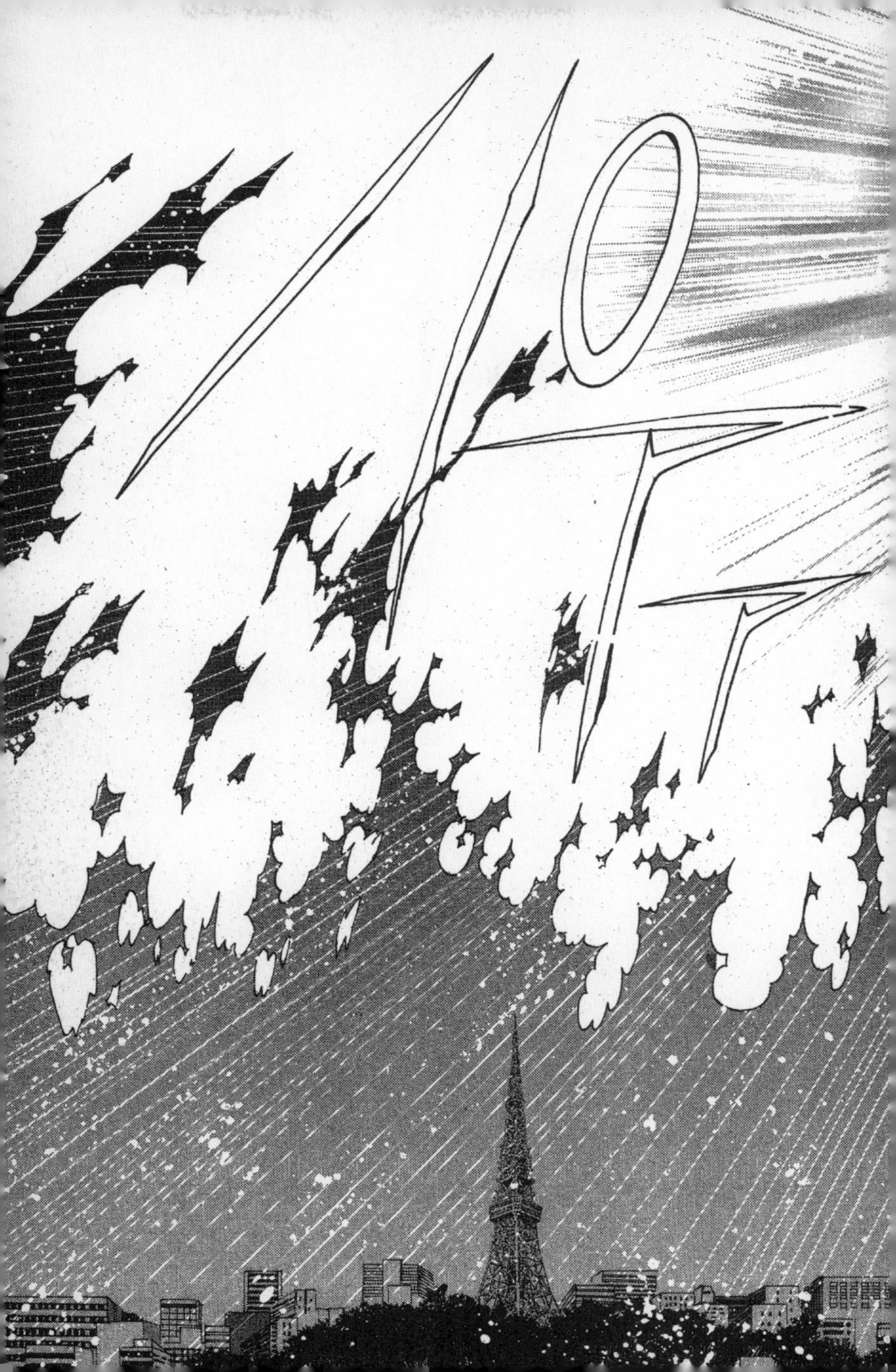

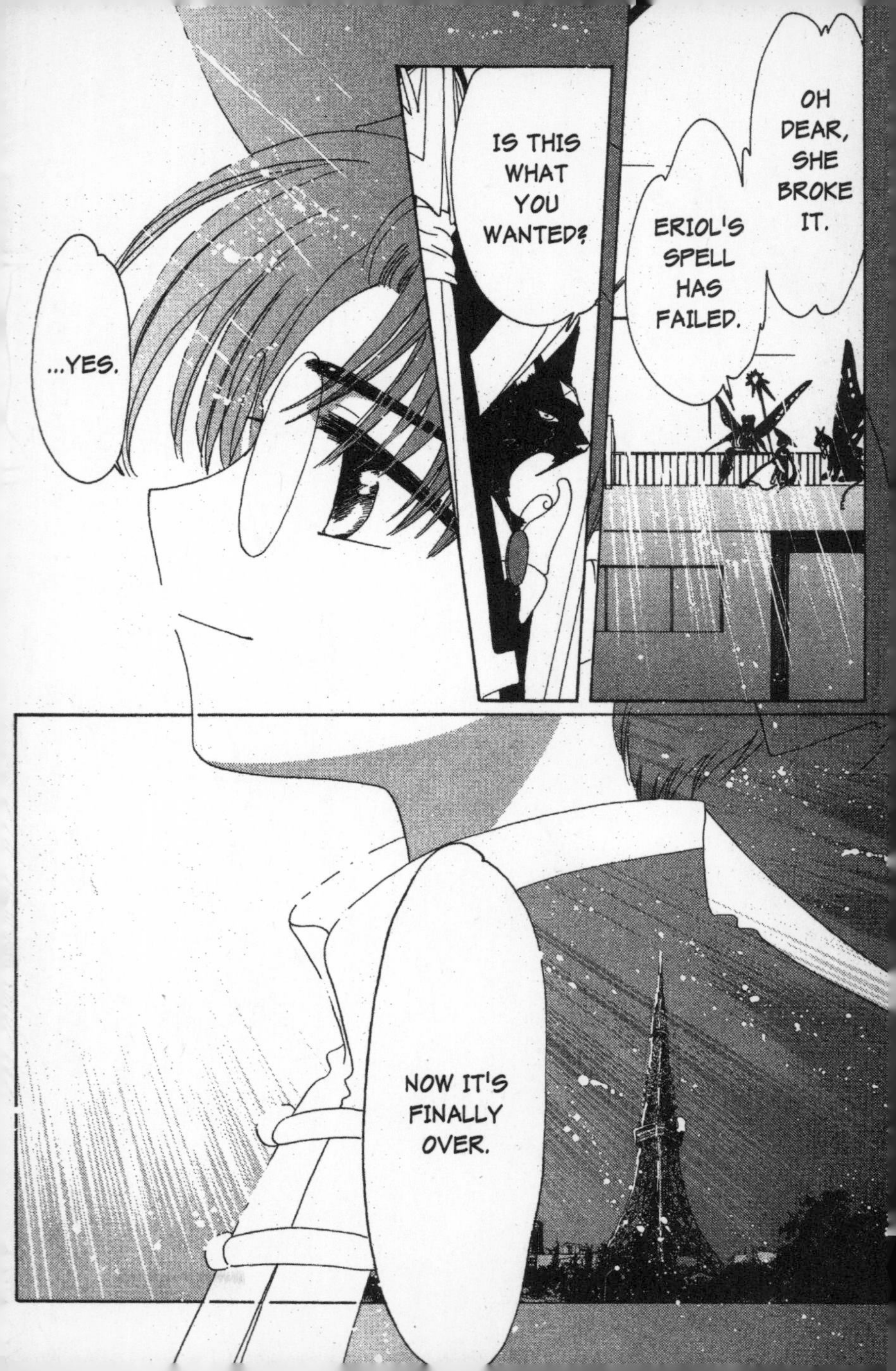
OH DEAR, SHE BROKE IT.
ERIOL'S SPELL HAS FAILED.
IS THIS WHAT YOU WANTED?
...YES.
NOW IT'S FINALLY OVER.

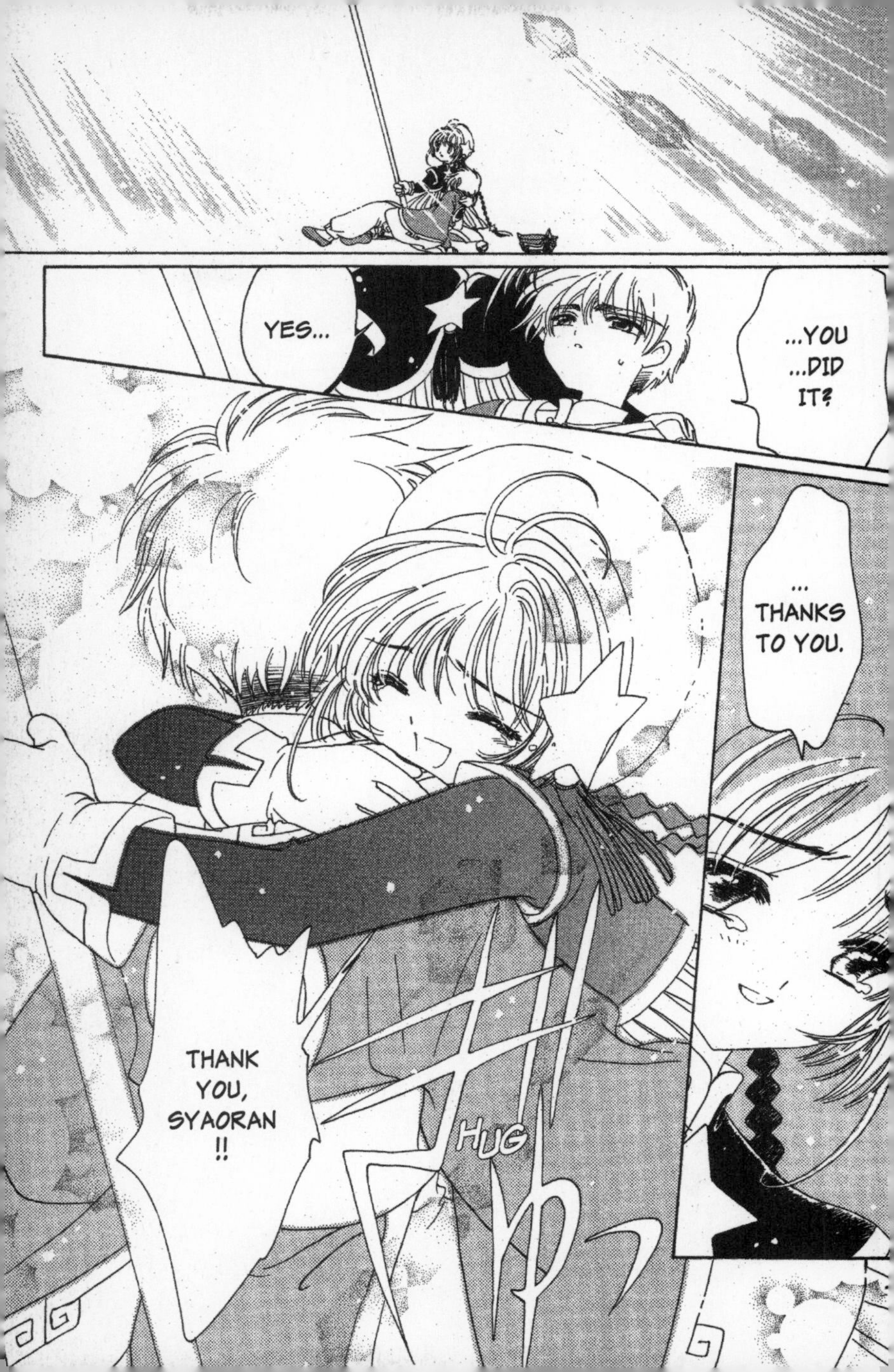
...YOU ...DID IT?
YES...
... THANKS TO YOU.
THANK YOU, SYAORAN !!
HUG

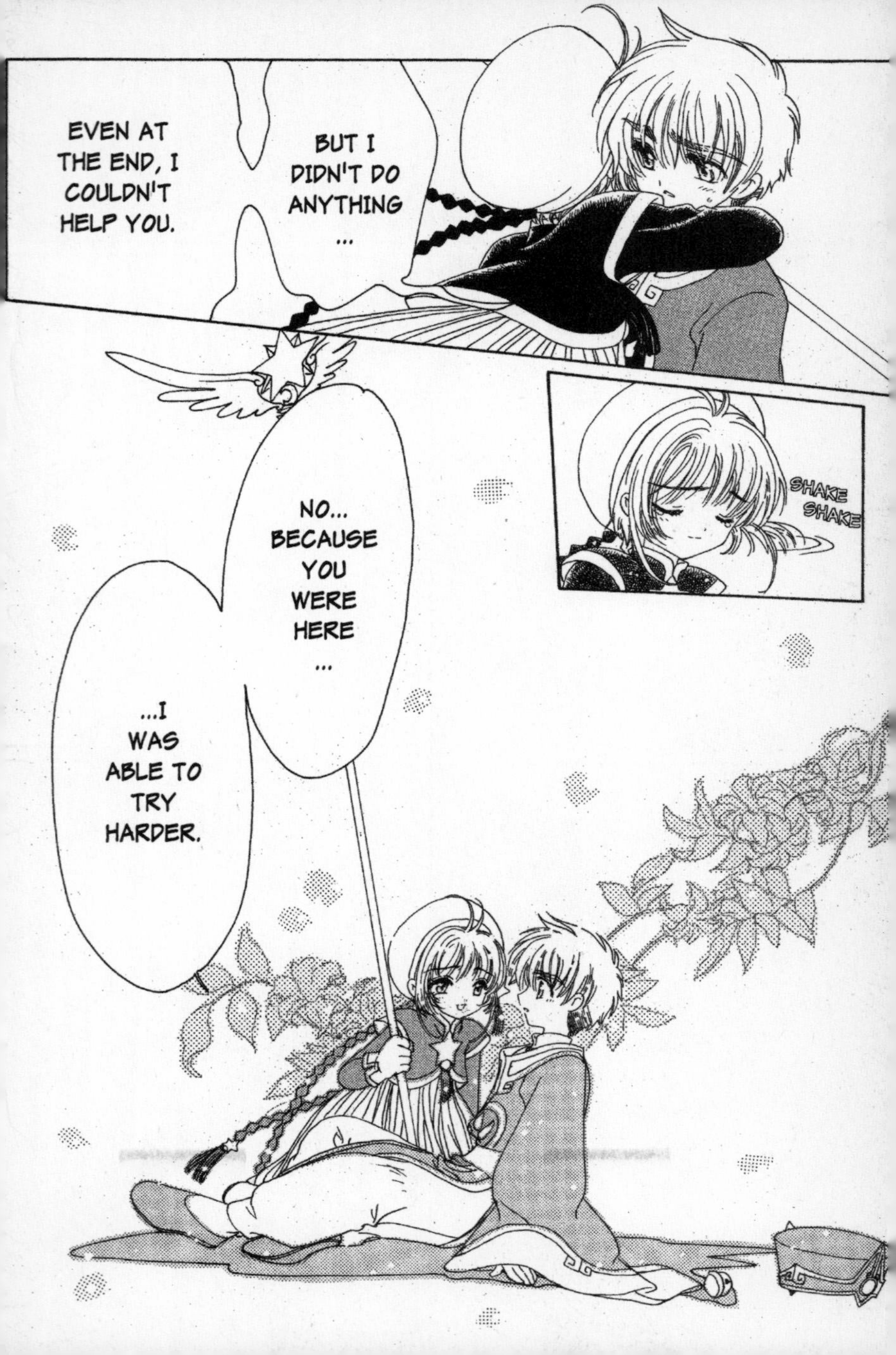
BUT I DIDN'T DO ANYTHING ...
EVEN AT THE END, I COULDN'T HELP YOU.
SHAKE SHAKE
NO... BECAUSE YOU WERE HERE ...
...I WAS ABLE TO TRY HARDER.

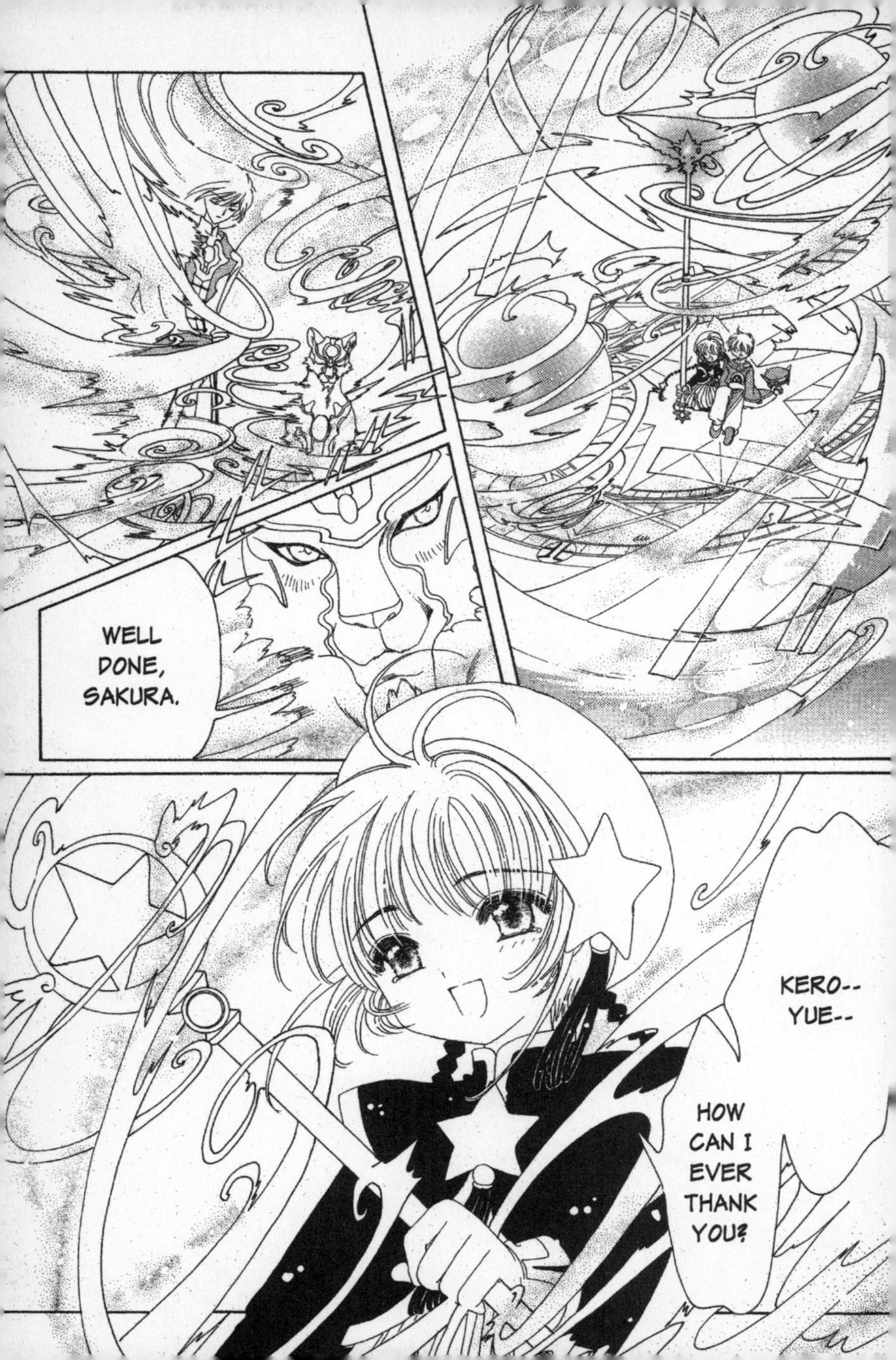
WELL DONE, SAKURA.
KERO-- YUE--
HOW CAN I EVER THANK YOU?

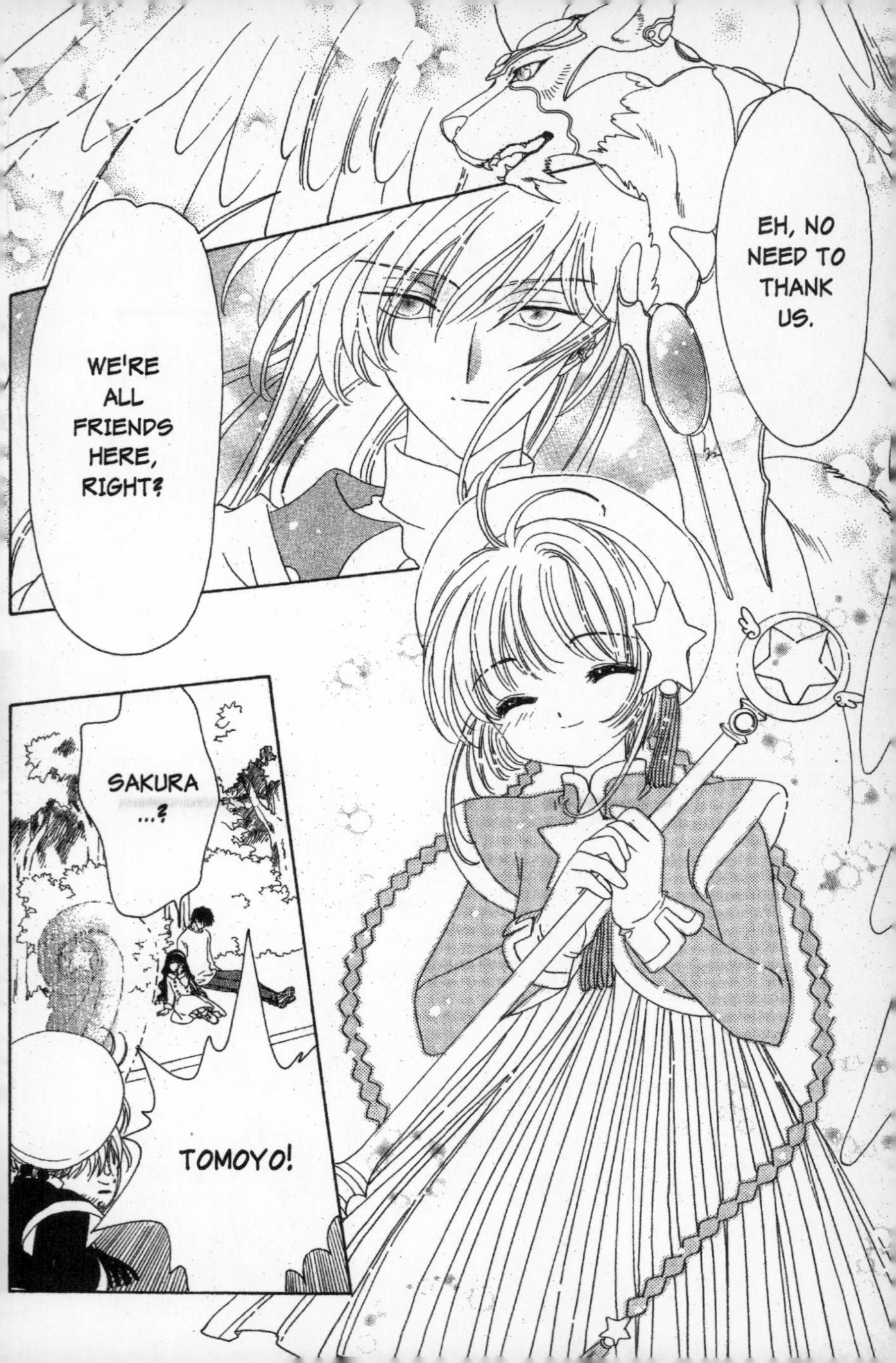
EH, NO NEED TO THANK US.
WE'RE ALL FRIENDS HERE, RIGHT?
SAKURA ...?
TOMOYO!

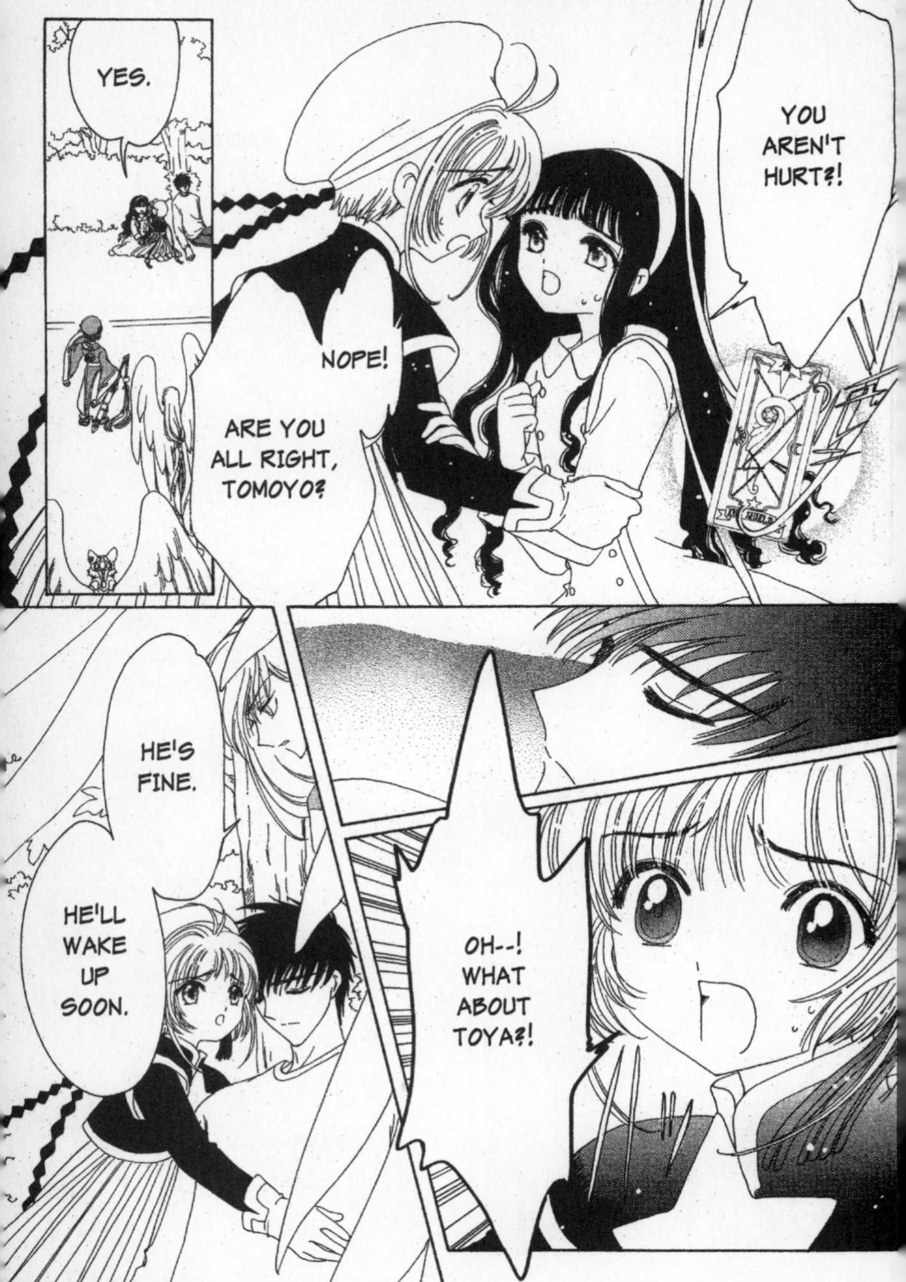
YOU AREN'T HURT?!
NOPE!
ARE YOU ALL RIGHT, TOMOYO?
YES.
OH--! WHAT ABOUT TOYA?!
HE'S FINE.
HE'LL WAKE UP SOON.

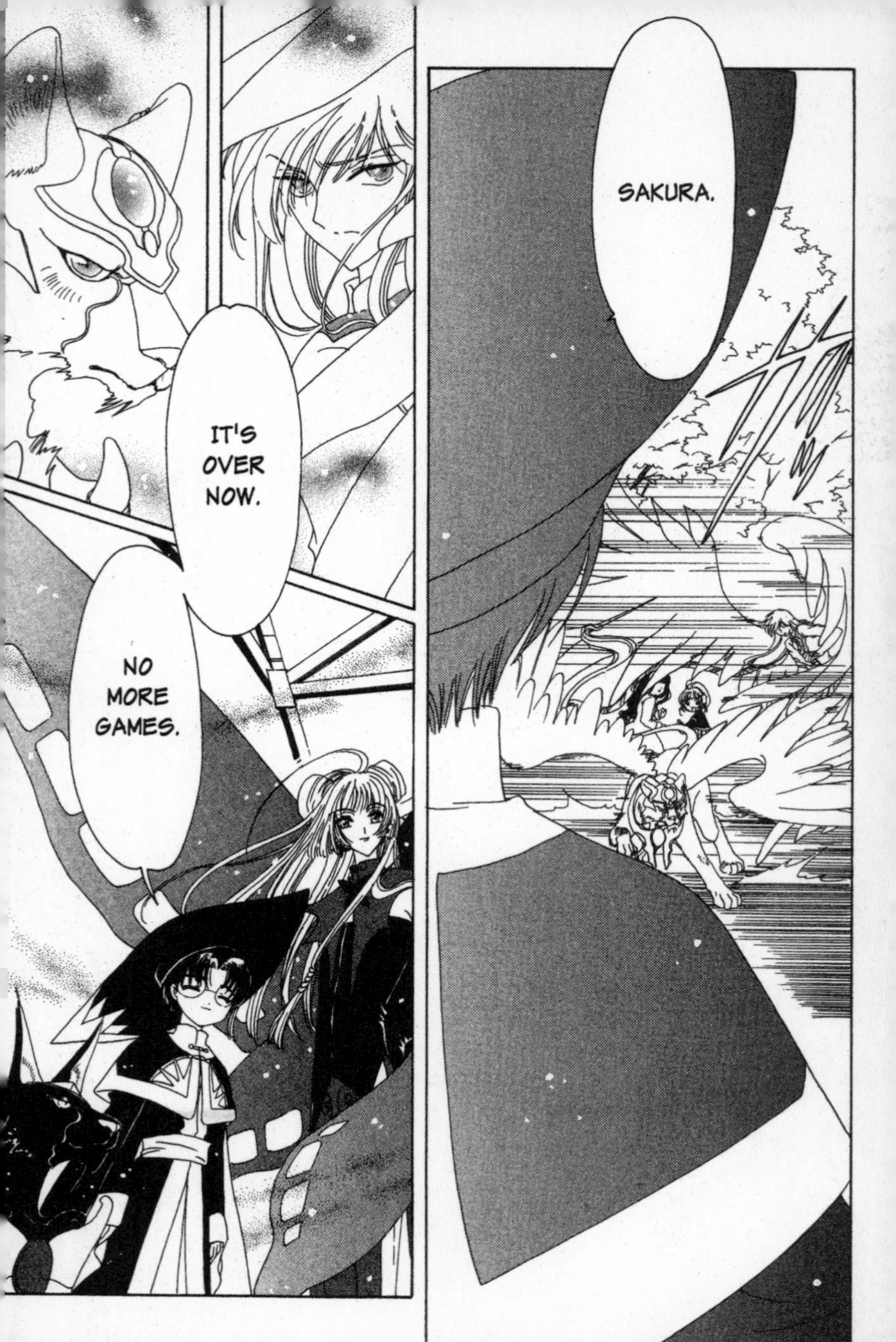
SAKURA.
IT'S OVER NOW.
NO MORE GAMES.

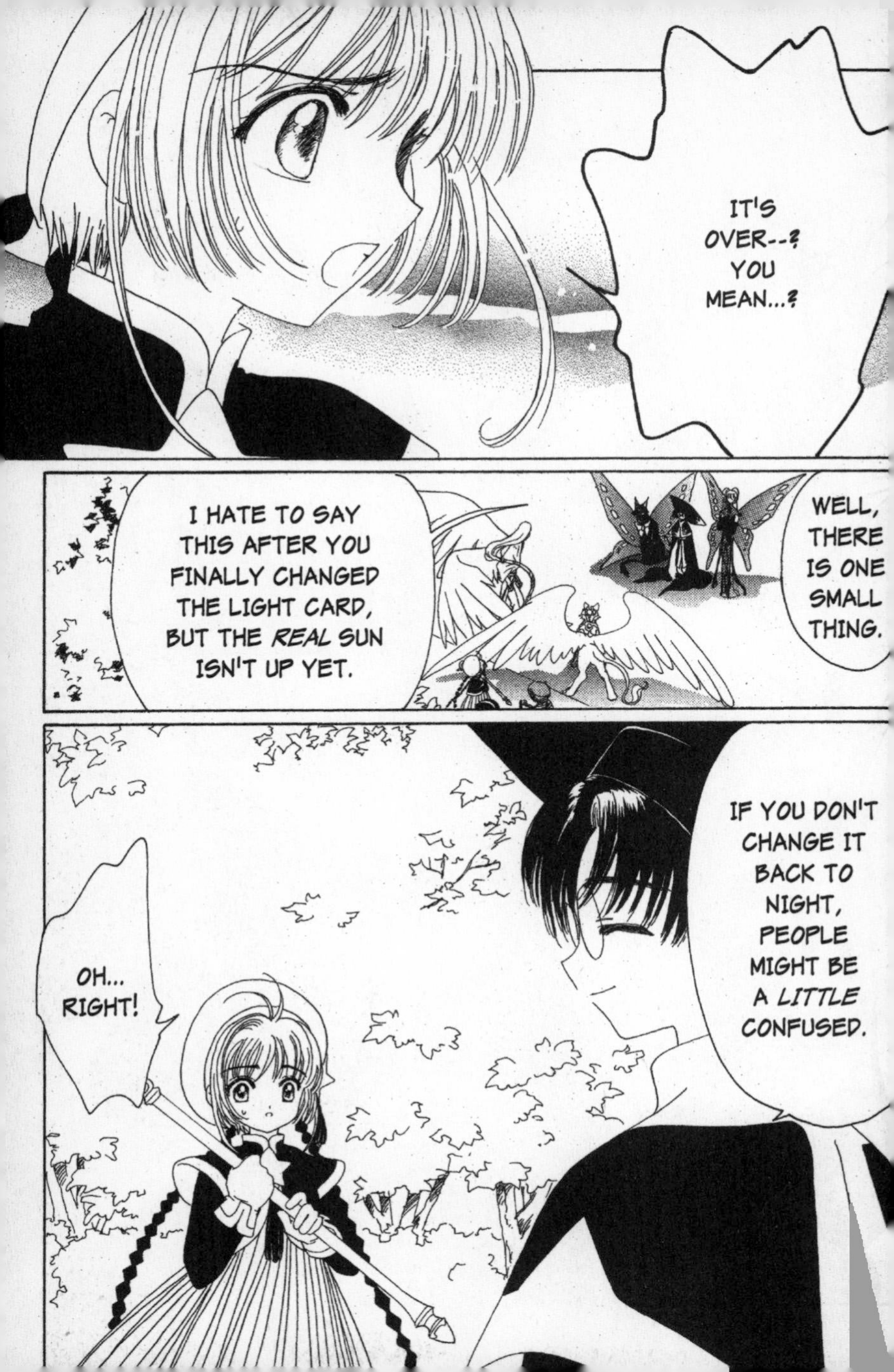
IT'S OVER--? YOU MEAN...?
WELL, THERE IS ONE SMALL THING.
I HATE TO SAY THIS AFTER YOU FINALLY CHANGED THE LIGHT CARD, BUT THE *REAL* SUN ISN'T UP YET.
IF YOU DON'T CHANGE IT BACK TO NIGHT, PEOPLE MIGHT BE A *LITTLE* CONFUSED.
OH... RIGHT!

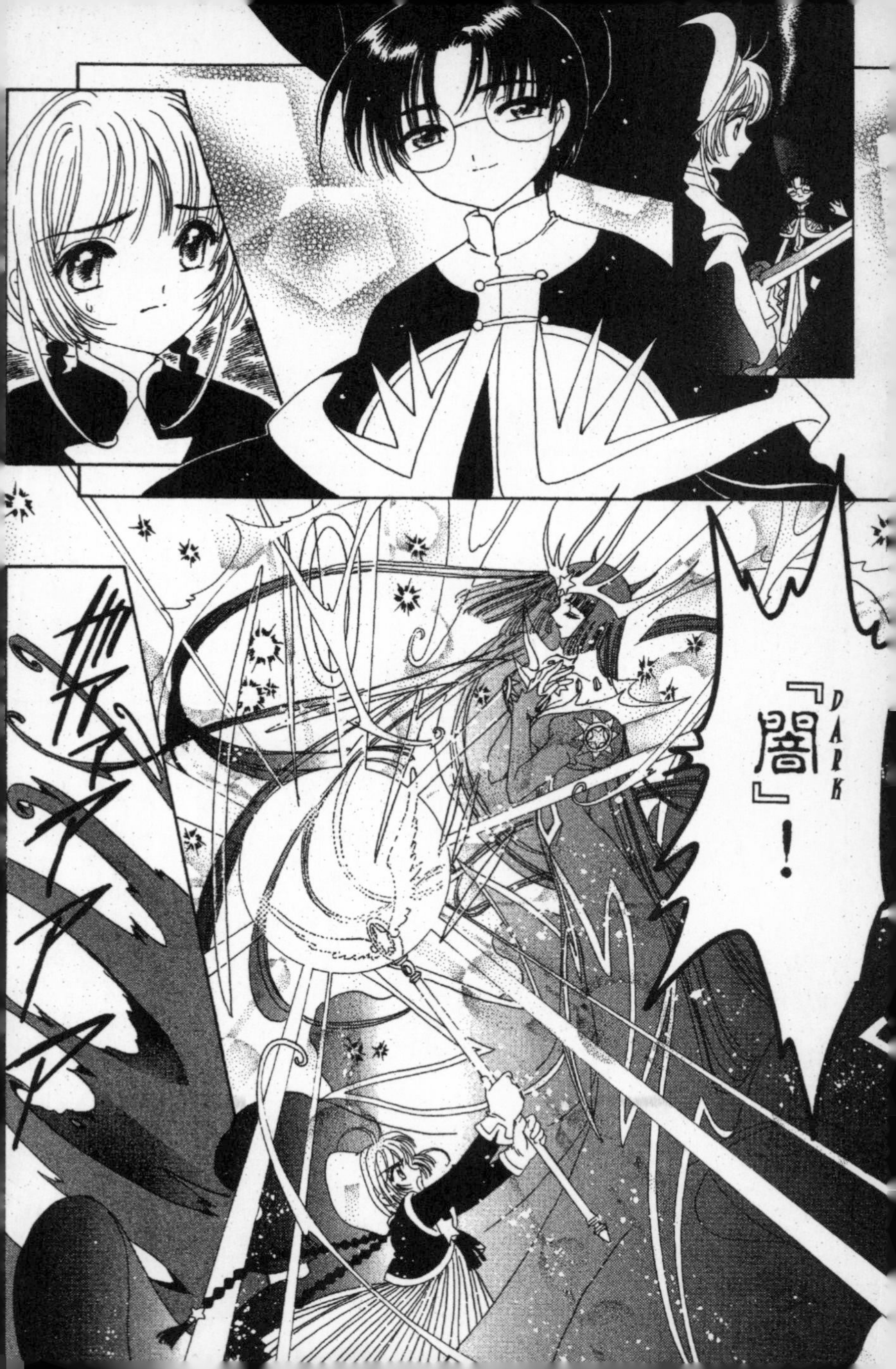
「闇(DARK)」!
ザァァァァァ

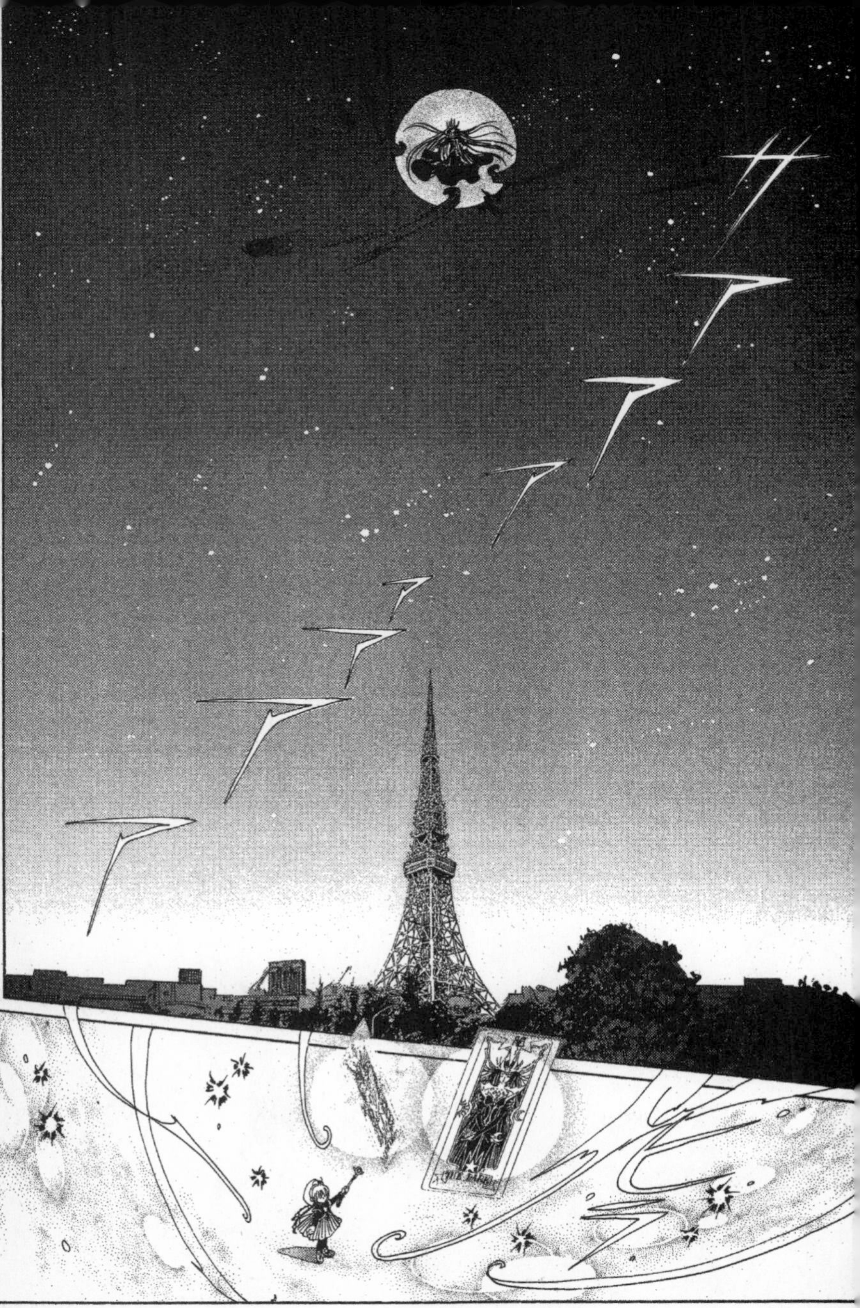
サァァァァァァァ

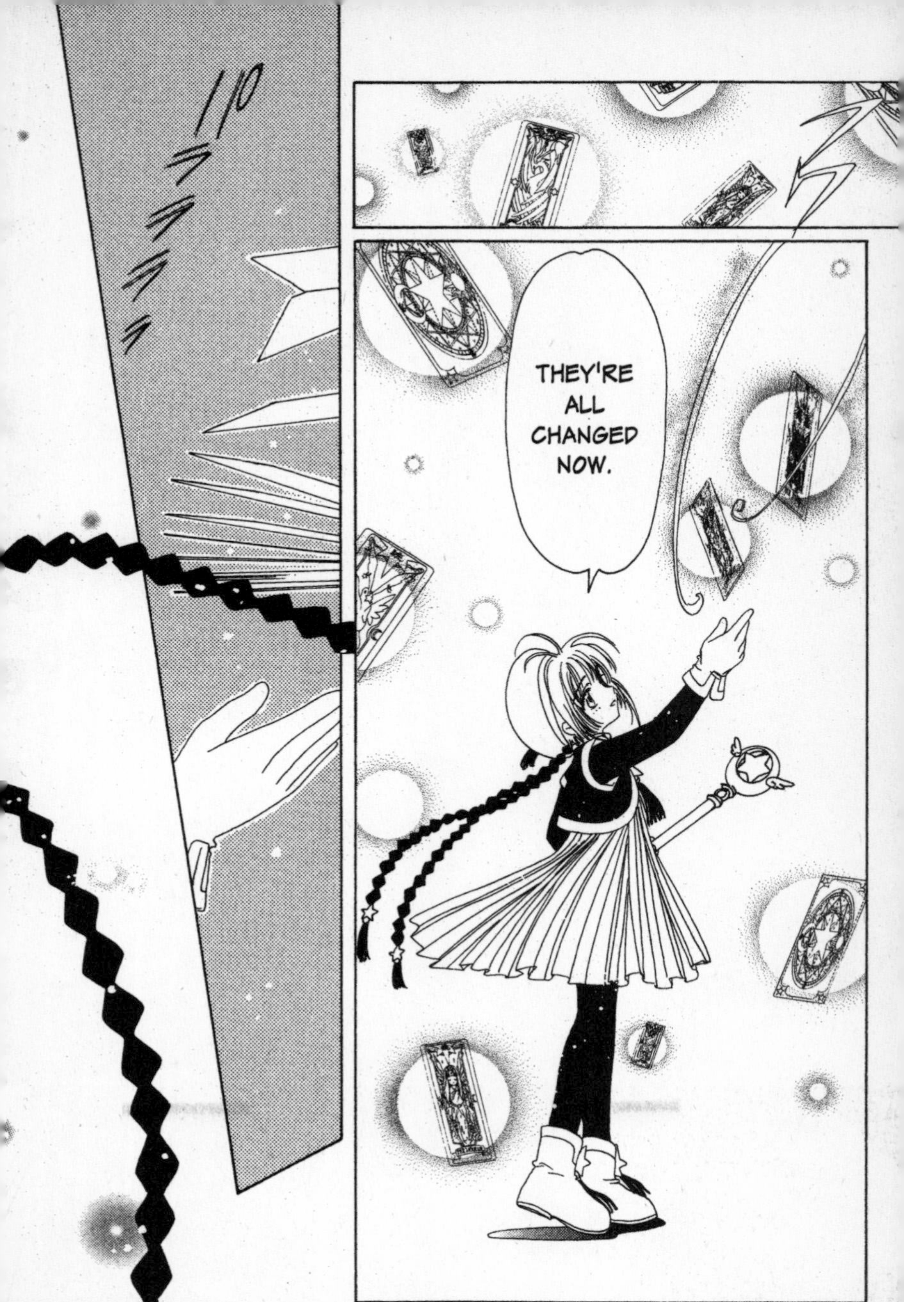
THEY'RE ALL CHANGED NOW.
パララララ

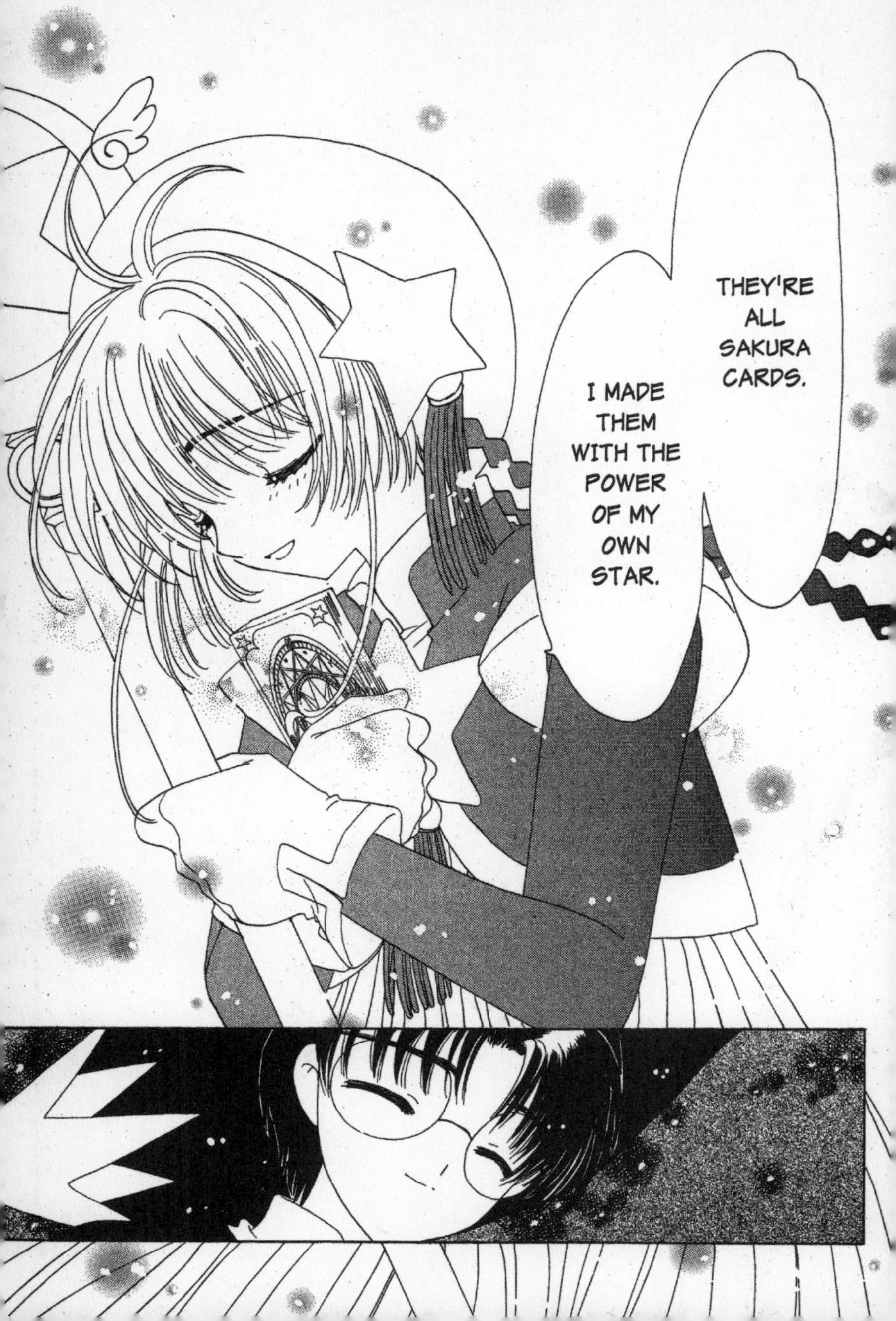
THEY'RE ALL SAKURA CARDS.
I MADE THEM WITH THE POWER OF MY OWN STAR.

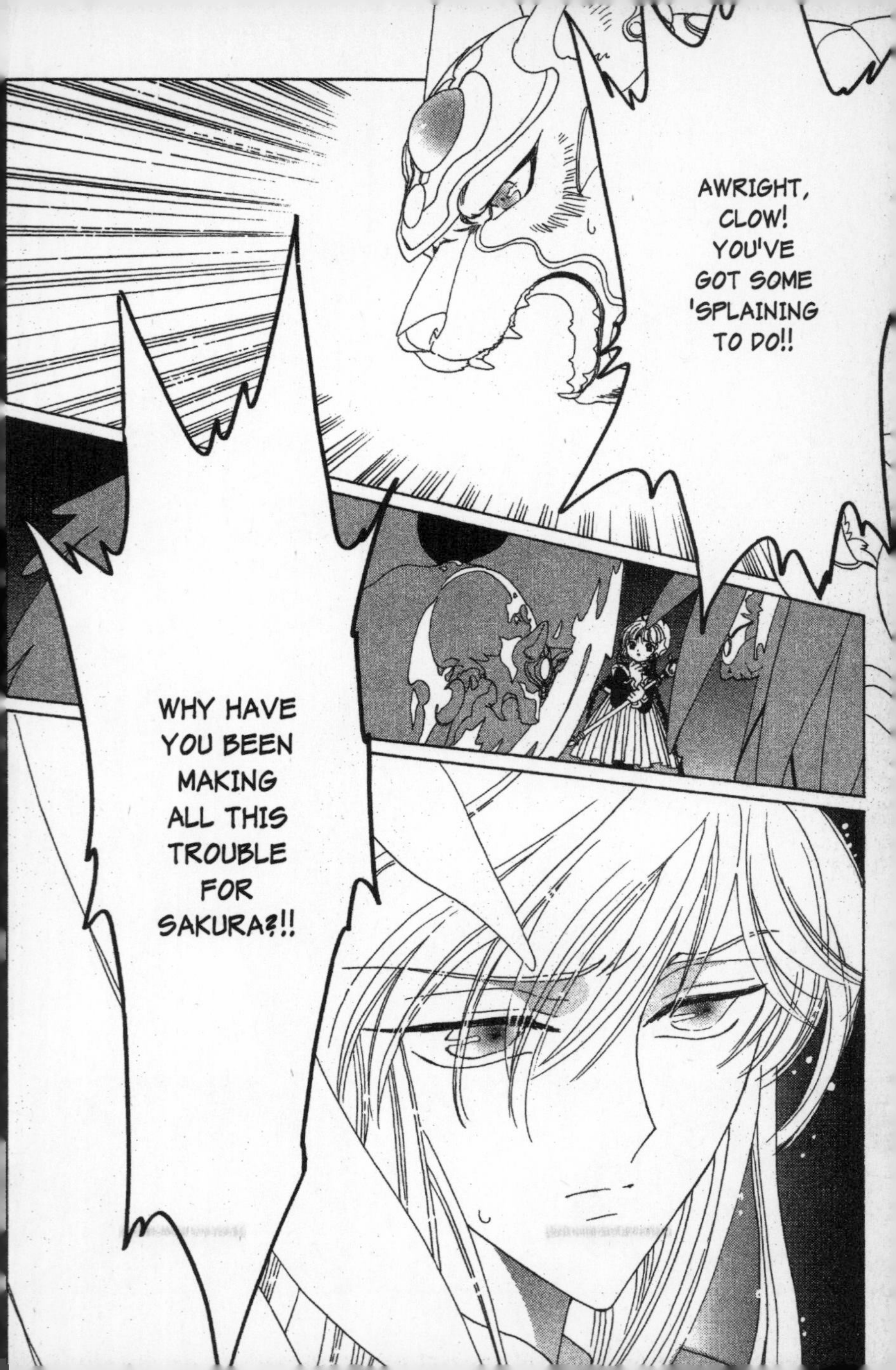
AWRIGHT, CLOW! YOU'VE GOT SOME 'SPLAINING TO DO!!
WHY HAVE YOU BEEN MAKING ALL THIS TROUBLE FOR SAKURA?!!

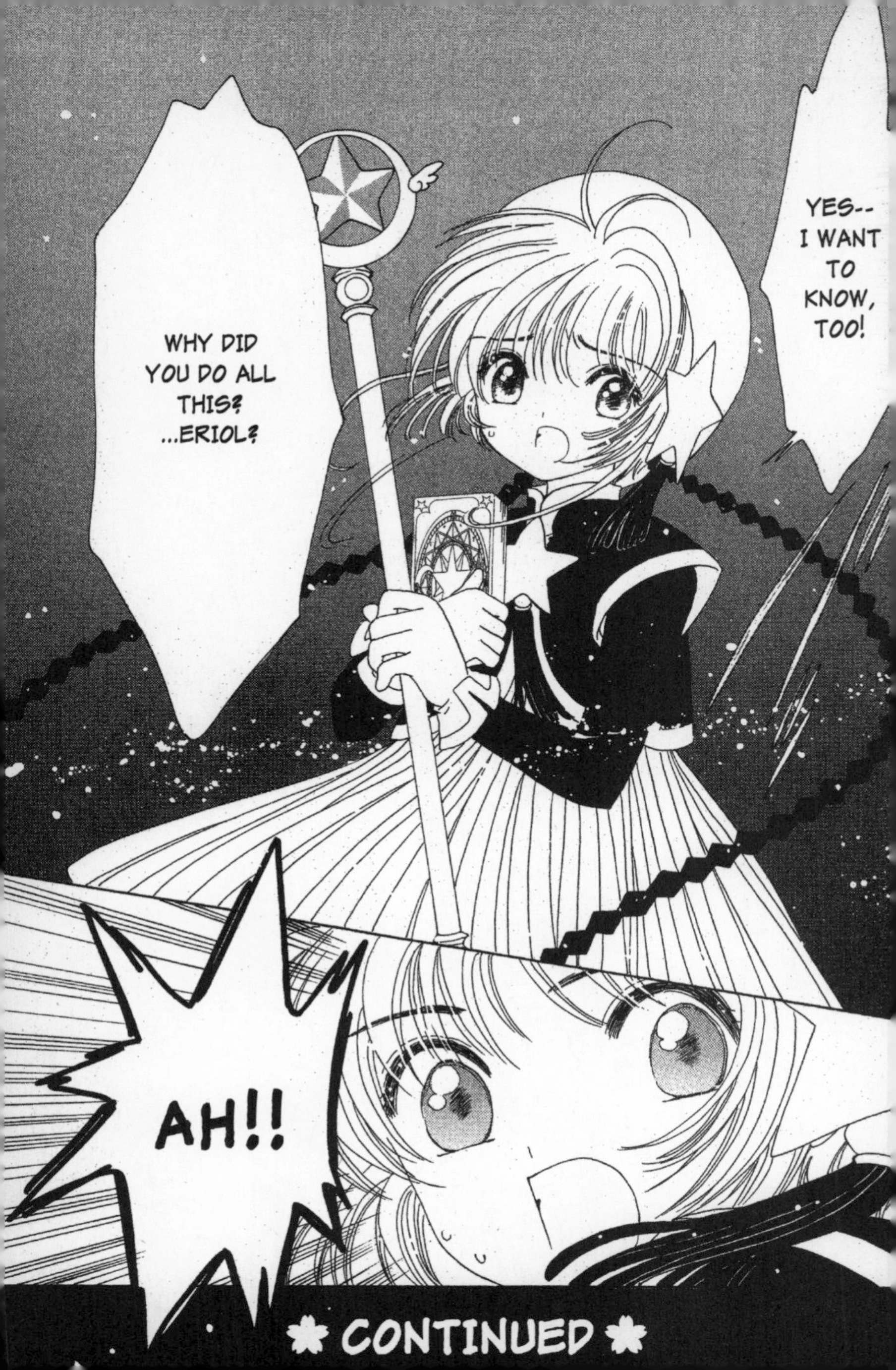
WHY DID YOU DO ALL THIS? ...ERIOL?
YES-- I WANT TO KNOW, TOO!
AH!!
CONTINUED

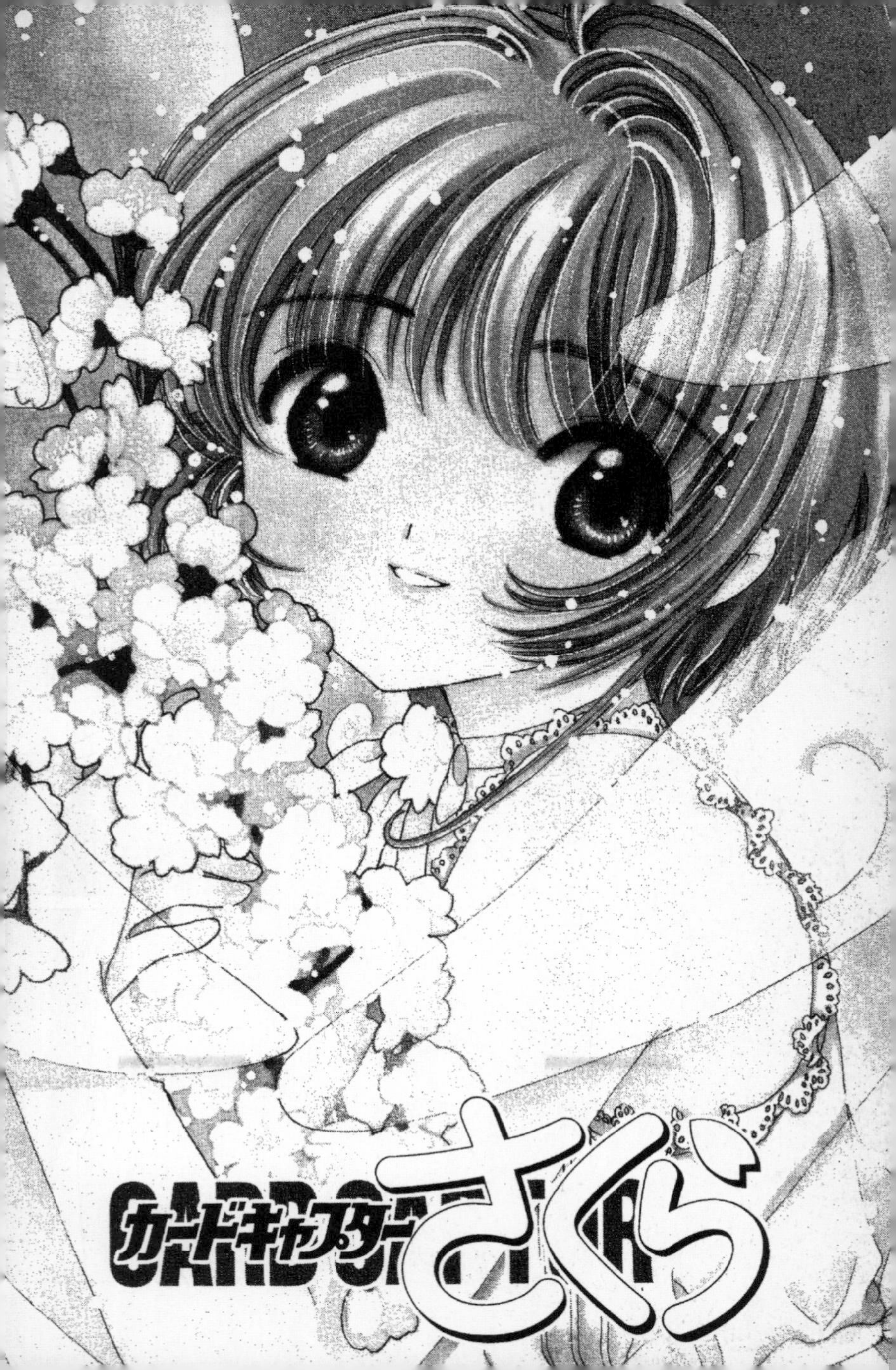
カードキャプターさくら

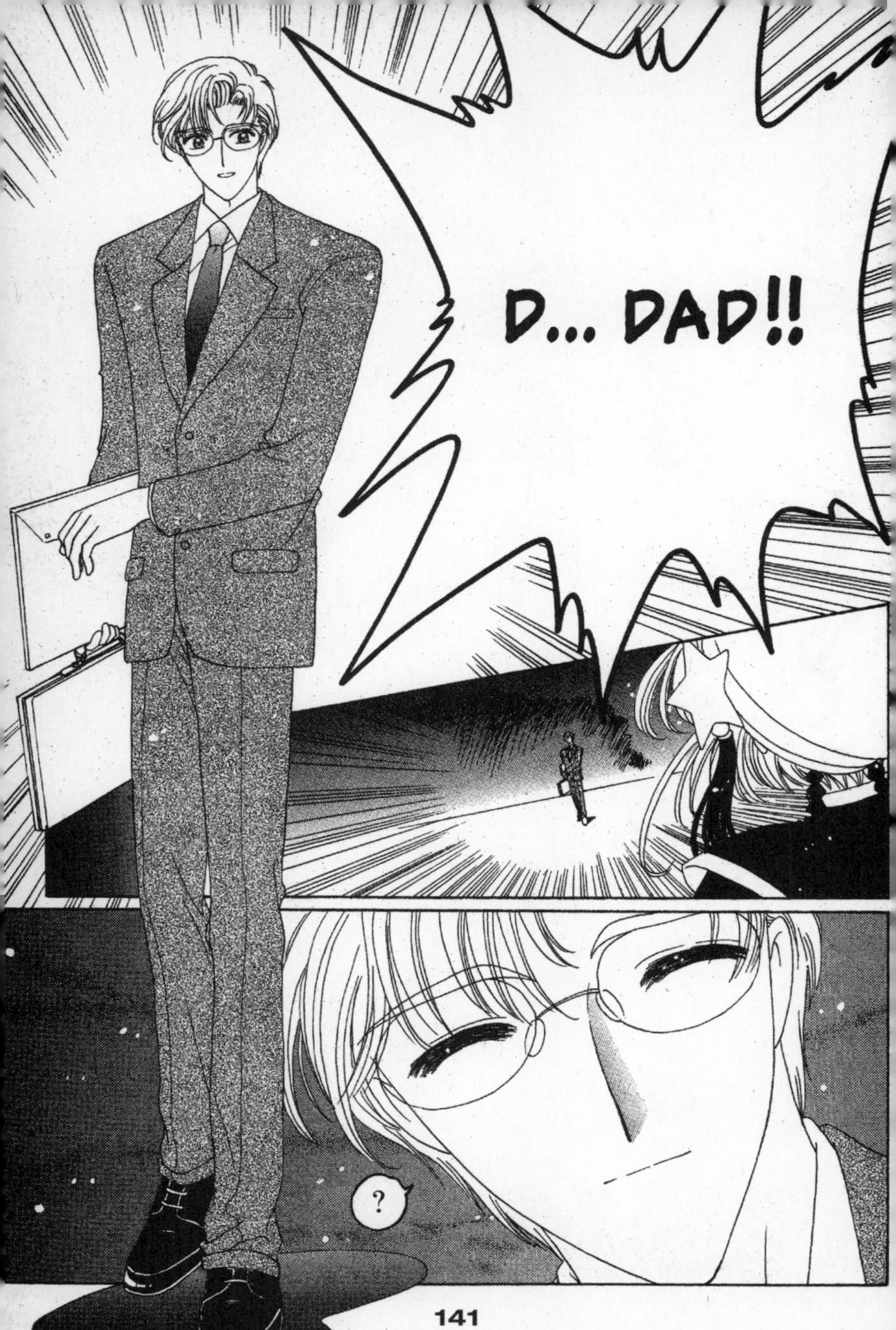
D... DAD!!
?

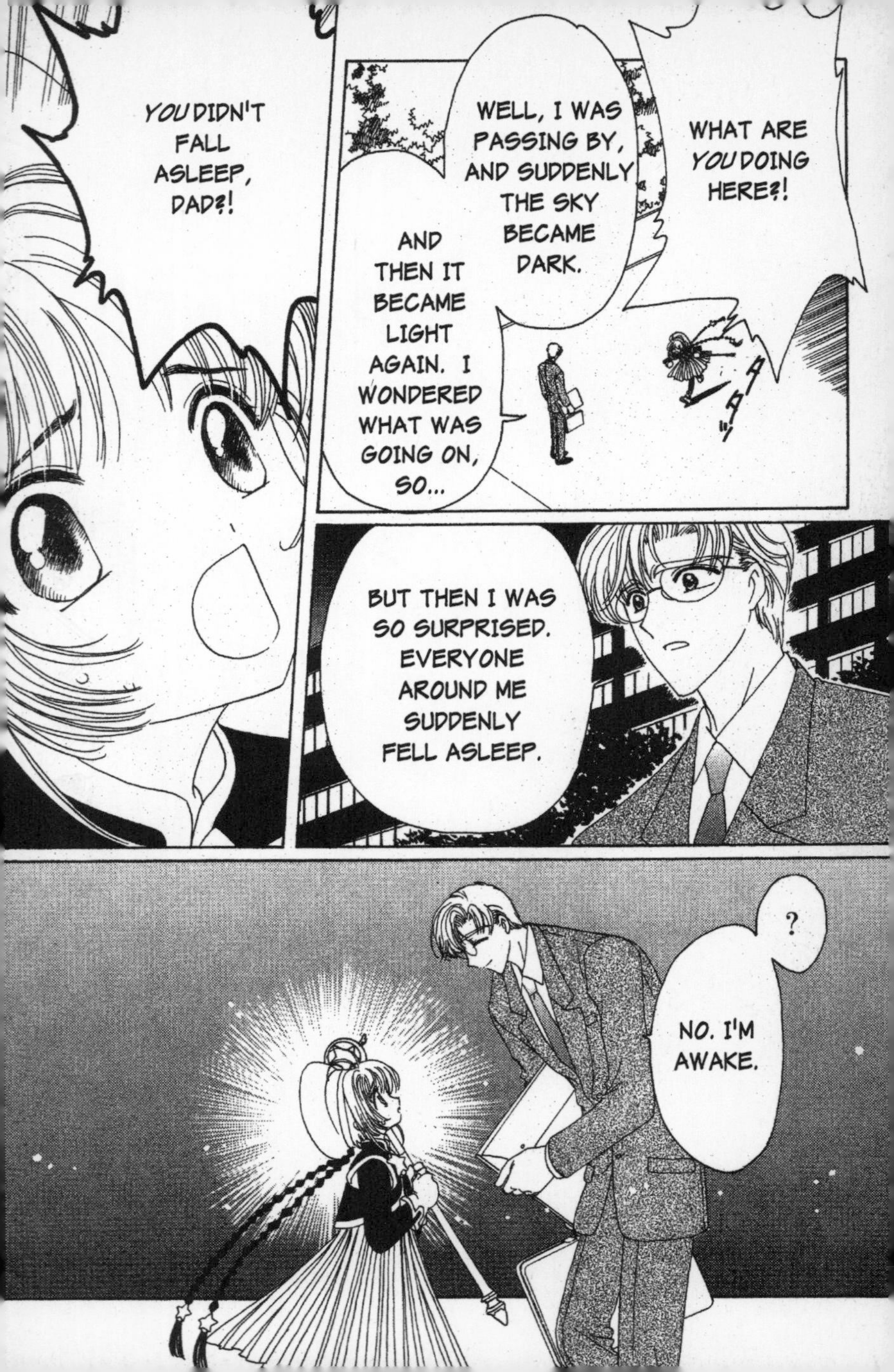
WHAT ARE YOU DOING HERE?!
WELL, I WAS PASSING BY, AND SUDDENLY THE SKY BECAME DARK.
AND THEN IT BECAME LIGHT AGAIN. I WONDERED WHAT WAS GOING ON, SO...
BUT THEN I WAS SO SURPRISED. EVERYONE AROUND ME SUDDENLY FELL ASLEEP.
YOU DIDN'T FALL ASLEEP, DAD?!
?
NO. I'M AWAKE.

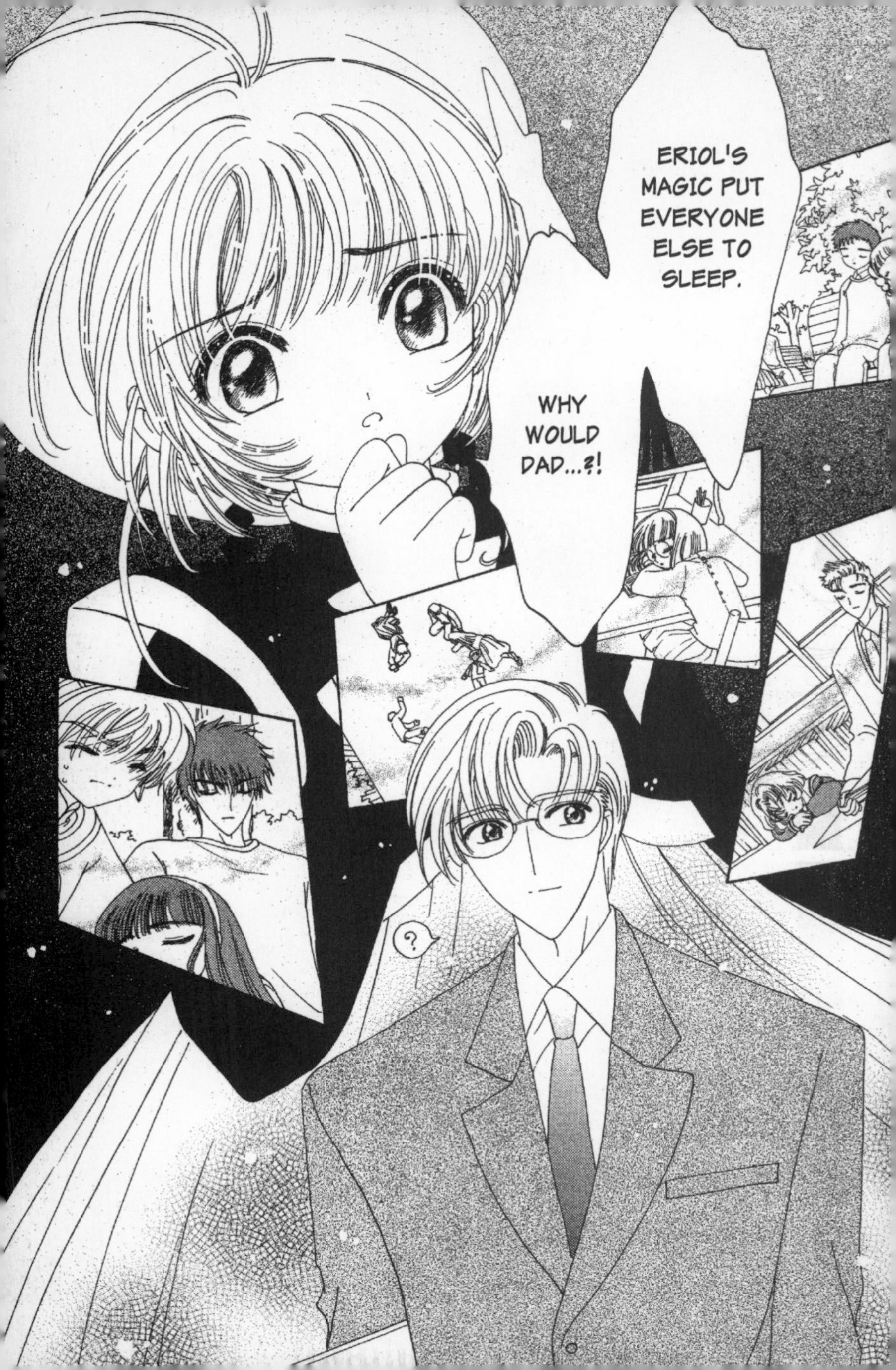
ERIOL'S MAGIC PUT EVERYONE ELSE TO SLEEP.
WHY WOULD DAD...?!
?

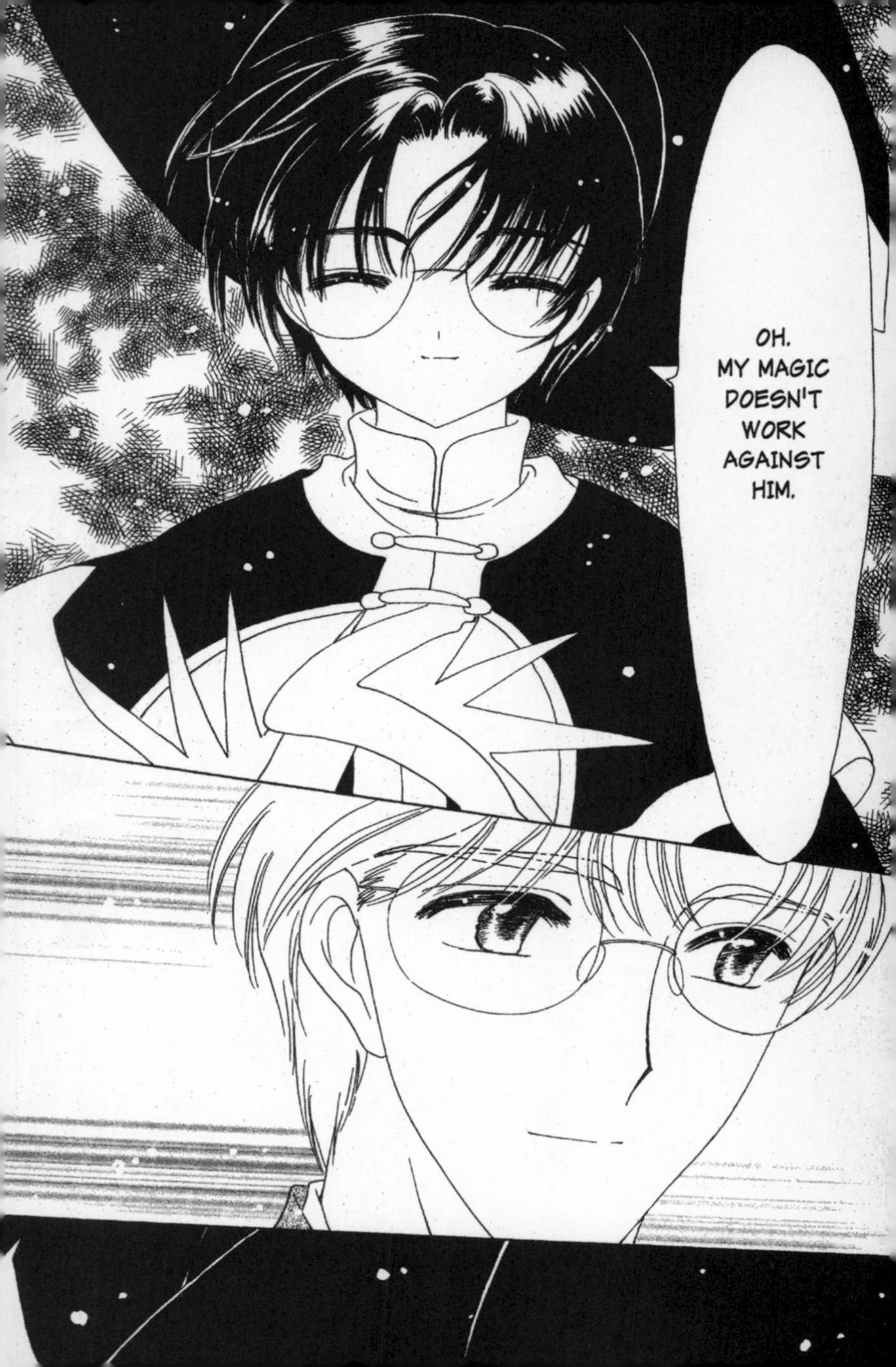
OH.
MY MAGIC
DOESN'T
WORK
AGAINST
HIM.

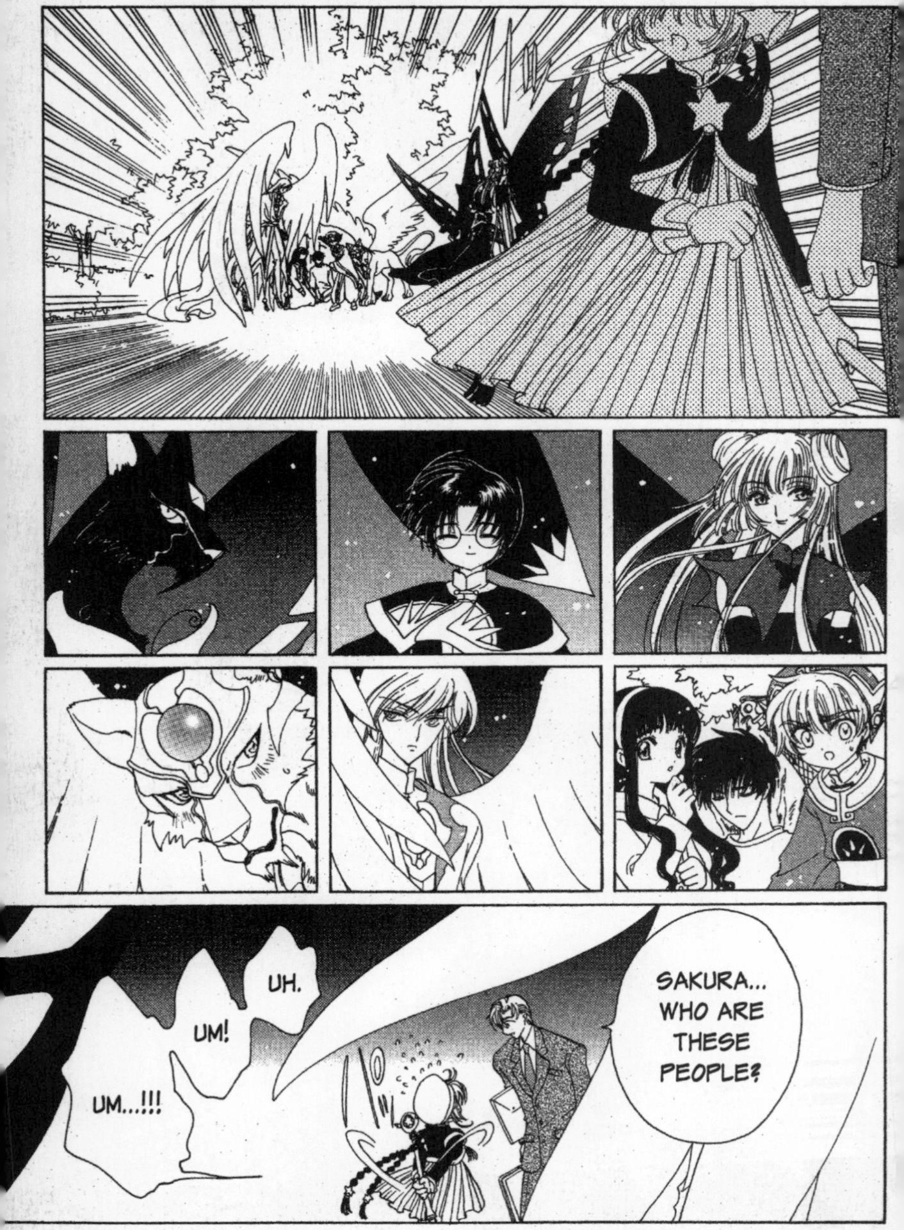
SAKURA... WHO ARE THESE PEOPLE?
UH.
UM!
UM...!!!

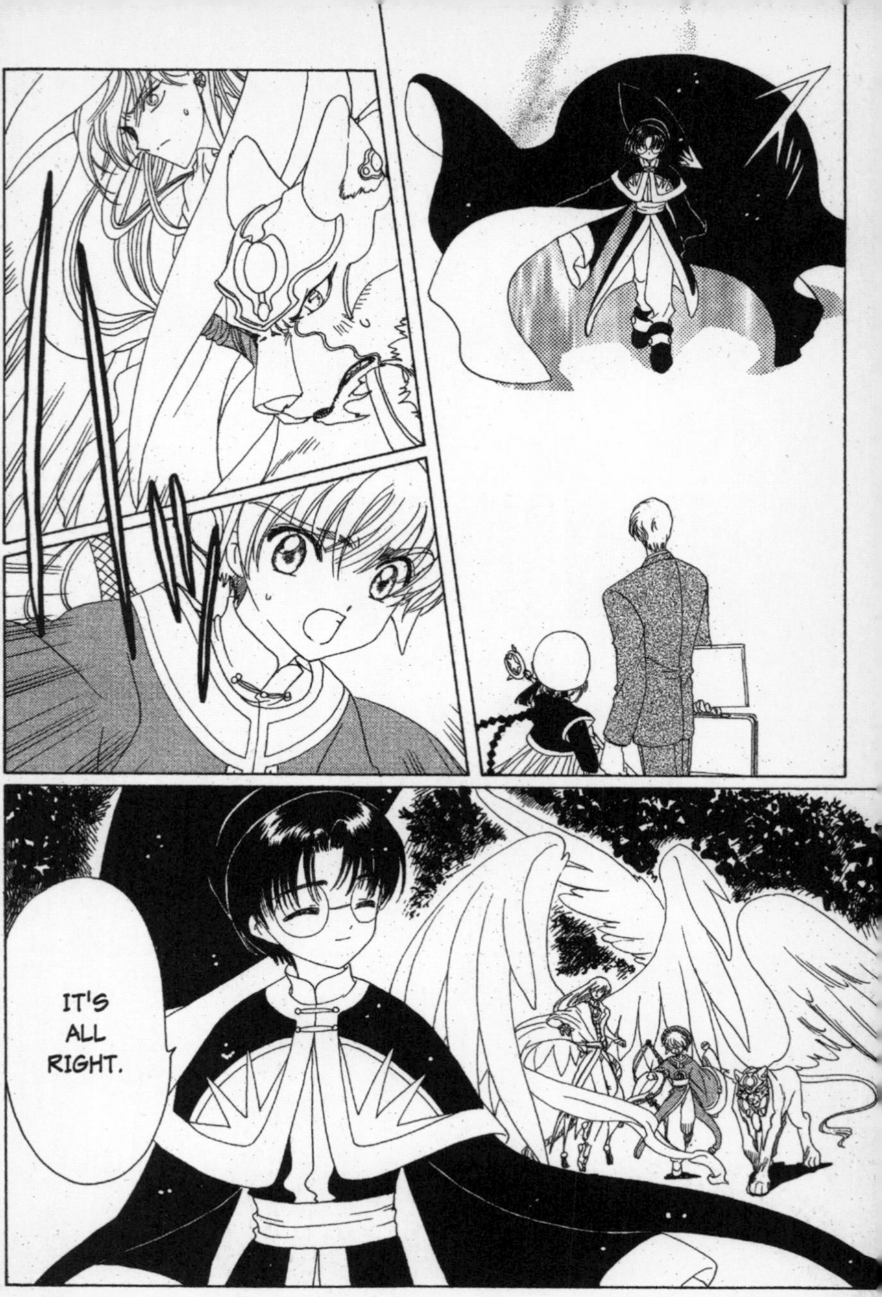
IT'S ALL RIGHT.

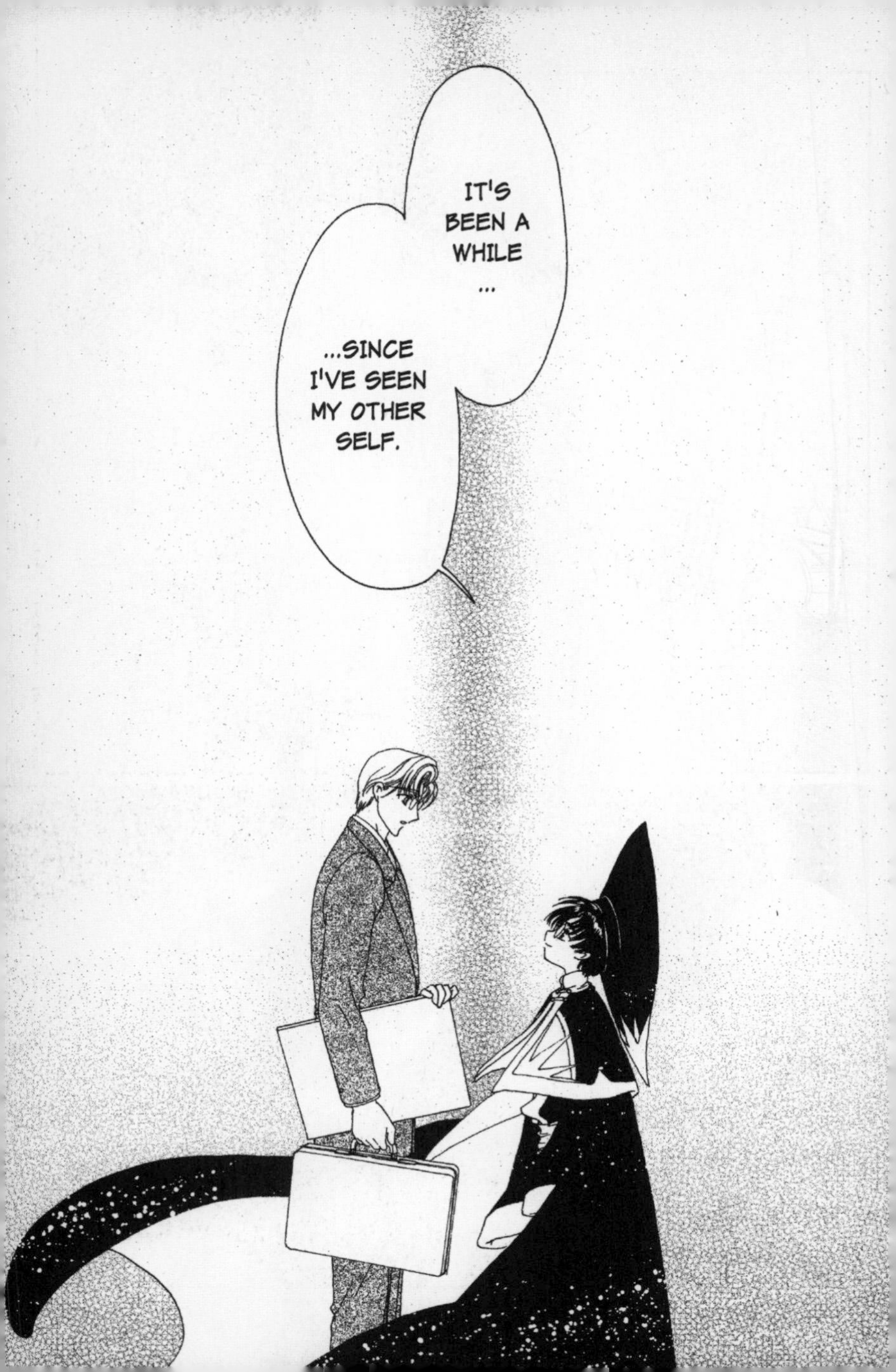
IT'S BEEN A WHILE ...
...SINCE I'VE SEEN MY OTHER SELF.

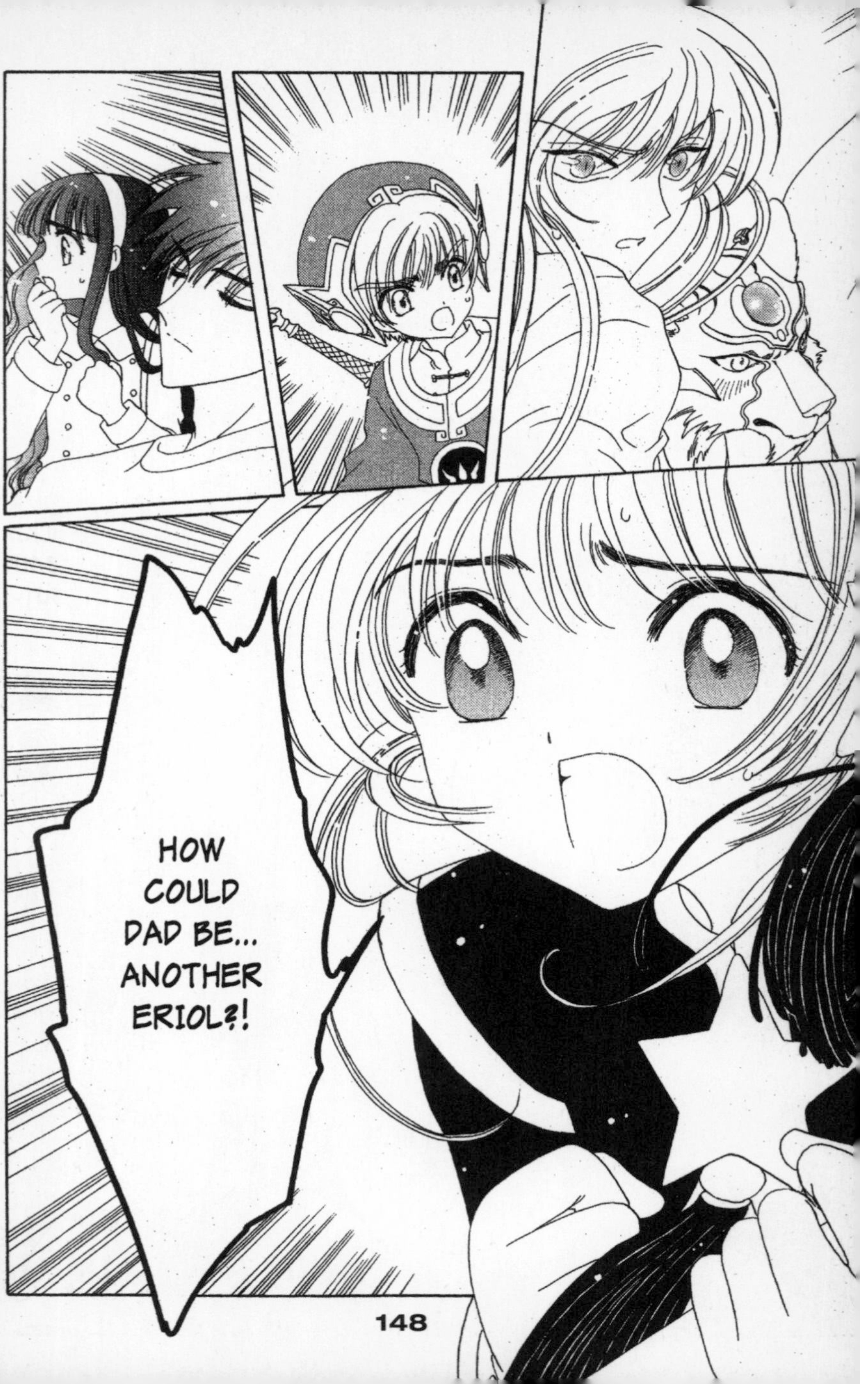
HOW COULD DAD BE... ANOTHER ERIOL?!

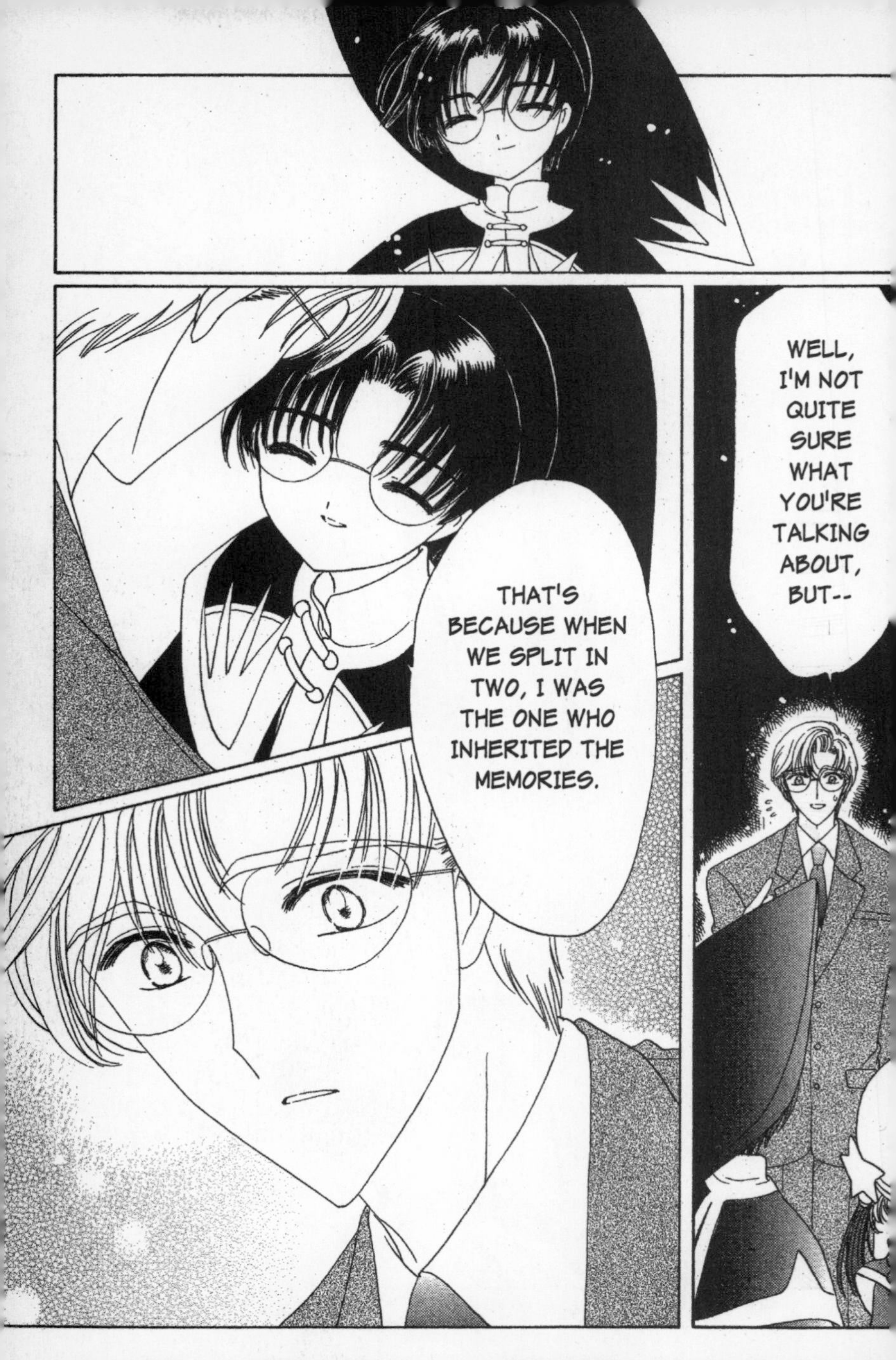
WELL, I'M NOT QUITE SURE WHAT YOU'RE TALKING ABOUT, BUT--
THAT'S BECAUSE WHEN WE SPLIT IN TWO, I WAS THE ONE WHO INHERITED THE MEMORIES.

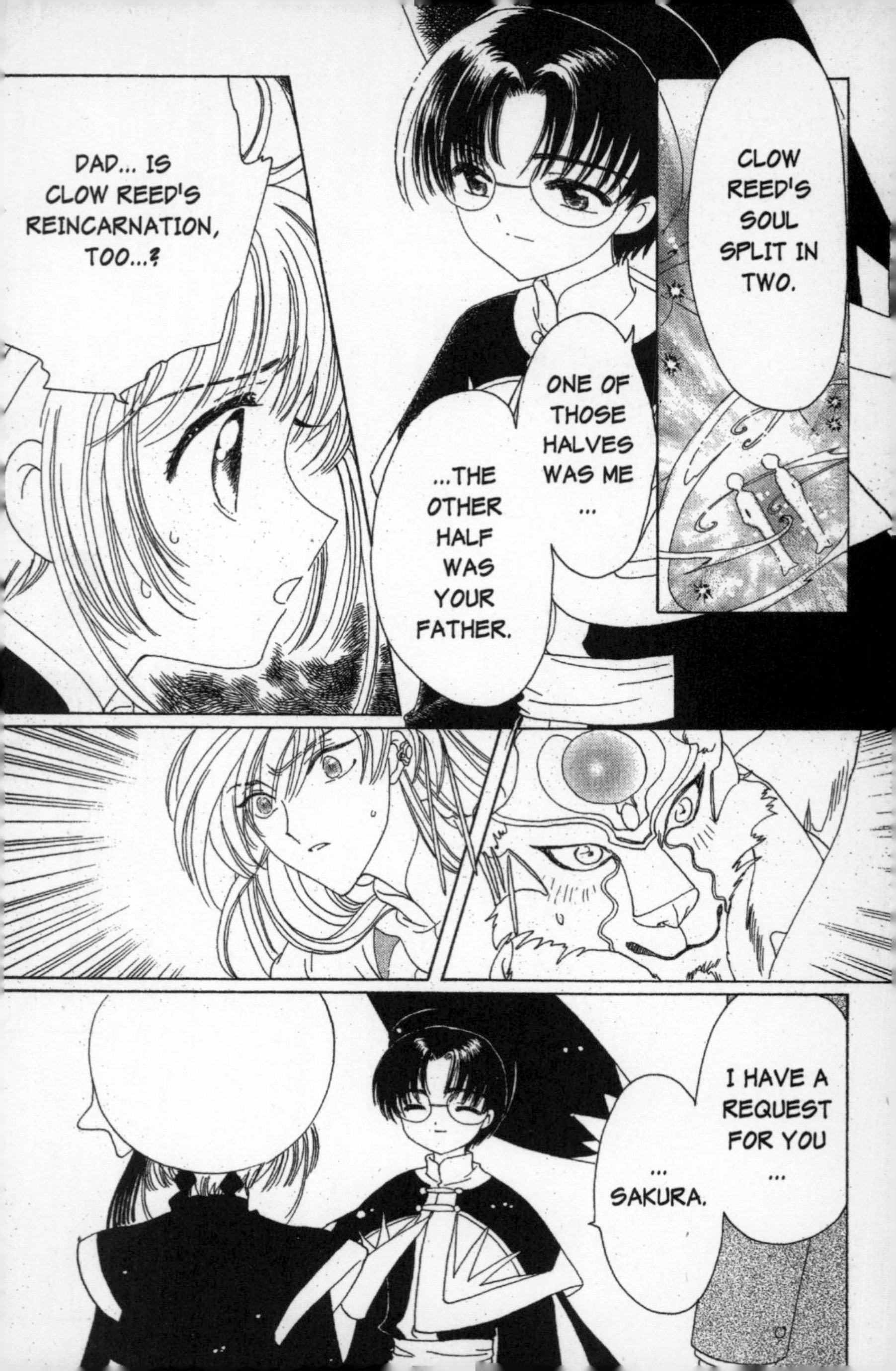
CLOW REED'S SOUL SPLIT IN TWO.
ONE OF THOSE HALVES WAS ME ...
...THE OTHER HALF WAS YOUR FATHER.
DAD... IS CLOW REED'S REINCARNATION, TOO...?
I HAVE A REQUEST FOR YOU ...
... SAKURA.

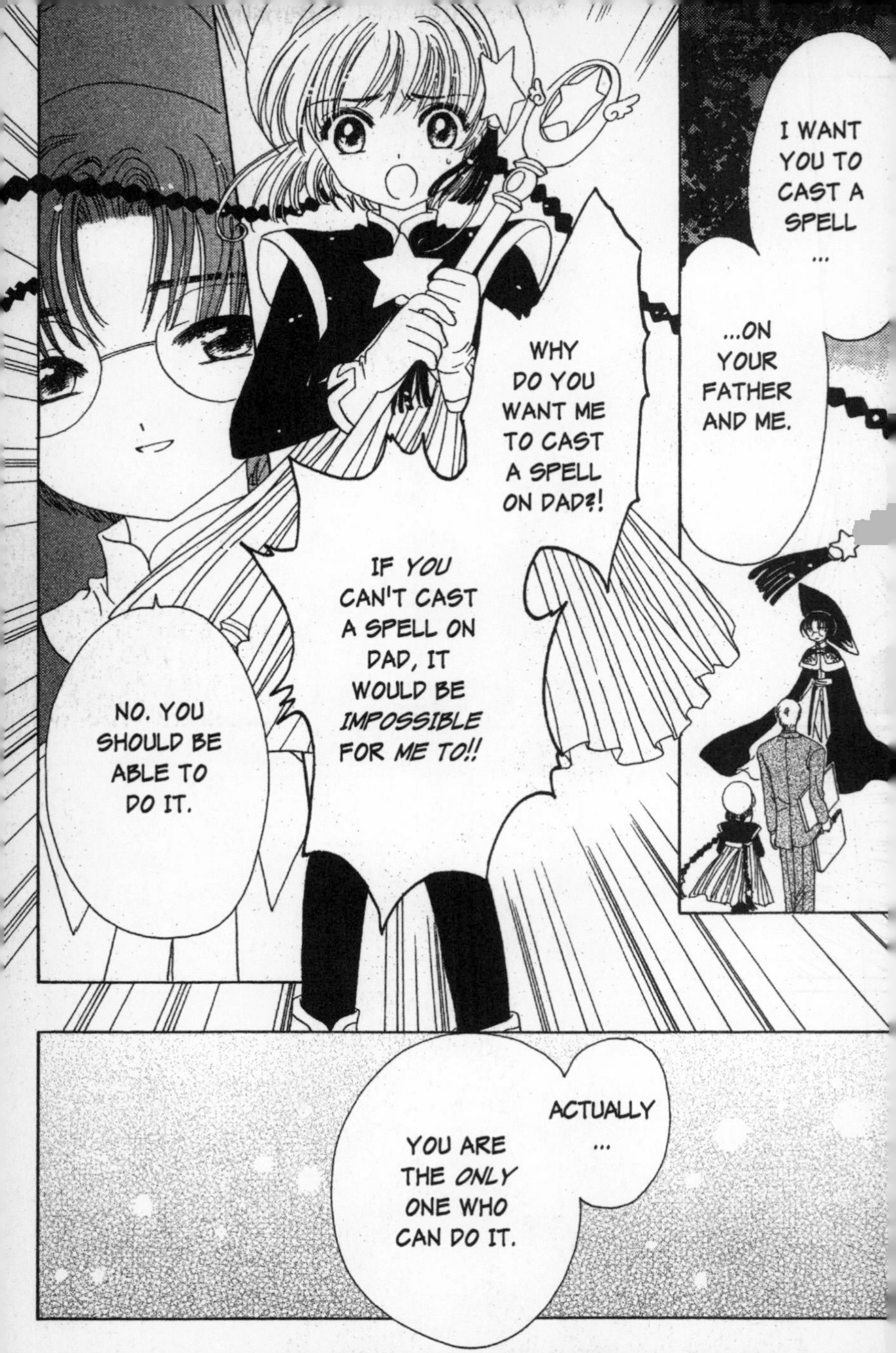
I WANT YOU TO CAST A SPELL ...
...ON YOUR FATHER AND ME.
WHY DO YOU WANT ME TO CAST A SPELL ON DAD?!
IF *YOU* CAN'T CAST A SPELL ON DAD, IT WOULD BE *IMPOSSIBLE* FOR *ME* TO!!
NO. YOU SHOULD BE ABLE TO DO IT.
ACTUALLY ...
YOU ARE THE *ONLY* ONE WHO CAN DO IT.

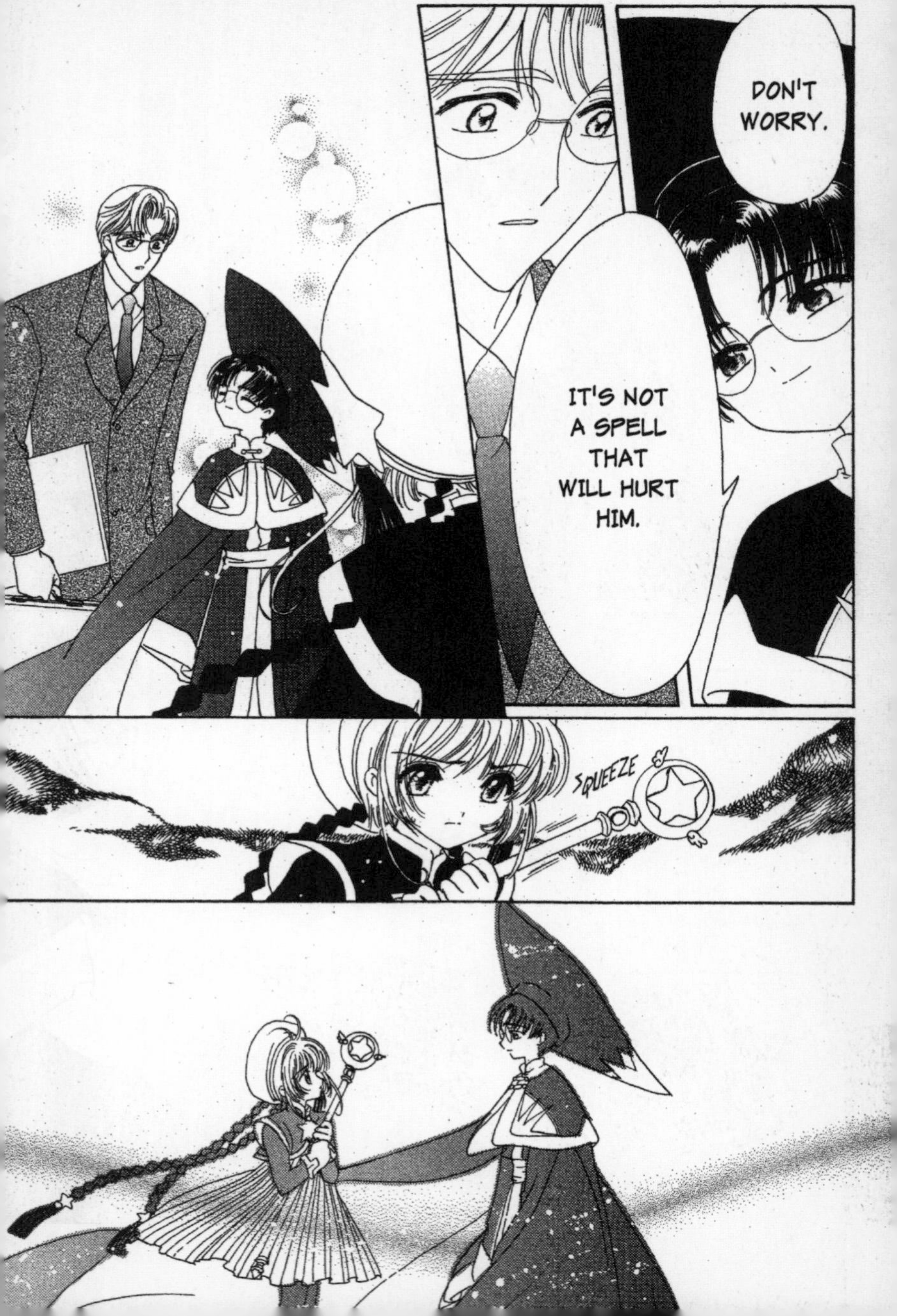
DON'T WORRY.
IT'S NOT A SPELL THAT WILL HURT HIM.
SQUEEZE

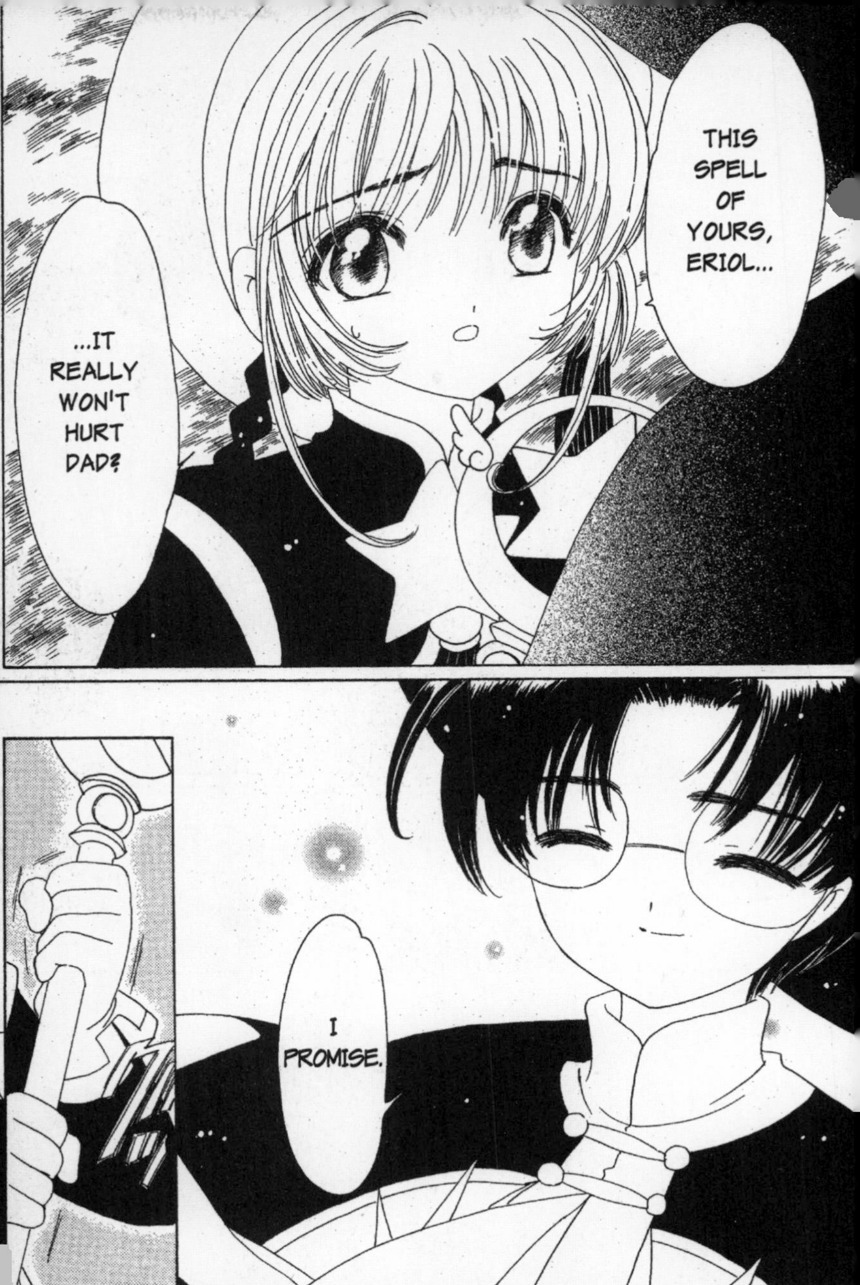
THIS SPELL OF YOURS, ERIOL...
...IT REALLY WON'T HURT DAD?
I PROMISE.

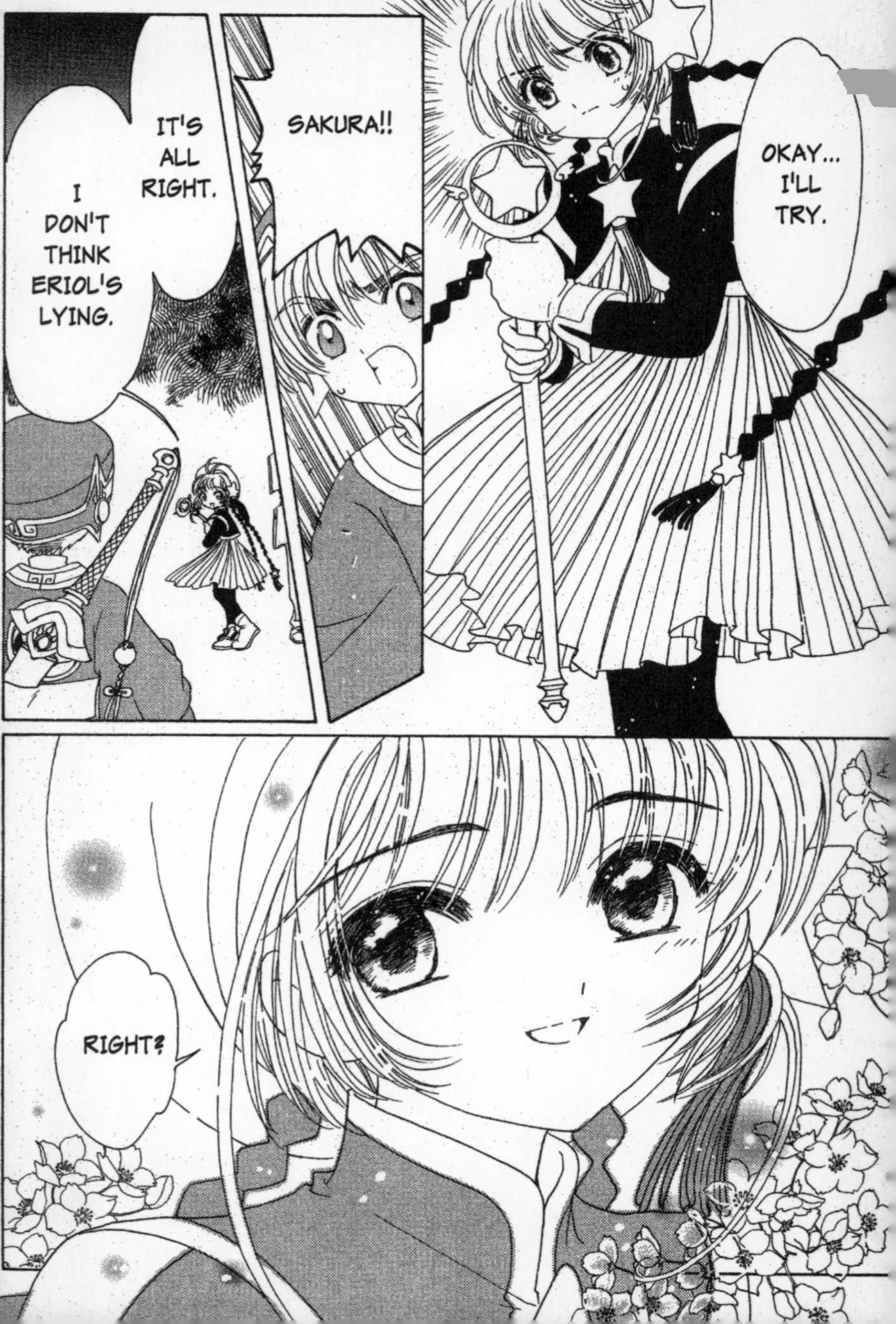
OKAY... I'LL TRY.
SAKURA!!
IT'S ALL RIGHT.
I DON'T THINK ERIOL'S LYING.
RIGHT?

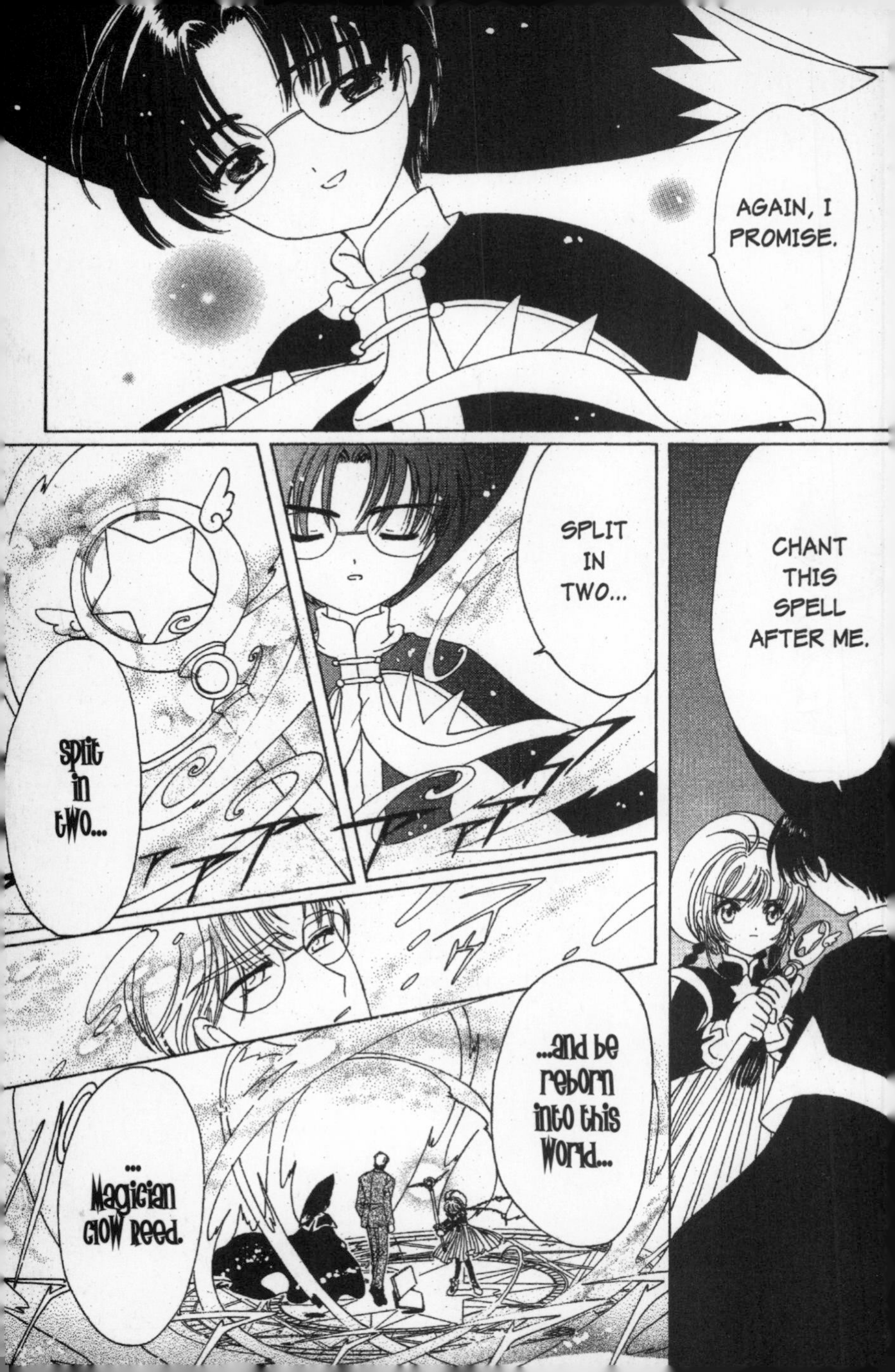
AGAIN, I PROMISE.
CHANT THIS SPELL AFTER ME.
SPLIT IN TWO...
split in two...
...and be reborn into this world...
... Magician Clow Reed.

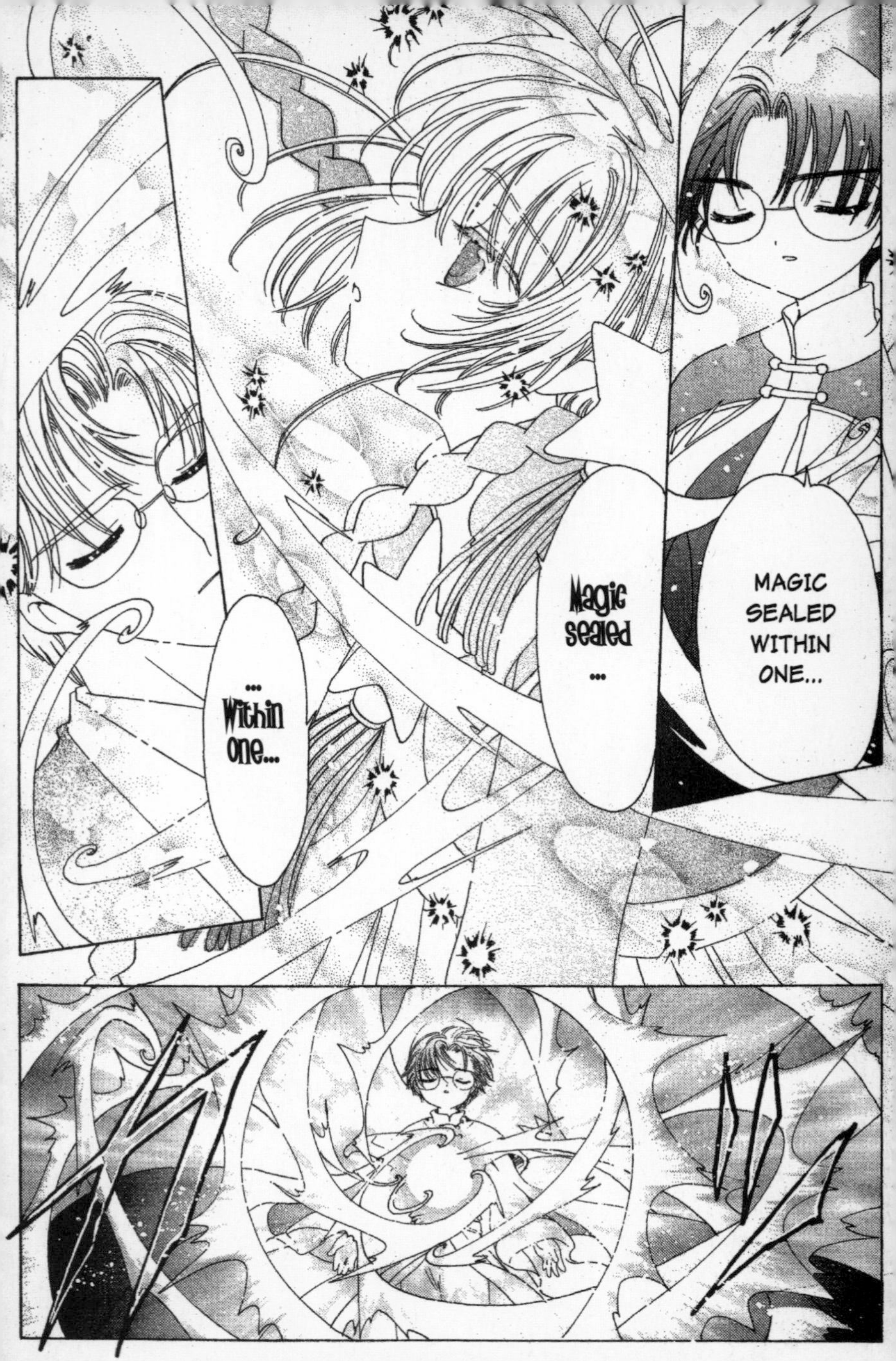
MAGIC SEALED WITHIN ONE...
Magic sealed ...
... Within one...

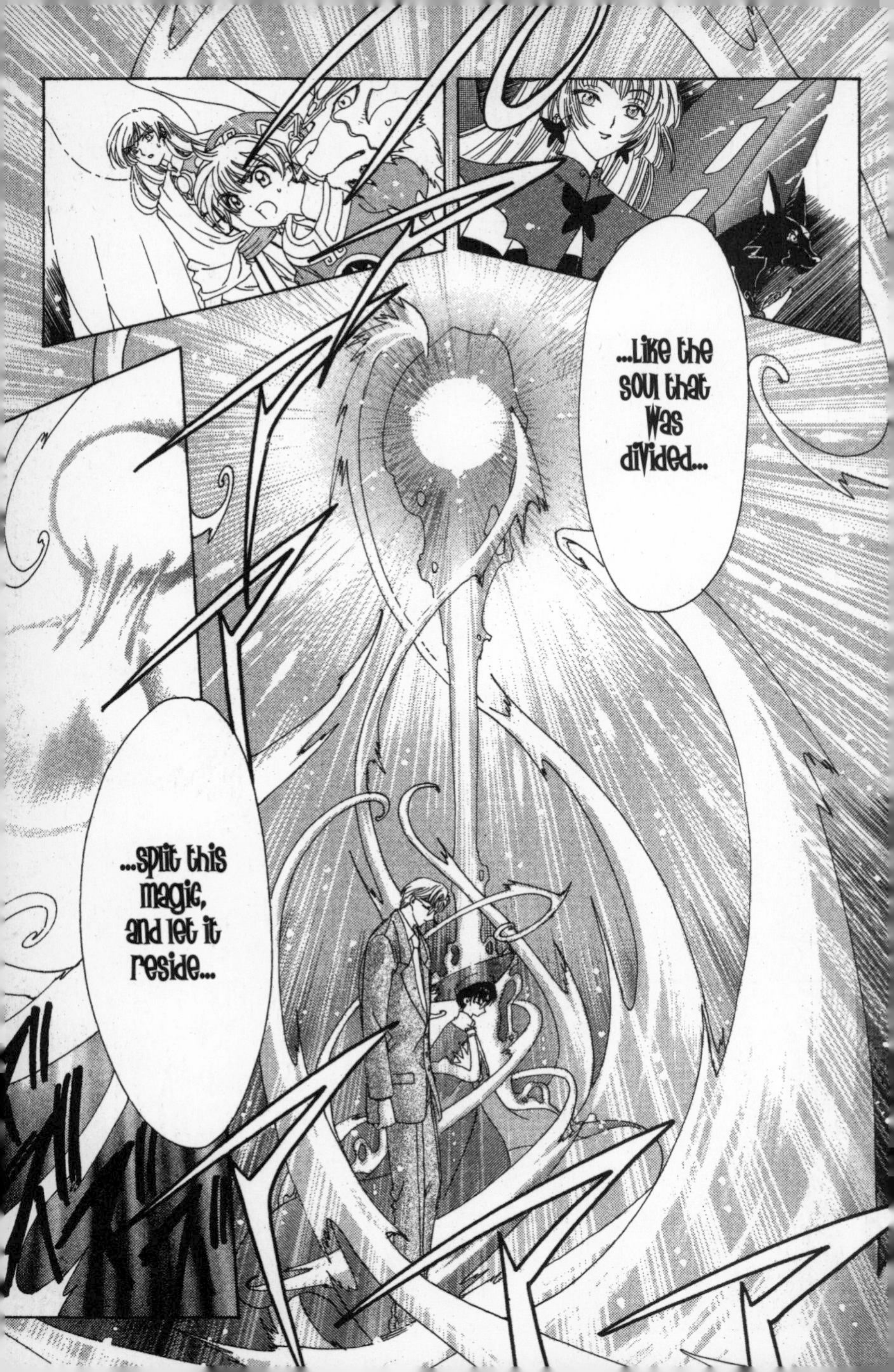
...like the soul that was divided...
...split this magic, and let it reside...

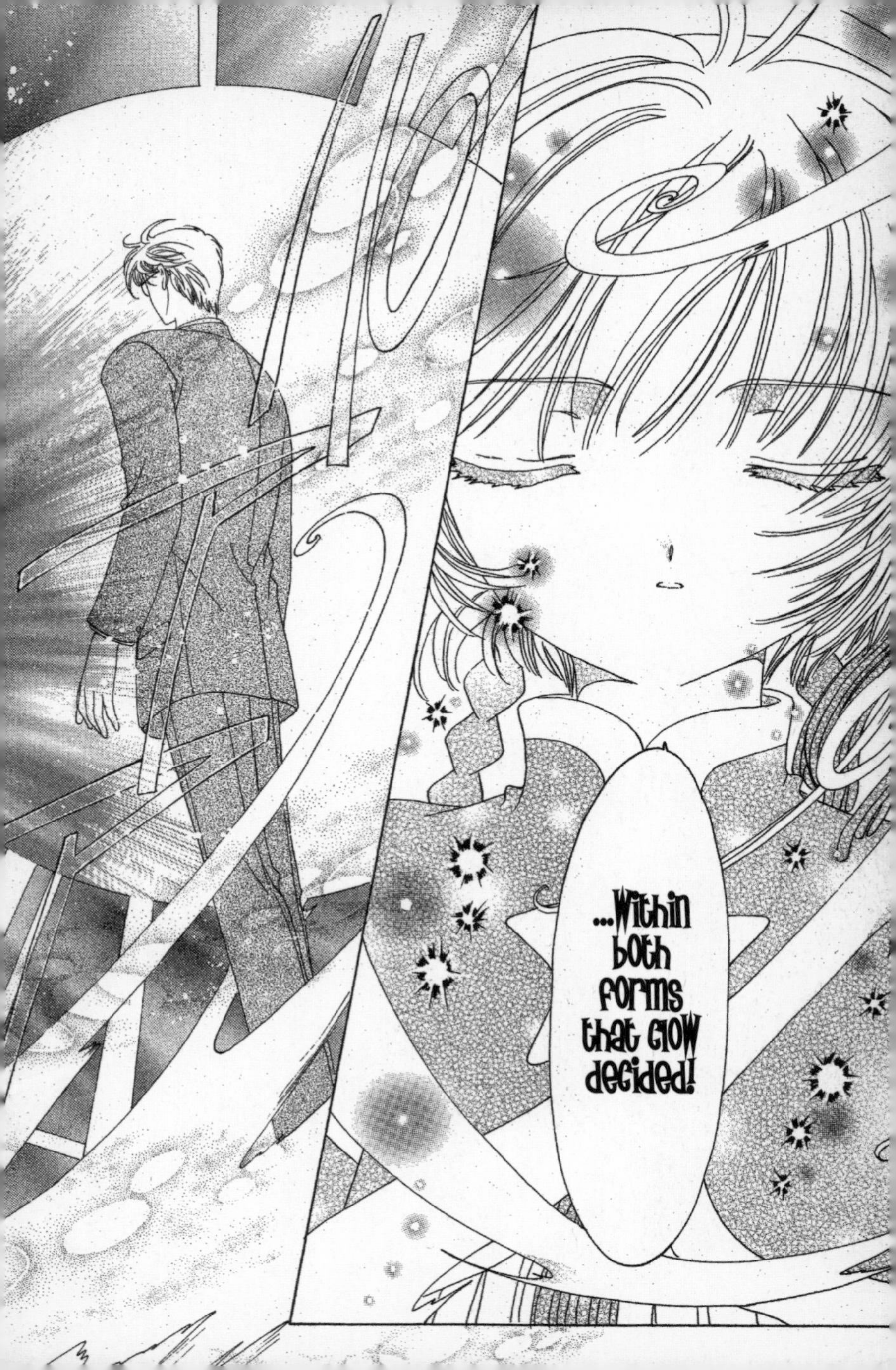
...Within both forms that Clow decided!

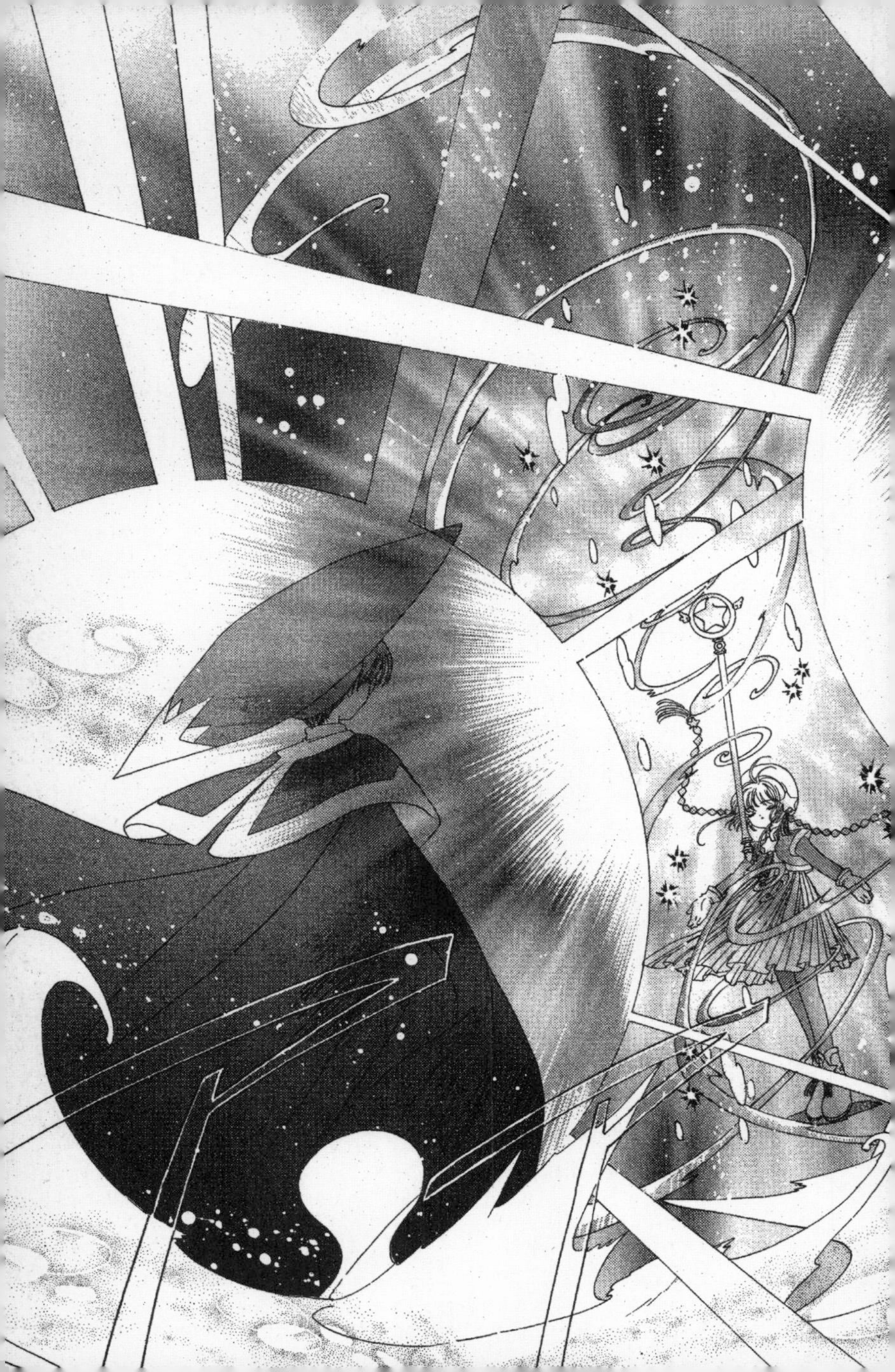

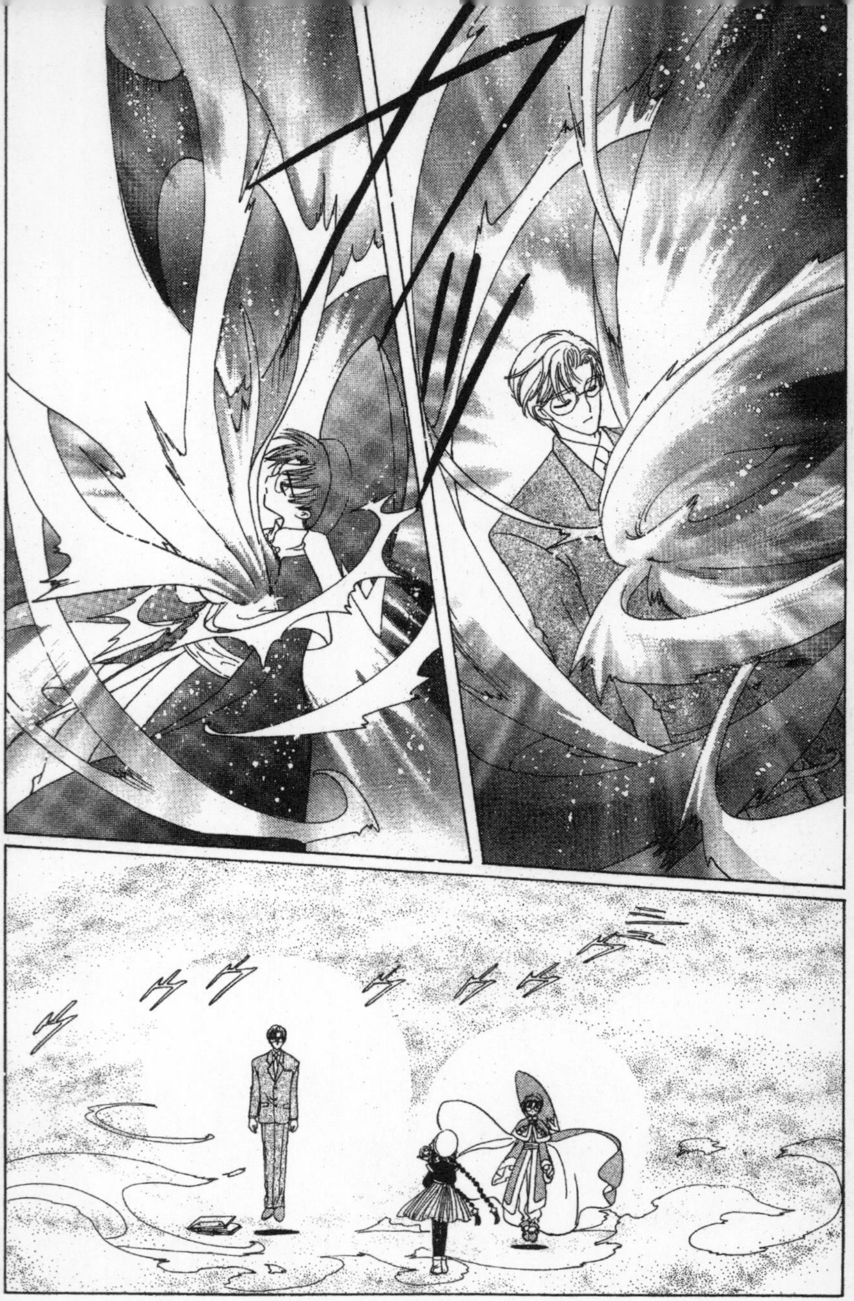

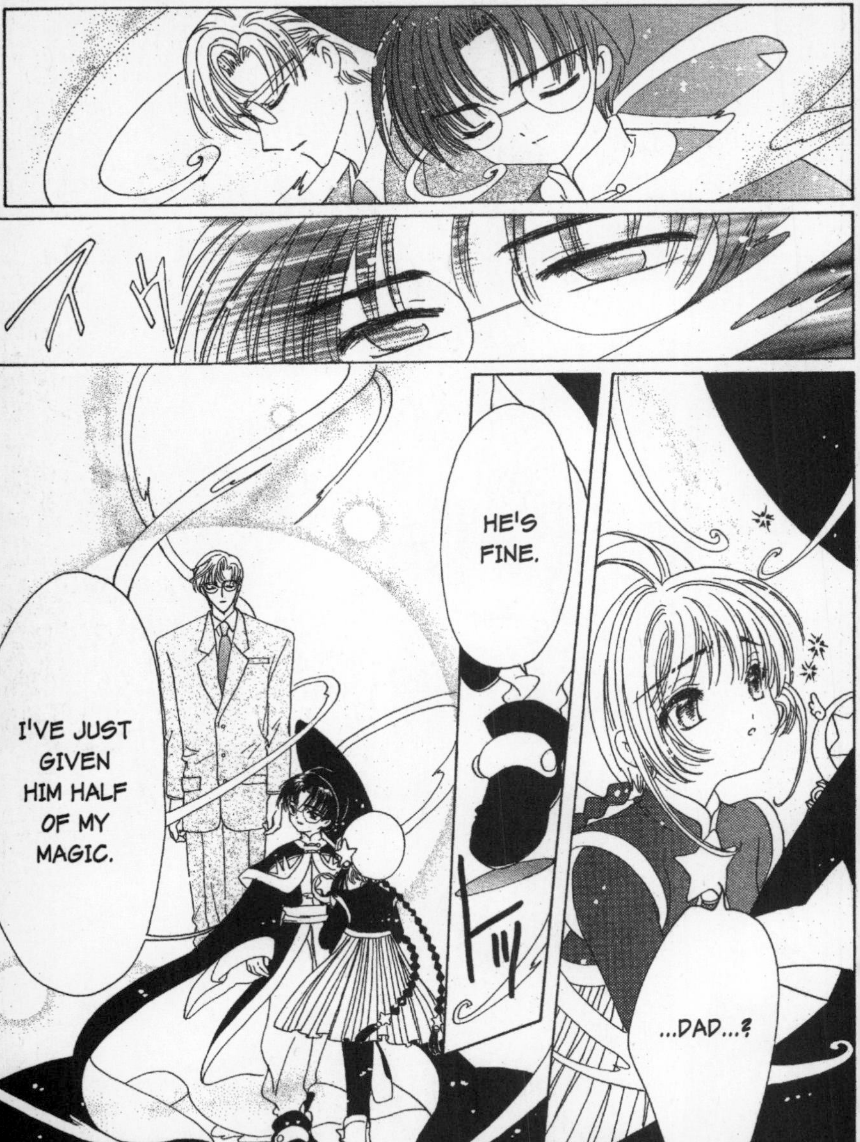
...DAD...?
HE'S FINE.
I'VE JUST GIVEN HIM HALF OF MY MAGIC.

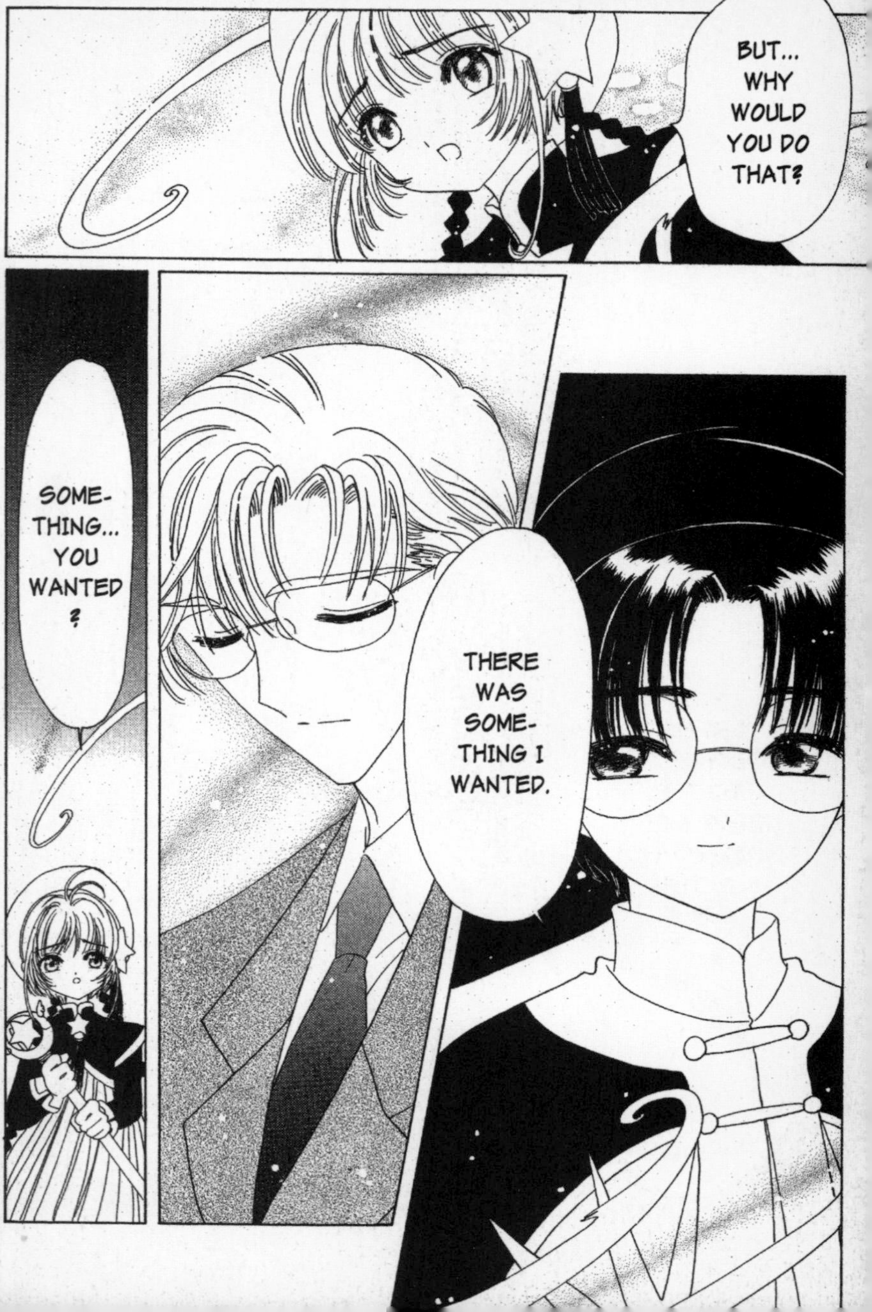
BUT... WHY WOULD YOU DO THAT?
THERE WAS SOME-THING I WANTED.
SOME-THING... YOU WANTED?

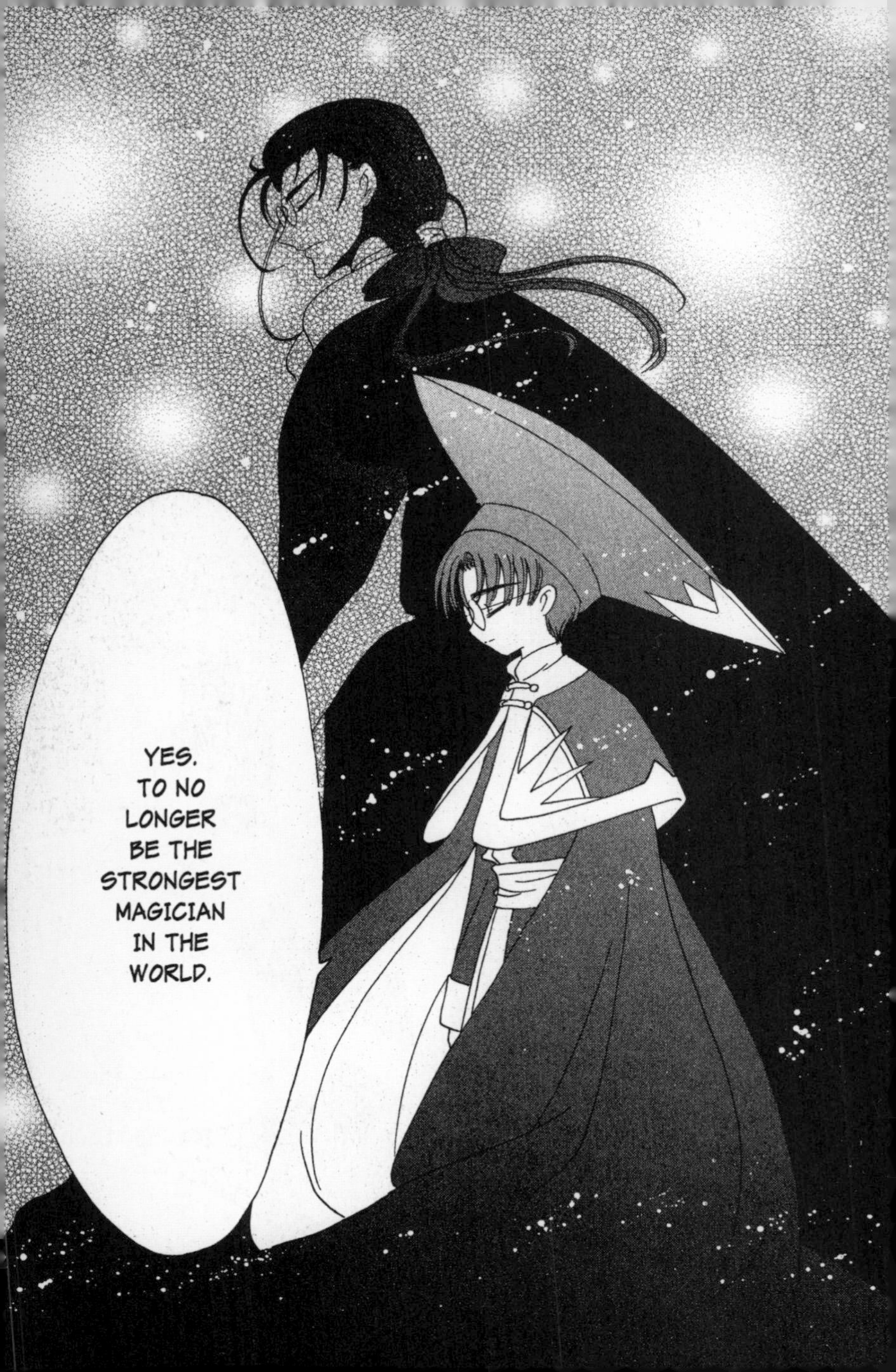
YES. TO NO LONGER BE THE STRONGEST MAGICIAN IN THE WORLD.

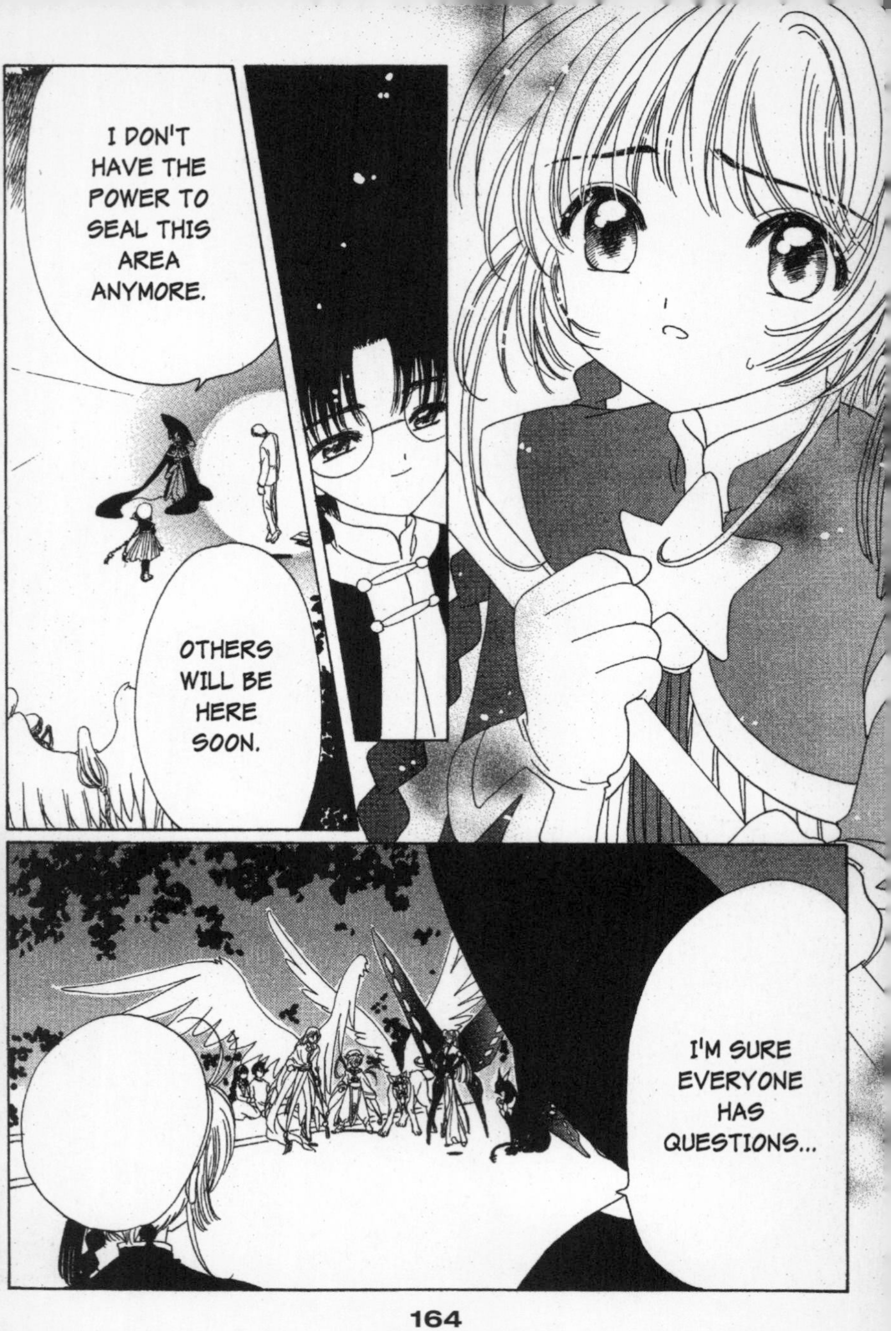
I DON'T HAVE THE POWER TO SEAL THIS AREA ANYMORE.
OTHERS WILL BE HERE SOON.
I'M SURE EVERYONE HAS QUESTIONS...

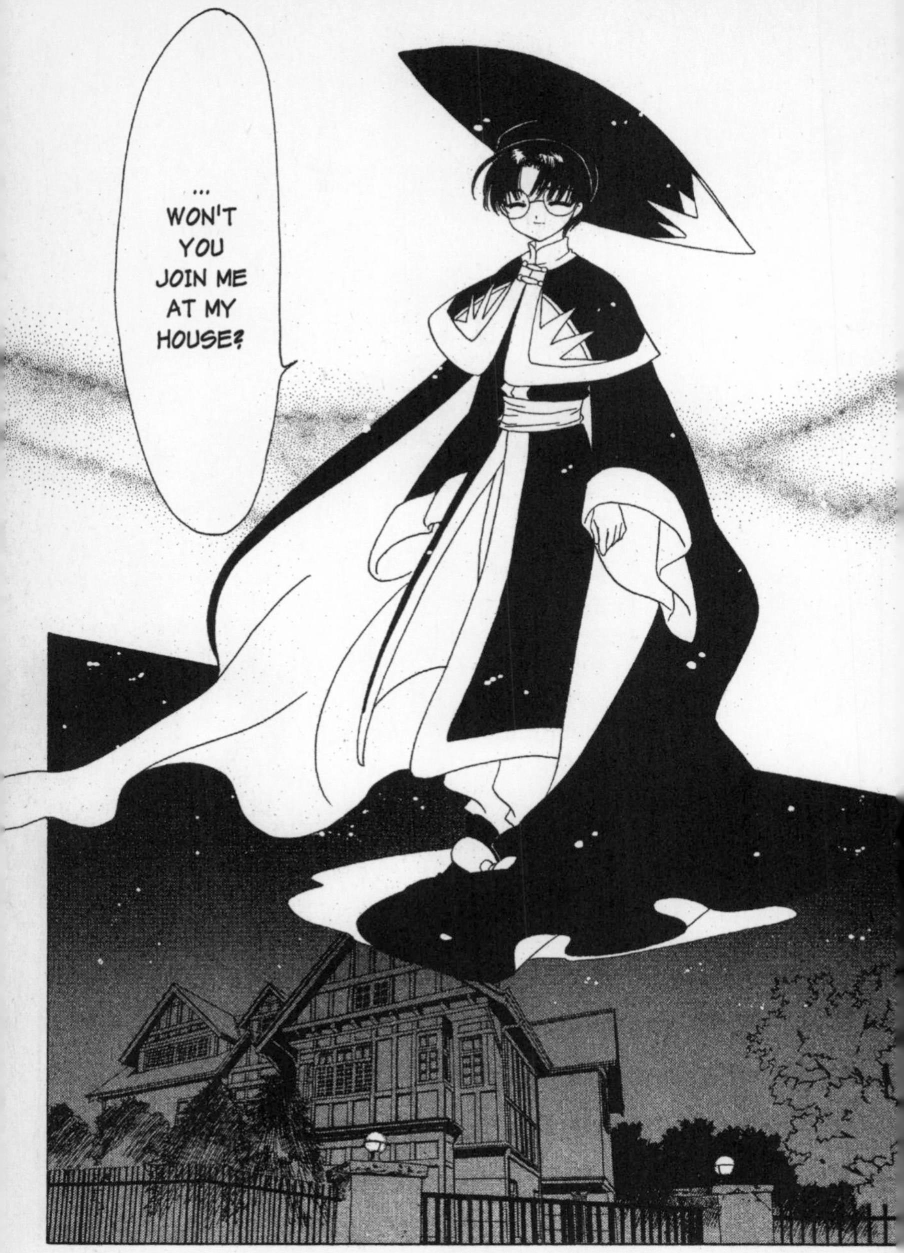
... WON'T YOU JOIN ME AT MY HOUSE?

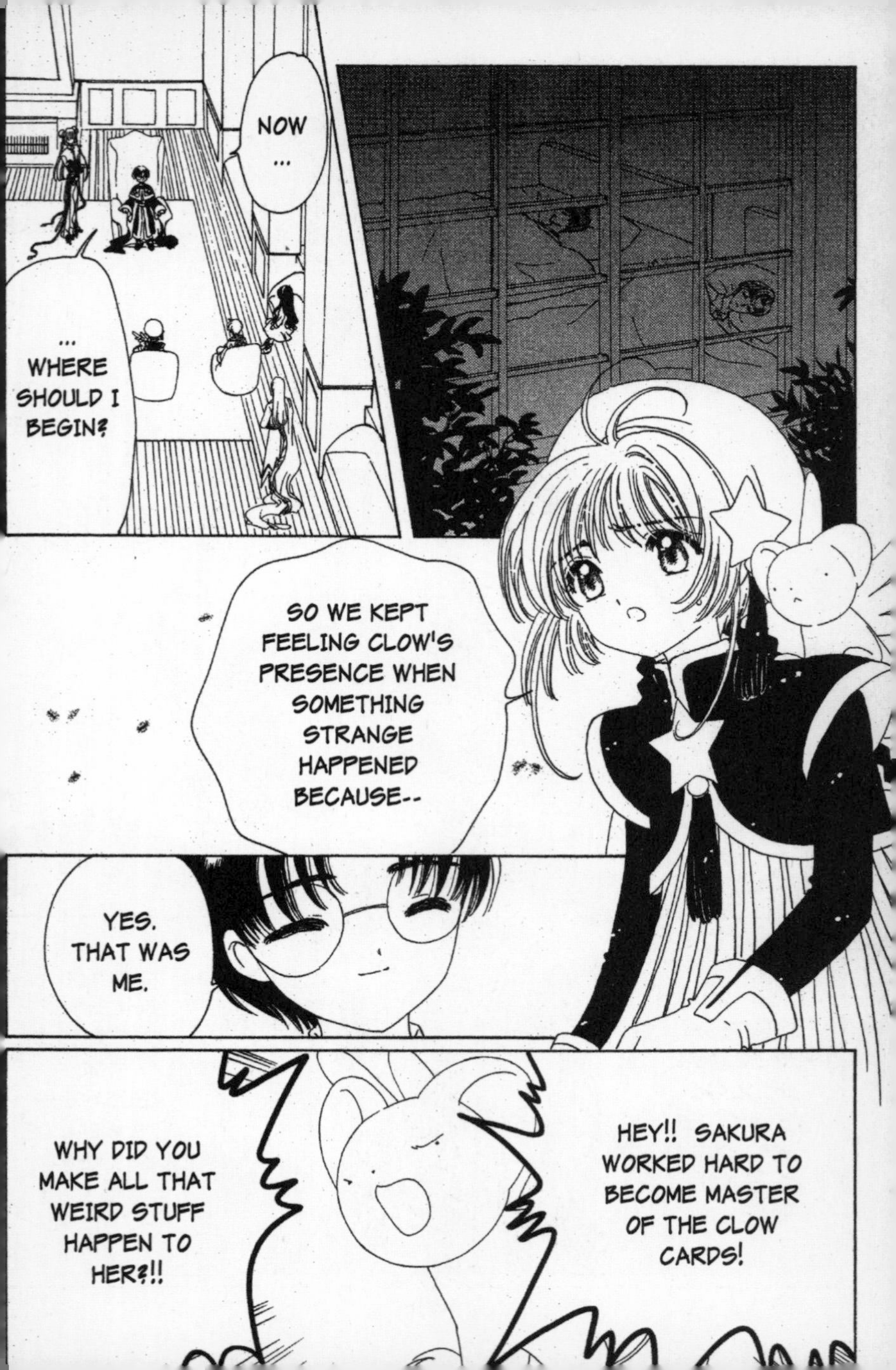
NOW ...
... WHERE SHOULD I BEGIN?
SO WE KEPT FEELING CLOW'S PRESENCE WHEN SOMETHING STRANGE HAPPENED BECAUSE--
YES. THAT WAS ME.
HEY!! SAKURA WORKED HARD TO BECOME MASTER OF THE CLOW CARDS!
WHY DID YOU MAKE ALL THAT WEIRD STUFF HAPPEN TO HER?!!

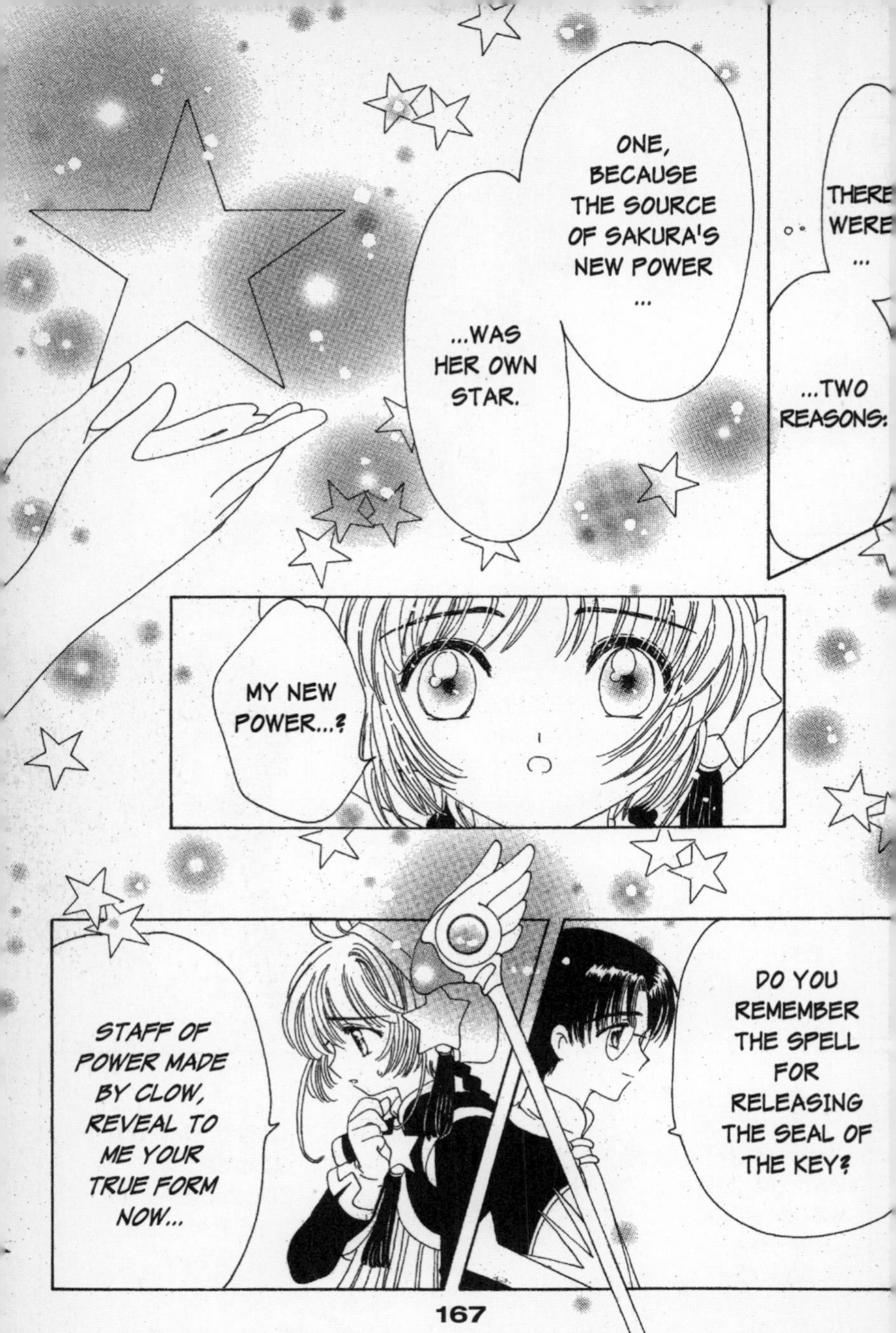
THERE WERE ...
...TWO REASONS:
ONE, BECAUSE THE SOURCE OF SAKURA'S NEW POWER ...
...WAS HER OWN STAR.
MY NEW POWER...?
DO YOU REMEMBER THE SPELL FOR RELEASING THE SEAL OF THE KEY?
STAFF OF POWER MADE BY CLOW, REVEAL TO ME YOUR TRUE FORM NOW...

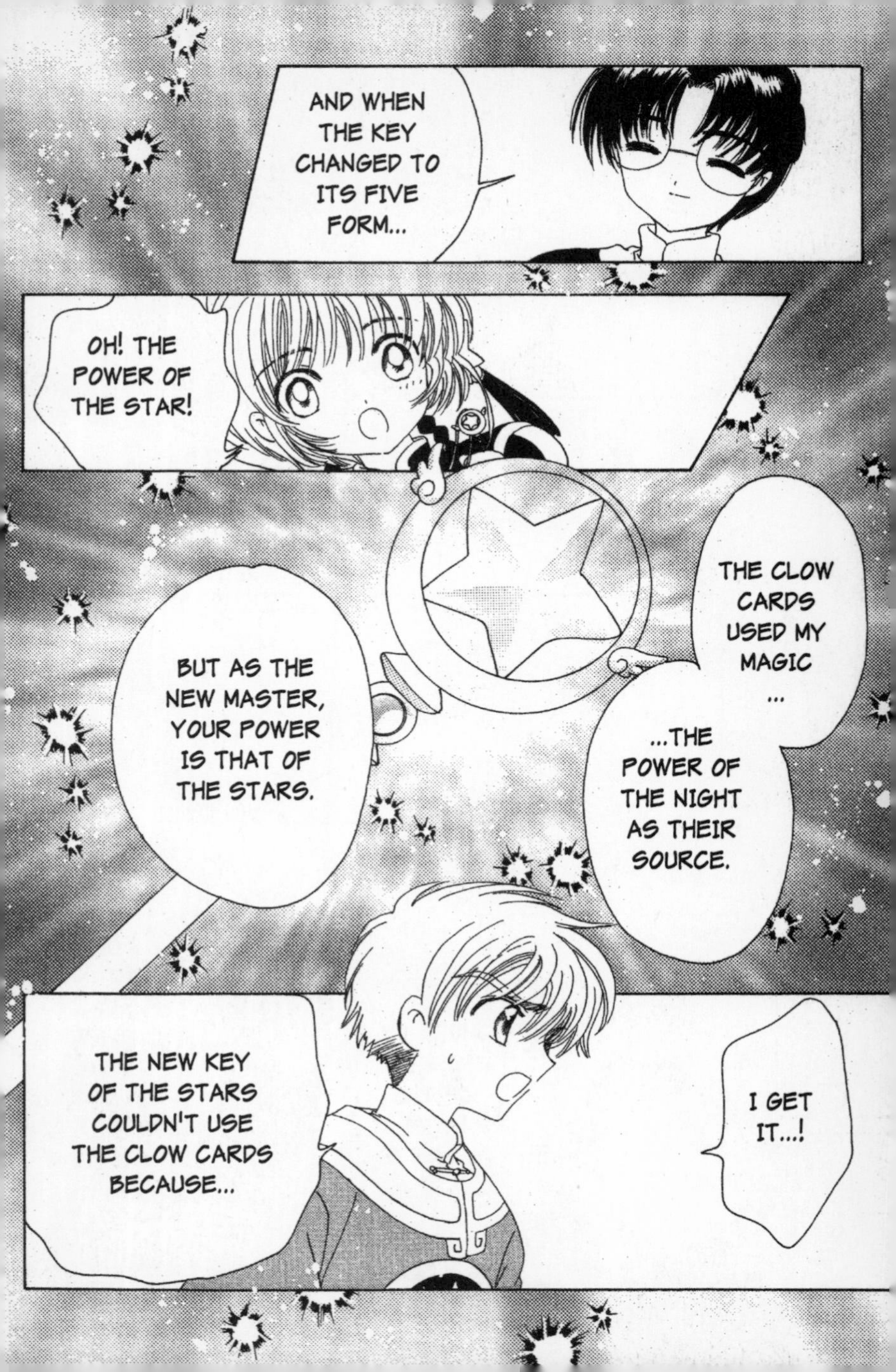
AND WHEN THE KEY CHANGED TO ITS FIVE FORM...
OH! THE POWER OF THE STAR!
THE CLOW CARDS USED MY MAGIC ...
...THE POWER OF THE NIGHT AS THEIR SOURCE.
BUT AS THE NEW MASTER, YOUR POWER IS THAT OF THE STARS.
I GET IT...!
THE NEW KEY OF THE STARS COULDN'T USE THE CLOW CARDS BECAUSE...

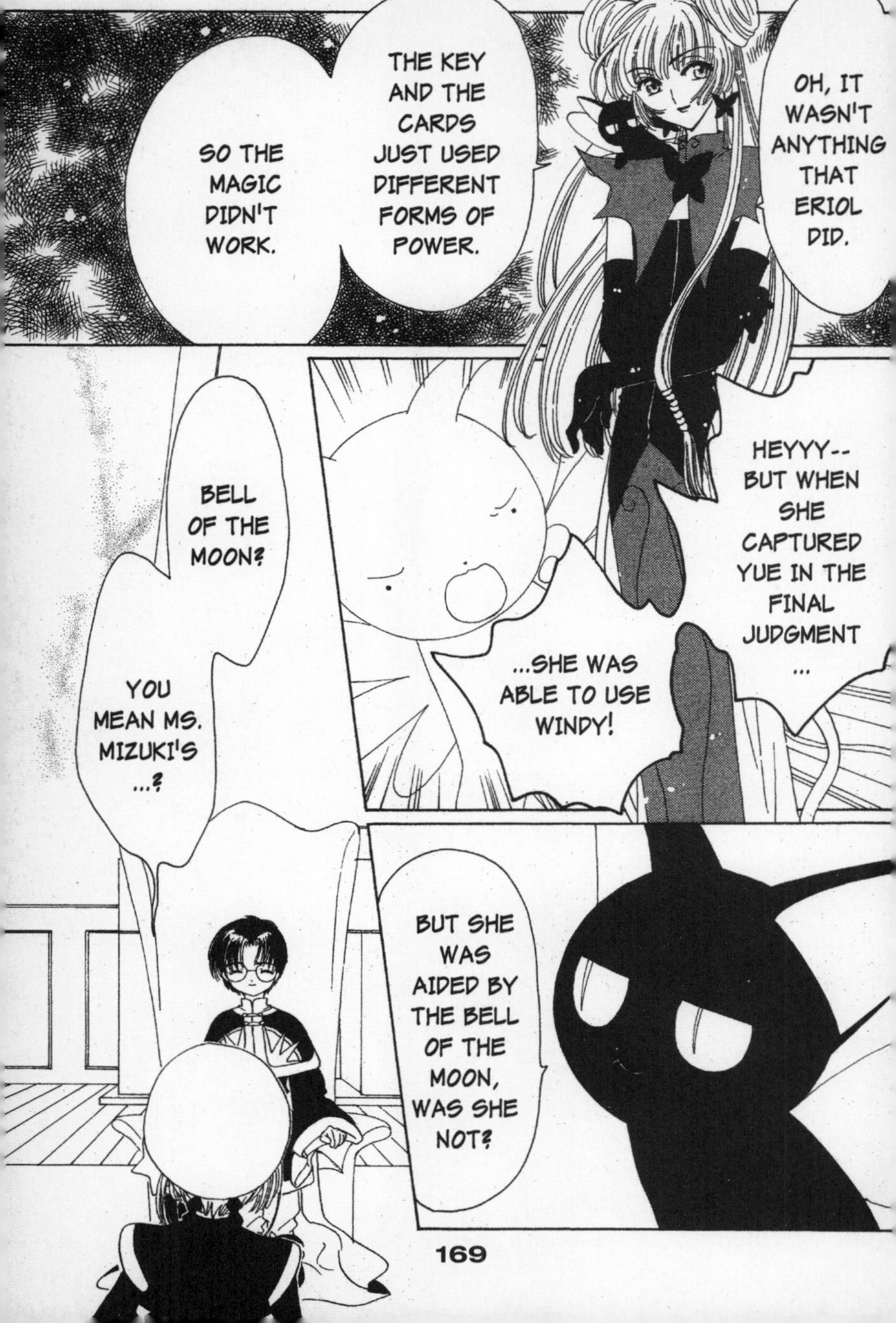
OH, IT WASN'T ANYTHING THAT ERIOL DID.
THE KEY AND THE CARDS JUST USED DIFFERENT FORMS OF POWER.
SO THE MAGIC DIDN'T WORK.
HEYYY-- BUT WHEN SHE CAPTURED YUE IN THE FINAL JUDGMENT ...
...SHE WAS ABLE TO USE WINDY!
BUT SHE WAS AIDED BY THE BELL OF THE MOON, WAS SHE NOT?
BELL OF THE MOON?
YOU MEAN MS. MIZUKI'S ...?

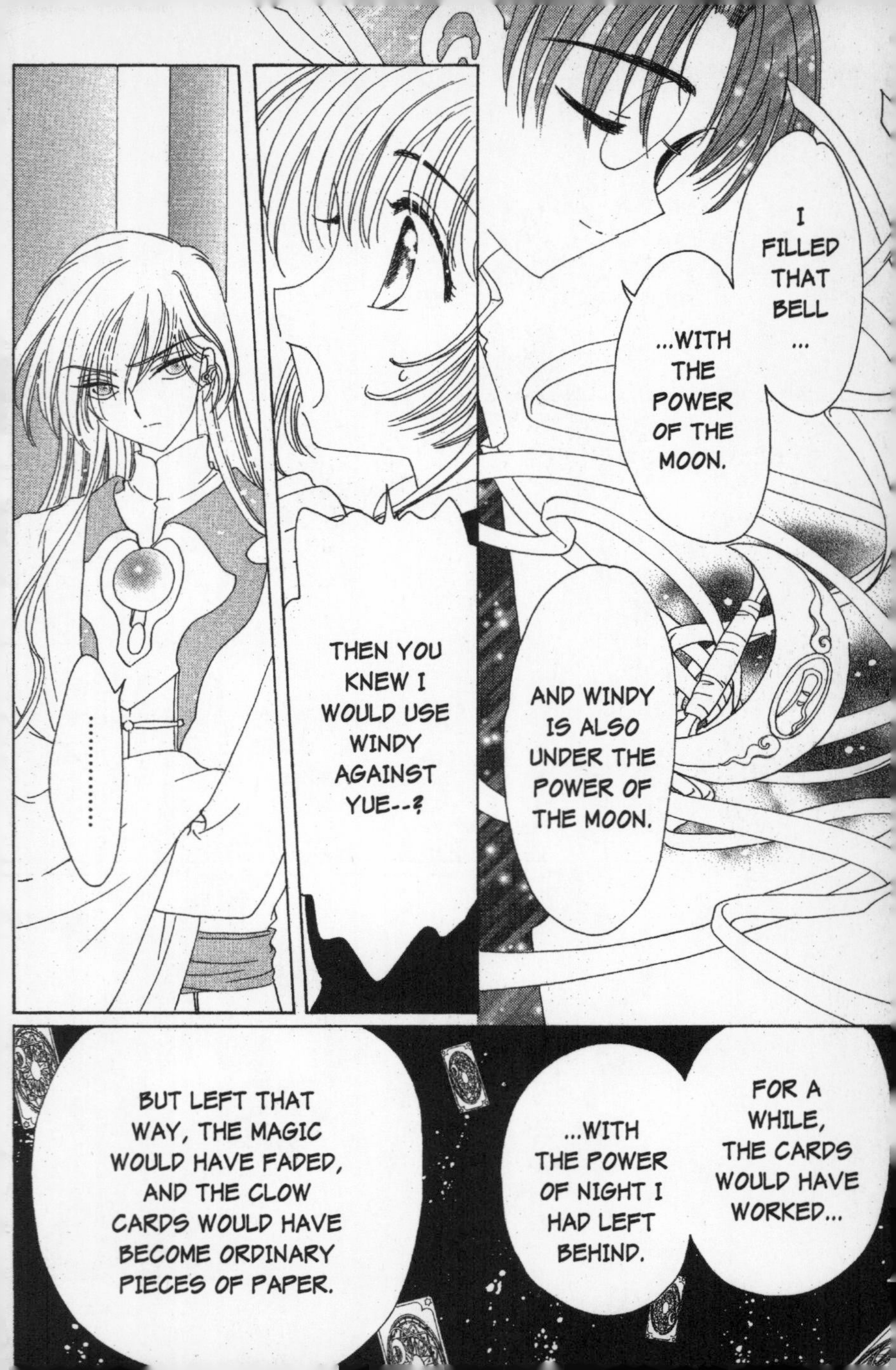
I FILLED THAT BELL ...
...WITH THE POWER OF THE MOON.
AND WINDY IS ALSO UNDER THE POWER OF THE MOON.
THEN YOU KNEW I WOULD USE WINDY AGAINST YUE--?
....
FOR A WHILE, THE CARDS WOULD HAVE WORKED...
...WITH THE POWER OF NIGHT I HAD LEFT BEHIND.
BUT LEFT THAT WAY, THE MAGIC WOULD HAVE FADED, AND THE CLOW CARDS WOULD HAVE BECOME ORDINARY PIECES OF PAPER.

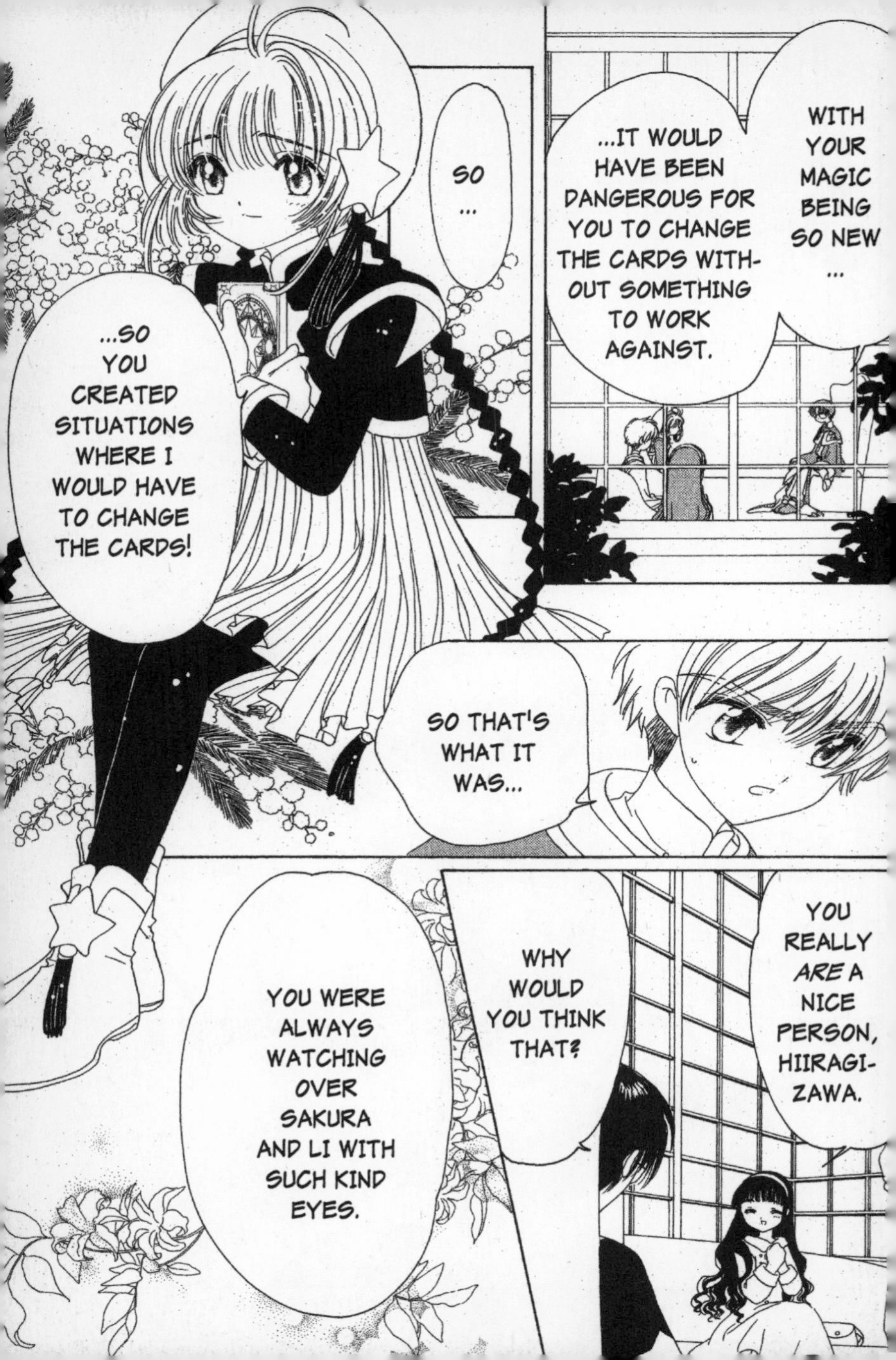
WITH YOUR MAGIC BEING SO NEW ...
...IT WOULD HAVE BEEN DANGEROUS FOR YOU TO CHANGE THE CARDS WITH-OUT SOMETHING TO WORK AGAINST.
SO ...
...SO YOU CREATED SITUATIONS WHERE I WOULD HAVE TO CHANGE THE CARDS!
SO THAT'S WHAT IT WAS...
YOU REALLY *ARE* A NICE PERSON, HIIRAGI-ZAWA.
WHY WOULD YOU THINK THAT?
YOU WERE ALWAYS WATCHING OVER SAKURA AND LI WITH SUCH KIND EYES.

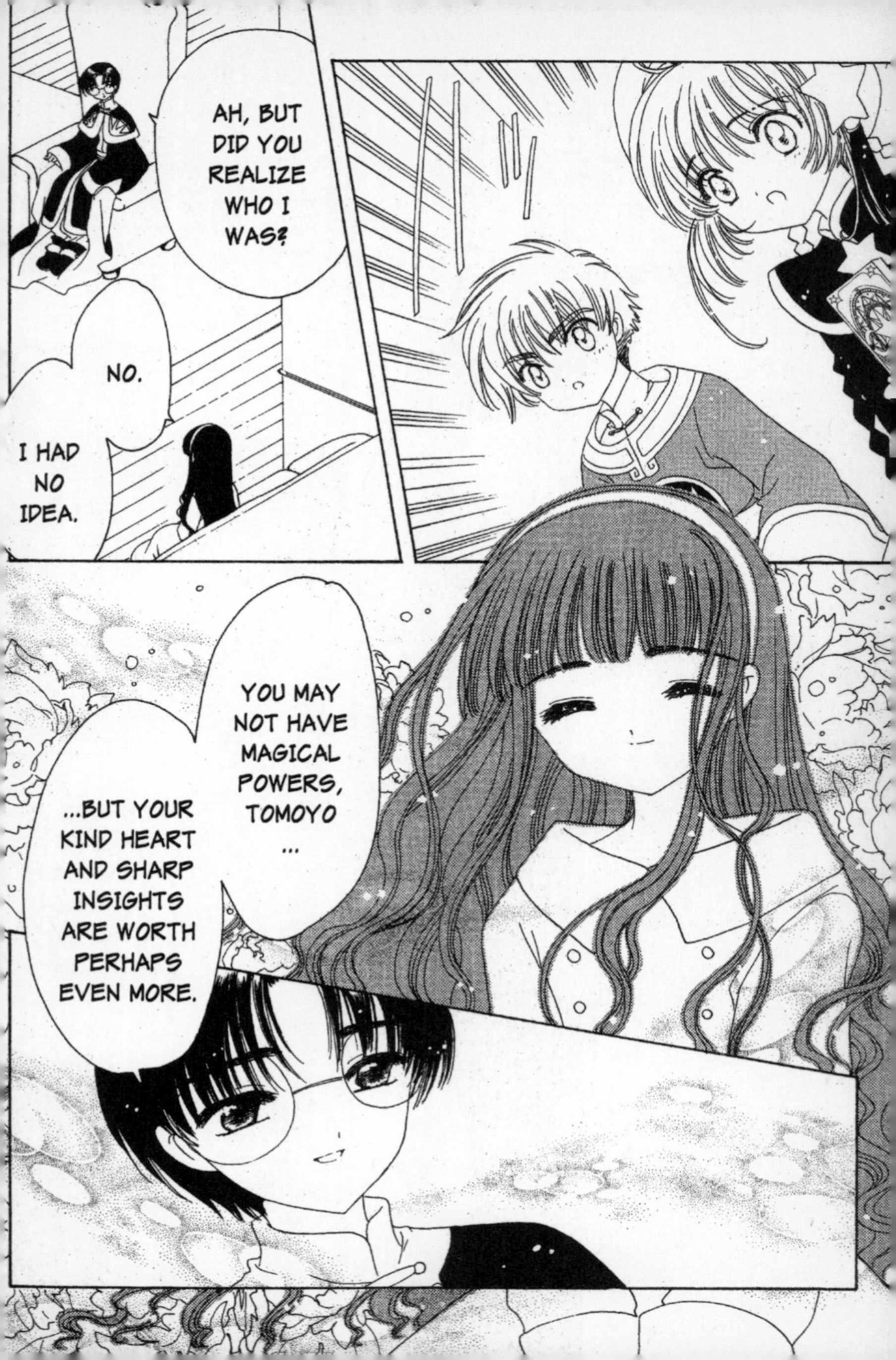
AH, BUT DID YOU REALIZE WHO I WAS?
NO.
I HAD NO IDEA.
YOU MAY NOT HAVE MAGICAL POWERS, TOMOYO ...
...BUT YOUR KIND HEART AND SHARP INSIGHTS ARE WORTH PERHAPS EVEN MORE.

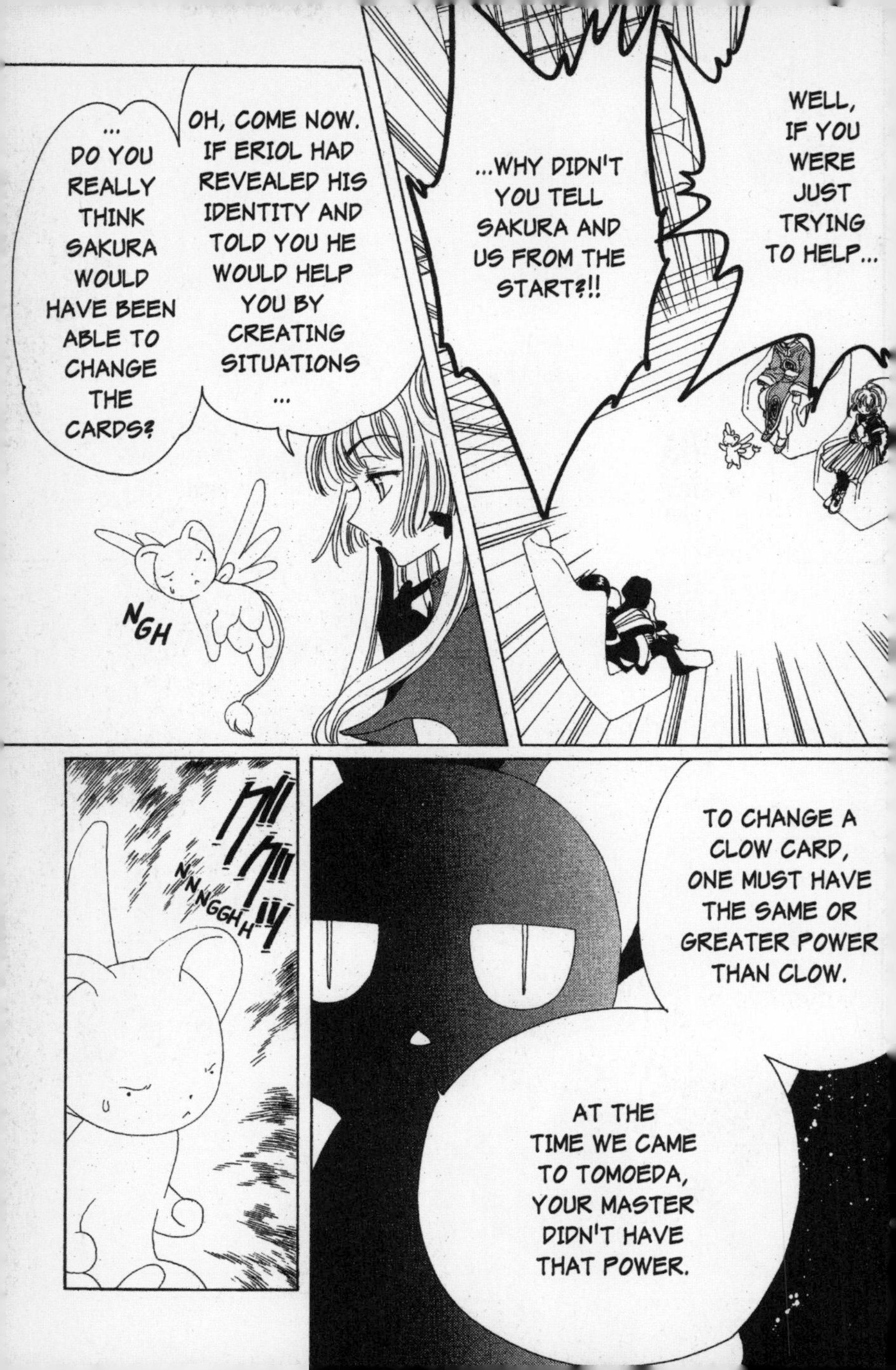
WELL, IF YOU WERE JUST TRYING TO HELP...
...WHY DIDN'T YOU TELL SAKURA AND US FROM THE START?!!
OH, COME NOW. IF ERIOL HAD REVEALED HIS IDENTITY AND TOLD YOU HE WOULD HELP YOU BY CREATING SITUATIONS ...
... DO YOU REALLY THINK SAKURA WOULD HAVE BEEN ABLE TO CHANGE THE CARDS?
NGH
TO CHANGE A CLOW CARD, ONE MUST HAVE THE SAME OR GREATER POWER THAN CLOW.
AT THE TIME WE CAME TO TOMOEDA, YOUR MASTER DIDN'T HAVE THAT POWER.
NNNGGHH

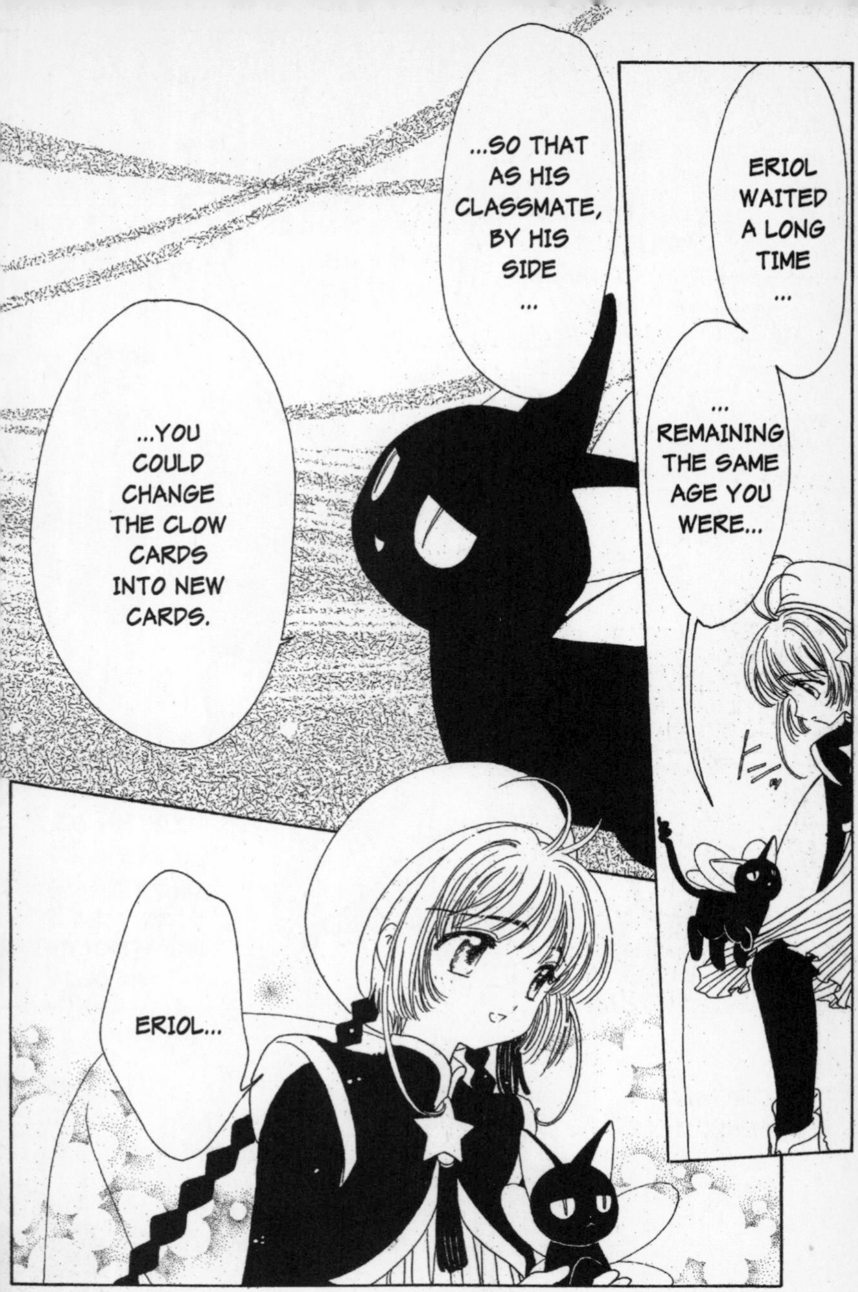
ERIOL WAITED A LONG TIME ...
... REMAINING THE SAME AGE YOU WERE...
...SO THAT AS HIS CLASSMATE, BY HIS SIDE ...
...YOU COULD CHANGE THE CLOW CARDS INTO NEW CARDS.
ERIOL...

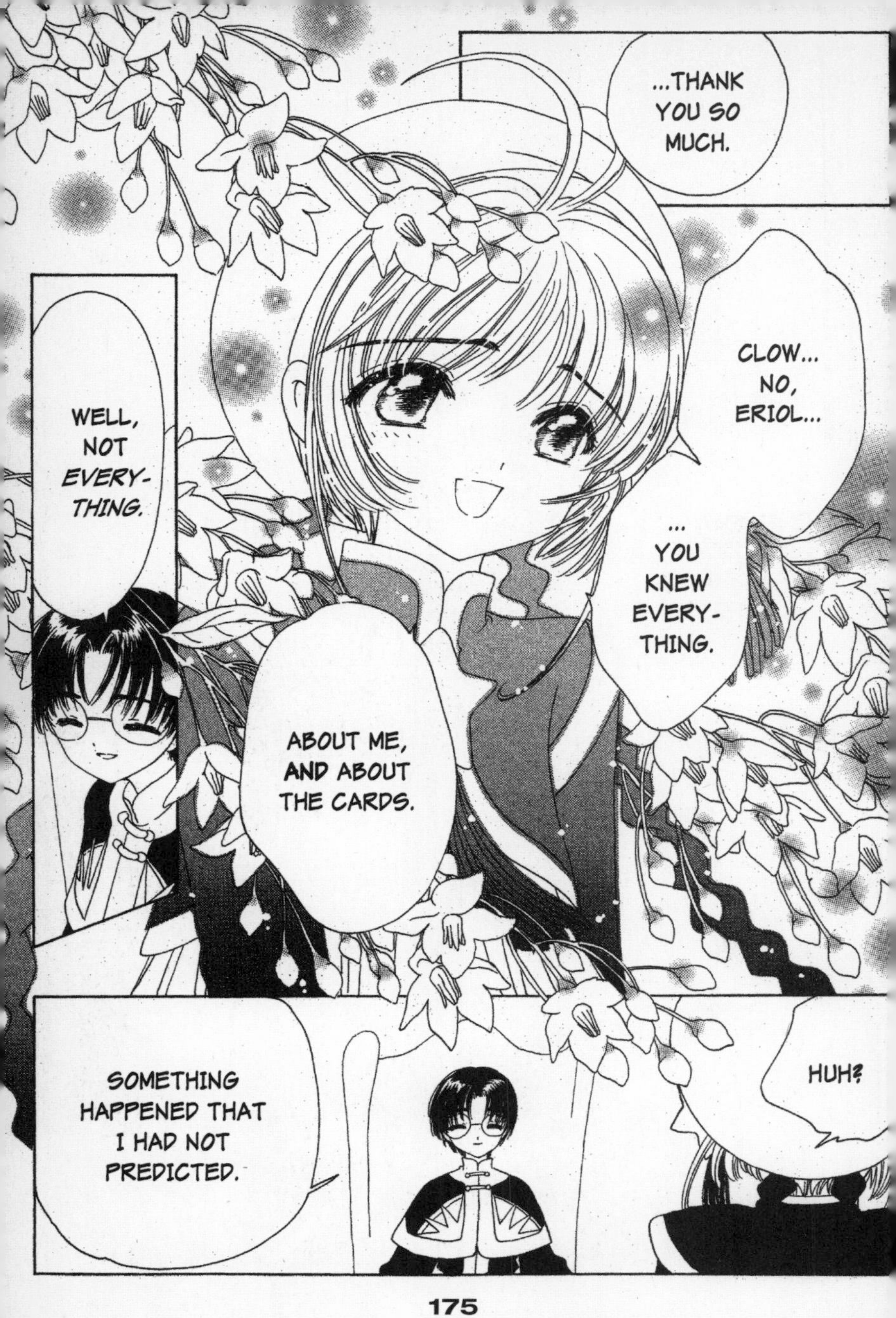
...THANK YOU SO MUCH.
CLOW... NO, ERIOL...
... YOU KNEW EVERY-THING.
ABOUT ME, AND ABOUT THE CARDS.
WELL, NOT *EVERY-THING.*
SOMETHING HAPPENED THAT I HAD NOT PREDICTED.
HUH?

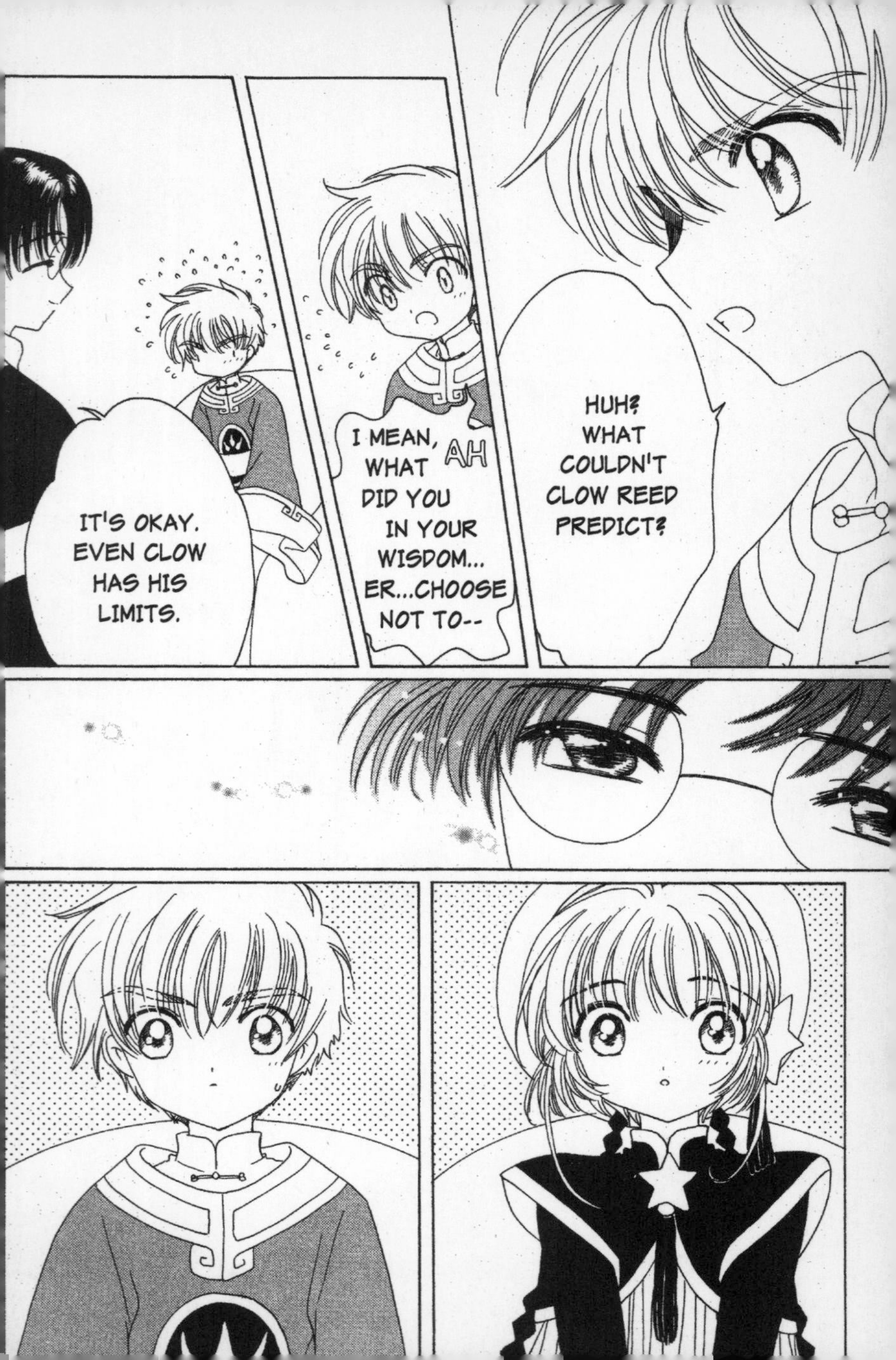
HUH? WHAT COULDN'T CLOW REED PREDICT?
AH
I MEAN, WHAT DID YOU IN YOUR WISDOM... ER...CHOOSE NOT TO--
IT'S OKAY. EVEN CLOW HAS HIS LIMITS.

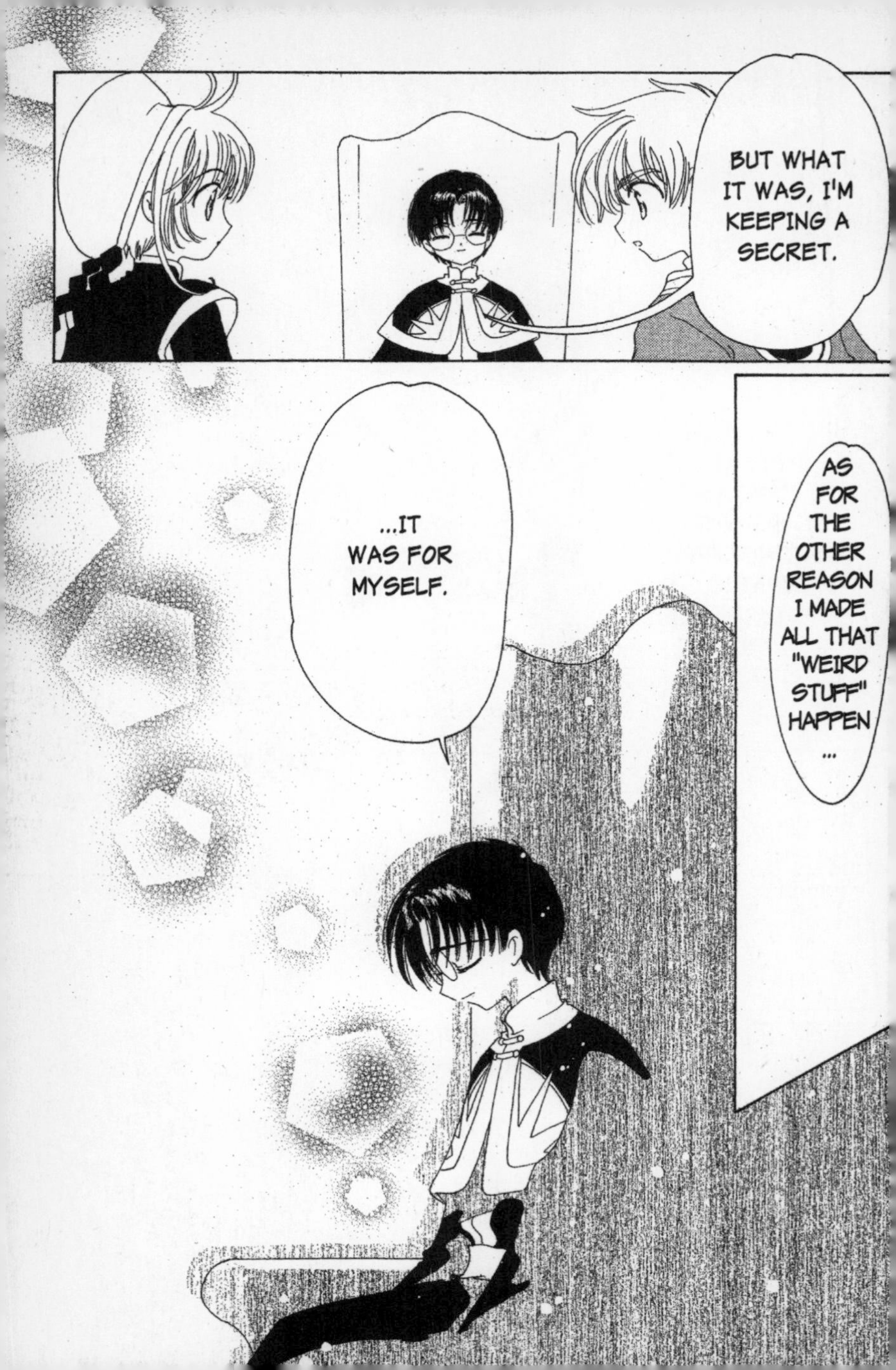
BUT WHAT IT WAS, I'M KEEPING A SECRET.
AS FOR THE OTHER REASON I MADE ALL THAT "WEIRD STUFF" HAPPEN ...
...IT WAS FOR MYSELF.

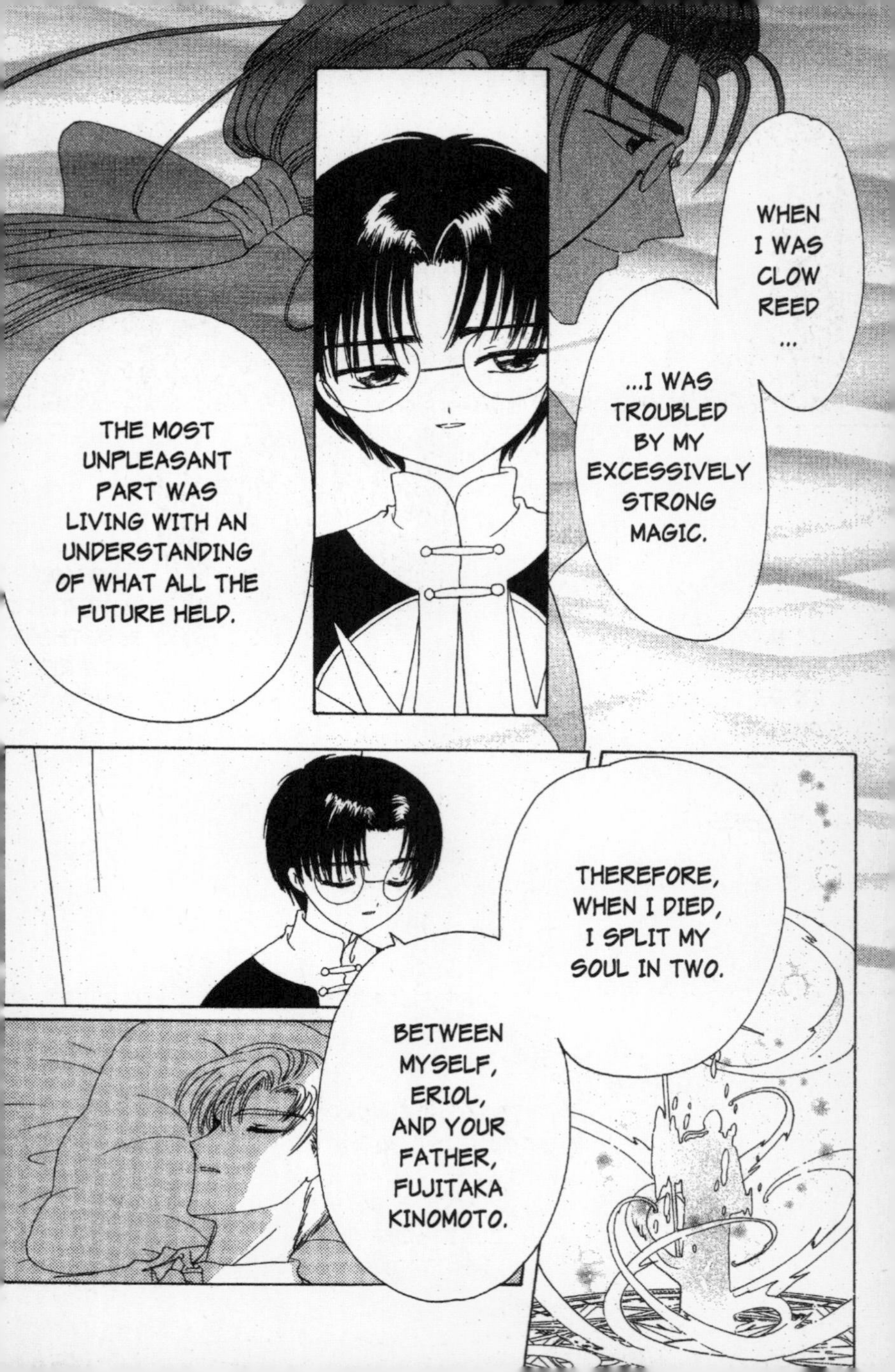
WHEN I WAS CLOW REED ...
...I WAS TROUBLED BY MY EXCESSIVELY STRONG MAGIC.
THE MOST UNPLEASANT PART WAS LIVING WITH AN UNDERSTANDING OF WHAT ALL THE FUTURE HELD.
THEREFORE, WHEN I DIED, I SPLIT MY SOUL IN TWO.
BETWEEN MYSELF, ERIOL, AND YOUR FATHER, FUJITAKA KINOMOTO.

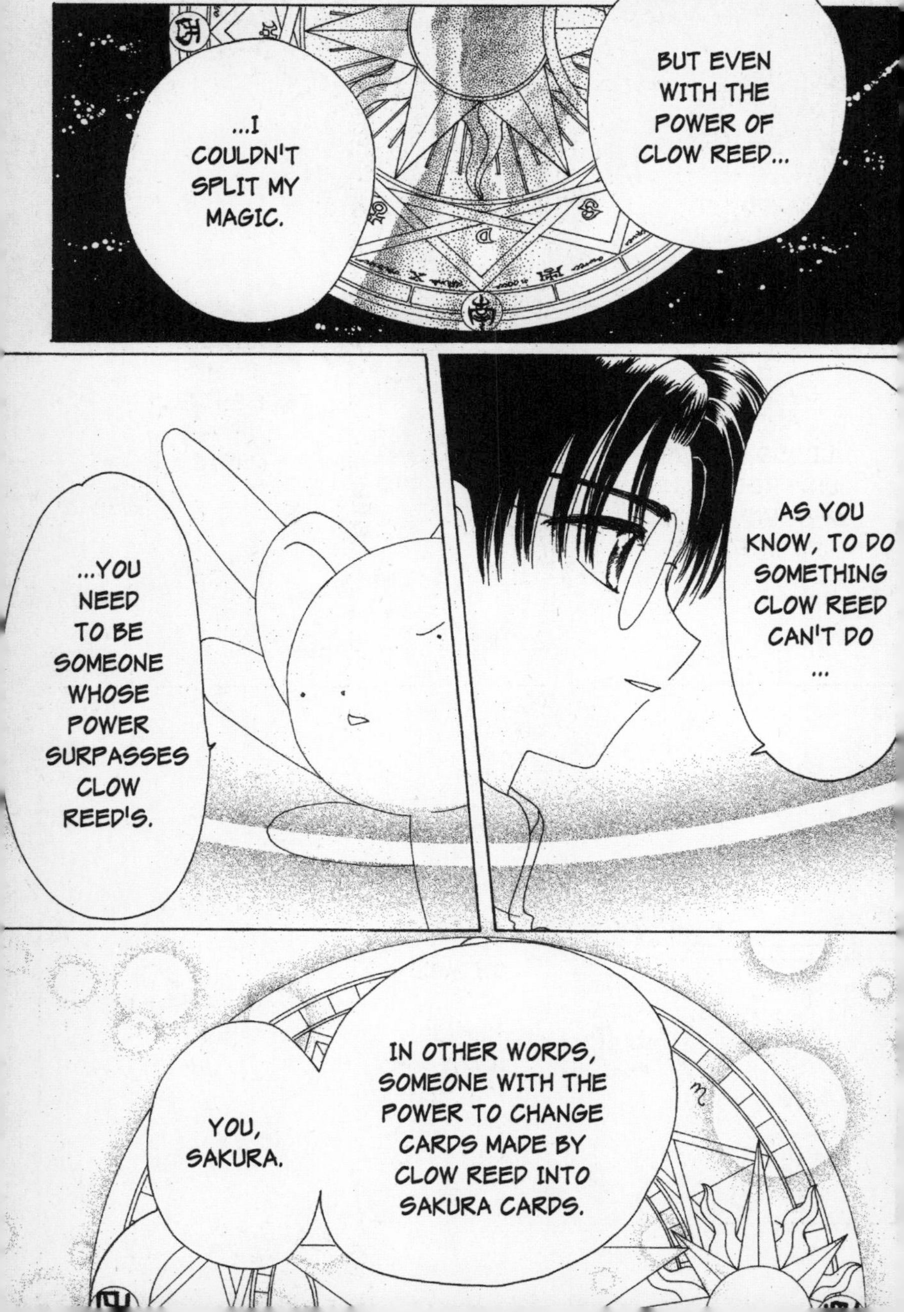
BUT EVEN WITH THE POWER OF CLOW REED...
...I COULDN'T SPLIT MY MAGIC.
AS YOU KNOW, TO DO SOMETHING CLOW REED CAN'T DO ...
...YOU NEED TO BE SOMEONE WHOSE POWER SURPASSES CLOW REED'S.
IN OTHER WORDS, SOMEONE WITH THE POWER TO CHANGE CARDS MADE BY CLOW REED INTO SAKURA CARDS.
YOU, SAKURA.

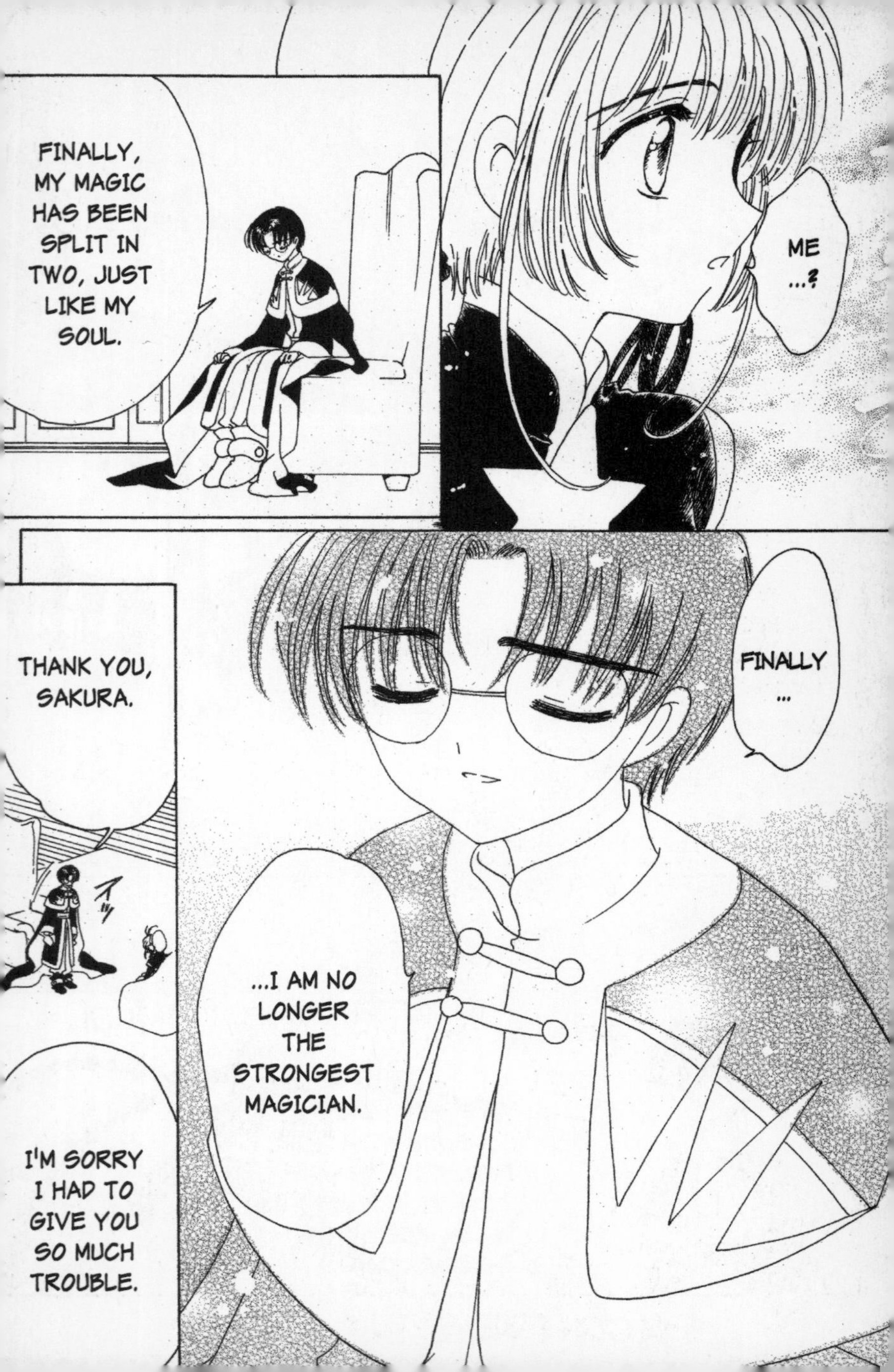
ME ...?
FINALLY, MY MAGIC HAS BEEN SPLIT IN TWO, JUST LIKE MY SOUL.
FINALLY ...
...I AM NO LONGER THE STRONGEST MAGICIAN.
THANK YOU, SAKURA.
I'M SORRY I HAD TO GIVE YOU SO MUCH TROUBLE.

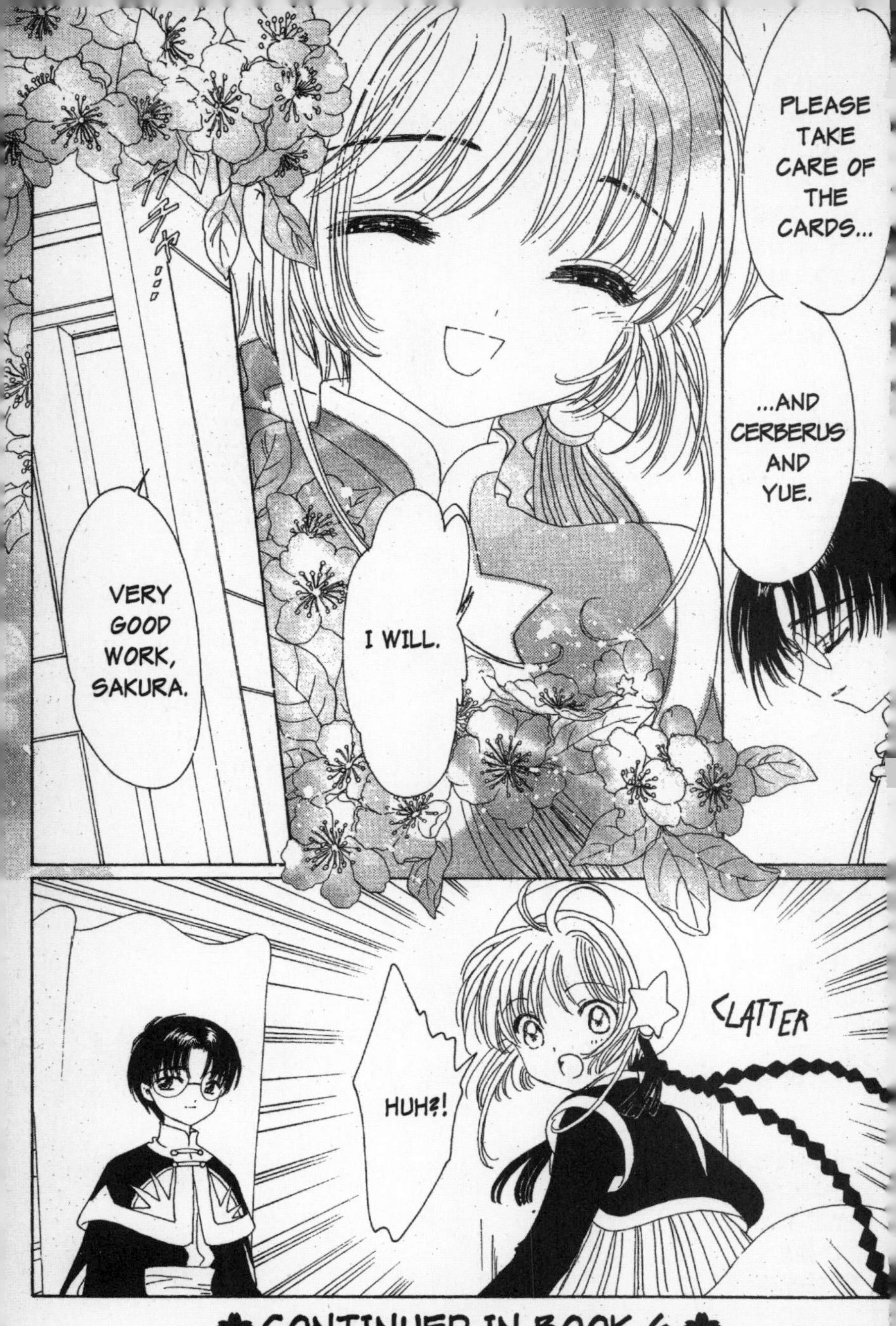
PLEASE TAKE CARE OF THE CARDS...
...AND CERBERUS AND YUE.
I WILL.
VERY GOOD WORK, SAKURA.
CLATTER
HUH?!

✿ CONTINUED IN BOOK 6 ✿

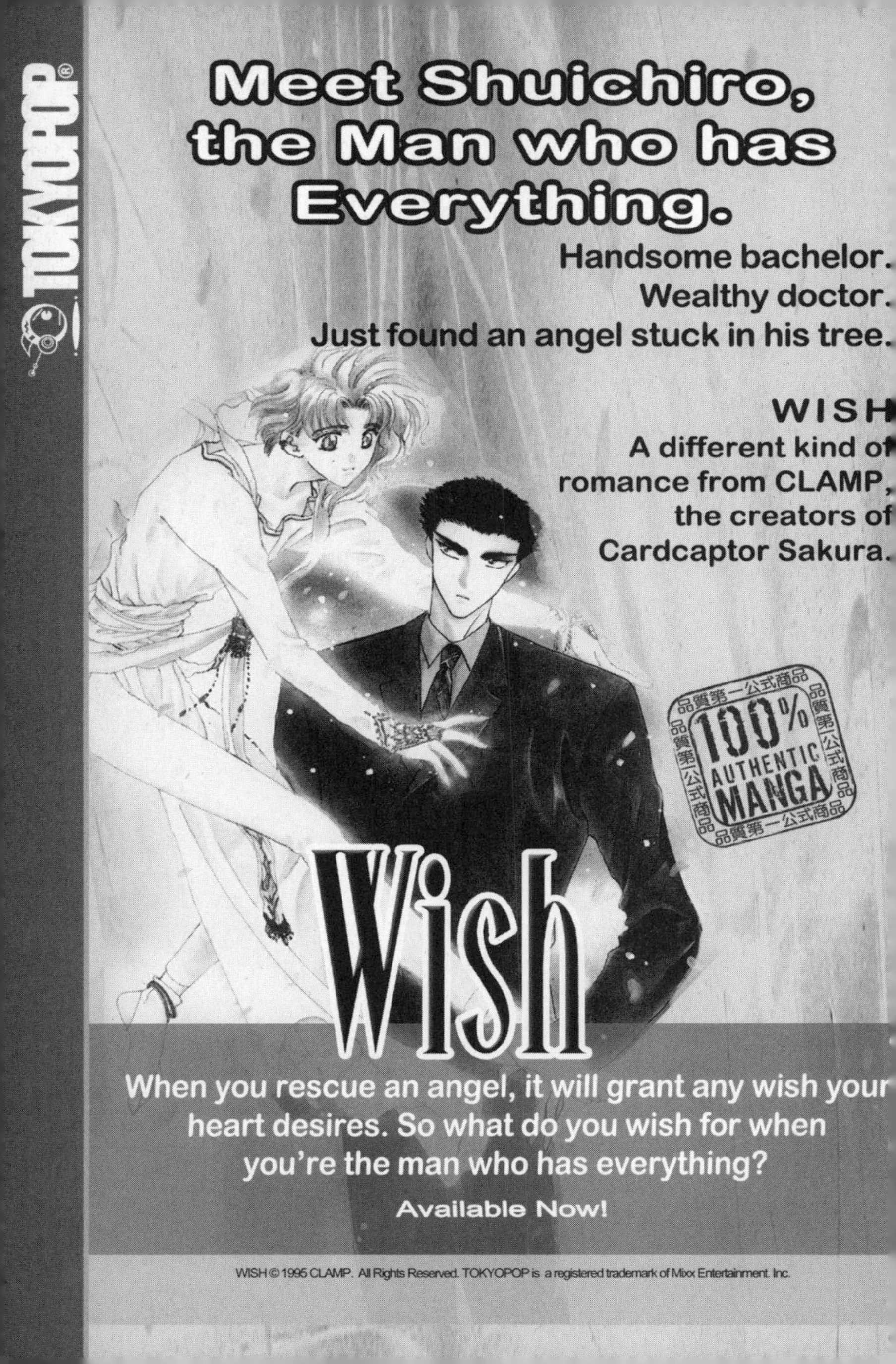
品質第一公式商品
100%
AUTHENTIC
MANGA

STOP!

This is the back of the book.
You wouldn't want to spoil a great ending!

This book is printed "manga-style," in the authentic Japanese right-to-left format. Since none of the artwork has been flipped or altered, readers get to experience the story just as the creator intended. You've been asking for it, so TOKYOPOP® delivered: authentic, hot-off-the-press, and far more fun!

DIRECTIONS

If this is your first time reading manga-style, here's a quick guide to help you understand how it works.

It's easy... just start in the top right panel and follow the numbers. Have fun, and look for more 100% authentic manga from TOKYOPOP®!